# FAMILY OF SPIES

# FAMILY OF SPIES

## Inside the John Walker Spy Ring

### PETE EARLEY

BANTAM BOOKS
TORONTO · NEW YORK · LONDON · SYDNEY · AUCKLAND

FAMILY OF SPIES

*A Bantam Book / November 1988*

N.P.

**Library of Congress Cataloging-in-Publication Data**

Earley, Pete.
   Family of spies.          *89 B3240*

   Includes index.
   1. Walker, John Anthony, 1937–      . 2. Walker
family. 3. Whitworth, Jerry.   4. Espionage—Soviet
Union—History—20th century.   5. Espionage—United States—
History—20th Century.  I. Title.
UB271.R92W3435  1988          327.1'2'0924   [B]   88-19432
ISBN 0-553-05283-7

*Published simultaneously in the United States and Canada*

*Bantam Books are published by Bantam Books, a division of Bantam Doubleday*
*Dell Publishing Group, Inc. Its trademark, consisting of the words ''Bantam*
*Books'' and the portrayal of a rooster, is Registered in U.S. Patent and*
*Trademark Office and in other countries. Marca Registrada. Bantam Books,*
*666 Fifth Avenue, New York, New York 10103.*

PRINTED IN THE UNITED STATES OF AMERICA

For Barbara,
my wife and best friend

This book is based upon exclusive interviews
with John Walker, Jr., Arthur Walker, Michael Walker,
and Jerry Whitworth, members of the most
damaging spy ring ever to operate in
the history of the
United States.

# CONTENTS

# PROLOGUE

Presidential candidate Ronald Reagan was overdue, and the crowd inside the SCOPE civic center in Norfolk, Virginia, became restless. One man in particular was impatient at the October 3, 1980, rally. He was a private detective who had volunteered to help provide additional protection for Reagan. The detective loathed delays. He was a meticulous man, a Navy veteran unaccustomed to the inexact schedules and last-minute changes that plague political campaigns.

The detective scanned the crowd as he waited in an aisle seat. From it, he could observe everyone in "his" row. If any of them interrupted Reagan's speech with catcalls or menaced the Republican candidate, the detective would act quickly to help subdue him. He took the assignment seriously. Earlier, he had told his girlfriend that if someone threatened Reagan's life, he would draw and fire the .38 caliber Smith & Wesson revolver that he carried in a holster on his hip.

Reagan's appearance at the back of the auditorium was greeted by screams and applause. Hundreds of hands reached out toward the candidate as he walked slowly down an aisle. The detective considered himself above political rally hysterics, but as Reagan approached, the detective impulsively stuck his hand into the aisle too and for a moment, it looked as if Reagan would touch it. But he didn't.

Almost frantic, the detective pushed forward into the aisle and actually touched the back of Reagan's jacket before being shoved aside by a Secret Service agent.

The detective stared at his hand with childlike awe. He had touched Reagan! He began to laugh loudly. He was the only person in the entire auditorium who understood the irony of this moment. It was his secret!

John Anthony Walker, Jr., a spy for the Soviet Union, had been so close to the next president of the United States that he had been able to brush Reagan's jacket. And John had been armed the entire time. He could hardly wait to tell his KGB friend.

"Nobody that day," John bragged later, "realized that a Russian spy had helped protect Ronald Reagan. I was simply the best!"

# PART ONE

## *UNMASKED*

*God hath given you
one face, and you make
yourselves another.*

**WILLIAM SHAKESPEARE**
*Hamlet*, act 3, scene 1

# 1

The telephone in room 763 of the Ramada Inn in Rockville, Maryland, rang at 3:30 A.M. on May 20, 1985.

John Anthony Walker, Jr., lifted the receiver: "Yes?"

"This is the front desk!" an excited male voice announced. "There's been an accident! Someone has hit your blue and white van in the parking lot! You'd better get down here quick!"

"Okay," John replied coolly. "Be right down."

John figured it was a trick. He had used the exact same ploy dozens of times himself while working on divorce cases as a private investigator. Obviously, someone wanted him out of his room. The only question was who?

John suspected the worst. He had driven to Maryland the day before, Sunday, May 19, from his home in Norfolk, Virginia, to deliver a package of stolen government secrets to an agent of the Soviet KGB. In return for betraying his country, John had expected to receive more than $200,000 in used $50 and $100 bills. But something had gone wrong during the exchange, very wrong.

Sitting on the edge of the motel bed, John began thinking back, retracing his steps over the past fifteen hours in an attempt to uncover some clue as to who was waiting for him downstairs in the lobby. Last night's meeting with the KGB had been arranged four months earlier, on January 19, when he had met his Soviet contact at a secret rendezvous in Vienna, a favorite meeting spot for the KGB and its spies. As they strolled past a window display of women's exotic lingerie, John had slipped his handler a small bag filled with rolls of undeveloped photographs of U.S. naval secrets. A few moments later, the Russian had handed John an envelope with detailed instructions for yesterday's meeting.

John had done his best to follow those instructions. Leaving home shortly after noon, he had driven from Norfolk along Interstate 64 toward Richmond, where he had connected with I-95, the superhighway that feeds into the nation's capital. For most of the trip, John had carefully observed the fifty-five-mile-per-hour speed limit, but at least once each hour, he had slowed his new Ford minivan to twenty mph, then accelerated to seventy mph, checking his rearview mirror to see if anyone else was imitating him. He had read about this evasive driving technique, called dry cleaning, in a popular spy novel. The drive proved uneventful. It was still too early in the year for the Sunday afternoon traffic snarls created by cranky, sunburned beach lovers crawling back to Washington from their weekend sojourns to the Atlantic Ocean.

John hated the four-hour trip to Washington. It bored him, and by the time he crossed the Potomac River to enter the Maryland suburbs north of Washington, he was anxious to check into the Ramada Inn and relax. But John had to make a test run first. Even though his Soviet handler had warned him against driving anywhere close to the location of their meeting prior to the agreed-upon time, John turned his van off the highway and drove toward Poolesville, a rural hamlet northwest of Washington. The locations that the KGB chose for exchanges were always remote areas and John, fearful of getting lost at night, had made it a practice to arrive several hours before the scheduled time to familiarize himself with the region. He drove quickly along the blacktop roads, picking out key sights—a small bridge, an elementary school, a grocery store—that would help him keep his bearings later that night. Once he felt comfortable with the course, he turned east and drove to the Ramada Inn in Rockville. As he pulled into the parking lot, John was confident that he hadn't been followed. Nothing seemed out of the ordinary. There was no reason to worry, he told himself, trying to settle the butterflies that always struck before a meet. This exchange would go as smoothly as the thirty other drops he had made in the Maryland and Virginia countryside during his eighteen years as a spy for the Russians. There was no reason to think otherwise.

John checked into his room, washed his face, and ate a steak dinner in the hotel restaurant. Refreshed, he returned to his van and drove toward Poolesville. It was near here, a few miles from the banks of the Potomac River, amid the rocky hills and tiny creeks, that John had been instructed to deliver his package of stolen secrets to a KGB agent. Such exchanges were the most hazardous part of his job as a spy. While the Russians felt safe walking the narrow streets of Vienna with John, any personal contact with him inside the United States was considered extremely dangerous. The Federal Bureau of Investigation, under Ronald Reagan, had been taking a much harder look at espionage than it had in the past.

For national security reasons, the FBI never reveals its counterespionage techniques. Even on the witness stand, FBI agents refuse to admit whether the agency photographs visitors to the Soviet embassy in Washington. But John's KGB handler had told him the practice was routine both in Washington and outside Soviet diplomatic posts in New York and San Francisco. He had also complained to John about other FBI practices. All telephone calls to and from the Soviet embassy in Washington are bugged, he claimed. Soviets who work in the United States are required to use diplomatic license plates on all their motor vehicles, tags issued by the State Department and coded each year with letters that identify the nationality of the motorist, making it easy for police and FBI to track them. Travel is also restricted. A Soviet stationed in Washington can't travel more than twenty-five miles from the embassy without special permission. While the State Department claims these restrictions were adopted only after travel by U.S. diplomats was curtailed in the Soviet Union, John's handler saw it differently. "Your government is very devious," he told John. "It forces us into action and then twists the truth. We were very courteous to your diplomats, but they took advantage, so we restricted them, and then your government said we were unfair and imposed restrictions. It was something they wanted all along, we think. There is always a hidden motive and secret purpose with your government."

To avoid detection by the FBI, the KGB choreographed every step of its meetings with John. After his initial contact with the Russians—when he walked into the Soviet embassy in Washington in late 1967 and offered to sell Navy secrets for cash—there was only one other face-to-face meeting in this country, a rendezvous two weeks later with a KGB agent in a shopping center. Thereafter, the Russians told him, they would meet in person only in Europe. Dead drops would be employed for all U.S. exchanges to minimize risk. Over the years John had performed so many dead drops that he had become an old hand. "You are the most experienced, the very best," his KGB handler once volunteered, massaging John's ego.

"Goddamn right!" John had replied.

John had begun his portion of yesterday's dead drop—just as the KGB instructions required—by turning onto a narrow road that meandered through a sparsely populated area. He altered his speed to check for tails, just as he had done earlier during his drive from Norfolk.

The Russians had placed an empty 7-Up can upright on the right edge of the road at a predetermined spot, an unobtrusive signal to John that his KGB contact was in the area and ready to make the exchange. The next move was up to him. Five miles later, he stopped to put a 7-Up can upright beside the road to signal that he was ready. He then continued on to the drop point, where he left his bundle of classified documents near a utility pole and a tree with a "No Hunting" sign nailed on it. John had prepared 129 stolen naval secrets for the KGB. The eight- by ten-inch copies of classified documents were wrapped in a white plastic trash bag to protect them from rain. Even the Soviets couldn't control the weather. He had hidden the bundle in the bottom of a brown paper grocery bag filled with an empty Diet Coke bottle, a used container of rubbing alcohol, an old box of Q-Tips, and a soap wrapper. At the same time that John was dropping off this package, the KGB was supposed to be dropping off a package of cash for him at a spot a few miles away. The Russians would also wrap John's bills in plastic and hide them in a grocery bag filled with trash.

Up to this point the drop had gone smoothly, but when John reached the Soviet drop point, he couldn't find the bag of cash. Worse, when he went back to his drop point to retrieve his bag of Navy secrets, it too had disappeared. He had checked both drop points several times during the night, conducting a methodical search through the weeds, bushes, and tall grass. Shortly before midnight, he had given up and returned to the motel.

Back in room 763, John thought at first that he had been discovered by the FBI, but he was confused because no one had tried to arrest him or keep him from leaving the Poolesville area. Maybe the Russians had simply screwed up, he thought, and left his money in the wrong spot. It had happened twice before.

The telephone call at 3:30 A.M. only added to his confusion. "I figured it was the FBI on the phone. Who else could it have been? It certainly wasn't the Russians," John recalled later. But the cockamamy story about his van being hit was too lame. "I just couldn't believe that anyone in law enforcement could be so dumb as to use that story about someone hitting my van. It just didn't make any sense. The FBI had to have known I was a private detective and had used the same trick a thousand times myself. It was just so incredibly obvious that I began to think, 'Hey, it might just be true. Maybe some drunk had hit my van.'"

Now, perched on the edge of the motel bed, John remained befuddled. His thoughts jumped back and forth. One moment, he was certain that he was about to be arrested by the FBI and then, just as quickly, he would decide the foul-up at the drop site and the mysterious telephone call to his motel room were merely coincidence. He was, after all, "the best." Besides, the dead drop had taken place on a Sunday night and he and his handler had laughed several times about how the "FBI doesn't work on weekends."

John walked to the window and peeked outside. He could see the motel parking lot, but not his van, which was parked around a corner. The fact that he didn't see a dozen police cars outside with their blue and red lights flashing gave him a bit more hope. Time was running out, though. If the FBI had unmasked him, it would be only a matter of minutes before federal agents came bursting through the door. The first thing he had to do was to destroy the envelope that the KGB had given him in Vienna. It contained hand-drawn maps of the dead drop route, an explanation of his every move, and black-and-white photographs of the drop points. There was only one problem. If he burned the instructions, he wouldn't be able to use them again, and the Soviets had told him that if a drop was ever aborted, both sides should simply try the exchange again exactly one week later. If he destroyed the instructions, he wouldn't be able to find the drop site the following Sunday and get his $200,000 payment—money he desperately needed.

Greed and ego quickly overruled caution. John scanned the room for a place to hide the envelope. There weren't many choices. Room 763 was standard motel fare: a double bed, a night table, two chairs, a small table with a smoked-glass ash tray, a dresser, mirror, and combination radio–television. Better to hide the envelope outside his room. Then, if it were found, the FBI couldn't prove that it belonged to him. John had noticed an ice machine next to the elevator bank when he first arrived. He could toss the instructions behind the machine and retrieve them later. But first he had to get to the machine, and that meant opening the door to his motel room and walking down the hallway and around a corner. John was petrified, but he had no choice. He had to leave his room.

Tucking the envelope under the pillow on the bed for temporary safekeeping, he slipped his .38 caliber revolver from its hip holster. "I didn't know who was on the other side of the door and if it was some kid waiting to rob me, I was going to waste him." He unfastened the chain lock and then, his hands shaking a bit and his lips dry, he jerked open the door. No one was there.

John stepped into the corridor, holding his handgun in front of him. The hallway was empty. Walking toward the elevator bank, he suddenly stopped near the exit stairway and placed his ear on the metal fire door. It was cold. He heard nothing from the other side. He twisted the doorknob and slowly pushed open the door. The stairwell was empty. His confidence renewed by his explorations, John dashed back to his room to retrieve the envelope. With his pistol in one hand and the envelope in the other, he returned to the hallway and raced toward the elevator bank and the ice machine around the corner.

"Stop! FBI!"

John spun to his right. Two FBI agents wearing bullet-proof vests had jumped out from a hallway opposite the elevators. Their blue-steel revolvers were pointed directly at John's heart.

What happened next is disputed. John says he immediately surrendered, dropping both gun and envelope instantaneously. But FBI agents Robert Hunter and James L. Kolouch described the arrest far more dramatically in sworn court testimony.

"Shortly after 3:30 A.M.," Hunter testified, "we heard John Walker's motel door open and close, and we heard footsteps. And I heard another door open and close, and footsteps again, and the door open and close again, which meant he came out and opened the door to the stairwell, obviously checking to see if anyone was there, and then returned to his room. We wanted to confront him by the elevator, not in the stairway, so we waited.

"We waited what seemed like a long period of time. It was quite exciting at that point, and a few minutes later, in fact approximately three-forty-five A.M., his door opened again, and I heard footsteps, and he quickly came around the corner and punched the elevator button with his left hand. As he punched the elevator button, agent Kolouch and I came out of our hiding spot in the hallway and he heard us as we moved and he immediately turned, a weapon in his hand.

"So we were standing there face-to-face, eyeball-to-eyeball, so to speak, with our weapons on each other."

QUESTION: He had a weapon in his hand at that point?
HUNTER: Yes.
Q: Where was it pointing?
HUNTER: Right at me!
Q: Well, who blinked first?
HUNTER: I'm sure he did; I didn't blink. We identified ourselves as FBI and told him to drop his weapon, and there was a confrontation that lasted a few seconds. It seemed like a long time, but it was a few seconds and he did finally drop the weapon.

"I didn't want to kill him," Hunter continued, pausing in his testimony for dramatic effect. "I wanted to talk to him. I needed to talk to this fellow. That's why I didn't pull the trigger."

FBI agent Kolouch gave a slightly different account of John's arrest during testimony at a different hearing. John didn't drop his weapon at first, Kolouch testified, but John's gun, he added, "was not pointed exactly—directly at us, but just about fifteen, twenty degrees off a direct line to us."

Whether or not John dropped his gun immediately or went eyeball-to-eyeball with Hunter seems immaterial now—to everyone but John Anthony Walker, Jr. During a series of long personal interviews after his arrest, John complained repeatedly that the FBI agents had embellished their testimony to make themselves appear heroic. "I didn't point my gun at either of them," John insisted. "I'm not that stupid. I'm a trained detective and I never point my gun unless I am going to fire it. Besides, do you really think those guys would have hesitated if I had swung around and aimed my gun directly at them? I dropped my piece and the envelope the second they yelled 'FBI.' " John was caught in a number of lies during interviews after his arrest, but he always shrugged off his falsehoods and his exaggerations as immaterial. The suggestion that an FBI agent might have added a bit of *High Noon* drama to the story of the arrest, however, infuriated him. "They lied!" he shouted at one point.

The second that John dropped his gun, both agents rushed forward. Kolouch pushed John against the wall, ripped his brown hairpiece from his head, quickly frisked him, and yanked off his thick-soled running shoes. Agent Hunter stood guard, his gun pointed at the back of John's now bald head. Other agents hurried out of hiding in room 750. Once Kolouch was certain John was not carrying concealed weapons, he hustled him into room 750 and ordered him to strip. Different agents seized each piece of clothing as he undressed, examining them in microscopic detail. They took away his metal-framed glasses and inspected them for microdots.

Naked, surrounded by FBI agents, without his toupee and nearly blind, John began to shake. Despite his experience as a private detective and his natural bravado, John Walker, Jr., was terrified.

"Fucking spy," he heard someone mumble. "Traitor."

John could tell from the agents' conversations that his motel room was being searched. He knew they wouldn't find anything. They already had what they were looking for: the envelope of instructions that he should have burned.

"You have the right to remain silent," agent Hunter said, reading John his rights under the Miranda ruling. He gave John a paper. "Sign this. It says I have read you your rights and you understand them."

"I can't," John replied. "I don't have my glasses and I can't read without them." Hunter barked an order and the glasses were quickly returned. Then Hunter asked if he wanted to tell them about the dead drop.

"I'm not saying a word without my attorney," John answered, regaining his composure. He noticed that an FBI agent was standing next to Hunter, jotting down notes on a pad. Anytime that Hunter said anything to John or he returned any comment, the agent noted the time and event. The FBI certainly wasn't going to screw up this arrest, he thought.

John was allowed to dress, then handcuffed and hustled out of the motel.

"Your next meal is going to be slipped under bars, Walker," John heard someone say.

Neither John nor the FBI agents with him—Hunter, Kolouch, and Jackson Lowe—said a word during the forty-minute ride to the FBI office in Baltimore. But after he was fingerprinted, photographed, and once again read his rights, John was pelted with questions.

"What were you doing last night?" Hunter demanded.

"Who were you meeting?"

"What are the instructions in the envelope for?"

John refused to cooperate. "I want an attorney," he said. "I have nothing else to say." The FBI agent standing near Hunter made a notation in his note pad: "6:21 A.M., interview ended."

Once the FBI makes an arrest, it usually hands the prisoner over to the U. S. Marshals Service, which oversees custody of federal prisoners. But the federal marshals' office in Baltimore didn't open until nine A.M., so there was little for the FBI agents and John to do for the next few hours but sit and stare at each other in the Spartan interrogation room.

Shortly after seven A.M., Hunter decided to unnerve John. He had a typewritten letter brought into the room and placed near John, who immediately began to fidget. John recognized the document. He had typed the letter himself, in his den at home, and sealed it inside the packet of Navy documents he had collected for the Soviets. Obviously, the FBI had picked up the grocery bag that John had left for the KGB. John's handler had warned him against including any personal remarks in a dead drop delivery. It was much safer to wait and talk in person in Vienna. But John had wanted to make certain the Russians realized how hard he had been working for them. He had asked them at an earlier meeting to consider giving him a $1 million payment in return for a steady supply of documents during the next ten years. John had included the typewritten letter in the dead drop package to help support his million-dollar request. He wanted to remind the Soviets that he had built an elaborate spy network and brief them on the ring's members and other potential recruits. John had been clever enough to use code names in the letter, but now he realized that the letter, along with the classified documents in the bottom of the grocery bag, would provide the FBI with enough clues to track down each member of his spy ring. John's twenty-two-year-old son, Michael Lance Walker, a seaman aboard the U.S.S. *Nimitz,* a nuclear aircraft carrier, had supplied all of the 129 documents in the grocery bag. Many of them were secret messages to the carrier or classified information about its mission. It wouldn't be difficult for the FBI to figure out that Michael had stolen them for his father.

The bag also contained personal letters to John from his best friend, Jerry Alfred Whitworth, a retired naval communications specialist, who had been an active member of the spy ring for ten years. John had included Whitworth's letters because the Soviets were particularly interested in him. It would not take the FBI long, John knew, to discover the identities of the two other men mentioned in his letter: Arthur James Walker, John's older brother and a retired naval officer; and Gary Walker, John's half brother, who was an Army mechanic. Arthur had provided John with a few rather useless classified documents, but Gary had never passed him anything. Gary was simply someone John had been trying to turn.

"Obviously," John said later, "I had put too much in my letter, but then, I never expected to get caught."

As he sat in the FBI interrogation room, John's thoughts turned to his own predicament. The documents that the FBI had recovered were an impressive cache. John remembered the most important ones: a thick study that identified problems with the nuclear Tomahawk land-attack cruise missile; a detailed explanation of how the Navy would respond if war broke out in Central America; schematics of the missile defense system aboard the U.S.S. *Nimitz* and its known weaknesses; an exhaustive study of how America's spy satellites could be sabotaged; and, as amazing as it sounds, some of the actual authentication codes needed to launch U.S. nuclear missiles.

These documents were just the tip of what John had passed through the years. If the FBI did a thorough investigation, as John suspected would happen, its agents would gradually uncover the full extent of his disloyalty and make a rather frightening discovery. From 1967 to 1985, John had sold the KGB vital U.S. cryptographic secrets that had enabled Russian agents to decipher approximately one million coded Navy dispatches, including messages about U.S. troop movements during the Vietnam War. He had wondered if American GIs had been captured or died in Vietnam because of information that he had revealed. Only the Soviets and their allies in North Vietnam knew for sure, but John realized that the sheer volume alone of the secrets that he compromised made him one of the biggest traitors in U.S. history, regardless of whether or not any Americans had died. He and his spy ring were part of an unprecedented breach in Navy security.

Besides selling U.S. cryptographic materials, John had also told the KGB how to strengthen Russian defenses and how the U.S. Navy intended to attack the Soviet Union if a war was declared between the superpowers. He had disclosed the precise location of sensitive underwater microphones used by the United States to track Soviet subs, and he had told the KGB where U.S. submarines would most likely be hiding if a war began.

There was no question, even in John's mind, that if the Soviet Union and the United States had gone to war, the Soviets would have enjoyed a dramatic edge because of what he had done.

Sitting in the conference room, John decided to see if he could throw the FBI off the trail.

"Who do you think I'm dealing with?" John asked, breaking his silence.

Hunter didn't hesitate: "The Soviets."

"There are lots of others out there interested in classified information," John replied. "Private intelligence-gathering organizations."

Hunter asked John to name the country that he was spying for, but John refused to say anything else. (Months later, a federal judge told prosecutors that they could not use as evidence or even make public John's statements that morning. The judge ruled that the exchange was improper because Hunter had not read John the Miranda warning *after* he had shown him the typewritten letter—even though John had already been read his rights twice that morning. It would be the only court battle that John would win.)

At five minutes before nine, John was finally turned over to federal marshals. As he was being taken away, he overheard Hunter tell another agent that a press conference had been called to announce the arrest. "I was amazed, totally bewildered," John recalled. "These assholes clearly didn't know who they were dealing with. Here I was, a person who had run a successful, perhaps the most successful spy ring in the nation's history, and all these bastards were worried about was getting out a goddamn press release. Getting public attention was more important than using me as a double agent."

John had always believed that he would never be prosecuted if he were caught. "I was too important as a double agent." Now the reality of his arrest was taking hold. To the FBI, John Anthony Walker, Jr., was just another criminal, a momentous one because his crime threatened national security, but a criminal just the same. John was incensed. How in the world could the government do something as stupid as prosecute him? he wondered. "I thought, 'I know more about espionage than the FBI and Central Intelligence Agency combined! For christsake don't these idiots know that they are blowing it!' "

John was taken to an isolated cell in the Baltimore City Jail, and it was there, after an hour of solitude, that he finally realized his days as a spy had ended. No one from the CIA was coming to his aid. No one was going to ask him to serve as a double agent the way they always did in the spy novels he loved.

John was exhausted, but too excited and nervous to sleep. Why had the FBI finally caught him? What mistake had tipped them off? The more he thought about his arrest, the more certain he became. He hadn't made any mistakes. Someone had turned him in. And there was only one person who would have done it—Barbara, his ex-wife. Barbara Crowley Walker. She had finally worked up enough courage to do it. It was difficult to believe, but it had to be her. His brother Arthur had warned him last fall, had told him that Barbara had called and threatened to turn John in.

"So what else is new," John had replied. Barbara, a self-admitted alcoholic, had threatened him so many times over the years that John had stopped taking her seriously. She was worse than the little boy who cried wolf.

Suddenly, several other events of the past few months started to come into focus. Like pieces of a mosaic, John saw the individual episodes begin to form a much larger picture. It was not only Barbara who had caused his downfall, but also his best friend, Jerry Whitworth; his own son, Michael; and even his own brother, Arthur.

"It's like an airplane crash," John recalled later. "Investigators check the wreckage and discover that it wasn't one single thing that caused the crash, but several different things that all came together."

A combination of all of their faults had led to his arrest. Each had failed him in his own way. "Why have I always been surrounded by weak people?" he asked later. "It was this group of misfits and weaklings that brought me down."

An astrologer once told John that he was a "double Leo" because of the location of the planets on his birthday, July 28, 1937. A "double Leo" is an extremely rare and gifted person, the astrologer explained, and John had believed her. "Double Leos are winners," he often told friends. "Take away all my money and throw me in the street naked. Within a week, I'll have gotten everything back and made even more."

Now that he had been arrested, he thought about the astrologer. She had been right. John Anthony Walker, Jr., was a winner, and he was not about to give the people he despised, such as his ex-wife, the pleasure of seeing him suffer. No, he thought, he was going to smile when they brought him in front of television cameras shackled in handcuffs and leg irons. His arrest and unavoidable prison sentence, he decided, would be "another adventure . . . a long-needed vacation." He would write a book while he was in jail about his experiences as a spy, and he would call it *John Walker, Jr.—Spy*. He would write two books, in fact, and call the sequel *John Walker, Jr.—Private Investigator*. He might even write a third about how to run a profitable small business. His arrest would make him famous. At last the entire world would know what only he and the Russians had known before: he was the best!

John began to unwind. He stretched out on the steel bunk, but tired though he was, he was still unable to sleep. "I kept thinking about Barbara and how she had snitched on me." Lying in the Baltimore jail, John decided that he had made only one mistake as a spy.

"I should have killed Barbara," he said later. "I should have assassinated her in the beginning. I should have put a fucking hole in her head."

With that final thought, he closed his eyes and fell asleep. He was awakened later that night for dinner. When the guards came for him, John began to chuckle mysteriously.

"The FBI was wrong," he noted later with sarcasm. "No one slid a tray under the bars of my cell. I ate in a jail dining room."

# 2

It was cold on the January 1986 night when I met John Walker, Jr., for the first time. He had been in various county jails in Maryland for seven months awaiting sentencing to a federal penitentiary. At this point John had not yet testified in public. Only his attorney, Fred Warren Bennett, and a handful of select FBI agents had discovered the damage he had caused.

I walked through the gloom and fog toward the Montgomery County Detention Center, a modern jail only a few miles from the site where John had made his last dead drop. I had been fascinated by him for months, by what it could be that would drive a man to sell his country's secrets to the Russians. I had read everything I could about him, talked with members of his family, learned as much as possible about John Walker, yet he was still an enigma. I wanted to know more, and I was here because now, for his own reasons, John Walker was ready to talk.

Directed to a small interview room usually reserved for attorneys and their clients, I sat in front of a heavy wire screen. A sign warned that it was unlawful to pass anything to a prisoner. The jail heating system had malfunctioned earlier that day and the tiny cubicle was sweltering. By the time John finally was brought in by a guard, I had removed my jacket and tie and perspiration had soaked my shirt.

John wore a jail-issued navy blue, short sleeve jumpsuit and thick black beach sandals. He carried a large brown folder filled with legal documents and yellow pads containing pages of scribbled notes. In his breast pocket were three freshly sharpened red pencils, all neatly aligned, points up. He had already outlined the main events of his life and he had reconstructed, he explained, his conversations with the KGB. He had provided all this information to the FBI, which had used a polygraph machine to verify its truthfulness, and now he wanted me to have it.

"I want the truth out," he explained. "I really don't know how anyone is going to be able to write very much bad about me if they are objective and report the whole picture and tell all the facts about my life and not a bunch of lies.

"Except for this one black mark," he continued, "I've led a very impressive life."

Within the hour, John was telling me why he had become a KGB spy. This is what he said:

"Everyone makes a big deal out of the fact that I became a spy. It's because spying is such an unusual crime, but what they don't understand is that I became a spy because that is what I had access to. If I'd worked in a bank, I would have taken money. If I'd had access to dope, I would have sold drugs. The fact that I became a spy is really insignificant. The point is that I became a spy because I needed money. It was as simple as that."

John paused and asked if my tape recorder was close enough to the wire grill to pick up his voice clearly. "When I was working as a private eye, I had a three-hundred-dollar recorder, not one of those cheap ones like you have there," he told me. I assured him that the recorder was reliable.

"You got to understand what I was going through at the time. My job in the Navy was extremely arduous duty. It was the worst duty I ever had in the military and for the first time I was having trouble keeping up. Meanwhile, I'm getting zero cooperation from Barbara. The marriage is vegetating. I was in Norfolk and the family was in Charleston, where we owned a small bar, so I'm running down to Charleston every weekend and Barbara is the pits. At this point, she is a problem drinker. God, I can see her now, a cigarette in one hand and a fucking glass in the other with her legs crossed at the end of this stinking line of bar stools.

"Sex between us is stopping and I mean stopping fast. There is no intimacy. I know that she is having an affair with someone. I don't know who, but I know. A husband always knows. A wife knows too. Your wife knows what you do and you know what she does without asking. You just know such things. You can sense them. I'm not the kind of person who would confront someone. If I walked in the house and caught my wife in bed with some guy, I would have backed out the door and laughed at the fucking dummies. I'm not the kind who would shoot them, that's for sure. I'm not saying it didn't bother me. Sure, it did, she was my wife, but I would have overlooked it. I didn't know at the time that it was my own goddamn brother who was screwing her. If I had figured it out I *would* have confronted him."

John paused and then grinned. "I would have said, 'Hey Art, I know you're fucking Barbara. Goddamn, I thought you had better taste.' "

He laughed and watched to see if I smiled. I did and then he said, "That's not really true. I was just trying to be funny, but this wasn't a funny situation. The truth was that my life sucked, really sucked."

Suddenly, it seemed as if John had become exhausted and a great burden had been placed on his shoulders. His speech slowed. "Anyway," he continued, "that's when I began to feel like I was back in the same hole that I had come from. I had an alcoholic father, and I saw the horrors of that and I promised myself that I would never be an alcoholic because I knew how destructive they were to the family and I didn't want to submit my kids to that bullshit. This is where the depression happened. Every chance that I got, I was trying to find some way to generate enough money to keep the bar going and Barbara wouldn't let up. . . . Nag, nag, nag. Yack, yack, yack. Where is the money coming from?

"I had a trailer behind the bar, sixty feet by twelve feet. It was the biggest you could get, so she wasn't living bad, but really strange things started happening. The kids were running wild. Things were out of control.

"It got to be too much. I was sitting in my goddamn room in the BOQ [Bachelor Officers' Quarters] in Norfolk, this shitty little room that the Navy gave me, and I was cleaning my pistol.

"It's hard to explain, it's irritating really because I'm a very rational person. You will find that out about me the more we talk. But I just couldn't handle another argument with Barbara. I was off submarines, which I missed, and I was stuck working on a desk and I really missed submarines, I mean, God I loved submarine duty, and Barbara had become a nagging bitch and a fucking alcoholic. I kept thinking, 'How can this be happening? How can my life be so screwed up?' I had a small insurance policy, ten-thousand-dollar whole life, I think, maybe more, but it was enough to pay off the bar debts and keep the place going for a while and I kept thinking about that money and how killing myself would get Barbara off my back too. It would have been more logical to divorce the bitch. I mean, the wife that I married at twenty was not the same person at thirty. I mean, I never would have considered even dating her if we'd met when we were both thirty.

"So I took the gun, the .38, I think, and I loaded the piece, I'm sure it was the .38, and I was in my room at the BOQ and I said, 'Screw it,' and I chambered a round and put that son-of-a-bitch up to my head, and I held it there and a few tears ran and I just couldn't do it. I just couldn't fucking do it, and I said, 'Fuck it Walker, you are already dead, man. You are just too dumb to know it. You are totally fucked up.' "

John sat quietly for several moments and then he looked at me and said, "All I really did was commit another form of suicide. I became a Russian spy."

I did not react. His answer sounded too pat, too rehearsed, yet believable, as if parts, if not all of it, were true. I *wanted* to believe John Walker. I *wanted* to believe that he was telling me the truth. But I wasn't certain.

We spoke a long time that night and John seemed pleased when I told him that I intended to talk to his mother, Margaret, and his father, John Walker, Sr.

"You'll love my mother," he said. "She's a typical sainted Italian grandmother. My dad is another story."

I mentioned several other persons with whom I wanted to speak, and then our time was up. But as the guard was leading him away, John turned and spoke to me.

"I know a lot of people will tell you lies about me," he said. "I don't know why people feel they have to do that. But they will. You're gonna have to be careful."

# PART TWO

---

# *THE PAST*

*For I the Lord your God am
a jealous God, visiting the iniquity
of the fathers upon the children
to the third and the
fourth generation . . .*

**Exodus 20:4**

*I'll meet the raging of the skies,
But not an angry father.*

**THOMAS CAMPBELL
"Lord Ullin's Daughter"**

# 3

At the turn of the century, Scranton, Pennsylvania became known as the Anthracite Capital of the World because it was located over the largest deposit of coal ever discovered in the United States. Immigrants seeking jobs deluged the booming industrial town, arriving from Wales, Ireland, Scotland, Germany, Poland, Lithuania, Italy, and Russia.

Arthur Scaramuzzo was among them. He stepped off a passenger car at the Lackawanna train depot in downtown Scranton in the spring of 1907, a sixteen-year-old boy from Italy with all of his possessions in one bag. Arthur could not speak, write, or understand English according to a note pinned to the breast of his thick wool jacket. Written by an immigration officer in New York City, the note said Arthur was seeking his father, Ralph, who worked in a stone quarry near Scranton.

Ralph had been the first member of the Scaramuzzo family to come to the United States. Like so many other immigrants, he sent for his family as soon as he could afford to. Arthur was the first to arrive. Eventually, Ralph earned enough to bring all four of his children to Scranton, but at Ellis Island his beloved wife, Rose, was declared "medically unfit" because she had cataracts. She was forced to return to Italy, where she died alone.

The quarry where Ralph Scaramuzzo worked was owned by Prospero Gaetano, another Italian immigrant. The two men had not known each other before Ralph applied for work, but their common heritage led to a quick and lasting friendship. So it was not surprising that Arthur Scaramuzzo was directed to Prospero Gaetano's house when he arrived in Scranton. The boy began work beside his father at the stone quarry the next day. It was exhausting, difficult labor. Arthur stood just five feet seven inches tall, but he had broad shoulders for a teenager, and strong arms. At night, he studied English.

A year later Arthur appeared again at the Gaetanos' door. This time he had come to ask Prospero Gaetano for the hand of his daughter, Angelina. At fourteen, she weighed a scant ninety pounds and still looked a girl, but she was a good cook and had been prepared by her mother to care for a husband and home. They were married April 28,

1908, in St. Lucy's Roman Catholic Church in West Scranton. The union lasted more than sixty years until their deaths, one year apart, in the early 1970s.

Scranton is a town where changes emerge slowly and memories linger. Children grow up in the same neighborhoods where their parents played as youngsters. Arthur and Angelina spent most of their lives just a few blocks from the church where they were married. He is remembered in West Scranton as a hard-working, pious man who was a good provider for his wife and eight children, four girls and four boys. Many nights, after a dinner of pasta, meat, salad, and bread—always torn from the loaf, never sliced—Arthur gathered his children around and told them funny stories, fairy tales that he made up as he went along. Afterwards he went down to the fruit cellar and brought them oranges and bananas.

Angelina was equally devoted to her family. She was always doing something for someone else: baking bread for a sick neighbor, mending clothes for her children, helping collect a basket for the needy at Christmas.

The Scaramuzzos were devout Roman Catholics, so much so that when Arthur added on to his simple, two-story frame house on Geraldine Court, he erected two shrines to the Virgin Mary in the entryway. It was not unusual, the children recall, to see Arthur and Angelina pray before the shrines at night before retiring, thanking the Virgin for what they considered to be an abundant life.

But one of their children, Margaret Loretta Scaramuzzo, looked at her parents' life a bit more skeptically than they did. Born in 1913, Peggy was a beauty. She had auburn hair, ebony eyes, and an unbridled sense of adventure. "Peggy wanted more from life than most of us," a cousin remembers. From the time she was a little girl, Peggy attacked life with a vengeance.

As a teenager, Peggy developed a beautiful singing voice and was soon a frequent vocalist at St. Lucy's. But while singing at church functions pleased her parents, Peggy sought a bigger stage.

Her mother and sisters sometimes had trouble accepting Peggy's passion for life. Once, when her mother asked Peggy to run an errand to the corner market, Peggy snapped, "No. There are some things a young lady just doesn't do." Angelina was forced to make the trip herself.

Peggy saw how hard her mother's life was, raising eight children and running the home. She saw the toll that her father paid for working as a stone mason. As a child, she had assumed these hardships were the routine ingredients of life. But as she matured, she started to look at her own neighborhood more critically. She saw girls only a few years older than she marry and turn, seemingly overnight, from gushing teenagers into dour wives left at home to change soiled diapers while their pot-bellied husbands tossed darts and drank beer at the neighborhood bar. She began to realize that although West Scranton was her parents' world, it didn't have to be hers. She had beauty and talent, and she didn't intend to settle for a young man who was content to come home each night with coal dust under his fingernails.

On a brisk December evening in 1932, Peggy met a man who also had big dreams. She had gone with her brother Frank to a nightclub called The American Beauty to hear a local band. During a brief intermission, a young man approached her.

"Hello, Miss Scaramuzzo," he said. "My name is Johnny Walker."

John Anthony Walker was unlike anyone Peggy had ever met. Lean and clean-cut, he was handsome by any young girl's standard. But there was something more to Johnny Walker than good looks. He had a certain elegance that other Scranton boys lacked, a certain charm and gentleness. He also had the most appealing voice Peggy had ever heard, a distinct baritone with a certain authority to its natural cadence, a smoothness that seemed to say, *Trust me, I know what I am talking about.*

Johnny had grown up in West Scranton, the son of James Vincent Walker, an engineer for a mining company, and Mary Ferguson Walker. He had two brothers and a sister, all of them smart and talented, like him. When Johnny was a student at St. Patrick's High School in West Scranton, underclassmen from the University of Scranton used to hire him to write school papers for them. Johnny was not just intelligent he was musically gifted. A love of music was just one of the things that brought Johnny and Peggy together. Fifty years later Peggy still recalled the night she met her future husband. "It was love at first sight," she told me tearfully, as we spoke in the parlor of her childhood home, which Arthur Scaramuzzo had bequeathed to his children. "Johnny was so handsome and I was so in love with him. We were so full of life. Nothing was going to stop us, man! Nothing!"

I asked Peggy, who was seventy-four years old at the time, about her wedding. But Peggy, who was still working an eight-hour job during the week and was mentally sharp, suddenly became evasive. "I can't remember when it was," she said, "but you know it was here in Scranton and it wasn't anything special."

I later discovered that Peggy and Johnny were not married in Scranton, but in Rockville, Maryland, on August 15, 1934. One month after the ceremony, Peggy gave birth to Arthur James Walker. The fact that Peggy was pregnant when she married was never mentioned within the family. Even Arthur claimed not to have known. It was the first of many family secrets to be revealed.

# 4

Washington, D.C., is much more glamorous than Scranton, and Johnny and Peggy soon were happily settled into a modest apartment at 43 R Street Northeast, a tidy section of rowhouses. Johnny worked at the Department of Commerce as a clerk in the National Recovery Administration, one of the overnight bureaucracies President Franklin Delano Roosevelt had created to help pull America out of the depression. Peggy took care of Arthur and soon found herself pregnant again. On July 28, 1937, Peggy gave birth to John Anthony Walker, Jr.

From the beginning, relatives recalled later, Peggy favored her second-born. Perhaps it was because her pregnancy with Arthur embarrassed her. For whatever reason, Peggy developed a special bond with John, whom everyone called Jack as a child, that grew stronger through the years.

It didn't take long before John Walker, Sr., grew tired of being a government clerk. Meetings and shuffling papers were not for him, he told Peggy. So when a better paying and more demanding job opened at the Bituminous Coal Commission, he accepted it and moved his family to Altoona, Pennsylvania. But before Peggy had a chance to unpack, Johnny quit this job to take an even better one in New York City. Could there be a better place for an ambitious young man and his family than New York City? he asked Peggy. Johnny had been offered a job by his father's cousin, Frank Comerford Walker, a prominent attorney, former Montana state legislator, Democratic Party official, and pal of FDR. On December 10, 1938, a group of Democratic stalwarts had formed a private corporation to raise money for construction of the Franklin D. Roosevelt Library, the first presidential library. Frank Walker had been elected president of the group, and he wanted Johnny to be its liaison with the Philadelphia construction company hired to build the library and with Dr. Fred H. Shipman, the library's first director. It was challenging and heady work.

An album of family photographs shows a beaming couple poised in the living room of an attractive fifth-floor apartment on Seventy-seventh Street in Manhattan. Johnny is pictured with his jacket tossed casually over his right shoulder, his left arm draped around Peggy. He is dressed in a crisp white shirt, tie, suspenders, carefully pressed trousers, and spit-polished shoes. Peggy is wearing a store-bought dress with matching hat and gloves. Peggy and Johnny spent hours keeping their family album current, she meticulously arranging each snapshot and Johnny drawing white ink doodles on the album's black pages. It was more than a scrapbook of family snapshots. It was a primer of a couple on the move.

Nearly all of the relatives visited the young couple in New York, and Arthur Scaramuzzo, in particular, was generous in his praise. The United States really was a land of unlimited opportunity, he proclaimed. He had arrived a poor immigrant, and his son-in-law had actually met the President of the United States!

Peggy and Johnny enjoyed not only the city, but also each other. There were occasional arguments—both were stubborn—but spats were rare. Peggy gave birth to James Vincent Walker, the couple's third son and last child, in New York City in 1939.

Some of Johnny's correspondence to the library's corporate board still exists in the archives at Hyde Park. The documents reveal a certain brashness. At one point, FDR's cronies asked Johnny to write a history of the library. His twenty-one-page account included not only compliments to FDR and the library's backers, but also several harsh criticisms. The board chose not to circulate it widely.

When his job with the library ended in 1941, Johnny turned once again to his politically powerful cousin for help. Frank Walker liked Johnny and thought he was bright and talented. He also knew that Johnny was a good salesman, an excellent musician, and a lover of the theater, so he helped Johnny get a job with Warner Brothers as a salesman/publicist. He was sent to Richmond, Virginia, to cover movie theaters in the Washington, Virginia, and Maryland region. The Walkers didn't like leaving New York, especially for a town as sedate as Richmond and a job that just didn't seem as exciting as the old one. But it was more glamorous working for the movies than for the federal government. The couple bought a bungalow at 712 Pensacola Avenue in a middle-class area of Richmond in a quiet, close-knit neighborhood.

"I remember the heat in Richmond," Arthur Walker recalled later. "I had been up north all of my life and I thought it was really hot in Richmond. Life was good there. We assimilated quickly into the neighborhood."

Because of his association with Warner Brothers, Johnny was regarded as a neighborhood celebrity, a glitter that gave Peggy and her three sons a special status too.

"Dad was really making decent money," Arthur recalled. "If a person made fifteen or twenty bucks a week back then, they were happy, and he made much more than that.... I remember him opening up a Christmas bonus check of a thousand dollars."

The Walkers' life might have seemed idyllic, but it wasn't. Johnny and

Peggy fought constantly. The exact cause of their unhappiness isn't clear. At the time, Peggy complained that Johnny's work took him away from the family too much and he wasn't helping around the house as much as she wanted. But as in many marriages, the most obvious complaints were just signs of deeper unrest. One night after suffering through one of Peggy's harangues, Johnny exploded and slugged her in the face. The next morning, after he had cooled, he apologized. "He was so upset that he began to cry," Peggy recalled. But the altercation was not an unfortunate aberration.

Some people can look back over the years and pick an incident that marked a dramatic change in their lives. Johnny Walker could cite the exact day his life turned topsy-turvy: September 19, 1944. While returning home from booking a movie in Emmitsburg, Maryland, his car and another vehicle collided in a spectacular accident. The only particulars about the mishap come from memory, and everyone who remembers the event tells a different story. But there is one thing that they all agree upon. Johnny Walker nearly died. His injuries were so severe that when the police arrived on the scene they didn't think anything could be done to save him. "The county coroner had already started filling out my death certificate when he discovered I was still breathing," Johnny told me later. He was rushed to the hospital in Gettysburg, where Peggy hurried to his bedside. The boys were left behind to be cared for by the family's live-in housekeeper, Emma Evans. The subsequent hospital bills and lawsuit against Johnny filed by the other driver drained the Walker family bank account.

After he recovered, Johnny lost his prestigious Warner Brothers' post and went through a series of other jobs—he sold pots and pans door-to-door, worked as a department store clerk, and drove a taxi—but none of them paid all the bills. Peggy was forced to find work. During the day, she labored at the Franklin Uniform Company; at night, she took photographs of couples at the Tantilla Garden, a nightclub that claimed to have the "South's finest ballroom." By 1947, the Walkers' home was a shambles. "I remember my father coming home from work and drinking himself into oblivion," John Walker, Jr., said. "My mother would start on him, bitching endlessly about money or shooting her mouth off about how he didn't do anything and couldn't care for the family, and pretty soon he'd punch her, and then all hell would break loose." All three boys recall being awakened at night by the sounds of their parents yelling and cursing each other. The boys shared a large upstairs bedroom in Richmond and during lulls in the fighting downstairs, one of them—usually John, the most adventuresome of the brothers—would creep down the staircase and peek around the corner to see what was happening.

One night John saw his father passed out drunk in a chair and Peggy lying on the floor amid broken dishes. She was sobbing. "Is she dead?

Did he kill her?" Arthur demanded when John came scampering back upstairs.

"Naw, she's still alive," John said, "but he got her good."

Jimmy began to cry.

"Shut up!" John shrieked. "You want him to come up here and beat us?"

It was a confusing time for Arthur, John, and Jimmy. They had always been proud of their father and, like most boys, had seen him as a larger-than-life figure and a role model. Before the accident, the boys had waited anxiously for Johnny to come home on weekends from his sales trips. Not now. "Suddenly, I wasn't talking about Dad like other kids did," Arthur recalled. "I wasn't proud of him anymore."

As a boy, John became furious when Johnny beat Peggy. "I didn't understand what was happening," John said later. "I didn't really appreciate my father's sober days because I was too little. My mother would tell me that he was a good man and that she loved him, and when he was sober, he was good to us, but it was a fucking horror movie when he wasn't."

Loud arguments, slammed doors, brawls, and drunken lectures were the norm. Arthur received the brunt of Johnny's anger toward his boys, but John was the one who became outraged by his father's behavior. After a confrontation, Arthur would hide in the woods near his home and simply wait for Johnny to go to bed. John seethed and plotted.

"I decided I had no choice but to kill him," John recalled. "I was probably ten or eleven years old, but I was serious. I was going to do it. In fact, I wanted to do it. I was going to kill my father because I hated him for what he was doing to my mother."

John spent a week planning the murder, considering various methods, rejecting them one by one. Finally, he hit upon an acceptable plan. "We had a cast-iron bed, a rollaway that was heavy. It probably weighed seventy or eighty pounds. Jesus, it was a monster, and I decided to use it to kill him."

The next time his father came home drunk, John intended to push the heavy rollaway to the edge of the stairway. When his father began climbing the steps, John would push the bed down on top of him. "Either the fall would kill him or he would be pinned under the bed and I could go down and hit him with a baseball bat and finish him off."

A few days after John had decided on his murder plan, Johnny came home drunk and got into an argument with Peggy. John quietly pushed the bed into position at the top of the stairs. He sat down and waited. The next morning Peggy found her son asleep next to the rollaway bed. Johnny had passed out in a living room chair and had never made it up the stairway that night.

On November 12, 1948, the Realty Industrial Loan Corporation foreclosed on the Walkers' house after Peggy and Johnny failed to make the $50 mortgage payment for the seventh month in a row. Peggy's swank studio couch, Johnny's piano, the boys' maple bedroom set, were dragged outside and sold to the highest bidder by the loan company to recover a $2,600 loan.

The glamor days of the $1,000 Christmas bonus and live-in housekeeper were long since over. Peggy had no choice but to telephone her father. "Papa, we need someplace to live," she said. Heartbroken over his daughter's financial plight, Arthur Scaramuzzo suggested that she and Johnny return to Scranton. He would find a place where she, Johnny, and the boys could live with relatives until they got back on a good financial footing. Peggy turned scarlet as she spoke with her father. She had never felt so humiliated in her life. John saw his mother sobbing as the family prepared to move to Scranton, and it made him angry.

"I wished," he told me later, his voice filled with anger, "that I'd never fallen asleep on the stairs that night and that my father had tried to come up them."

# 5

As he had done twice before, Johnny Walker sought Frank Comerford Walker's help when he returned to Scranton in early 1949. Frank delivered by getting Johnny a job in the business end of the Roosevelt Theater in Scranton. Everyone in the family except Jimmy, who was only eleven years old, went to work. Peggy took photographs of school-children for Prestwood's Photo Studio; Arthur was a stock boy at Belinski's Market after school; John sold the blue streak edition of the *Scranton Tribune*. The boys were farmed out to relatives until Peggy and Johnny had saved enough to rent a two-bedroom apartment over the theater. Johnny joined Alcoholics Anonymous and there were fewer confrontations at home. But the family had changed.

It was time, Peggy had decided, to accept the harshness of life. She no longer paid attention to Johnny's talk of making it big and leaving Scranton. She would dream through her children now, especially through her cherished son John. Of the three, only he seemed to have what it would take to break away from Scranton and its tedious, blue-collar life-style.

On most nights, Peggy could see John through her kitchen window as he stood across the street from the theater selling papers to people leaving the last show. A determined and frugal boy, each night, he tucked aside half of the $1.25 that he averaged. Peggy helped him hide his money from his father. When he earned his first $10, she took him to the bank to open a savings account.

While John was selling newspapers on a particularly harsh February night in 1949, he saw a small boy pedaling his bicycle toward the theater. It was so cold that the boy's wool mittens had frozen to the handlebars of his bike. Most of the color had left his face and he was puffing.

"Whatcha doing?" John asked.

"Deliverin' the *Trib*' to people's homes," Joey Long answered. "Just finished. How 'bout lettin' me come behind your stand and warm up?"

John nodded, eager for the company. That night's meeting was the beginning of a friendship that lasted more than thirty years. Joey Long, a year older, was a husky, uncomplicated boy who was honest, worked hard, and never got into any trouble. As youngsters, John and Joey created their own adventures.

"John and I would talk about getting away and seeing the world," Long later remembered. "He was very aggressive, very sure of himself. He wasn't lazy. He wanted to get ahead. He was very tight with his money. He told me he was saving it, but I didn't know what for. He used to say that his father was a failure and he didn't want to be that way."

When Joey turned seventeen, he joined the Marines. John went with him to the recruiter's office and helped Joey fill out some of the necessary forms. Afterward, Joey pestered John about signing up, but John wasn't interested in a military career. He had other plans.

Joey was not John's only "best friend." A short time after the Walkers moved to Scranton, John met Charles "Chas" Bennett, a thin, bespectacled boy one year younger than him.

John's friendships with Joey Long and Chas Bennett were completely separate. Each one was *his* friend and John never made an effort to bring them together, nor did he encourage them to become friends with each other. But there was something else about his friendships with Joey and Chas that was peculiar.

When Joey Long was with him, John was a rambunctious adventurer who was polite, respectful, and honest. But when he was with Chas Bennett, it was a different story altogether. "On the surface, Jack [John still was known as Jack during this period] was never in any trouble," Charles Bennett recalled. "But believe me, what you see on the surface with Jack is not what you get. Trust me. I knew him like a brother, better than anyone else. Jack is cunning, intelligent, clever, personable, and intrinsically evil."

John and Chas stole eggs and threw them at streetcars, rolled used tires down hills at cars passing below, threw rocks through windows at St. Paul's Catholic School. They soon graduated to more serious pranks. They stole money from purses and coats left unattended during school functions and stole coins from the tiny canisters in church sanctuaries where worshippers left donations for the poor and money to pay for prayer candles.

Once they stole a tin of hosts. The next day at St. Paul's, Chas asked several girls in between classes if they wanted to "receive communion."

"I didn't realize until much later," Charles Bennett recalled, "that I was always the one passing out the hosts while Jack lurked in the shadows watching."

Years later, Charles Bennett still talked about John's influence over him. "It was almost hypnotic," he said. "I can't explain it, but he became my Svengali. There was just something intriguing about him that drew me to him. He had a certain manipulative power."

He added, "Jack was constantly calculating, his mind was active all the time. There was no spur-of-the-moment action, no random conversation. If you said something, he was filing it away, figuring out how to use it in the future."

The boys' misdeeds became more and more dangerous. John made a pair of brass knuckles and got into a fist fight in order to use them. He and Chas began setting fires. In 1950 John went to work as an usher at the Roosevelt Theater and pulled a prank that terrified Chas. One of the pictures playing that summer was *Winchester .73*, a hard-driving western that starred Jimmy Stewart and Rock Hudson. As part of a publicity stunt, the studio sent theaters replicas of a Winchester rifle. John borrowed the rifle one night and invited Chas and another boy to go "shooting" with him. They hiked into the mountains overlooking the city and took turns shooting empty beer bottles and discarded cans. But John got bored and when it was time for him to shoot again, he moved to a nearby ledge and began firing at the headlights of the cars on the main highway below.

"I was terrified," Charles Bennett recalled, "not of the police, but what my father would do if he had found out. But Jack didn't seem to care and I remember thinking after that incident that Jack *wanted* his father to find out what he was doing. I think he really wanted to strike back at his father and embarrass his old man."

# 6

Johnny and Peggy moved across town in 1951, into a house in the same West Scranton neighborhood where both of them had grown up. Neither Arthur nor John wanted to enroll at St. Patrick's High School. They had heard stories about the strictness of the nuns and priests there, and it was much smaller than the public schools that Arthur and John liked. But Johnny Walker didn't care what his sons wanted. He had graduated from St. Patrick's and felt the rigid discipline would be good for his boys. Peggy also liked the idea because she was turning more and more to the Church for solace, returning to the teachings that had sustained her parents.

The school was run with absolute authority. Answers were black and white; actions were good or evil. There was no room for gray, whether it was a question of school rules or Catholic dogma. Physical punishment, a crack on the knuckles with a ruler or a swat with a wooden paddle, came quickly and often. Students were required to say the rosary every day. A photograph of Pope Pius XII was displayed next to a picture of President Harry Truman in the principal's office. The three-story brick school building looked more like a fortress than a school. To John it became a prison.

He developed an intense distaste for organized religion, but while he shared his feelings with his brother, John was cagey enough to conceal them at school. Open confrontation with the priests and nuns would have been catastrophic. Instead, he resisted tacitly, doing as little homework as possible and showing no interest in any school function. He even refused to have his picture taken for the yearbook. He wanted no part of St. Patrick's.

Meanwhile, Arthur thrived at the school. Academically, he had his ups and downs, but he excelled in sports, particularly football, scoring three touchdowns and averaging four yards per carry as a running back for the Paddies during his senior year. Arthur also was into basketball, baseball, and track, played the trumpet in the band, and was the hero in a senior class play. Just before graduation in 1952, his classmates named him the most popular student in the school.

John and Arthur had always depended upon one another—each filling in for the other's weaknesses—but after the move to West Scranton they began to grow apart. The separation was partially because of girls. John wasn't interested in them; Arthur was obsessed. Years later, Arthur would claim that he was a virgin when he married and was rarely unfaithful to his wife. Others, including John, would recall how Arthur had had a string of girlfriends and how he had, in fact, lost his virginity as a teenager when the family lived in Richmond. At St. Patrick's in 1952, he met Rita Clare Fritsch, a prim and proper blonde pixie with large black-rimmed glasses and a pug nose. Rita fell in love with Arthur, but not with his family. She had heard from her mother that Johnny was a drunk. Rita also had trouble getting along with Peggy, who seemed jealous of her son's new interest. The more serious Rita and Arthur became, the more time Arthur spent at the Fritsch home.

Arthur was not the only member of the Walker family spending less and less time at home. Johnny had quit his job at the Roosevelt and gone to work as a disc jockey at radio station WARM. The most popular radio deejays in Scranton were on the air in the afternoon and early evening. Being a newcomer, Johnny was stuck with the graveyard shift. But he didn't mind the schedule because it gave him the opportunity to experiment with different formats. Within a few months, he had developed a show called *The Night Walker*. Johnny played soft music and read love poems over the Scranton airwaves. Sometimes he would whisper into the microphone as if he were confiding in an unseen lover. The show was an overnight sensation and Johnny was, once again, a celebrity, especially among women. The circuits overloaded whenever Johnny asked listeners to phone in and request "that special song for someone you love." Soon he was earning $4 an hour, at a time when some workers in the Lackawanna Valley were earning that amount for a full day's work.

For a while, Johnny's success made family life much easier. The tranquility did not last, however. Trouble seemed to follow Johnny. Merchants began to complain that he was not paying his bills. There were shocked whispers that he had been seen around town with various women. Gossip escalated after a loud public argument between him and a bartender ended in Johnny's being kicked out of a popular nightclub. Johnny and Peggy began fighting physically again. Some of the brawls were so violent the police were called in by neighbors.

When Arthur graduated from St. Patrick's, Johnny took him aside and told him that he was going to college. Arthur didn't want to go, but his father insisted. Perhaps he had failed his boys, but he wasn't the first father to get mired in alcohol, and his problems didn't mean that he didn't want his sons to succeed. Arthur dutifully enrolled at the University of Scranton, but by the end of the first semester it was obvious that he was in over his head. Without telling his parents, he went downtown to see a Navy recruiter. He chose the Navy, he confided to me later, because he liked the uniform.

Johnny was furious when Arthur broke the news, but there was little he could do. Peggy was certain that Arthur would be killed. Arthur listened to them complain for nearly an hour, then went over to Rita's. To Arthur's irritation, it was nearly a year before he was called to active duty. Rita saw him off.

By the time that Arthur left, John, too, had found a means of escape from the family. He had used some of the money he had saved from working various jobs to buy a baby blue 1949 Ford for $590, a hefty sum in 1954. Johnny had hoped that his son would use the money for college tuition, but John showed even less interest in a college degree than Arthur had.

John loved his car, in the way that only teenage boys can. He washed and waxed it faithfully, shampooed its interior, and fidgeted with its engine. On May 27, 1955, John was sitting in a soda shop on Jackson Street with a boy nicknamed Smiley, who suggested that if John needed money for new tires, they could break into a gasoline station and either steal some money or tires for his car. John agreed, but the first station they broke into didn't have anything worth stealing. The next few hits also turned up little. Frustrated, they decided to go after a bigger score—Cuozz & Gavigan's, a men's clothing store.

John and Smiley removed the cover from a ventilator and lowered themselves inside the rear of the building, but found the door into the main store barred. After several minutes, the two boys began climbing out of the store, only to be met by Patrolman William Shygelski, who had heard noises from the rear of the clothing store while walking his beat.

Shygelski ordered John and Smiley to stop, but neither did, and the foot patrolman drew his revolver and began firing at them. John ran to his car and sped away. Undeterred, Shygelski flagged down a passing car and gave chase. It never occurred to John that Shygelski might commandeer a car, so he assumed he was home free. Slowing down to avoid attention, he stopped at a red light at North Hyde Park and Jackson. Before the light turned green, Shygelski's car sped up, and he jumped out, gun in hand.

"Stop! Police!" he yelled. John jammed the gas pedal to the floor as Shygelski dropped to his knee and fired twice more. He had taken aim at the Ford's gas tank, but his shots hit the bumper. Shygelski chased John at speeds up to eighty-five mph until John finally lost him.

A few days later, the police captured John on the basis of a tip from his mother. During several hours of questioning, John confessed to the attempted burglary and told about Smiley. The police called Johnny Walker to see if he wished to post his son's bail. "No, he might learn something if you keep him in jail a few nights," Johnny replied. John was taken to the Lackawanna County Jail and locked in a cell with adults. The next morning, Johnny Walker took Jimmy to see John.

"Now you take a good look at your brother," Johnny told Jimmy. "See what happens to bad boys?"

John begged his father to post bail, but Johnny declined. John Walker, Jr., claimed years later that an adult in the jail attempted to rape him that night. The attack was stopped by others in the cell. "I hated my father so much that night," John said. "He had left me there knowing something like that might happen." One week later, John appeared before Judge Otto P. Robinson. The Reverend John W. Casey, pastor of the Walkers' church, spoke on John's behalf. "John Walker," he said, "is an exceptional student and, it is hard to say this under the circumstances, but in school he has been a fine student."

Mother Vincent, principal of St. Patrick's High School, was not quite as enthusiastic. John had missed fifteen out of 180 days of school, she reported. His conduct was "generally good" and his scholarship was "fair."

The judge was unmoved by statements of the pastor and the principal. John and Smiley were sentenced to indefinite terms at the state correctional institution at Camp Hill. "I can't see anything in favor of either one of you. You are just two crooks," Robinson said. But because this was the first time that either boy had been to court, Robinson suspended the sentences and put the boys on probation. "This is a chance for you fellows to go straight," Robinson lectured. "Don't make another mistake. You've got to be honest or you go to Camp Hill. Learn the Ten Commandments and obey them and you won't be in further trouble."

No one bothered to tell Arthur about John's brush with the law. "I came home on leave on my birthday and when I found out, I took John outside and said, 'Hey, what's going on?' I could see that he was really getting screwed up because of the situation at home, my dad's drinking and such, and I felt that the Navy was really taking care of me. I was already a petty officer and I really loved submarine duty, so I said, 'John, you got to go into the Navy, man! You got to get out of this house.' "

It took Arthur only thirty minutes to convince John. He marched his brother straight down to the recruiting office. "We walked in," Arthur recalled, "and I was in my Navy blues and I said, 'I got my brother here and he wants to join up,' and this recruiter starts going crazy because he is so happy. Well, John went through the basic questions and when the recruiter came to the one about having committed any criminal acts, John said that he had been arrested and the recruiter slowed down a bit, and then the recruiter says, 'What did you do?' and John tells him, and this guy flips out and says, 'Sorry, we can't take you unless you get the judge to lift your probation.' So John and I walked across the street to the courthouse and went up and I found the judge and said, 'Your Honor, my brother wants to join the Navy and I think it would really help him out.' Well, we talked for a while and the judge agreed and called the recruiter, and the next thing you know, John is in the Navy. I went back to submarine duty and John went off to boot camp."

Years later, I asked John about his troubled childhood. At first, he claimed that the only crimes that he committed were the failed burglaries that he and Smiley attempted. When I told him about Charles Bennett's statements, John grudgingly acknowledged that he had been involved in some childish pranks, but considered them examples of "typical fifteen-year-old behavior."

"I'm not saying that I didn't do things that I shouldn't have done," he explained. "Breaking into those places was wrong, but you got to remember that I didn't have anything because my old man was a drunk and that was really the big factor.

"Look, I bought the family car, not him. Talk about role reversal. He used to come to me to borrow the keys and then he never would bring it back when he promised, and when he did the back seat was filled with beer cans and whiskey bottles.

"The reason that I was breaking into a clothing store was not because I needed money, it was because I needed clothes. We didn't have any money because my father drank it up. The same was true about glasses. One reason I did lousy in school was because I couldn't see. I would borrow Chas Bennett's glasses to look at the blackboard and write down the next assignment. We'd be standing on the street corner and he'd say, 'Hey Jack, here comes a girl,' and I'd say, 'Quick, give me your glasses so I can see. Is she cute?'

"So I know what I did was wrong," John concluded, "but I was just a kid and I didn't want to ask my mother for money, and those burglaries, if you call them that, were the entire extent of my criminal career. That was it. I made a mistake and broke into those stores, but I was hardly a criminal. I don't think most people would even call what I did a crime if they knew the facts. I was just a kid trying to support himself."

Interviews with John's teenage friends, as well as police and court records, give a rather different picture of John's past. During questioning in June 1955 by Scranton detectives James Walsh and Leo Marcus, John confessed to six other burglaries besides the four that he and Smiley committed on May 27.

There is reason to believe John was involved in other crimes as well that until now have not been revealed. Three months before his arrest, on February 11, 1955, a teenage armed bandit held up a Scranton Transit Company bus at 11:25 P.M., escaping with $38 in cash. The gun-toting robber was never caught. John bragged about committing the robbery to his brother, Jimmy, and showed him a money changer that he took from the bus driver and the gun that he had used. John also showed up at Chas Bennett's house the morning after the stickup.

"I asked him what was going on," Bennett recalled, "and Jack said to me, 'I robbed a bus last night. I put a mask on and I waited until it got to the end of the line and then I robbed everyone.' "

Another person also knew that John was a thief.

"I used to come home on leave and find John peddling things," Arthur Walker told me one afternoon during a reflective moment. "John would be selling things really cheap, like brand new Arrow shirts for one dollar, and whenever anyone asked him, he'd grin that grin of his and say they'd fallen off a truck. I knew, but I honestly thought the Navy would straighten him up."

# 7

John's first letter from boot camp was dated October 28, 1955, three days after he left Scranton. Addressed to Jimmy, it had $10 tucked inside for Peggy. Before John left, he and Peggy had agreed that if he wanted to write both parents, he would address his letters to Peggy and Johnny, but if he wanted to tell his mother something without his father knowing or if he was sending Peggy cash, he would send the letter to Jimmy.

Peggy put John's letter in an empty shoebox along with a second one, which came a week later. She still has them.

"I loved the Navy and it quickly became my home," John recalled. "I had an inferiority complex at first because I hadn't graduated from high school and I had gotten into trouble. But everything went right for me from day one. Just excellent! I couldn't believe it, and then I realized that I was obviously sharper than most of the others."

His letters to Peggy support John's recollection. "Today, as we were marching along," John wrote, "the CO could no longer stand the second platoon leader, so he kicked him out. Everyone knew he was about to pick a new man for the job. Well, it didn't take him long to decide *I* was the best man."

John liked the role of leader and worked hard to keep it. "I wanted to be the best." After boot camp he went to radio operators' school in Norfolk and immediately applied for submarine duty. Arthur, who had been assigned to the submarine U.S.S. *Torsk* for two years, had convinced John that there was no better assignment. Most sailors considered duty on diesel submarines arduous and dangerous because they were cramped, noisy, and unpredictable. When a diesel submarine submerged in icy waters, it got so chilly inside that crew members joked they could see each other's breath. In the tropics, the temperature inside the boat could soar to over a hundred degrees. The air inside tasted thick and viscous, as if you had an oily film on your tongue. There was no privacy in the tight quarters.

But Arthur loved submarines. "A submarine crew is a special breed," he told John. "Each man has a specific responsibility and if he doesn't perform it, he not only jeopardizes the mission, but also the lives of every man aboard. There is no room on a submarine for someone who is second best."

John wanted to follow in his brother's footsteps, but a Navy doctor ruled that John was unfit for submarine service because of poor eyesight, so he was assigned to the U.S.S. *Johnnie Hutchins,* a destroyer anchored in Boston harbor. John was upset, but Arthur buoyed his spirits. "We'll find a way to get you on a sub," he promised.

John reported to the *Hutchins* early one morning in June 1956. By dusk, he had investigated every part of the antiquated training vessel and learned its history. The boat had been named to honor the son of a Texas tenant farmer who had been killed in 1943 during a battle off New Guinea. When a Japanese bomb exploded and killed the helmsman, Johnnie Hutchins, despite the fact that he was severely wounded, pulled himself to his feet just in time to spot a torpedo headed directly toward his ship. He turned the craft away from the torpedo and died.

The men aboard the *Johnnie Hutchins* had also served their country well in the war. The *Hutchins* had singlehandedly sunk three Japanese midget submarines off the coast of Okinawa in 1945. The heroism of both sailor and ship inspired young recruits, even cynical, street smart ones like John. Late at night, he fantasized about taking charge of the *Johnnie Hutchins* during some future sea battle and leading its crew to victory.

The destroyer made two training cruises in 1956. Hugging the coastline, it moved slowly north to Quebec, Halifax, and Newfoundland. Later, the fifty-seven trainees and officers on board headed south to the Caribbean and Cuba. Both trips were considered routine by the Navy, but not by John. During liberty in Canada, John and a throng of other sailors went to a whorehouse. John had lost his virginity in the backseat of a car before he joined the Navy, but this experience was his first with a skilled partner and it marked the start of what became an addiction. John paid to have sex with scores of prostitutes during his twenty-year naval career. There was something alluring about the murky underbelly of life that drew John like a siren's song. Bleak harbor hotels, lurid bars, and crude hookers fascinated him. The inherent danger of these places only added to his excitement. He felt comfortable in a cheap bar with his hand on a hooker's thigh.

"I'm not the kind of person who confuses love and sex," John explained. "Sex is not love. Sex is a muscle spasm that you have with someone, and that's all. It's entertainment. Love is something else."

When the *Hutchins* docked in Boston, John began frequenting the roller rink at Revere Beach near Broad Sound. On weekends, the owners of the rink stopped all skating at nine P.M. and held a dance on the huge wooden floor. John never had trouble finding a date. Although he looked scrawny beside his brawny sailor pals, he had a pleasing face. He wore his inky hair close-cropped and was clean-shaven; in fact, he could go without shaving for a day without anyone noticing. And he still had the same mischievous grin. But his greatest weapon seems to have been full-moon eyes underscored by dark shadows that gave him a melancholy look that girls described as "dreamy." Most of the girls who attended the dances at the skating rink were looking for mates. They would gladly have quit their jobs as waitresses, carhops, or factory workers to marry a sailor and start a family.

In an October 7, 1956, letter to Jimmy, John handed out a lot of advice and then went on to boast about the action at the Revere rink. The letter was a mixture of genuine concern and cockiness. "How are you doing in school?" John wrote at one point. "Just remember those little nuns are *real* dumb. You can always pull the wool over their eyes."

The letter also contained four bright red-and-white stickers marked *CONFIDENTIAL*. When John returned to Scranton for a weekend visit, his brother asked him how he had come by them.

John explained that the Navy used them to identify radio messages that were considered sensitive. Confidential was the lowest of these classifications and the only one that John had access to. Next was secret, followed by the highest classification, top secret. "The Navy likes to classify everything," John explained. Even radio messages that he sent to shore for supplies such as toilet paper were classified confidential. "Can you believe that?" Jimmy seemed uneasy. "Look," John said. "I put them on as a joke. It really isn't any big deal."

# 8

Barbara Crowley didn't want to go, but her friend Mary Ellen kept asking. There's nothing wrong with two teenage girls attending a dance at the Revere rink, Mary Ellen had insisted. Most of the sailors who patronized the rink were respectable; many were away from home for the first time. It was the older sailors that a girl had to watch out for, and they prowled Boston's seedy bars, not its roller rinks.

As far as Barbara was concerned, only "sleazy" girls went to the skating rink at Revere Beach. She wanted to attend the dance held each Saturday in the grand ballroom of an expensive downtown hotel. "It's where all the college kids go!" she explained. But Mary Ellen protested that they weren't college students, and besides, mingling with fraternity boys made her uneasy.

"Everyone bleeds the same blood," Barbara snapped.

The two girls continued to argue until Barbara gave in. "I'll go, but I'm not interested in getting involved with any sailors," she said.

Barbara had worked hard to pull herself up from a humble background, and she was adamant about marrying someone from a better social class than the one she had been born into. "My family was as poor as you can get," Barbara told me years later. Born on November 23, 1937, she was one of seven children of George and Annie Crowley, native Bostonians. "As far back as I can remember, we were on some kind of welfare, and it's hard to get poorer than that."

When Barbara was a small child, her father worked as a welder for Bethlehem Steel in the vast Boston shipyards. Annie took in laundry and ironing to supplement George's meager earnings. The family lived in a modest house in Chelsea, a working-class neighborhood in Boston. When Barbara was five, her father fell from a scaffold at the shipyards and injured his arm. Doctors discovered during an examination that he had multiple sclerosis, a degenerative disease that impairs the muscles and damages the nervous system. A short time after the accident, he became bedridden. "My mother went to work as a waitress," said Barbara's older sister, Annie Crowley Nelson. "My brothers sold newspapers and I baby-sat. Everyone had a job because my father was sick for a long time before he passed away."

Barbara was just eight when her father died. A year later, her mother married another Boston laborer, Oscar Knight Smith, who moved the family to Mercer, an isolated hamlet in central Maine. Smith found a job at a local paper mill, but his meager salary was barely enough to keep the family fed, clothed, and sheltered. Shortly after the wedding, Smith got sick and doctors found a brain tumor. It was not the first. Years earlier, doctors had removed a section of his skull to extract another tumor. The surgery on this second tumor left Smith partially paralyzed. Once again, the family was in wretched financial shape.

"I was in ninth grade and it was Christmas when my stepfather suddenly told me that I wasn't going to go back to school," Barbara Walker complained bitterly to me. "He told me that I had to get a job, and he and my mother sent me to a fish factory where I cut frozen fish.

"Friday," Barbara Walker continued, "was my mother's favorite day because that is when she came to pick up my paycheck."

Barbara told me that she hated her stepfather. "I left home on my eighteenth birthday—the minute I was legally old enough," she said.

Barbara moved in with the family of a friend in Boston and eventually went to work as a keypunch operator at the Federal Reserve Bank.

At nineteen, she was an attractive young woman. She was five feet two inches tall, and weighed only a hundred pounds, but she had a Jayne Mansfield figure and shoulder length black hair. "Barbara was a very strong-willed person," Annie Crowley Nelson said of her younger sister. "She was intelligent and was not snotty, but she carried herself with a certain pride."

It took Barbara time to warm to strangers, and it was her haughtiness that first attracted John Walker, Jr., when they met at the rink. "Barbara could turn her nose up at anybody. She had that Boston better-than-you attitude," he recalled. "She was good looking and was a real working girl. She got up every morning and took the 8:05 subway to work. She seemed to know exactly what she wanted out of life, and she was just what I wanted in a woman."

John pestered Barbara for a dance, but she refused because he was a sailor. He jokingly told her that he could tell her fortune, but she continued to ignore him. When the dance ended, Barbara's friend Mary Ellen announced that John had offered her and the sailor she had met a ride home. Reluctantly Barbara agreed to go along, but when John was a block away from her house she made him pull up to the curb and told him she would walk the rest of the way. "I didn't want John to know where I lived. I didn't want to see him again." But Mary Ellen had given Barbara's telephone number to John that night, and he called her the next day. "If you don't go out with me, I'll throw rocks through your windows," he said, laughing. Barbara declined, but John persisted. Finally, she agreed to a date—a tour of the U.S.S. *Johnnie Hutchins*. Afterward, she and John ate fried clams and butterscotch sundaes at Howard Johnson's.

The next evening they went out again, and soon John was dining regularly with Barbara and her surrogate family. By the summer of 1957, Barbara and John were in love. They also had two large problems. John's tour on the U.S.S. *Johnnie Hutchins* was coming to an end. The destroyer was going to be decommissioned in Bayonne, New Jersey, and John had been told to pack his seabag. "I'm in love with Barbara," he told a shipmate. "She is the first person I have ever really loved, but I don't want to get married. I love the Navy and my job and I don't want to get tied down yet."

Barbara's doctor had told her that she was going to have a baby. She hadn't planned on getting pregnant, but she hadn't taken any precautions either. She had simply hoped it wouldn't happen. She told John the day that she found out. He knew that he didn't have to marry Barbara. Other sailors talked about women they had gotten pregnant and left behind. Barbara should have been more cautious, John said. "My first reaction was just to get the hell out when she told me that she was pregnant," John remembered. But the more he thought about marrying Barbara, the more he liked the idea. "I thought, 'Hey, this could be really good. I could have one of those great Italian families like my grandpa Scaramuzzo, you know, where I would come home from work and Barbara and the kids would be waiting for me and I would sit around and tell them stories like Grandpa did.' Only I was going to do it right, not like my father and mother had done."

Before John decided, however, Barbara told him that she had a secret she wanted to share. Her mother and stepfather had returned to Boston to live, but she had never mentioned them to John. She asked John to drive her to a store in a poor section of Chelsea, but wouldn't tell him why. When they got there, he followed her upstairs into a cramped apartment. "It was a disaster inside," John told me. "Barbara began introducing me to all these people who were living there and then she told me that this was her real family, not the nice Italian family that she was living with."

After they left the apartment, Barbara said, "I've not always been proud of my family, but I wanted you to meet them and know that I want something different from this for myself."

A few days later, she confronted John. "Well, what are we going to do—get married or what?"

"Oh, all right," John replied. "Let's get married."

They eloped to Seabrook, New Hampshire, where a motel operator telephoned the police, who quickly drove around and informed the flustered couple that in this state they had to be twenty-one years old to get a marriage license. Barbara looked in a world almanac at a public library and discovered that couples could get married in North Carolina without waiting, if the woman was at least nineteen years old, and so they were married June 4, 1957, in Durham. Barbara telephoned her mother to announce her news, but John didn't tell anyone at first. He did, however, send a telegram to Arthur, who was stationed in Norfolk, asking for a $100 loan. Arthur and Rita had been married less than a year and didn't have much income, but Arthur immediately withdrew the money from their savings account and was about to wire it to John when Rita caught him.

"Why does he need the money?" she demanded.

"He didn't say," Arthur replied.

"Then call and ask him!"

Arthur telephoned John. "Rita wants to know what you need the hundred bucks for, John." John could hear Rita coaching Arthur in the background. "Tell him if he got some girl pregnant, he doesn't have to marry her," she was saying.

"I need the money for rent," John said.

"Rent?" Arthur repeated for Rita's benefit. "Did he get somebody pregnant?" Rita asked.

"I got married," John said. "Now are you going to send the money or what?"

Arthur wired the $100 that afternoon.

Now that Arthur and Rita knew, John decided to call his parents. His father sounded genuinely happy, but John could tell that Peggy was merely feigning enthusiasm. "If you're happy, then I'm happy, Johnny-boy," she told him with deliberate cheerfulness.

When Barbara developed toxemia, her doctor took John aside and warned him that the baby would probably be born dead. John was more worried about Barbara. He asked for permission to be with her in the delivery room, an unusual request in 1957. As John stood beside her, holding her hand, Barbara gave birth on December 27 to a pale but healthy girl. They named the baby Margaret Ann, after their respective mothers.

"We named her after you, Mom!" John told Peggy when he called her from the hospital. She sounded thrilled, but couldn't help but feel sad after she hung up the receiver. Later she explained that she had been thinking about her own marriage and comparing it to her son's. She and Johnny had met at a dance, too. She and Johnny had been anxious to better themselves. She had gotten pregnant and gotten married in a brisk ceremony. She and Johnny had started out, just as John and Barbara were doing, not as newlyweds with time to learn about each other, but as a trio. Clutching her rosary, Peggy prayed.

# 9

Navy life was hard on the new family. Six months after Margaret was born, John had to report to the U.S.S. *Forrestal*, an aircraft carrier in Norfolk. The transfer sounded terrific at first. Arthur and Rita were in Norfolk and John was eager for Barbara to meet them. And the *Forrestal* was not just any aircraft carrier. It was the newest carrier in the fleet, the first ever designed to accommodate jet aircraft, and the largest ship in the world. It was longer than ten football fields placed end to end, and it reached thirteen stories above the water. Capable of holding ninety aircraft, it could move at an astounding speed of thirty-three knots. Assignment to the 5,499-man crew of the *Forrestal* reinforced John's belief that he was one of the Navy's rising stars.

"I was really developing good self-esteem and self-confidence. By this time, I had aced the high school GED and had no difficulty passing a two-year college equivalency test. I was studying like a maniac and making every rank at the absolute minimum time. The thing I liked about the Navy was that promotions were based upon how well you did on exams, not how well you kissed ass. Your commanding officer might despise you, but if you did a good job, the Navy had to promote you, and I was thriving on that kind of competition."

Unfortunately, John's transfer to the *Forrestal* was a disaster. John and Barbara had assumed they could all stay with Arthur and Rita in Norfolk until they could find an apartment, but when they arrived, they discovered that Arthur and Rita were away on vacation. "We had to rent the first apartment that we saw, and we slept on the floor that night because we didn't have enough money for a motel room and didn't have any furniture," said John. "We were really pissed at Art and Rita." A few days later, John learned that the *Forrestal* was about to leave on a seven-month cruise of the Mediterranean. Barbara was unnerved. What would she and the baby do while John was at sea? She didn't know anyone in Norfolk. John telephoned his parents in Scranton and made arrangements for Barbara and Margaret to move in with them.

John and Barbara were both miserable during the separation. John had promised her that he wouldn't go ashore when the *Forrestal* docked in foreign ports because they wanted to save his pay to buy furniture and rent a nice apartment. John was also afraid he would be tempted by hookers if he left the ship. So when his shipmates went carousing, he stayed aboard and studied for his next promotion. At first, he received long, passionate letters from Barbara, but suddenly she stopped writing, and after four months of silence, John sent an angry telegram. Barbara replied with a curt: "Everything fine. Love you."

"The reason I stopped writing," Barbara claimed later, "was because I didn't want him to know what his mother was doing to me, the hell that she was putting me through. Pop [Johnny] and I did all the housecleaning and I did all the cooking and she didn't do anything but go to work and come home and bitch, bitch, bitch."

Peggy recalled Barbara's stay differently, describing her daughter-in-law as lazy. "She expected to be waited upon." Perhaps it was jealousy over John, but Barbara and Peggy couldn't stand each other. As soon as John's cruise was over, he and Barbara returned to Norfolk. "I'm quitting the Navy as soon as I can," John suddenly announced one afternoon to Barbara and to his brother Arthur. "I can't stand these goddamn aircraft carriers anymore."

Arthur urged John to reconsider. "Try to get on subs once again," he pleaded. But John had already tried and been rejected once more. "There might be a way for you to get assigned to a submarine through the back door," Arthur volunteered. The next morning, Arthur drove to the personnel office at the Norfolk Naval Base, headquarters for the entire Atlantic fleet, and with luck was able to get John's orders changed. He had been scheduled to go to another aircraft carrier, but instead was sent in May 1959 to a sub tender, the U.S.S. *Howard W. Gilmore,* based in Charleston, South Carolina. John was thrilled by the move. Arthur hadn't gotten him on a sub, but this was close enough.

Barbara, meanwhile, gave birth to Cynthia, the couple's second child, that same month. Two months later, Barbara was pregnant again. The couple's third daughter, Laura, was born April 24, 1960. Barbara and John had been married less than three years, but they already had three daughters and their roles as husband and wife had been clearly defined.

"My job is to earn an income for my family," John told Barbara the first time that she asked him to help change a diaper. "I work hard sixty hours a week on the ship and I'm not going to come home and change diapers or do dishes. You don't work and you are the wife, so that's your job."

It made sense to Barbara. "I did very little to cross John or upset him early in our marriage," she told me later. "I wanted things to be perfect when he was at home. If there was something that I really wanted to do and he didn't want to do it, that was okay. If I really wanted to do it, I put it off until he was at sea."

By May 1960, John had earned a total of five promotions, but he and Barbara were still living on about the same amount of money that they had when first married, even though their family now numbered five. "Every time John got a promotion and more pay, we put the raise into our savings account on the theory that if we don't have it, we won't miss it," Barbara explained. They also adhered to a strict credit policy: anything bought on credit had to be paid off within two years, and nothing new could be purchased on credit until all previous charges were paid. Saving money was an obsession with them, a testament that showed how much they cared for each other. Barbara bought powdered milk for her daughters even when she could afford fresh milk. John wore his shoes until they could no longer be resoled. Both refused to tip waitresses.

"When I first met Barbara," John said, "I told her my plans for life. I had no intention of doing my twenty years and retiring and having nothing to show for it. I was going to save my money and invest it and have something going for me when I got out—a business run by someone else. Barbara knew that. She had to be prepared for it because I wasn't going to be like my dad with no money, no future, nothing going for him."

In June 1960, John passed an eye exam and was judged fit for submarine duty. It was the third time he had taken the test, and the only reason he passed was that the Navy had lowered its vision requirements. Five months later, John moved Barbara and his daughters back in with Peggy and Johnny in Scranton and left for sixteen weeks of training at the Navy submarine school in New London, Connecticut.

Barbara found life in Scranton more depressing than ever. She fought with Peggy constantly. A short time after Barbara arrived, Johnny moved out of the house and back in with his mother in Scranton. Barbara dashed to phone John and tell him that his mother had driven Johnny away. John rushed home and upbraided Peggy. "If you were half the wife that Barbara is, he wouldn't have left you," John said. Peggy seethed. It wasn't really her boy talking, she said later. "It was that witch, Barbara."

After completing submarine training, John was assigned to the U.S.S. *Razorback,* a diesel submarine stationed in San Diego, and he moved his wife and children there. The *Razorback* left on an extended cruise days after John arrived. On June 28, 1961, Peggy finally received her first letter from him. He had been at sea for four months and his letter contained an apology for his angry outburst at her over Johnny and was filled with sweet references to Barbara, whom he called Bobbie.

Much to my surprise this afternoon, I received a phone call from Bobbie. I feared the worst, but she was just lonesome and wanted to call. In a way I wish she hadn't called; it only made me very homesick. Like all women, she started to cry and I swore I would have also if there weren't so many sailors around. So, if you get a chance, I'd rather have you write Bobbie than me. I think it's harder on the girls than the men.

After the U.S.S. *Razorback* returned, it was sent to San Francisco and John moved his family into subsidized Navy housing on the base. For the first time in their marriage, John and Barbara had a normal nine-to-five life together for a long period. They also allowed themselves some spending money to eat at restaurants and see movies. John bought a bicycle and rode it to the ship each day to save money.

The togetherness, however, wore thin. John discovered that Barbara spent most of her time talking about their three daughters and he was quickly bored by domestic discussions. She in turn grew weary of John's endless sea stories. One evening John came home early from a short test cruise on the submarine and found the house in disarray. Dirty clothes had been dropped on the floor, and the kitchen was jammed with several days' worth of dirty dishes and silverware. Barbara, who was pregnant again, and the three girls were nowhere to be seen. When they arrived home a few hours later, John was waiting on the front step.

"What the hell is going on?" he demanded.

"I was too tired to clean up tonight so I took the girls to a drive-in movie," Barbara said.

John told me later during an interview that this incident was a turning point.

"I have always been a neat person," he explained. "I can't stand an untidy house and that incident stands out in my mind. To put it in perspective, I was literally busting my ass, trying to get ahead at work, but my wife, who I thought was in the same mold, was becoming a typical lazy Navy wife who didn't want to do anything but sit at home and raise kids. I began to sense that she was not the woman who I thought I had married. We had gotten married at an early age and both of us had a lot of growing up to do and I was growing up in a much different direction than she was. Things in the marriage were still okay, but I was beginning to see long-range things in Barbara that I was not happy with. Laziness was the main thing, which resulted in her being what I would call a slob.

"She had started watching television, and it seemed that she was watching it twenty-three hours a day and doing absolutely nothing to progress or improve herself. Technically, we were both high school dropouts, but I had done something about that. I had gotten my GED. When we first met, I viewed Barbara as someone who was poor as hell, but who had lots of ambition. She had pulled herself out of the sewer, and I figured she would claw her way to the top. We were very similar in that way. We were aggressive and had high aspirations. We were going to make something of ourselves. But after a few years of marriage, it became clear to me that she was falling to the side. She wasn't doing anything. She talked about getting her GED. She talked about it endlessly, but she never went after it. I'll give her this much: raising kids is tough. But I was out at sea a lot and I still managed to study hard enough to make all of my ranks."

In the spring of 1962, John moved his family again—the fifteenth move in five years—to Vallejo, California, where he reported for duty on the U.S.S. *Andrew Jackson,* one of the Navy's new nuclear-powered submarines. It was a trying time. Barbara was having a difficult pregnancy and had started complaining about John's refusal to help around the house or care for the children—Margaret, age four; Cynthia, age two; Laura, age one. Despite her badgering, John refused to lift a finger. "The Navy is my job. The house and children are yours!"

Barbara went into labor on November 1, 1962. John had planned to play in a baseball game that day with some fellows from the radio crew, so he dropped Barbara at the hospital entrance and then went on to the game. Barbara gave birth to a boy. As she was being wheeled back to her room, she thought back to Margaret's birth when John had insisted on being with her in the delivery room. They had been so much in love. She began to cry.

John had always wanted a son, and when he heard that Barbara had given birth to a boy, he rushed to the hospital, armed with long-stemmed roses and a large box of chocolates.

"I had always planned to name our first son John Anthony Walker the third," Barbara Walker told me later. "Every time I got pregnant, I prayed it would be a boy so that John could have a son who he could pass his name to. On every previous pregnancy, I was going to name the baby John if it were a boy.

"But when I had my baby boy, John wasn't there. He was at some damn baseball game with his pals," she said. "So I named my son Michael Lance Walker, and when John found out he was furious."

It was one of the sweetest moments in her life, Barbara Walker recalled.

# PART THREE

## TRAITOR

*The man who pauses on the paths of treason,*
*Halts on a quicksand; the first*
*step engulfs him.*

AARON HILL
*Henry V,* act 1, scene 1

# 10

The three-inch-thick book had a bright red cover with the warning *TOP SECRET—SPECAT* printed on it in bold letters. The acronym SPECAT, short for SPECIAL CATEGORY, meant that even military personnel with top secret clearances couldn't examine the book without special authorization. John knew why. The book contained the plans for the beginning of World War III.

John lifted the cover of the red binder and read the title: *Single Integrated Operational Plan (SIOP)*. Even the title was secret. Officially, no such plan existed. The SIOP (pronounced *sigh-op*) was the Pentagon's road map for a full-scale war with the Soviet Union. It contained a list of all U.S. nuclear weapons and their targets.

In the early 1960s, mapping Armageddon was even more intricate and difficult than it is today because each U.S. missile carried only one nuclear warhead and the nation's most powerful nuclear bombs would have had to be carried into the Soviet Union and dropped by B-52 bombers because they were so big. The trajectory of every nuclear missile, whether it was fired from land (intercontinental ballistic missiles) or sea (Polaris missiles), had to be precisely calculated to make certain that no missiles collided in the air and to ensure that some flight paths into Russia were kept open. These pathways, called target windows, had to be kept clear so that the B-52's could carry out their missions.

John had been given permission by the captain of the nuclear submarine U.S.S. *Simon Bolivar* to see the SIOP. The captain had received a message from Atlantic fleet headquarters in Norfolk saying that another U.S. submarine had developed mechanical problems and was limping back to port. Until that submarine was repaired, the *Bolivar* had to cover some of its targets.

It took John just a few minutes to log the *Bolivar*'s new assignment, but the SIOP fascinated him and he read every possible detail before locking it up in a safe.

"It was incredible," he recalled later. "Haven't you ever wondered if the United States would go after the eastern bloc countries like Yugoslavia and Czechoslovakia if there were a full-scale war? Haven't you ever wondered if we would hit China and what cities would be blown up in Russia and in what order? Well, here it was—all of it—in my hands, and I was reading it! I mean, this was your wildest fucking nightmare and it was right before my eyes!"

It was at this point that John remembers wondering how much the Soviet Union would pay for stolen U.S. military secrets, but he insisted that his curiosity was nothing more than just that—an innocent inquisitiveness. His thoughts, he said, were similar to those of a man who inherits a valuable heirloom. He has no intention of selling the family treasure, yet he still wonders how much it would fetch from a collector. Knowing the Soviets might pay thousands of dollars for a copy of the SIOP made John's access to it that much more savory.

John had entered the Navy's submarine force at a pivotal time in its history. In the 1950s, the United States and the Soviet Union had both moved to enlarge and modernize their postwar submarine fleets. The first dramatic step for the U.S. Navy came with the successful launch of a submarine powered by nuclear energy. Suddenly diesel submarines were obsolete. Atomic-powered submarines were legitimate underwater vessels, capable of remaining submerged for months. Almost overnight, the importance of submarines increased. Difficult for the enemy to track, they became the silent eyes of the Navy. The next major improvement came in 1961, when ballistic missiles were added to the submarines' armory. No longer were submarines confined to firing torpedoes at ships. Now they could attack entire cities.

John joined the submarine fleet just as it was being converted from an aged diesel flotilla into a modern nuclear armada. His first submarine assignment had been to a diesel-powered vessel, but a year later he joined the crew of the new, nuclear-powered U.S.S. *Andrew Jackson*. One year after John came aboard, the *Jackson* moved to the East Coast, where it launched the first Polaris "A-3" missile on October 26, 1963. The two-stage, 30,000-pound Polaris "A-3" could hit a target 2,875 miles away—nearly twice the range of previous Polaris missiles. For the next two years, John roamed the Atlantic and the Mediterranean on the *Jackson*. Barbara and the four children lived in Navy housing in Charleston specially built for Polaris missile crews.

The workings of nuclear submarines and Polaris missile launches were not the only bits of front-line technology John was privy to. Depending upon which Navy official was speaking, the Russians were either nipping at our heels in submarine development in the fifties and sixties or were years ahead of us. To counter the Russian threat, whatever its size, the Pentagon devised numerous anti-submarine-warfare techniques. The most impressive was SOSUS, an acronym for Sound Surveillance System. SOSUS was nothing more than a giant underwater ear in the form of several hundred specially built hydrophones installed by cable-laying ships on the continental shelf off the East and West Coasts. The architects of America's nuclear submarine program had adopted a one-reactor, one-propeller design and paid extraordinary attention to making U.S. nuclear submarines as noiseless as possible. However, the Russians had focused on speed, and built nuclear subs with two reactors and twin propellers that created a much more jarring wake than our single blade. The Russians also bolted pumps, motors, and other internal machinery directly to the inner hull of each submarine, which resulted in the broadcasting of the slightest vibration or clatter into the sea. By the time that John joined the *Jackson* crew in 1962, the Navy had perfected SOSUS to the point that a Soviet submarine could not leave its home port on the Barents Sea or the Sea of Okhotsk and head for deep water without being detected by SOSUS ears. By the mid-sixties, the U.S. Navy had so thoroughly bugged the continental shelf that it was impossible for a foreign submarine to approach the U.S. coast without each mile of its voyage being carefully tracked by SOSUS. The hydrophones, later enhanced by computers, worked so well that SOSUS operators could tell from the sound of propeller wash not only the location of a submarine but also its type.

The SOSUS system was another top secret that made John pause and wonder: "How much would this be worth to the Reds?"

John didn't consider such thoughts unique. "Everyone aboard a submarine talked about these things," he insisted. "It was always in a joking way, such as 'Hey, I'll bet the Reds would pay a bundle for this,' but it was standard conversation in the radio room." In interviews with me, John's shipmates denied such conversation ever took place. Any mention, even in jest, of selling classified information to the Russians would have been seen as suspect behavior and probable cause for investigation, they claimed. But John insisted that the value of classified material was a frequent topic and that the Navy unwittingly encouraged such speculation because it bombarded submarine crews with warnings about techniques the Soviets used to discover Navy secrets. "The Navy was paranoid about nuclear submarines and it stressed the importance of keeping information secure. Naturally that made you wonder: 'How much would this stuff be worth?' "

While John was a radio operator on board the U.S.S. *Andrew Jackson,* he underwent his first and only "background investigation," conducted by a naval investigator named Milo A. Bauerly. There was little reason at the time for Bauerly to be suspicious of John. During his nine years in the Navy, John had earned seven promotions, each on schedule. His commanding officers called him "bright, energetic, and enthusiastic." His neighbors and friends assured Bauerly that John didn't have a drinking or drug problem. He appeared to be happily married, was not in any financial trouble, was not a homosexual, and had no known contact or friendship with foreigners. Bauerly knew about John's criminal record as a teenager—the matter was serious enough to make him read the sealed juvenile court records in the Scranton courthouse. But participation in a single bungled burglary of a clothing store seemed insignificant when compared to his pristine Navy record. John was not the first case Bauerly had seen of a troubled teenager straightened out by the Navy. Based on Bauerly's findings, the Navy granted John a clearance on December 29, 1964, to work with top secret and cryptographic materials.

John developed a reputation as a clown aboard the *Jackson*. During one cruise, he mixed several spoonfuls of peanut butter with other ingredients and beat the concoction into a mixing bowl until it had the same texture as human excrement. Having formed the peanut butter into a coil, he placed it on a piece of paper on an ensign's desk. Needless to say, the officer was horrified when he discovered the substance.

"What the hell is this?" he demanded.

John stuck his finger in the peanut butter and then pressed it to his lips.

"Tastes like shit, sir!" he replied calmly.

When the *Jackson* moved from San Diego to Charleston, John and Barbara began to live a little higher on the hog. "We bought this little bar and two or three barstools, and we really stocked up the bar well," John said. "It was the first time that we could afford to buy expensive liquor, and when I came home at night, Barbara would be waiting with a drink and we would both have one before dinner, just like we saw on television and in the movies. I drank scotch and Barbara drank gin and tonic, and Margaret [age eight] was big enough that we even had her mixing them for us."

John was on a ninety-day rotation at the time, which meant that after three months at sea, he spent three months at home. After each cruise, John came back armed with bottles of cheap, tax-free liquor. The Navy limited the number of bottles a sailor could bring home, but John paid nondrinkers to buy him their allotments. "I think all of us had a drinking problem during those years," said Donald Clevenger, a crewmate of John's and a friend of the family in the mid-1960s. "Our life-styles were built around parties and booze. There always seemed to be a group of people at Johnny's house, a special gang. Usually they were radio people from the boat . . ."

In August 1965, one of John's commanding officers transferred to the nuclear-powered submarine U.S.S. *Simon Bolivar*, and he asked John to transfer with him and run the *Bolivar*'s radio room. John quickly agreed. "I was beginning to peak. I was at the top of my profession."

On the *Bolivar*, John befriended Bill Wilkinson, one of the radio operators of lesser rank who worked for him. Wilkinson, a wiry, feisty Louisiana boy with an uncultivated style, became John's drinking buddy and sparked John's interest in politics, debating the civil rights movement and segregation with him for hours on end. Wilkinson was a racist—he later became Imperial Wizard of the Ku Klux Klan—and John delighted in teasing him about blacks. All John had to do to rattle Wilkinson when the two men went on liberty was to tell him that his dinner had been prepared by a black. Wilkinson would rather starve than eat it.

John joined the John Birch Society, an ultraconservative political group, and had Barbara host several coffees for members and recruits. He enrolled in a book club that mailed him one "great book of the western world" each month. John and Barbara read the first book that arrived in the mail and discussed it, but later she fell behind on the reading and dropped out. John didn't. He read each book—Greek mythology, Plato—not because he enjoyed them, but because he was trying desperately to better himself.

"What I was trying to do during this period in my life," John said, "was constantly improve and learn." At the time few people realized John's motivation. "The only reason I joined the John Birch Society was because it was good for my career. I mean, what could be more natural. The Navy is an anticommunist group. So are the Birchers. It just made sense. It was all show." So were the books. He made certain that his boss and the radio crew aboard the *Bolivar* saw what he was reading.

In the spring of 1966, Barbara received an upsetting telephone call from a close buddy of John's. "I think my wife is in love with your husband," he warned her. A few minutes later, the sailor's wife knocked at her door. The woman announced that she was leaving her husband for John. Barbara poured her a cup of coffee and began gently asking her a series of questions.

"How did you get here, dear?"

The woman, who was only twenty-two, said that she had driven over in her husband's car. "If you get divorced, you are going to lose that car," Barbara said. "Now, are you going to go to work or what?" The woman said she hadn't thought about that. "Well, your husband isn't going to support you anymore if you divorce him." Barbara spent almost an hour explaining "reality" to the woman. After she left, Barbara began dealing with her own situation.

"She had given me every indication—she had said everything but they had had an affair. . . . It hurt me a lot that John had slept with someone else, but I did not blame the other woman. He had set her up for the kill. She was young and didn't know better."

Barbara was furious at John, who was away on a ninety-day Polaris cruise. She did not know that John already had had several sexual liaisons in foreign ports with hookers by this time. She had never suspected him of adultery. Her fury was tempered, however, by the same "reality" that she had described to the young woman. Even if a judge required John to pay child support and alimony, his Navy pay wouldn't be sufficient for her and the children to continue living as they were. After all their years of penny-pinching, John and Barbara had finally achieved a financial status that allowed them some luxury, and Barbara didn't want to give that up. Not yet. She was still in love with John, too. They often fought and she was angry at him much of the time, but there were still some good times between them. Just a few months earlier, they had taken a second honeymoon. Barbara had flown to Spain and met John when he was on liberty. They had bought a fire-engine red MG Midget and driven the back roads of Spain, Italy, and France. It had been a magical trip. Barbara recalled eating Brie and drinking Chablis with John while watching the sun set over the Rock of Gibraltar. They made love one night in the outskirts of Paris in a tiny room John had rented from a farm family. The next morning they ate breakfast with the couple and their gaggle of children.

"I knew my husband was changing. I had married a young sailor who liked to be called Jack, but Jack was becoming John and there was a difference," Barbara Walker told me later. When I asked her to explain, she said that John Walker was only twenty-eight years old in 1966, but he looked much older. He had lost most of his inky black hair and his melancholy eyes were concealed behind thick black-framed glasses. His skinny frame had puffed out.

"John was worried about getting old. He suddenly had to have a sports car and he kept talking about how we needed more money and nicer things."

Barbara convinced herself that John's sexual escapade in Charleston was merely a passing fling. When he returned home from sea, Barbara didn't mention the telephone call from his buddy or her encounter with the sailor's wife. Barbara had decided that the best way for her to keep John from straying was to work harder at pleasing him when he was at home.

On July 6, 1966, John and Barbara bought a small house and 4.87 acres of land in Ladson, South Carolina, roughly fourteen miles north of Charleston. John and Bill Wilkinson had talked about becoming business partners, but couldn't agree on an investment. John wanted to buy an apartment house in Charleston, but Bill wanted to buy a franchise for a miniature golf course. The Ladson property was a compromise. They intended to convert it into a storage lot for cars. The lot was Bill's idea. "What's the first thing a kid does when he joins the service?" Bill asked John one day. Before John could answer, Bill said, "Why, he buys himself a car and then he gets orders to go to sea and has to find somewhere to put it." It was a position that Bill had found himself in shortly after he joined the Navy. The owner of a car storage lot had shown Bill how to cancel his car insurance and use that money to pay a storage fee.

Converting the property into a storage lot would cost a lot more than the $1,400 in working capital that John and Bill had pooled. "That's when Johnny got the idea of turning the place into a bar," Bill Wilkinson recalled, "and I came up with the name House of Bamboo, because I'd been to a bar named that in Houston, Texas, that I thought was classy."

With help from local teenagers, the men set to work remodeling the house, but a few weeks after they started, Bill announced that he was dropping out of the partnership. "How can you do this to me, Bill?" John complained, but Bill said he didn't have a choice. He and his wife had separated earlier, but now they wanted to get back together and Wilkinson needed his share of the money to bring her home from her mother's. John reluctantly returned Bill's money and decided to change the name of the still unopened bar to the Bamboo Snack Bar.

John and Barbara had already signed a $15,400 mortgage to buy the Ladson property. Without Wilkinson as a partner, John had to take out a second mortgage of $4,250.

In September 1966, Arthur Walker's ship, the U.S.S. *Grenadier,* arrived in Charleston for repairs. He headed directly for John's apartment, and by nightfall, he had agreed to come into the bar as a partner for $1,000.

Barbara was apprehensive about opening the bar, but she said she put up an enthusiastic front. "I knew that it wasn't going to work. How could it? Johnny was leaving for sea duty, Art was going to go back to Key West, and I was going to be stuck running it, cleaning toilets, and serving drunks. It had to fail, I mean, what did I know about running a bar? Nothing."

Barbara was also worried about Arthur's influence on John. "The two of them began to party again and this upset me. I knew Art's reputation because Art had told John about women he had slept with and John had told me. So I knew about it, but Rita didn't."

In order to save money, John, Barbara, and Arthur started the painting and final renovations of the bar themselves, but they hadn't finished when John had to leave for a cruise aboard the *Bolivar.*

What happened next is disputed by Barbara and Arthur, but this is how Barbara tells the story. "John was going to sea and he was worried that Arthur wouldn't do his share of painting at the bar, so he insisted that Art stay in our apartment. He wanted Art there every night to guarantee that the next morning he would be ready to go back to the bar and help with renovating it.

"One night, after John had gone to sea, Art and I went to the bar and painted or something, and when we got back to the apartment that night it was really late, and I was unhappy and tired, and here is good old Art—someone who says he cares and is very compassionate.

"I told Art that I was going to take a shower and go to bed, so I took my shower and put on pink pajamas—we aren't talking negligee, I mean, who looks sexy in pink pajamas?—and I came back in the living room and the lights were turned low and there was music on and Art was sitting at the bar, and he said, 'Let's have a drink.' So I sat down on the bar stool ... and then Art says, 'Oh let's dance,' and I think, 'Barbara, this is not a brilliant thing to do—dancing in your pajamas,' but I did it anyway, and one thing led to another and Art kissed me and I felt bad, real bad, and I said to him, 'I really wish that wouldn't have happened,' and he got nervous and decided to leave and he says, as he is running out the door, 'Don't feel like you've been compromised.'

"The next day, Art came back and we worked at the bar, and then we went to the apartment and we had some drinks and we were sitting on the couch and he kissed me, and this time we didn't stop and I had sex with my husband's brother.

"John almost caught us when he came home. He came into the bar and Art was standing there and John announced that he almost came home early the night before, and I thought, 'What if he had?' He would have caught us in bed together—he would have caught me in bed with his brother."

Arthur admitted to having sex with Barbara, but told me that the encounter occurred later, after Barbara and John had opened the bar and moved into a trailer behind it.

According to Barbara Walker, her sexual relationship with Arthur lasted for the next ten years. Arthur Walker claimed Barbara exaggerated. He admitted to having sex with Barbara twice, once in 1966 and again in 1968.

A few weeks after John arrived home from the *Bolivar* in the fall of 1966, Barbara decided to tell him about her affair with Arthur, but she changed her mind at the last minute. "I wanted to tell him that I had slept with his brother because I wanted to hurt him like he had hurt me, but I just couldn't do it."

As luck would have it, just before the bar was finally ready to open, John was promoted to the rank of warrant officer and received orders to report to the naval base in Norfolk.

"I begged John not to open the bar. We just didn't have the money to back us and we were going to fall flat on our asses, but there was no way to stop him and Arthur. They were going to own a bar. It sounded so grand and they loved telling their sailor buddies about it."

John and Barbara struck a deal. He would move to Norfolk, and she and the four children would stay behind in Charleston. If the bar didn't show a profit after one year, they would sell it. John and Barbara had exhausted all of their savings and had borrowed every cent they could by the time the bar opened in September 1967. Now they were trying to maintain two households, pay interest on their bank debts, and operate the bar on John's salary of $120 per week. From the day it opened, the bar lost money.

While John was the partner who insisted on the bar opening, Barbara also proved to have a touch of foolishness when it came to business deals. At one point, a customer told Barbara that he had helped survey the land in Florida where Walt Disney intended to build a new park called Disney World. Barbara listened intently as he talked about the fortune she could make by buying several pieces of Florida property near the future vacation spot. Barbara telephoned John that night and suggested they close the bar and use whatever money was left to buy real estate in Florida. When he refused, Barbara became enraged and accused him of being a coward. She slammed down the telephone receiver.

A short time after the bar opened, Arthur's boat left Charleston and he returned to Key West, Florida, where he was stationed. Rita, his wife, soon learned about the $1,000 that Arthur had invested in the bar and insisted that Arthur get the money back and any profits owed him. John exploded when Arthur's letter arrived. "There aren't any goddamn profits," he wrote in a blistering return letter to Arthur. "Not only am I not sending you any money, but as a partner, I expect you to cover this month's losses. I expect a goddamn check from you!"

Near bankruptcy, John still refused to close the bar. Instead, he borrowed $700 from a now-defunct amusement company.

By November 1967, John was making the four-hundred-mile trip from Norfolk to Ladson nearly every weekend. He refused to acknowledge that no woman could raise four children, run a business, and survive on his hand-to-mouth budget. Barbara just wasn't working hard enough, he said, and he was angry because she had started to drink to ease her pain.

They argued and Barbara told John that she had had enough of his money-losing operation. She had reached the end that afternoon when one of their creditors came in and demanded that Barbara pay for equipment that she and John had leased. "I tried to explain that we didn't have the money," Barbara told John, "and then he told me that if we didn't have it, then he was going to take it out in trade with me in the trailer for an hour."

John didn't react.

"Is that what you want John? You want me to prostitute myself for your damn bar?" Barbara shouted.

"Do what you have to do," he replied. "But I'm not closing this bar." They had sacrificed for years to save enough money to buy a business, John said. He wasn't going to call it quits now and lose everything.

"I'm not going to end up like my old man," John said.

# 11

From its exterior, the operations headquarters of the U.S. Atlantic Fleet looks more like a furniture warehouse than a gold mine of highly sensitive military secrets. But the drab, concrete building off Terminal Boulevard in Norfolk is a bustling command post that controls the precise movements of a horde of complex fighting ships. The Navy has neatly divided the world into four geographic arenas—the Atlantic, Mediterranean, Eastern Pacific, and Western Pacific—and established huge communication centers in each sector. Day after day thousands of scrambled messages from naval stations, warships, submarines, and spy satellites flow into four centers, technically called Naval Communication Area Master Stations, or NAVCAMS. All ships operating in the Atlantic are directed from within the windowless, two-story operations building in Norfolk.

In April 1967, John became a watch officer in the message room responsible for communicating with every U.S. submarine operating in Atlantic waters. If a nuclear submarine came upon the *Leninsky Komsomol,* a Russian sub, off the coast of France, the encounter was immediately reported to the office where John worked. If hostilities erupted in the Middle East and the Pentagon decided to dispatch more submarines to the Mediterranean, John was the man who contacted an Atlantic-based submarine and directed it through the Strait of Gibraltar. While he was on duty in the message room, John was required to read every top secret message that was sent to or received from a submarine in the Atlantic.

Sometime in December in 1967 John stole his first top secret document for the Soviets. John said later the theft was an "impulsive" act caused by his deep depression over his marital and financial problems.

"It was late one night and there were eight or nine people on the watch. This other guy and I were talking about how much classified information was worth, and this guy jokingly says that it would be easy to steal documents. I said, 'Well, who are you going to sell them to? What are you going to do, walk up to the front door of the Soviet . . .' and I stopped without finishing the sentence because I was thinking, 'Hey, he's right, and that's exactly what I'm going to do! It's my way out! I'm going to steal classified information and take it to the Soviet embassy.' After the guy left my desk, I kept thinking, 'Naw, you don't really want to do this,' and just as quickly I'd say to myself, 'Oh yes you do!' and so I did it right then, just like that, totally on impulse."

A casual conversation with another sailor might have nudged John across the Judas line, but there is strong evidence that his actions were not quite so capricious. John himself remembered he had been curious about the value of stolen military secrets since the day he had first peeked into the SIOP and learned the locations of key SOSUS hydrophones. And he chose the first document that he stole with great care.

In the mid-1960s, the message center where John worked was housed in two modestly furnished offices. The larger front office contained two rows of dull gray government-issue desks, filing cabinets, a paper shredder, a copying machine, and a small enclosed area where a radio operator worked. The watch officer's desk where John sat was separate from the other five desks in the room. Located in a corner, facing the wall, it gave John a measure of privacy.

A doorway near John's desk led to a smaller room that contained banks of cryptographic machines and teletypes. The cryptographic machines were used to unscramble ship-to-shore messages and to encrypt shore-to-ship transmissions. The crypto room also contained two small safes and a huge walk-in vault built into one corner of the room. The vault was protected by a thick steel door with a combination lock. There was a desk inside the vault and two more combination safes. The Navy's most critical codes were kept inside the two small safes in the vault.

In the 1960s, the Navy used direct high-frequency radio transmissions to send messages between ship and shore rather than bouncing transmissions off satellites. Because the signals were easy for the Soviets to monitor, the Navy encrypted ninety-nine percent of all its messages before they were broadcast. The content of the message was regarded as immaterial. If John needed to tell a sailor aboard a nuclear submarine that his wife had just given birth to a boy, he encrypted the message just as he would if the president decided to launch a missile strike. As a consequence, the Soviets could never be certain when they overheard a scrambled radio transmission whether it was important.

Like the other military services, the Navy relies on the National Security Agency in Fort Meade, Maryland, for its codes and cryptographic machines. During John's tenure at Norfolk, the codes were delivered by the NSA under armed guard to the Navy Accounting Center in Washington, where they were distributed to the Armed Forces Courier Service for delivery to a specially trained naval officer at each station and on each ship known as the Registered Publications System (RPS) custodian. The RPS custodian manned the desk inside the message center vault in the crypto room, keeping a detailed record of who saw the NSA codes and why. At the time, the Navy changed its codes each day. In this way, even if the Russians were lucky enough to unscramble a radio transmission, they would know the code only for twenty-four hours. When it was time to change the code, the RPS custodian removed one month's worth of codes, called keylists, from the vault and placed them in one of the safes outside the vault for the watch commander. The keylist told the watch commander how to change the various dials, rotors, plugs, and wires on the cryptographic machines so that they would encrypt and decipher messages according to the code for that day.

Since John was a watch officer, he knew the combination of the safe where the current month's worth of keylists were kept. John also had obtained the combinations to the vault and the two safes inside it.

The first document that John stole was a keylist for a KL-47 cryptographic machine. The KL-47, which dated back to the 1940s, was one of the oldest cryptographic machines still in use in the message center. (The exact date, name of its inventor, and technical drawings of the KL-47 machine are still classified.) John chose the KL-47 because its settings were still changed each day by hand, rather than by computer cards. The keylist for the KL-47 was written out on a single eight- by ten-inch sheet of paper.

"I chose the KL-47 more for its appearance than for its actual worth. It was one of the only cryptographic machines that were used during World War Two, so it was outdated and really only used for a backup in the sixties, but it still had a very high classification and that was impressive as hell. I remember the keylist had the words TOP SECRET— SPECAT, printed in big bold red letters across the top of the page."

John wasn't certain whether an employee at the Soviet embassy in Washington would recognize the keylist for a KL-47 cryptographic machine, but he was confident that the simplest embassy worker would understand the words Top Secret.

There was another advantage to selling the Russians the keylist for the KL-47. If the CIA or Navy learned somehow that the KL-47 had been compromised, they would have a much more difficult time tracing the leak to John than they would if he gave the Russians the keylist to one of the NSA's most up-to-date systems. "The KL-47 had been around for twenty years, and God only knows how many people had used it during that time."

The hardest part of stealing the KL-47 keylist was not removing it from the safe, John explained later, but copying it. Because he was the watch officer, John could remove the KL-47 keylist and study it at any time without arousing suspicion, but making a copy of any top secret document was immediately suspect.

Some time after midnight, John opened the safe, removed the keylist, and took it to his desk. He had been working the evening shift, but he waited until he had rotated onto the morning watch to steal the document because this was the only shift where the watch officer was the highest ranking person in the message room. With his back to the other six or eight men in the message center, he hid the keylist under some other papers on his desk, then walked casually over to a file cabinet where another sailor had left a magazine. Back at his desk, he tucked the KL-47 keylist between the magazine's pages.

John waited for nearly a half hour before he stood up and walked across the room to the copying machine that was enclosed in a small glass office. He had been watching and no one had gone near it that night.

"I figured that if I was going to get caught, it probably would happen the very first time I tried stealing a document," he recalled. His fears were prophetic. When John reached the copy machine, he placed the magazine on the glass, closed the plastic cover, and made a photocopy of a page of the magazine. He looked around the room behind him. No one was watching, and so he placed the keylist face down on the glass and quickly closed the plastic cover.

"Hey, Skipper, you can get into a lot of trouble for what you're doing!" a voice said.

John spun around. One of his men was standing a few feet behind him, coffee cup in hand. John was about to have diarrhea.

"You know better than to copy personal items on that machine," the sailor said. "Naughty, naughty, naughty." He laughed and John feigned a chuckle. When the sailor turned and walked away, John struggled to regain his composure. Then he pressed the copy button. This was the closest that John ever came to getting caught while actually stealing a top secret document.

# 12

John was sure he would be arrested leaving the operations headquarters, but no one bothered him. He had returned the KL-47 keylist to the safe and simply folded his copy, tucked it into his pants pocket, and walked right past the armed Marine guards. Still, he was unable to sleep when he got back to his room and, after four hours of fidgeting, dressed and drove to Washington.

"I was afraid someone had seen me. Maybe they were just waiting to arrest me in Washington at the front door of the Soviet embassy."

John wasn't really certain about how to approach the Soviets. Obviously, the most direct way was to march up to the embassy. But what then? Did he simply ring the doorbell and announce that he wanted to become a spy? Would the Soviets believe him or think his actions were a trick? And what if the FBI was watching? As he drove, John decided to rely on an old Navy acronym: KISS—Keep It Simple, Stupid. "The simpler it was, the less there was for me to screw up." It became his golden rule for spying.

Just outside Washington, John looked up the address of the Soviet embassy in a telephone book. He drove into the city, parked the MG, hailed a cab, and gave the driver an address several numbers higher than the embassy so that he could get a good look at where he was going before he got out of the cab.

The embassy of the Union of Soviet Socialist Republics is less than four blocks from the White House. The grandiose stone mansion in the 1100 block of Sixteenth Street Northwest had been built at the turn of the century by Mrs. George M. Pullman, widow of the railroad sleeping car magnate, but the grande dame never got around to occupying the rectangular, four-story structure. Instead, it became the embassy for the last czarist family, the House of Romanov. By the mid-60s, it had become a forlorn place with pale gray wooden shutters that were always closed.

The taxi dropped John a block north of his destination. As he covered that block, his eyes darted from side to side, searching for the G-men he suspected of lying in wait. As he got closer, John saw a gold plaque by the front door of the embassy with the cyrillic letters CCCP on it. Rather than walking to the huge wooden door, he continued on all the way to the corner of Sixteenth and L streets. He paused, turned around, and realized that he had just made his first mistake as a spy. He should have walked directly into the compound. "I was simply giving the FBI a second chance to see me."

John hurried back toward the building, quickening his pace. "A car had just left the embassy and this big Russian was closing the iron gate behind it. The embassy had a fence around it. I slid through the gate, really startling this guy."

John announced that he wanted to see the embassy's "security manager." The Russian at the gate didn't seem to understand.

"Embassy security! Where's the director?" John repeated, almost panicked. This was taking too long. He didn't want to be standing in front of the embassy any longer than necessary. But the Russian still didn't react. John walked past him to the front door. He jerked it open and stepped inside, startling a young woman perched behind a tiny desk.

"I need to see the man in charge of your security," John stammered, trying to sound in control of his emotions. He heard the front door open and close behind him. The gatekeeper was now standing between him and the door. The receptionist looked nervous, and after a few moments she disappeared behind a door at her right.

John had been so overwrought outside the embassy that he really hadn't examined the man at the gate closely. Now he saw that he was a "perfect specimen of an iron curtain goon—direct from central casting." The Russian stood well over six feet tall, had broad shoulders, and a prizefighter's nose. The receptionist finally reappeared and motioned John into a small office where she pointed toward a wooden chair. John sat and waited.

After several minutes, a slender man in his late twenties entered the office. "Why did you come here?" the man asked, his English betraying a Slavic accent.

John stood. "Are you with embassy security?" he asked.

"Why did you come here?" the man repeated calmly.

John suddenly realized that he and the slender Russian were not alone in the room. The goon had quietly joined them and was standing, once again, behind John.

"I am interested in pursuing the possibilities of selling classified United States government documents to the Soviet Union," John said, repeating the lines he had practiced during the drive to Washington.

The embassy official showed absolutely no emotion.

"I want to sell you top secrets," John repeated. "Valuable military information. I've brought along a sample." John removed the KL-47 keylist from the front pocket of his jacket and handed it to his Russian inquisitor, who studied it cautiously. He turned and left the room.

"It suddenly hit me that I was no longer on U.S. soil," John Walker told me later. "They could have killed me right there if they wanted to."

The embassy official appeared distressed when he returned to the room. Marching over to John, the Russian demanded in an excited voice to know why the keylist wasn't signed. John explained that NSA keylists always had a Letter of Promulgation on the back of them that identified them as NSA keylists, but sometimes the statements were signed and sometimes they weren't. The missing signature didn't mean anything, he said. It was just a sign of sloppiness. The Russian appeared unconvinced. He asked John his name. The question caught John off guard. For some reason, he had assumed that he could sell military secrets to the Soviets without telling them his name. He quickly decided to lie. Several names zipped through his mind, but he worried that he might stumble if he picked a name that was too different from his own. He remembered KISS.

"James," John said. "My name is James."

"James what?"

"Harper," said John. Like Johnnie Walker, James Harper was the name of a brand of whiskey. It would be hard to forget. (An American named James Harper was arrested in 1985 and charged with espionage in a case unrelated to Walker's.)

The Russian asked John for identification.

"Is this necessary?" John protested.

The Russian insisted. He had to see some sort of written identification. John opened his billfold and withdrew his military identification card. The Russian reached out for it, but John didn't hand it to him. Instead, he held it up so the Russian could read it.

"John . . . Anthony . . . Walker . . . Junior," the Russian read aloud. "Thank you . . . Mr. Harper."

John's face felt warm.

The Russian smiled and sat down behind the desk across from John. He motioned John to sit. "Please," the Russian said, "enough foolishness. We desire the document that you have brought. We want more such documents. We welcome you, friend. So please let me have your identification."

John pushed his ID card across the desk. The Russian excused himself once again and left the room. Five minutes passed. Then ten. He figured the Russian was making a copy of his military identification card, but didn't understand why it was taking so long. John kept looking at the time. He was going to be late for the midnight watch. He should have allowed more time for the transaction. Howard Sparks, the watch officer John relieved, was going to be angry. Only a few weeks earlier, John's car had broken down while he was driving back from Charleston to Norfolk. John had been more than an hour late and Sparks hadn't been happy about it. John would be calling attention to himself by being late again.

When the Russian returned to the office, John complained, "I have to get back to work." The Russian said it was necessary for them to proceed slowly.

"The hell it is," John said. His sudden display of backbone caught the Russian off guard. The Soviet apologized, explaining that he and John still had to talk about several crucial things, such as security precautions, John's access to other documents, future meetings, and, most important of all, John's motivation.

"Is your coming here political or financially motivated?" he asked John.

"Purely financial. I need the money."

The Russian nodded sympathetically. He began asking John questions about his life-style. Was he married? Did he have a drinking problem? Did he use drugs? The exchange reminded John of a job interview and he felt uncomfortable once again. This was taking too much time. John needed to get his payment for the KL-47 and get the hell out of there. "I've got to get back to work," John complained again, but the Russian continued with his questioning. "He reminded me of a salesman following a written script," John said later.

At one point, the Russian asked John if he had ever read any writings by Karl Marx. Before John could answer, the embassy official began explaining the superiority of Marxism over capitalism. John had had enough. "Look," John said, interrupting the Russian, "here is what I had in mind." John quickly offered to, in effect, sign a "lifetime contract." He would supply the Russians with classified information, primarily NSA keylists, in return for a regular salary, "just like an employee."

The Russian seemed stunned at the idea of paying a spy a weekly salary. How much did John expect to receive under such a system, he asked. The fee was negotiable, John said. Between $500 and $1,000 per week. John handed the Russian a copy of his duty schedule for the next month so that they could choose a date for their next meeting.

It would be better if there were no face-to-face meetings, the embassy official said. But John would have to meet with a KGB contact at least one more time to discuss dead drops, his salary request, and what kind of documents he could provide. The Russian told John to draw up a "shopping list" of classified information at his disposal. John should return in two weeks to a shopping center in Alexandria, Virginia, and stand outside the Zayre store there at precisely 2:00 P.M. He should carry a folded *Time* magazine under his right arm, the Russian said. He could enter the store and make a purchase if he wished or wait outside and window shop while he waited for the contact.

"A man will approach you and call you 'Dear Friend,'" the Russian said.

John took a piece of paper out of his coat pocket and began writing down the instructions. "You mustn't do that," the Russian said. "It isn't safe."

John continued to write. "I got a bad memory for some things," he said.

The Russian left the room. When he returned, he handed John an envelope. It contained bills—all fifty-dollar bills.

"One thousand dollars," the Russian said. He then placed a sheet of paper on the desk and asked John to sign it. John looked at it but balked because he couldn't read Russian.

"What is this?" he asked.

"A receipt, of course," the Russian replied.

John signed it.

The Russian motioned John toward the hallway, where several men were waiting. One stepped forward and handed John a heavy, full-length coat and broad-brimmed hat. John put them on and was led to a side door of the embassy where a car was waiting. The men crowded around John, dwarfing him.

"Good-bye, dear friend," the embassy official said.

The cluster of Russians moved quickly outside and pushed John into the center of the back seat. No one talked. The car raced down the alley that separates the embassy from *The Washington Post* building and pulled onto a main thoroughfare. During the next half hour the car raced around northwest Washington, until it finally came to a sudden stop in a residential neighborhood. Within seconds, John was shoved out and stripped of the hat and coat. The embassy car sped away.

John was convinced that he would be arrested at any moment by the FBI, but after standing alone for several minutes on the sidewalk, he began to feel euphoric. He had done it! He removed the envelope from his jacket and fanned the bills.

"I knew I was about to make a lot of money," he said later. "One hell of a lot of money."

# 13

Barbara couldn't believe that John suddenly had enough cash to repay the $700 loan from the amusement company and buy Christmas presents for the family. John and Barbara both liked to buy lots of presents at Christmas. It was the only time of the year when they were extravagant. Even when they were first married and penniless, they had had department stores put purchases in layaway as early as June for Christmas. They would pay a little each week. There hadn't been many presents for Christmas last year because every cent had gone to renovating the bar. This year had been looking bleak too, until John arrived in Charleston with a billfold full of cash. Barbara was suspicious and demanded an explanation. John lied. "I got a second job." He said he had made extra cash working for a car rental agency, helping to move an excess of cars from Norfolk to Washington. Barbara didn't believe the story, but she didn't press John for answers. Instead, she cooked a big Italian dinner, exactly as John wanted, and Arthur and Rita joined them. Temporarily detailed to Charleston once again, Arthur had driven home to Key West and brought Rita and the kids up to John's for Christmas. Barbara felt awkward when Rita first arrived, but once she realized that Rita didn't know about Arthur's sexual encounter with her, she relaxed.

John was soon back in Norfolk and en route to Washington for his second meeting with the Russians. He was still bewildered by the fact that he hadn't been arrested. The FBI must have seen his clumsy entrance at the Soviet embassy, he thought. Federal agents were probably searching through military records at the Pentagon at this very moment trying to match his face with a name. "I really believed that after I went into the embassy, I would be arrested within a few days," John said, "and then I figured it was just a matter of weeks. It took me a long time to get over the feeling that someone was looking over my shoulder and about to arrest me."

John had brought a small packet of classified information with him on this trip, along with the "shopping list" of classified documents that he could supply the Soviets. By now they would have had time to check the authenticity of the KL-47 keylist with their own cryptographic experts. Obviously, they would want John to supply them with the next month's KL-47 keylist and, if possible, a technical manual that showed exactly how the machine was wired.

Because of his training as a cryptographic repairman, John knew that the keylist he had sold the Russians was actually only half of the solution that they needed to read the messages encrypted on the KL-47 machine. If the Russians were lucky, ingenious, and unrelenting, they might be able to break the KL-47 code and transcribe some messages, but it would be extremely difficult without access to an actual KL-47 machine. Compared to today's computer designed and enhanced cryptographic machines, the KL-47 appears amateurish, but it still contained enough tricks to make unlocking its code formidable.

Like all cryptographic hardware, the technical details of the KL-47 machine are still classified, but it operates on a rather simple theory. The machine looks like an old-fashioned typewriter except that it has a large open bin on its top. This bin contains twelve rotors, or wheels, attached to a center core that can be removed from the bin. Each wheel rotates independently with the letters of the alphabet and numbers on its edge. To encrypt a message, the operator sets the twelve rotors to a series of predetermined locations. The rotors then act like the keys on a normal typewriter, except that they are misaligned. For example, when the operator types *A* on his keyboard, a rotor on the KL-47 machine whirls around and prints a different letter—such as a *K*. To unscramble the message, all the person receiving it must know is the transpositions on the current keylist, for example, that *K* actually stands for letter *A*. The KL-47 machine, however, is more complicated than that. Each time the KL-47 operator types a letter, the machine *chooses* a different rotor to type the letter. As a result, the letter *A* might be printed as a *K* the first time and as an *L* the second time that it is typed. The word *AGAIN* would come out as KMLZP, even though the letter *A* is typed twice. The military further complicated the KL-47 machine by designing it so that only eight of its twelve rotors work at any given time. The KL-47 keylist that John had sold the Soviets told them exactly how each rotor was aligned, but without a wiring diagram of the machine, the Soviets didn't know the sequence of the rotors. John would have supplied that information if he had had access to the technical manual for the KL-47 machine, but he couldn't find one. He did have access, however, to the keylists and to technical manuals for at least four other types of cryptographic machines, devices used much more frequently than the KL-47. John had written the names of the machines on a sheet of paper for the KGB; the KWR-37 machine, KW-8 and KY-8 systems, and KG-14 machine were included. John also had written the word SOSUS on the notepaper to show the KGB he had access to much more than just cryptographic devices. He knew the location of key SOSUS hydrophones off the Soviet land mass, the Aleutian Islands, and Iceland. He also wrote down the acronym SIOP (Single Integrated Operations Plan), which referred to the nuclear battle plan he had seen while aboard the U.S.S. *Simon Bolivar*. John hadn't seen a recent SIOP, but he could still recall several specifics about the document that the Russians might pay for.

The Russians had asked John to compile a list of Navy personnel at the message center, with a short biography of each sailor there. The KGB especially wanted to know about any of his co-workers' weaknesses: married men with mistresses, drug addicts, alcoholics, homosexuals, officers in financial trouble. John had worked diligently and composed an elaborate report on his peers.

Since his meeting at the Soviet embassy, John had begun to pay conscientious attention to every message that crossed his desk, making copies of several dozen of the most interesting, including the precise location of ships and submarines operating in the Atlantic and specifics about each ship's destination and mission. Some of the messages contained general information such as "rules for peacetime engagement" that told a ship's crew how and when it could respond with gunfire if it came into contact with a Soviet vessel. John had also copied messages that Navy ships had filed when they sighted Russian ships and submarines. These messages would help the Russians to know when they had been observed by U.S. ships and when they had avoided detection.

Even though his shopping list contained a tantalizing collection of classified information, John wanted something more to astound the KGB and crystallize his importance in their minds. He had saved the best for last. At the bottom of his shopping list, John wrote, "Keylists and technical manuals for the KW-7, also known as Orestes."

In the 1960s, the KW-7 was the most important cryptographic equipment in the United States, used by the Navy, Air Force, Marines, Army, and the CIA.

Intelligence experts divide information into two types: tactical, or "real time intelligence," and strategic, or "long-term intelligence." Tactical information is generally less than six months old, usually involving specific information about an individual operation, such as the exact time and location of a bombing raid in North Vietnam. Strategic intelligence tends to be much more general. Once the Soviets had access to the keylist for the KW-7 machine, they would be only a step away from being able to read thousands of U.S. military messages, including some tactical information because the KW-7 was being used extensively in Vietnam. Selling the Russians the keylist for an antiquated KL-47 cryptographic machine would allow a peek through a keyhole at U.S. military secrets. Supplying the Russians with the KW-7 keylist was much more damaging, more like throwing open the entire door. The Soviets would still have only half the puzzle—the keylist—but John had access to technical manuals that could be used to reconstruct a KW-7 machine.

John understood the consequences of selling the Russians the keylist and the technical manuals for the KW-7. If the United States and the Soviet Union went to war, the Russians would be able to read Navy messages both tactical and strategic. John knew that giving the Russians access to the KW-7 cryptographic machine could cost American lives in Vietnam. If the Russians shared tactical intelligence gained through the KW-7 machine with the North Vietnamese, the lives of both U.S. pilots on bombing raids and of grunts engaged in ground combat would be jeopardized.

John considered the ramifications before he included the KW-7 machine on his shopping list, but in the end, he couldn't think of any reason not to sell it. He had convinced himself that the United States and Soviet Union were never going to war and that the Russians wouldn't share intelligence information with the North Vietnamese. The KW-7 was simply too valuable for the Russians to share with the Viet Cong. Already John's sense of his own importance as a figure in the cold war had grown to monstrous proportions.

"I decided," John told me during one of our first interviews together, "that if I was going to be a spy, and I clearly was going to be one, then I would be the best damn spy there ever was, and that meant giving them everything. And that's exactly what I did."

John met his Russian contact outside the Zayre store in Alexandria as scheduled. He was looking in a display window when a voice behind him said, "Hello, dear friend. Please do not turn around, but walk with me."

John did as he was told. From an occasional glimpse, John knew the man was about six feet one, had dark brown hair, wore glasses, and was clean shaven. This KGB agent had a clear, pleasant voice that reminded John of his father. In his thirties, John guessed, but didn't wear a wedding band. Only one rather obvious mannerism betrayed the fact that he was not an American. The Russian was holding his cigarette pinched between thumb and forefinger. Americans hold cigarettes between their first two fingers.

"How did you get here?" the Russian asked.

"I drove my car from Norfolk as instructed," John replied.

"Did anything unusual happen?"

"No," said John, who was uncertain what the Russian meant.

The Russian asked John if he had seen any cars more than once during his trip, which might mean that they had been trailing him.

"No, I don't believe I was followed," John answered.

During the next ten minutes, John and the Russian walked through a neighborhood near the shopping center. The Russian spoke slowly and calmly about John's new career as a spy. The KGB would pay him a salary of $4,000 a month in return for cryptographic information like the KL-47 keylist. He'd get extra money if he obtained specific items that the Russians needed, but he would never receive less than $2,000 each month as long as he had access to cryptographic materials.

John quickly agreed to the terms and the Russian turned to security. John should never telephone the Soviet embassy. He should tell no one, including his wife, that he had become a spy. He should be extremely careful with his money and not spend it lavishly by buying a new car, fancy clothes, or a new house. Copying documents was risky. John would be given a Minox camera to photograph them. He could steal them, photograph them, and return them. This procedure was much safer than trying to use a photocopy machine.

The KGB agent described how a dead drop was performed and gave John some pointers on how to detect whether he was being followed. "If you are on foot, get into a taxi but only go a short distance—two or three blocks perhaps—and then get out. Watch behind you this entire time and see if anyone does the same." John could also lose someone who was following him in a car by walking up a one-way street against traffic.

As they spoke, John realized the Russian seemed to be following a carefully crafted script, just as the embassy employee had. As the lecture on security drew to a close, the Russian asked John if he had access to a technical manual for the KL-47 machine. John told the KGB agent that the operations headquarters in Norfolk didn't have one. In that case, the agent explained, John would be given a hand-held device invented by the KGB specifically to read the internal wiring of the KL-47 machine. He would receive it and a Minox miniature camera in the next dead drop. John should hide the "rotor reader" because it would be a dead giveaway to anyone who knew anything about cryptology.

"What about the pill?" John asked.

The Russian didn't understand what pill John was talking about.

"Aren't you going to give me some sort of pill that I can take if I'm arrested so I can commit suicide?" John asked.

The Russian appeared confused. "No, we don't do that," he responded.

The Russian asked John to give him the keylist for the KL-47 machine and any other material he had brought with him.

"I didn't know I was supposed to bring it out here," John replied.

"Where is it?" the KGB agent asked.

"I put it in a locker at National Airport," John said. The Russian stopped walking. He warned John that lockers were routinely checked and he suggested that John get the documents immediately. "I will contact you there," he said, turning briskly and walking away.

John hurried to the airport. He had hidden the documents because he hadn't wanted to carry them to the shopping center, fearing that the FBI would be waiting there to arrest him.

The main terminal was crowded as usual. John stopped short of the lockers and surveyed the crowd. A man in a two-piece gray suit standing near the lockers was reading a newspaper. A woman sat nearby knitting. John wondered if they were watching for him. He didn't move for several minutes. Then a woman with two youngsters came up and embraced the man with the newspaper and they all left. John decided he was being paranoid. Opening his locker quickly, he grabbed the package of documents and rushed out through the glass doors. A few feet later he heard the Russian's voice behind him.

"Hello, friend," he said. "Let's walk into that parking lot." A car pulled up beside them as they neared the parking lot entrance, and the KGB agent took John's package and handed it through an open window to a man inside the car, which sped away.

"Did you bring your shopping list?" the Russian asked. John handed him the notebook paper. When he finished reading it, the agent said that he was particularly interested in the last item on the list—the KW-7 keylist and technical manuals.

"I can get those, but it could be difficult," John said. The Russian indicated that he would pay John a bonus of $1,000 or more for the KW-7 keylist, particularly if he could get it within a few weeks. The Russian handed John a packet containing instructions for the dead drop and listing the steps John must follow if he wished to contact the Soviets in an emergency. If they needed to get in touch with him, they would send a birthday card signed "Your dear friend," his cue to go to a prearranged location in Washington where he would find instructions and a package.

"Do you understand everything that I've told you?" the Russian asked, after passing him the envelopes. "Yes," John assured him. The Russian handed him another envelope that contained cash.

"We will not meet again face-to-face for a long time," the Russian said, "but we will become good friends and we will communicate in the dead drop packages. We want you to know that we are very concerned about you. Many people who come to us help us for years and then retire. We hope you will be one of them.

"Good-bye, dear friend," the Russian said, gently patting John on the shoulder. The patting must have been a signal because a car pulled up alongside seconds later. The agent quickly stepped inside and was gone.

John kept on walking for several minutes and then hurried back to his car to count his money. The Russians had given him his $4,000 salary, plus an extra $1,000.

Sometime in early January 1968, John delivered the keylist for a KW-7 machine by leaving a copy of it in the bottom of a bag of trash during a dead drop in a Virginia suburb of Washington.

On January 23, 1968, the U.S.S. *Pueblo* was captured by the North Koreans in international waters off their coastline. The *Pueblo* was a secret intelligence-gathering ship outfitted with sophisticated eavesdropping gear that had been dispatched by the Navy and the NSA to "sample electronic environment off east coast North Korea" and to "intercept and conduct surveillance of Soviet naval units operating Tsushima Straits."

One crew member of the *Pueblo* was killed and the other eighty-two were captured during the surprise North Korean attack. During the next eleven months, the crew members were held hostage and tortured in North Korea.

After John Walker was arrested, FBI agents quizzed him extensively about the timing of his delivery of the KW-7 keylist. Agents repeatedly asked if he knew anything about the *Pueblo* capture. John vehemently denied any connection between the two events. FBI agents handling the Walker case remained suspicious about the timing of John's disclosure of the KW-7 keylist and the seizure of the *Pueblo*. At one point, the FBI theorized that the Soviets might have urged the North Koreans to attack the *Pueblo* because the KGB had access to the KW-7 keylist. The Russians had to have known that the *Pueblo* contained extensive cryptographic equipment, including the KW-7, the theory went.

John considered the FBI theory "totally preposterous" and, in all fairness, it is difficult to believe that John's delivery prompted the Russians to undertake such a convoluted and risky action.

But after the *Pueblo* crew was released on December 23, 1968, a naval investigation revealed that the attack had happened so quickly that the ship's crew had failed to destroy several important cryptographic machines before being captured. The most serious loss, according to disclosures only made public by the Navy in recent court documents, was the confiscation of a working KW-7 machine. U.S. intelligence sources now believe that machine was subsequently delivered to the Soviets.

Regardless of what prompted the attack, and whether or not John's delivery played any role in it, the end result was the same. In early 1968, the Russians suddenly obtained a working KW-7 machine and its daily keylists.

Because the KW-7 was so widely used and so vital to U.S. military communications, the NSA decided not to scrap it after the *Pueblo* incident. Instead, the NSA modified the KW-7 machine on the theory that its changes plus the daily keylists would be adequate safeguards to keep KW-7 encrypted messages secret. What the NSA didn't know, of course, was that John was providing the KGB with keylists and all of the KW-7 technical manuals. As soon as the NSA devised a way to modify the KW-7 and sent out the new technical manual, John photographed the document and delivered the film to the Russians.

In the first few months that he was a spy, the KGB gained access to the United States' most widely used cryptographic system, thanks to John Walker and the seizure of the U.S.S. *Pueblo*.

It was as if the U.S. Navy had opened up a branch communications office directly in the center of Red Square, and it marked the beginning of the deciphering of more than *one million* classified U.S. military messages.

# 14

Fear of arrest nagged John during the early months of 1968. Each morning his first thought was, "Today is the day that I will be arrested." His anxiety surfaced periodically during the day in sweaty palms and feet that tapped restlessly. Even asleep, John could not escape his uneasiness. He had nightmares about being arrested in the message center and dragged outside into an angry mob of sailors.

"I spent the money from the Soviets as soon as I got it. There was no point in being frugal because I felt I was going to be arrested at any minute," he said. "I lived from dead drop to dead drop."

John earned $725 per month as a Navy warrant officer. The Soviets were paying him $4,000 per month. Though the KGB warned him not to attract attention by spending lavishly, John couldn't resist. In April 1968, he rented a three-bedroom apartment in a swanky Norfolk complex and told Barbara that it was time for her and the children to come join him. Barbara was stunned by her new home. The apartment featured luxuriant wall-to-wall carpeting, up-to-date kitchen appliances, pristine rooms, and a doorman. John was the only warrant officer in the building, but none of his co-workers at the Navy message center was suspicious when John bragged about his "new pad" because they had heard him boast about what a good investment the Bamboo Snack Bar had become.

"I thought Barbara would love the apartment and wouldn't have a thing to nag me about, but I was wrong," John said. She complained that their furniture wasn't good enough for their new home. Much to Barbara's surprise, John offered to buy all new furnishings without regard to cost. Barbara had always felt she had a hidden talent for interior decorating, and during the next few days, she inspected dozens of colors, fabrics, and wall coverings. Whenever she asked for money, John reached into his front pants pocket and removed a thick wad of folded $50 bills that he enjoyed flaunting. By the time Barbara was finished, John had spent $10,000 in cash.

Barbara knew immediately that John had lied to her about having a second job, but she didn't pester him about it. The family was reunited and neither she nor John had to scrimp anymore. The days of powdered milk and resoled shoes appeared to be over, and Barbara was glad.

With John's encouragement, she began schooling her children in the social graces that befitted the family's new financial status. Barbara bought a small wooden table, which she placed in the kitchen. Margaret, aged ten, Cynthia, nine, Laura, eight, and Michael, six, were required to eat dinner there each night until they had mastered sufficient table manners to join Barbara and John in the dining room. Dinner became an elaborate ritual whenever John worked the day shift. When he arrived home, Barbara met him at the door clad in a cocktail dress, a martini and folded newspaper in her hands. John relaxed alone in the living room for several minutes. After he finished the newspaper, Barbara brought in hors d'oeuvres. Dinner was served when John sat at the head of the table. It ended when he finished eating and Barbara scurried to clear his plate. After dessert, John talked about his day, and then it was time for each child to tell "something new which they had learned that day."

"I always felt so stupid," Cynthia Walker said of the nightly after-dinner ceremony. "We always went around the table and Margaret was first. She always had something new that she had learned, and then it was Laura's turn, and she always told some fantastic story even if she had to make it up. It didn't matter what Michael said because he was so cute that no one cared. And then it would be my turn, and I wouldn't know what to say so I'd sit there and be ridiculed and called stupid."

Dinner was not the only drill in etiquette. After school, Barbara had her daughters practice walking across the living room without dropping a book that she placed on each of their heads. "When you walk into a room, you should own it," she lectured. "Every eye should be on you and you alone." Meticulous grooming and wearing fashionable clothes became important. Barbara enjoyed dressing all her daughters alike, and she spent time doctoring Cynthia's straight brown hair with sugar water to make it curl like her sisters'.

John bought an eight-millimeter movie camera and began taking family movies. "I hate home movies where some kid comes out of the ocean and waves into the camera and says, 'Hi,' " Barbara Walker said, recalling her husband's toy. "So I began writing scripts for the children to perform."

Like most Navy wives whose husbands spent long periods at sea, Barbara was used to handling family finances. But after she joined John in Norfolk, he insisted on keeping track of the money. One night Barbara asked him to tell her why he seemed to have an endless flow of cash. "It's better for you that you don't know," John replied cryptically. The next day, he brought a hypodermic syringe home from work and placed it in the middle drawer of his desk. He had used the syringe at the message center to squeeze oil into hard-to-reach gears in cryptographic machines, but John knew that Barbara's curiosity would eventually lead her to his desk and he thought the syringe might make her think he was trafficking in illegal drugs. John stacked five pennies in the desk drawer near the syringe. When he carefully opened the drawer a few days later, the pennies were no longer neatly stacked. The Russians had told him about the penny trick. It was an inconspicuous way to tell if someone had been snooping in his drawer. Barbara didn't ask any more questions about the cash after he planted the syringe, John recalled.

On May 20, 1968, the submarine message center where John worked was ordered by Vice Admiral Arnold F. Schade, commander of the Atlantic submarine force, to send a top secret dispatch to Francis A. Slattery, commanding officer of the nuclear submarine *Scorpion*. The sub had just left Gibraltar on its way to Norfolk from a three-month Mediterranean cruise when Schade ordered it diverted toward the Canary Islands and six Soviet warships. The *Scorpion* was told to monitor the Russian ships, which included a nuclear submarine. Shortly after midnight on May 22, the *Scorpion* filed a routine position report with the Norfolk message center; it was six hours away from the Russian warships. The submarine missed its next routine position report and suddenly didn't respond to a series of attempts by the message center during the next twenty-four hours to contact it. Schade immediately received permission to launch a discreet, quick search for the *Scorpion*. Two squadrons of destroyers, several airplanes, and a nuclear submarine were dispatched. During the next four days, John and his colleagues worked round-the-clock as concern over the missing submarine mounted.

When the *Scorpion* didn't return to Norfolk on schedule May 27, the families of its ninety-nine-man crew patiently waiting at the Navy dock discovered for the first time what John and other watch officers already knew. The *Scorpion* was missing. The Navy quickly declared an alert and organized a full-scale search. Within thirty-six hours, top secret dispatches were received indicating that SOSUS hydrophones had overheard the *Scorpion* being rocked by a series of explosions. The sensitive hydrophones also had recorded the sound of the sub's hull being crushed by water pressure as the boat sank two miles to the Atlantic Ocean floor.

Because the *Scorpion* had been on a mission to monitor Soviet warships, there was immediate speculation that it had been attacked. The crypto machines in the message center worked nonstop as the investigation increased to a frantic pace.

The sinking of the *Scorpion* devastated Norfolk, the sub's home port. The sailors in the message center were especially upset. "The *Scorpion* was under our control when it went down," recalled John Rogers, the message center officer in early 1968 who was John Walker's direct boss. "We felt a special responsibility for it. It was one of ours."

Barbara Walker was shaken by the disaster too. She and other Navy wives talked for hours about the tragedy and the distraught families of the dead crew. But John displayed little outward emotion. "The Navy is full of risks," he told Barbara. "Putting your life on the line is simply part of the job. That's what they pay you for."

The *Scorpion* incident troubled John more than he let on, however. Had something he sold to the Soviets played a role in the disaster? he wondered. The Navy was still speculating in the summer of 1968 that the Russian warships might have attacked the *Scorpion,* and that made John very uncomfortable. What if Navy investigators somehow found out that he was a spy? What in the world were the Soviets up to? He was scared, but not enough to stop collecting material for the KGB. The increase in top secret messages brought on by the *Scorpion* tragedy gave John a mother lode of classified documents. He methodically copied dozens of them, including papers that outlined how the Navy conducted its search, what kinds of information had been detected by the SOSUS hydrophones, what the U.S. naval intelligence knew at the time about the Russian ships, and possible theories about why the submarine had gone down. The KGB told John in the notes left at dead drops that it was delighted with the material.

Five months after it sank, the broken remains of the *Scorpion* were found 400 miles south-southwest of the Azores. In December 1984, *The Virginian-Pilot and The Ledger-Star,* a Norfolk newspaper, published a series of previously classified Navy documents that concluded that the *Scorpion* sank after one of its own torpedoes exploded aboard the boat. The torpedo explosion theory is the most logical explanation the Navy found for the sinking, but no one is one hundred percent positive to this day about what actually caused the boat to sink. There are some sailors who still believe the Russians might have been involved in the tragedy.

Copying messages about the *Scorpion* was much easier than obtaining keylists. Most secret messages were routinely photocopied after they were deciphered so copies could be delivered through the chain of command. The military is notorious for duplicating its paperwork, and it was not difficult for John to make an extra copy of a sensitive message for the KGB. He hid the copies in plain sight.

"The best place to hide something is right under someone's nose,"

John bragged. "I put copies of messages in a file folder and stuck them in the back of a file cabinet that no one used." If someone accidentally found the file, they would most likely assume it was there because it was supposed to be. "The Navy never throws anything away and no one knows why some things are kept," John explained. "Once we were going through some files in a ship and came across a bunch of old World War II battle plans."

When John first told me about how he hid documents "in plain sight," he acted as if it were something that he had thought up himself. Later, he told me that the KGB had first suggested it to him in various instructions left at dead drops. I don't think John ever realized that the concept was not something that the KGB had originated, but was made famous in Edgar Allan Poe's short story, "The Purloined Letter."

John did receive a used Minox camera from the KGB with a small chain that looked like a carrying strap but actually was used for focusing the camera. The chain was the exact distance that John needed between his camera and a document. All he had to do to take a perfect picture was hold the chain on a document and pull the Minox back until the chain was taut. The Russians provided John with high-speed black-and-white film and told him to use a 150-watt bulb when photographing documents. John took the photographs inside the crypto vault when he was working the morning shift and free of supervision.

He also used the KGB's rotor reader to determine the KL-47's circuitry. Once again, John applied KISS. During an early morning watch, he innocently announced that he needed to inspect the KL-47 machine because it was garbling messages. None of the men under his command flinched and John quickly put the hand-held rotor reader to work.

"A K mart store has better security than the U.S. Navy," John told me later, laughing. Still, he was worried. He felt it was only a matter of time before he was arrested.

One morning, he decided to learn how to sail; he immediately fell in love with the sport and bought a twenty-four-foot sailboat. In the beginning, John took Barbara and the children out on the boat. But, Barbara would complain and the kids would fidget. Soon he was sailing exclusively with younger sailors who worked for him at the message center. John supplied the sailboat and a metal washtub filled with ice and beer; the sailors brought the girls. "I loved sailing. If I wasn't at work, I was on my boat."

Barbara stopped fixing elaborate dinners after John bought the sailboat because she never knew when he would come home. She found herself being left behind on weekends with the children.

"Barbara really bitched about the sailboat and finally I told her, 'Hey, some men play golf, others play tennis, and still others play handball, and they may or may not include their wives in these activities. I'm telling you right now that sailing is my thing. I need my time away, and sailing is it, and I don't want to hear any bitching about it,' " John said. "Of course, Barbara hated that. She couldn't understand what I would call absolutely normal male behavior in ninety-five percent of all American households where the husband goes out on Saturday morning to play golf. 'Why don't you want to stay home with me and the kids?' she'd moan, or she'd demand that I take her with me every time I went out on the boat, and finally I said, 'Look Barbara, this is just the way it is. Sometimes you can come out on the boat with me, but other times I am going to go with my friends; and if it's going to upset you so much, tough shit, because you are not going with me and that's final.' "

While John was gone one afternoon in 1968, Barbara discovered a metal box hidden in the bottom drawer of his desk at home. Inside were several rolls of film, and black-and-white photographs of country roads with trees and bushes marked with hand-drawn arrows. There was a map too, and a hand-printed note that said, in part, "information not what we wanted, want information on rotor." In big red block letters at the top of the note were the words, "Please Destroy." The box contained $2,000 in cash too. During the next couple of weeks, Barbara tried to make sense of her discovery. She finally confronted John.

"Tell me about the box," she said. "What does it mean?"

"I'm a spy," John replied. "That's where I get all the money."

Eighteen years later, after John was arrested, Barbara Walker recalled her exchange with John in testimony before a secret federal grand jury in Baltimore, Maryland. She was under oath when she testified.

QUESTION: What occurred during the confrontation?
ANSWER: I called him a traitor.
Q: When you called him a traitor, what was his reaction?
A: He told me to shut up, that someone might hear me.
Q: Was there a physical confrontation as well?
A: Yes.

Barbara Walker later said that John had punched her in the face, giving her two black eyes. But that was not all that she blamed on John.

Q: Would it be fair to say, Mrs. Walker, that you are an alcoholic?
A: Yes, it would.
Q: Is that a condition which began to develop around the time that you are telling us about now?
A: Yes.

John Walker denied Barbara's claims that he had beaten her physically and driven her to drink. When we spoke, John said that he was aware of Barbara's implication that she had objected to his spying out of a sense of loyalty to her country. The issue of patriotism *never* came up, John insisted.

"Barbara's big concern was the same that it always had been," John said. "She wanted to know why I didn't love her anymore. Why I didn't want to spend time with her and the kids, or just her. And I said, 'Hey, you want to know why I don't love you anymore? Let me count the ways, Barbara! Where do you want me to begin?' You see, Barbara was contributing nothing to my life at the time, almost like my father was with my mother.

"I swear that's how the argument began. It didn't have anything to do with patriotism. She concocted that stuff about calling me a traitor to make herself look better. Hell, she wanted to know how I did it—she began asking me all kinds of questions because she thought it was exciting—and then she said to me, 'Can I get involved in this with you?' and I said, 'Barbara, I'm going to get arrested any goddamn minute. Why do you want to get involved?' and she said, 'Because I want to prove my love for you. This is something we can do together.' That's what it was all about. Not patriotism.

"It was really sad because she never did figure out how to keep me happy."

At the time John made those statements to me, he was clearly angry at Barbara for turning him in to the FBI. He wanted to hurt her. But John insisted he was telling the truth.

When I told Barbara Walker how John had described their confrontation, she began to cry. She also appeared irritated that someone might actually believe him. "I've told the truth," she said. "I called him a traitor and he hit me. I love my country."

Barbara Walker acknowledged that she had questioned John about his spying and had volunteered to go with him on a dead drop. The explanation that she gave me was almost identical to what she told the grand jury during her sworn testimony.

Q: Did you offer to go with him on a drop?
A: Yes. I did.
Q: Why did you offer to go on the drop?
A: Since the marriage and our family structure was falling apart, I thought that if I showed him that I cared, that would help things to change.

Barbara Walker hammered home that same point to me during our more than thirty conversations. "Family always came first to me," she said repeatedly. "You got to understand that." At the same time, she rarely mentioned patriotism.

Barbara Walker's testimony before the grand jury also included an exchange that inadvertently supported John's explanation for why he became a KGB spy.

Q: Did John ever tell you why he was engaged in this activity?
A: The business in South Carolina was failing, and I was trying to maintain household expenses, plus the business, and I often would

take my engagement ring to a pawnshop and pawn it. Every time I did, I told him about it.

Q: He told you that he was doing it for the money?

A: Yes.

Money and family. They were the two themes that continued to surface whenever I spoke to John and Barbara.

While Barbara and John disagreed about what happened the day she learned he was a spy, both agreed about what happened next.

John saw Barbara's willingness to go with him on a dead drop as a "great opportunity."

"I knew," John told me, "that wives couldn't be forced to testify against their husbands. If she went with me, then, even if I divorced her, she would still be my accomplice."

Barbara did drive John to his next dead drop. He sat beside her in the front seat scanning the route with a pair of high-powered binoculars for possible FBI agents. Barbara told me later that she was petrified during the exchange. But she didn't make any mistakes or panic when John first jumped from the car to drop his trash bag of documents, and later to pick up his KGB cash. The KGB had put two soft drink cans in the trash bag that John retrieved. Neatly tucked inside the cans were fifty-dollar bills, each rolled tight like cigarettes. Back home that night, John asked Barbara to set up her ironing board and press each fifty-dollar bill so that it would lay flat. She obliged.

"At that point, as far as I was concerned," John later told me, "Barbara was just as much a spy as I was!"

The distinction that Barbara Walker had betrayed her country, not for money—as he had done—but because of a misguided love for him and a devotion to her children never crossed John's mind.

# 15

In the summer of 1968, John Walker made a startling discovery. His money hadn't made any of his personal problems disappear. In fact, he was more miserable now than he ever had been.

The swanky apartment, expensive furnishings, and elaborate dinners hadn't helped his marriage. "Barbara kept nagging me," John claimed, "worse than before."

Barbara had become deeply depressed and began drinking more and more. John's military career also was in trouble. "I kept thinking that I was going to be arrested and I couldn't concentrate at work. Promotions suddenly didn't matter. Nothing mattered because any minute I was going to get arrested. I just knew it."

John had received high marks in late 1967 from his first boss at the Navy message center, John Rogers. "John ran his watch well," Rogers recalled. "There were no boo-boos. Traffic moved good. He was a smart-ass sometimes, but as far as I was concerned, he did a hell of a good job in the sub center when he worked for me." But by July 1968, John's work was becoming slipshod. Bill Metcalf, who became John's boss that summer, considered John an abysmal watch officer. "My boss and I used to go to sea periodically and when we got back, we never knew what the hell was going to be wrong because Johnny Walker had been left in charge," remembered Metcalf. "You could bet that he'd gotten into some type of a jam with his smart mouth. He just wasn't as interested in doing as good a job as the other watch officers."

John knew he was headed for disaster, but he didn't know how to deal with his own paranoia. At one point, the KGB warned John in a note that the FBI had developed a new sophisticated homing device that it used to follow a suspect's car. The device not only kept agents abreast of the location of the car, but also signaled when its automatic transmission was put into neutral or park. John had always been afraid the FBI would tail him to a dead drop. Now he was even more worried that a swarm of FBI agents would arrest him when he stopped to pick up his KGB cash. John began renting cars in Washington because he thought they would be more difficult for the FBI to bug. He also began leaving his car's automatic transmission in "drive" when he stopped during a dead drop. He kept the car from moving by jamming on its emergency brake. This worked fine until the emergency brake on one of his rental cars broke. He ended up chasing the unoccupied car down a deserted country road while carrying a trash bag filled with KGB cash.

"I was going wacky," John recalled. "I couldn't sleep. I was miserable and I seriously considered killing myself again because my life was such a nightmare."

John's colleagues noticed that John was more nervous than usual and that he suddenly had more money than before, but still no one suspected him of being a spy.

John bragged constantly about the money he made from leasing his bar, so much so that Howard Sparks, a fellow watch officer, visited it one day when he was on an assignment in Charleston. Much to John's relief, Sparks reported that the place was filled with customers.

Bill Metcalf, meanwhile, disliked John. "The problems with Johnny Walker involved moral turpitude. The guy just didn't have any moral standards as far as I was concerned. He constantly bragged about women and if a woman looked twice at him, why he'd be unzipping his britches. But there was never any hint that he was mishandling cryptographic material."

In August 1968, John held a beer party on his sailboat, and a dozen young sailors and their girlfriends came. Jimi Elizabeth Thomas, an exuberant nineteen-year-old student at Old Dominion University in Norfolk, was one of the guests. Jimi's initials spelled JET and her friends nicknamed her Jimi-Jet because she lived her life like a jet-propelled aircraft breaking the sound barrier. No one talked faster, drank more, smoked as much, or danced longer than the light-brown-haired, buxom farm girl who seemed to end all of her sentences with a self-deprecating laugh.

"John was the only person at the party in uniform," Jimi Thomas recalled when we spoke, "and he was at least ten years older than the rest of us. He seemed so mature and interesting because he had so much more experience than any of us. We talked and talked and talked and, of course, we drank. Oh did we drink! Alcohol turned out to be a predominant part of our relationship. Anyway, John eventually asked me for a date and I said yes. I think he told me that he was separated or divorced, I can't remember which, but it wasn't important at the time because I probably would have gone out with him anyway. The hard cold truth is that my standards were unfortunately not what they should have been at the time."

Jimi came from a conservative, lower middle class family in Kinston, a rural North Carolina community, and she was eager to probe the fancy life that John quickly offered.

"I loved to dress up and we would go to the nicest restaurants in Norfolk, and I loved it, just loved it. John would buy dinner and we would drink and listen to bands and I knew it had to cost a bundle, but it didn't seem to matter to him, not at all. I wanted both worlds: my campus life with the fraternity parties and school friends, and also the life of fancy restaurants and dress-up." Jimi saw John only on week nights because weekends were reserved for campus functions. The arrangement suited him fine because it left his weekends for sailing and didn't raise any suspicions at home.

Being with Jimi was a wonderful diversion for John. He delighted in showing her how to open lobster claws and marveled at her bubbly excitement over ordering for the first time from a menu written only in French. He explained his money by telling her that he was in the Mafia—a confession that excited, rather than repelled, Jimi-Jet.

Barbara Walker also was seeing someone else during this time period. In September 1968, Arthur and Rita moved from Key West to Virginia Beach, a community that abuts Norfolk, and Barbara and Arthur resumed their sexual relationship.

Once again, their accounts of what happened differ. Arthur told me that he and Barbara only slept together once in Norfolk, but Barbara insisted that Arthur had a key to the back door of her apartment.

"Art used to go to lunch with John and find out exactly what he was doing that afternoon to make sure that he wasn't going to come home unexpectedly," she told me. "He would rush over and we'd go to bed."

I noticed Barbara Walker's obvious distaste for Arthur whenever she spoke about him. "He is much worse than John," she told me several times. When I asked Arthur about this, he told me that Barbara had always been jealous of his seemingly idyllic marriage to Rita. Rita Walker also made the same comment separately to me. At one point after Arthur was arrested, Barbara Walker telephoned Rita Walker and told her the names of several women who, she claimed, Arthur had had sex with while married to Rita.

One of the enigmas of the Walker spy case concerns a statement Barbara Walker made to the FBI about her bedroom escapades with Arthur in Norfolk during the fall of 1968.

Barbara claimed that she told Arthur that John was a spy. Arthur responded, she said, by saying, "If it's any consolation to you, I did the same thing, only on a smaller scale and for a shorter period of time." Barbara Walker said she was so stunned by Arthur's response that she didn't ask him any other questions. The FBI was shocked by Barbara Walker's comment and immediately speculated that Arthur might have become a KGB spy prior to John. But even though Barbara Walker passed a polygraph test that indicated she was telling the truth, the FBI was never able to find any evidence that Arthur Walker had been involved in espionage before his brother.

Arthur Walker vigorously denied that Barbara ever told him anything about John's espionage. When I asked him about her statements, Arthur said it was possible that Barbara "might have thought she told me something like that" but during the heat of passion, he either misunderstood her or wasn't paying any attention.

"Barbara likes to speak in riddles," he said. "She might have said, 'John is doing something illegal,' or 'John is doing something immoral,' and I might have responded by saying, 'Well, so have I,' but she never told me that John was a spy. That's not something you'd forget."

Whatever revelations Barbara made to Arthur in 1968, both she and her husband were busy with their secret lovers. In November, John took Jimi-Jet to Washington with him. She stayed in a motel while he, unbeknownst to her, went on a dead drop exchange. After he returned, they drove to Baltimore for a night of drinking at various striptease bars.

Before Jimi left college on Christmas break, John bought her a diamond dinner ring, and on Christmas Eve, he sent her three poinsettias. Her parents and friends were impressed, but Jimi was beginning to feel uneasy. "I didn't love Johnny Walker," she recalled. "I loved the good times that he could offer, but I didn't love him and he knew that. The interest that held me was his money and the good times. It was all materialistic."

When Jimi returned to school in January, she decided to stop seeing John, but he telephoned her room and announced that he had made reservations for a trip to Miami. "I'd really never been anywhere and I wanted to go. Of course, we flew first class—John always did—and once again, it was nonstop drinking. But John took me shopping and bought me anything I wanted—anything. He never bought anything for himself, but he spent money on me."

John was getting his money's worth. "Jimi was literally saving my life," he recalled. "She was the only good thing I had going at the time."

When Jimi told John she didn't love him and felt uncomfortable with their relationship, he reacted by spending even more money on her than before and planning more exotic adventures. "John was not a demanding lover at all," Jimi Thomas told me. "Twice during a weekend was fine with him. He seemed more interested in being close to someone." When the college semester ended in May, she returned to Kinston and did not contact John.

That fall John was told that his work at the message center was becoming unsatisfactory. He decided to ask for a transfer, in part because he felt it might be safer for him to spy in a new job farther away from the FBI and Washington. He was ordered to report in mid-September to radioman school at the Naval Training Center in San Diego, California. On September 10, 1969, John's first formal negative evaluation was placed in his file.

Chief Warrant Officer Walker is an individual with excellent potential as a communications specialist. However, during this reporting period he has allowed his performance to fall below his previous level. The apparent lack of interest in his job, with the consequent reduction in the reliability of his performance, have contributed directly or indirectly to numerous serious mistakes."

The Navy knew something was wrong with John, but no one bothered to investigate what it might be, despite his top secret/crypto clearance and abundance of cash.

John told Barbara that he would send for her and the children after he got settled in California. Then he telephoned Jimi and asked her to fly to Norfolk for a final weekend together. He took her to dinner at the Officers' Club.

"He was on edge," Jimi recalled. "He wanted me to be close to him. There was a special plea for that. I don't know what he was searching for, but he wanted something. He wanted a relationship with someone."

While John and Jimi were at the club's bar having drinks, a co-worker of John's approached and began talking to Jimi. He had been attending an aloha party in one of the club's back rooms and he took a Hawaiian lei off his neck and draped it around Jimi's. As John and Jimi drove away from the club that night, John reached over and snatched the lei from Jimi's neck.

"It was the first time I had seen him angry," said Jimi. "He was a very unhappy man."

Jimi, who later became a born-again Christian, never heard from John Walker again.

# 16

The KGB had been upset when John first announced that he was being transferred to San Diego. In a dead drop letter, it assured John that it understood the unpredictable nature of military service, but it also urged him to be extremely cautious and it asked John to describe in detail why he was being moved. John hadn't told the KGB that *he* had requested the transfer. He was afraid the Russians wouldn't understand why he was moving from one of the best spots in the Navy for a spy to a post where he would have almost no access to classified information. As a result, the Russians suspected the worst. In its note to John, the KGB asked if the Navy was moving him because it was suspicious and wanted John out of the critical message center. "PLEASE BE CAREFUL!" the KGB wrote. "FOLLOW ALL SECURITY PRECAUTIONS EXACTLY!"

The KGB's concern seemed genuine and that pleased John, but the KGB note also carried a not-too-subtle reminder. John's spy salary would drop to $2,000 a month if he was unable to keep a steady flow of keylists coming. "The only lever the Soviets had on me was money, and they didn't hesitate to use it."

Before he left Norfolk, John had averaged one dead drop exchange per month. But the KGB told John that it wanted him to make only two or three dead drops per year once he moved to California.

"I was astonished when they told me to cut back," John told me later during one of our sessions, "because it meant that they really didn't care how current the material was that I was delivering. That *is* really significant because classified information is time sensitive and its value drops the older it gets."

John told me that at first he couldn't understand why the KGB was willing to wait six months for a cryptographic keylist. "What the KGB was really telling me was that its agents were perfectly happy to tape record all Navy cryptographic broadcasts on the air for six months and then use the keylists that I sold them to decipher the messages. It was just insane. I kept wondering, 'How can they do this? What does it mean?' and then it finally came to me. It finally made sense."

John decided that the reason the Soviets were willing to wait for cryptographic keylists was because there was no reason for them to hurry.

"All this talk about us going to war with the Soviets is bullshit," John told me, in a bit of self-rationalization. "There never is going to be a war between the Soviet Union and United States. If anything, we are going to be allies in the next war against some Middle Eastern or Central American country. It became very clear to me. That is why they didn't care when they got my stuff. You see, it really didn't matter."

The longer that John was a spy, the more certain he became that he was correct and by the time he was finally arrested, John could cite several examples to prove his theory. This became one of the most frequent subjects of our conversations together. John insisted on explaining his reasoning over and over again, as if saying it repeatedly somehow made it true.

"It's all a silly game," he said. "Look, the Russians weren't interested in a hell of a lot of stuff that they should have been anxious to get." When John first offered to brief the KGB about his experiences on nuclear submarines, it demurred, he claimed. When John volunteered to go after top secret "intelligence messages"—special dispatches between the Navy and the NSA and CIA agents—the KGB became alarmed and ordered John to stick to providing cryptographic material and classified information that flowed through regular Navy channels. The KGB showed less interest than John expected in his recall of the SIOP and the location of SOSUS hydrophones. But the most obvious confirmation of John's "it's-all-a-big-game" theory was an incident that occurred shortly after the *Scorpion* disappeared in 1968. John cited the episode to buttress his hypothesis, but in telling it to me, he revealed just how insanely far he was willing to go as a spy to help the Soviets.

As a message center watch officer in Norfolk, John was part of a two-man team responsible for deciphering and implementing the order from Washington that authorized a wartime launch of Polaris nuclear missiles. The Navy held a drill after the *Scorpion* disappeared to test its nuclear firing procedures. "We didn't know until the last moment whether it was practice or genuine," John remembered. "That's how real it was." After the drill, John wondered how much the Soviets would pay him to sabotage the real thing. John outlined his idea in a dead drop letter. In return for $1 million, John told the KGB that he would refuse to transmit "the order to fire" and make certain that hundreds of Polaris missiles were either not fired or were significantly delayed. John was flabbergasted when the KGB showed no interest at all in his offer. "I couldn't believe it. I mean, here I was, one of the men who actually turned the key, and the Soviets didn't care. They didn't give a damn! The KGB could have totally nullified the most important part of our triad of nuclear defense. I could have kept all the Polaris missiles from firing. Not one single Atlantic fleet submarine would have launched a nuclear missile against the Soviet Union, and they didn't care! I mean, doesn't that seem a bit strange? Wouldn't that action have been worth one million dollars to the Soviet Union—to keep all the submarines in the Atlantic from firing? But they didn't even ask me about it. They didn't even ask! How could they not ask?"

When I suggested to John that the KGB might not have trusted him to carry out his part of the bargain during a nuclear attack, he became incredulous. "I had already betrayed my country," he replied. "Why wouldn't they trust me to not turn the key?" No, there could be only one reason for the KGB's lack of interest. "All this talk of war between the superpowers is nothing but talk," John concluded, "and I saw no reason why I shouldn't profit along with all the goddamn ship contractors, arms dealers, and politicians who push this fantasy of an inevitable war."

# 17

The "practical application laboratory" at the Naval Training Center in San Diego where John had gone to work was made up of three mock radio rooms, similar to ship radio rooms except the laboratory's cryptographic equipment didn't actually work. John was able to steal a few things at the school for the KGB. Some classified documents crossed his desk, but mostly John stole SITSUMs, or Situation Summaries. These were short intelligence reviews of Navy operations around the world, and the KGB found them useful. But what the Soviets really wanted were keylists, and they pressured John to get them. When he couldn't, the KGB cut John's monthly salary from $4,000 to $2,000.

The salary cut bothered John, but he didn't feel any immediate financial pinch and didn't see much use in complaining or trying to find some way to obtain keylists. Barbara and the children liked San Diego, and John was more relaxed than he had ever been. He decided that a sabbatical from spying wasn't all bad. He wasn't nearly as worried about being unmasked as a spy now, in part because Washington, D.C., and the FBI were physically so far away from San Diego. John knew this was foolish. The FBI would go anywhere in the country to catch a spy. But the distance still was psychologically comforting. He also wasn't making as many dead drops or photographing as much material as he had in Norfolk. John's attitude about being captured was changing.

"I really went through several periods as a spy. In the beginning, I felt like I was going to be caught any minute. There was a lot of fear, but after a couple years, I got into a what-the-fuck-is-happening mode. How can this be—that I'm not being arrested? It just didn't make any sense that I hadn't been captured. Then, after I'd been in California for a while, I began to enjoy myself. There was a certain thrill to it all and a metamorphosis began to take place. I began to realize that the FBI is not like it is on television. You see, the FBI doesn't really do any investigating. It doesn't know how to investigate. The FBI is not powerful at all because its agents are really just bureaucrats and they have the same inherent ineptitude of all government bureaucrats. All they do is spend their days waiting for some snitch to call them and turn someone in. That's how they operate, and I was beginning to sense that."

John and the KGB used a series of signals to contact each other when he did have a delivery. John would fly to Washington, rent a car, and drive to Sixteenth Street, a major north–south route in the northwest section of the city. He was supposed to use a piece of chalk to mark a signal at a prearranged spot along the busy street. The signal was changed after every drop, but it always was a single letter or number, such as A, F, 6, or 7, and John always drew it on Sixteenth Street near the Walter Reed Army Medical Center on a Thursday. At various times during his spying career, John drew his signal on the wall of a corner appliance store, a bridge abutment, a stone retaining wall, and on the side of an apartment complex. The Soviet embassy also is on Sixteenth Street and John assumed that an employee drove to work each Thursday along the route and watched for his mark. The exchange always took place two days later, on Saturday, at precisely 8:00 P.M. at one of the KGB's suburban dead drop sites. If the Soviets failed to show, John knew he had to repeat the procedure the next week and keep trying until the exchange was completed.

Sometime in 1970, John is not exactly certain when, he flew to Washington and went through the various steps to make a dead drop. But when he arrived at Sixteenth Street, John noticed that it looked like rain. He was supposed to mark the letter X in chalk on the first concrete rail of a bridge, but he was worried about the weather. A heavy downpour might wash off the chalk mark, and John did not want to return to Washington in a week to repeat the procedure. After several minutes, he decided to improvise. He drove to a convenience store and bought a tube of bright red lipstick. Hurrying back to the signal spot,

John waited for a lull in the traffic, then he scribbled the letter X in lipstick on the post. John was pleased with his ingenuity, but the Soviets were not. That Saturday, the KGB left John a blistering note. "The KGB was superpissed," John recalled. He had violated proper security procedures by using lipstick. Was he trying to be funny? He could have jeopardized the entire operation. He was getting sloppy and complacent. The KGB lectured him about the necessity of maintaining proper security at all times. Any deviations could bring about a disaster. The letter made John angry, but it also scared him. For the first time, he explained later, he realized that the information he had passed to the KGB was useful to the Russians only as long as the United States didn't know they had it. "I was certain that the KGB was prepared to kill me if it felt I was going to blow it and tip off the Navy," John said. "The fact that they had received keylists, especially for the KW-7 machine, and had been able to decipher messages, was much more important than my life."

He promised himself that he was going to be more careful.

# 18

John and Barbara had rented a cozy, three-bedroom house in San Diego. James and Frances Wightman lived across the street. Jim worked at the Naval Training Center personnel bureau close to John's office, and the two men often stopped after work for drinks. Fran Wightman and Barbara also developed a friendship that turned out to be much closer than their husbands' relationship. On most days, the two women met in Fran's kitchen for coffee. They enjoyed getting away from their children, and it gave Barbara a chance to seek advice from Fran, who was ten years her senior.

Jim and Fran both liked the Walkers, but they found the couple different from their other military friends. John simply had much more money and he treated his wife worse than anyone that Fran and Jim knew.

"I can't think of one endearing thing that I've ever heard John say in front of anyone about his wife," Jim Wightman told Fran one day. "He acts like he doesn't love her at all." Fran agreed.

One weekend, Barbara Walker knocked on the Wightman front door. Her hair was tangled, her face was smudged with motor oil, her blouse was splattered with brown stains. Barbara said she needed Fran's help. John and some friends had sailed on John's sailboat from San Diego to Ensenada, Mexico. She had driven down to join them and then had returned home. On the way back to San Diego, she had trouble with the car's engine. When she finally got home, John called, furious because Barbara had left Ensenada without noticing that his eyeglasses were on the car's dash. John had two sets of glasses, but the pair that he was wearing in Ensenada were shaded, making them unusable at night. John told Barbara to return to Ensenada with his eyeglasses.

"I'm afraid to go in my car and alone at night," Barbara told Fran.

"Don't worry, dear, I'll go with you and we'll take my car," Fran quickly replied.

During the eighty-mile trip to Ensenada, Barbara told Fran more about John's telephone call. "Barbara said that John was really angry at her and had called her a 'damn bitch,'" Frances Wightman recalled later. "When we got to Ensenada, John was in this bar, sitting with dames all around him. It was clear what he was up to, and Barbara just handed him his glasses and left without John even saying thank you."

A short time after the eyeglasses incident, Barbara and Fran decided to exercise at a nearby health spa. As the two women were riding to the spa, they saw John driving in the opposite lane. He was in his red MG convertible and he had a young girl next to him.

"I feel sick," Barbara suddenly announced. "Please take me home."

"Oh, come on, let's go to the health spa and forget about this," Fran said, but Barbara was visibly shaken and insisted that Fran drive her home.

A few days later, Barbara tried to push aside the incident by telling Fran that the girl was a hitchhiker who simply got a lift from John. Before long, John dropped all pretense of treating Barbara fondly around the Wightmans.

As he had done in Norfolk, John invited the sailors who worked for him at the Naval Training Center aboard his sailboat for parties and weekend outings. In July 1970, a new instructor at the radio school, Jerry Alfred Whitworth, took John up on his offer. John liked Jerry from the moment they met. Jerry was "much more intellectual" than the twenty-five other instructors directly under John's command. As far as John was concerned, most chief petty officers "were guys who had a cigar clenched in their teeth, a cup of coffee in their hand, and a pot belly hanging over their belts." But Jerry looked and acted more "like a college professor." Jerry smoked a pipe, wore a well-trimmed black beard, was slightly bald, and loved discussing the "philosophy of objectivism" as expressed in the writings of novelist Ayn Rand, his favorite author. Jerry was thirty-one years old, two years younger than John, when they met. He was six feet two inches tall and weighed an athletic 180 pounds.

There was something else about Jerry that John recognized immediately. He was vulnerable.

"Here was a guy who looked poised and self-assured, but who really had a thing about friendship," John recalled later. "Jerry really needed to have friends. He needed people to like him."

It was really not surprising that John recognized this trait. With only a few exceptions, all of John's closest male friends had shared a similar personality quirk and all of them had been manipulated by John.

Charles "Chas" Bennett, John's young pal in Scranton, described John's power over him as being akin to a "mystical spell." John's best friend aboard the *Razorback*, Donald "Cleve" Clevenger, a roly-poly Missouri native, also had been dominated by John. After John's arrest, Clevenger was still full of misguided admiration in interviews with me about John: "Johnny Walker is the smartest man I've ever known. He is the only person I know of in the Navy who was smart enough to do what he did." Even Bill Wilkinson, the snarling Southern racist whom John befriended aboard the *Bolivar,* acknowledged that John had once held a certain authority over him.

In each case, John had befriended people who admired him and whom he felt he could manipulate. John and I discussed this later. He said, "I think it is because I was always doing something interesting and exciting and they weren't. I was the high point of their lives because they didn't have anything else going for them."

So it was not unusual that John's dominating personality and Jerry's insecurity brought them together like the opposite poles of magnets, each drawing closer to the other to satisfy his own need.

Few of their co-workers understood the friendship that was developing between John and Jerry because the men were so different. Michael O'Connor, an instructor and pal of Jerry's, asked him once why he was so buddy-buddy with John.

"I was surprised," recalled O'Connor, "that someone with Jerry's knowledge, attitude, education, general wherewithal, meaning that he was a squared-away individual, a cut above the average person on the street, and apparently having some direction in his life, why he would associate with such a dingdong as Walker."

Jerry couldn't answer Michael's question. He wasn't certain why he liked John so much. But he was loyal to John and defended him around the other instructors. "If we got into a discussion about the attributes of Walker, it was a no-win situation for Jerry and it was certainly a no-win situation for me," O'Connor said. "We avoided that topic and we had a mutual understanding. I didn't care for Walker and Jerry knew that."

Jerry Whitworth's direct supervisor at the radio school, Bob McNatt, also found Jerry's friendship with John Walker unusual. "Even though he was the boss, Walker was a flake, a jerk," recalled McNatt. "I had been in the Navy eighteen years by then, and I had seen a lot of people like Walker. He was really interested in things outside his Navy job, like his sailing and flying his airplane. He just didn't seem to care about the job that we were doing, and he never demonstrated to us that he had any special skills or that he knew anything about what we were doing professionally. The truth is that Walker essentially spent all his time talking about and looking for sex."

McNatt was unimpressed when he first met Jerry Whitworth, but the two men soon became friends. "When Jerry Whitworth checked into school, he had a beard and mustache, and guys like me looked at guys like that and said, 'Oh Christ, here comes another one.' But Jerry surprised me. He was extremely competent. He was clearly one of the best in our profession. He was smart, clean-cut, a good thinker, and very serious. He always seemed to be thinking of bigger and better things—not get-rich-quick schemes—but philosophical issues. God, the only thing that I could see that those two had in common was that Jerry liked to sail and John had the boat."

In truth, Jerry Whitworth did not like John when they first met. He thought him vulgar and crude. But Jerry wanted to learn how to sail and John was eager to teach him aboard his new sailboat, appropriately named *The Dirty Old Man*. Sailing became the bridge that brought the two together.

"I worked hard at teaching Jerry how to sail," John told me during an interview, "and he learned quickly and was very good. I treated him like an equal and never pulled rank on him when we were together on the boat, even though I was an officer, and I think that impressed him. The truth was that I genuinely liked Jerry, a lot. I also wanted him to like me."

As always, John had an ulterior motive. His budding friendship with Jerry Whitworth corresponded with his first thoughts about taking in a partner as a KGB spy. "I knew that I would eventually have to go to sea again, and I couldn't think of any way to make drops while I was out in the Pacific," John recalled. "If I had a partner, then there would always be at least one person able to make dead drops." But John didn't see his interest in Jerry as being sinister, rather, "I felt as if I was doing him a favor, considering him as a partner."

Soon the teacher and pupil spent all of their free time sailing. Wednesday nights, in particular, found them together competing in local sailboat races. John had joined the San Diego Yacht Club, one of the city's most prestigious boating associations, and the club held weekly "beer can races"—impromptu competitions in which the winner often was determined not by speed, but by how much beer the boat's crew consumed before crossing the finish line. John sailed every Wednesday night and Jerry was always his first mate, following his every command. It wasn't long before John told Jerry that he was his "best friend," and three months after they first met, Jerry penned this note in *The Dirty*

*Old Man*'s guest book: "My experience on the *DOM* has been the best!"

Unbeknownst to Jerry, John was constantly testing him during their outings on the boat.

"I wanted to determine if he had larceny in his heart," John recalled, "so I began asking him what appeared to be innocent questions."

The questions were asked when only the two of them were aboard and they were posed as if John were merely engaging Jerry in one of those philosophical discussions that both enjoyed.

One night, John and Jerry were returning to San Diego from Mexico when John brought up the subject of movies. It was a clear night, cool with a black, star-studded sky. John and Jerry were sitting on the deck in their swim trunks as the boat edged along the coast at four knots. Both had been drinking heavily.

"I finally got around to seeing that hippie movie," John said.

"Which one?" asked Jerry.

"The one where those hippie faggots go riding across the country on motorcycles," John replied.

"You mean *Easy Rider*," said Jerry, referring to the 1969 film that starred Peter Fonda and Dennis Hopper.

"Unhuh, that's it," said John.

Jerry had seen it several months earlier and had recommended it.

"Well, what'd you think?" Jerry pressed.

"I thought it sucked! I was the only person in the fucking theater who cheered when those idiots got shot by rednecks," John said, laughing. "I was the only normal person in the entire theater obviously!"

Jerry laughed too and then, after several minutes of silence, he said, "I'd like to do that—ride my motorcycle across the country."

"You going to finance it by selling drugs like they did?" asked John.

"You know," Jerry said, "I might do something like that if I only had to do it once. You know, make one big score and end up with a large sum of money so I could do whatever the hell I wanted to do for the rest of my life."

John didn't push the subject. "I didn't respond," John said years later. "He had already told me what I wanted to know. The *Easy Rider* remark wasn't that significant on the surface, but it was probably the two hundredth remark that I had gotten from Jerry, and together they told me exactly what I wanted to know about him."

On another late cruise, Jerry let something slip that further bolstered John's intuition. Jerry told John that he had been married once and hadn't notified the Navy when his wife divorced him. Instead, Jerry continued to draw extra pay for housing that married sailors received and eventually pocketed $6,000 of illegal gains.

There were other lures that John used to strengthen his bond with Jerry. Whenever possible, John used his rank as chief warrant officer to favor the radioman first class. In July 1971, John picked Jerry to chaperone approximately a hundred high school students who had been invited to spend a week at the Naval Training Center as a reward for winning local science contests.

"When I selected Jerry, it really pissed off some of the higher ranking chiefs. They didn't like the fact that I had chosen him over them and they didn't like the image that Jerry presented because he was younger and had a beard. But I chose Jerry because I was impressed with him and because these kids were at an extremely delicate age, from thirteen and sixteen years old, and I didn't want to have some fat-ass chief of mine screwing some little sixteen-year-old and getting the Navy sued by her parents."

The chaperone's assignment turned out to be a landmark event for Jerry Whitworth because it was during the high school visit that he met his future wife, Brenda L. Reis. Several young girls were enamored of their gregarious guide, and Jerry corresponded with a few teenagers for a while after they returned home. Brenda was different from the others, however. The slightly pudgy sixteen-year-old from Grand Forks, North Dakota, didn't lose interest in her Navy guide.

Shortly after he began corresponding with Brenda, Jerry mentioned her to John. He was not seriously interested in her romantically, he explained. "She just seems like a nice girl who is fun to write to." Besides, Jerry already had a romantic interest in San Diego. Shirley McClanahan was a tall Navy dental technician at the Naval Training Center with bright red hair, brown eyes, and a slightly chunky but attractive figure.

John encouraged Jerry to invite Shirley to the beer can races, and he did.

"I remember Jerry asked me to go with him and John on the sailboat, and I had never been sailing before," Shirley told me later. "It was just exhilarating. I couldn't get enough of it."

Soon Jerry and Shirley joined John every Wednesday night aboard *The Dirty Old Man* at the San Diego Yacht Club. They always had a good time, but Shirley usually felt uncomfortable around John's dates.

"I always liked Johnny, but I couldn't believe how different he and Jerry were," Shirley recalled. "Jerry rarely used profanity and was laid back and meek almost. He was a sensitive, caring type guy. But John, oh God! was he ever *Mr. Crude*. If you were a woman, all he wanted to do was get into your pants. That was his thing. Women had one use for him. He tried to go to bed with every woman he met, I think, and you should have seen the dogs that he took out on the boat when his wife wasn't along. Some of them were real sleaze bags."

John's poor choice in women wasn't related to any problem with his looks or money. After he turned thirty, he had developed an obsession about being well-groomed. Gone was his pasty complexion: he was tanned and his skin looked weathered. Gone was the pudgy waistline: he had dieted and exercised. Gone too was the balding head: he had bought himself a $300 hairpiece. He wore a thick gold chain around his neck and kept his shirt unbuttoned almost to the waist. He favored brightly colored plaid hip-hugger pants with bell-bottom cuffs and black half boots.

Shirley didn't think Barbara Walker was much better than most of John's dates. "I couldn't stand John's wife," Shirley told me later. "She used to sit on the boat and drink, drink, drink. She was only in her thirties, but she was dowdy. In my opinion she was just as crude as John in her own way."

Shirley decided that she and Jerry should introduce John to her roommate and close friend, Mary Ann Mason, who also was a dental technician at the Naval Training Center.

Mary Ann was a voluptuous twenty-two-year-old blonde who reminded John of Jimi-Jet, especially after Mary Ann explained her attitude about life. "I don't worry about tomorrow," she said, "I just see how much fun I can have today."

Born in Michigan, Mary Ann was raised by an aunt and uncle. When she was sixteen, she returned to her parents' home, only to find that she couldn't stand her father. She quit school and struck out on her own. After several years of bumming around the country in the late sixties, she joined the Navy, even though she had trouble accepting its spit-and-polish regimen.

John was anxious to date Mary Ann, but she was apprehensive because he was married. "Based on my past experience," she told John, "all married men ultimately have to come clean with their guilt and tell their wives what they have been doing. I don't need your wife waving a revolver at me."

"She'll never know," John assured her. "Believe me, I can keep a secret."

Mary Ann agreed to continue going out on John's boat when Shirley and Jerry were along, but she refused to see John alone.

Just as he had done with Jimi Thomas, John came up with novel ways to change Mary Ann's mind. He asked her if she wanted to go flying with him. "I just got my pilot's license," he said. "Help me celebrate." He took her horseback riding at dusk on the beach. "You've got to see the sunset. It's fabulous." He bribed her with weekend trips to posh Mexican seaside resorts, and he bankrolled lavish shopping sprees. "John never showed up without flowers or perfume," Mary Ann Mason remembered. "He was very generous and he wasn't pushy at all. We dated a long time before we went to bed together. I liked that, because most guys would buy you dinner and then expect you to go to bed with them."

John loved being with Mary Ann, and he hated going home at night to Barbara and his children. "Mary Ann was as nutty as a fruit cake and just a lot of fun," John recalled. She was everything that John liked in a woman and Barbara was not. Mary Ann wasn't dependent on him. She didn't nag him. She never told him that she loved him and she never asked him if he loved her. The truth was that John was bored with Barbara and his children. They were dead weight that held him back. He had little patience for them and was becoming more and more resentful at home. He complained when his daughters needed braces for their teeth and he began asking Barbara about how she spent "his" money.

John was different around Mary Ann. He showed great patience when they were together and seemed obsessed with every detail of her appearance and her personal life.

Mary Ann really liked John, but she didn't love him and she wasn't certain whether it was John or the good times his money provided that attracted her the most. John didn't seem to care.

One night, after several hours of heavy drinking and a few joints of marijuana, John told Mary Ann about his past. He spoke for a long time, and even though her mind was numbed by an alcohol- and marijuana-induced high, she still recalled clearly years later the overriding subject on John's mind. "John told me his father had been forced to leave his family and now he was thinking about doing the same thing. He talked a lot about his father."

John never told Barbara about Mary Ann, but she knew he was sleeping with someone else. "I think he wanted me to know about his infidelities," Barbara Walker said. "I think he was proud of them. He would come home at three or four in the morning, and he used to delight in leaving his shirts with makeup all over them for me to find."

After one such incident, Barbara, in a moment of desperation, picked up one of John's lipstick-stained shirts and threw it at him.

"I'm not washing this," she screamed. "You can let the little whore who got the makeup on it wash it."

John just laughed.

Frances Wightman pushed Barbara to rebel against John and his playboy life-style. "Why don't you stand up for yourself?" Fran demanded during one of their afternoon kitchen sessions. "Why don't you tell John to go straight to hell?"

Barbara Walker became so upset by Fran's straightforwardness that she could barely speak. "Barbara said she couldn't leave him," Frances Wightman told me, recalling the conversation, "and I said to her, 'Johnny is treating you like dirt, Barbara. Why the hell can't you leave him?' and she said, 'How am I going to support four kids by myself without a high school diploma?' I told her, 'Barbara, start stashing some money aside and enroll in a course at Patrick Henry High School,' which was close by. 'Go get your diploma and get out of this situation.' But she just wouldn't do it. She wouldn't stand up for herself.

She was beaten down and had no self-respect. He didn't love her or the kids, except for maybe Michael, but Barbara loved him. She *really* did. It was sick."

Laura Walker recalled during an interview later that "San Diego was the turning point" for the entire family. "This is when my father no longer cared about anyone but himself, and he let everyone know it, and it is when my mother began turning to alcohol because of the way that he treated her," Laura told me.

Frances Wightman saw the signs of alcoholism too. "I think Barbara literally gave up. She just retreated."

One afternoon, after several drinks, Barbara took off her wedding band and engagement diamond and threw them in the trash. John didn't even notice.

"I remember watching this television show called *Land of the Giants* one afternoon in our house," Michael Walker said, recalling his childhood in San Diego. "I was on the sofa with my head propped on the armrest when I stuck my hand between the cushions and I felt this gun. I thought it was a toy at first, but when I pulled it out, it was real. It was loaded and everything. It was my mom's nickel-plated .38, and I put it back between the cushions after I found it, and I went to Margaret's room, and we called all the kids together and the first thing I said was, 'Hey, Mom is going to shoot Dad.' I just knew it. See, I knew that they were fighting at this time because I had seen them fighting a few months earlier when my dad and I were playing pool. We were playing away and my mother came in the room, and my dad says, 'Mike, go to your room,' and I was shocked because my dad and I never let anything interrupt our pool games. So I was shuffling my heels, heading for the hallway when I hear this *Wham!* and I turned around and he had decked her, knocked her flat on the floor with his fist, and I thought, 'This is it. We are all going to die.' So I knew that things between my parents were bad. That's why I figured when I saw the gun in the sofa that Mom was going to kill him. We were convinced, all of us kids, that it was going to happen, so we sat by the front window so we could warn my dad when he came home from work. We were really getting tired of waiting. It kept getting later and later, and my mother was sitting in the next room getting drunk, and here comes the MG up the driveway. We kids started screaming out the window, 'Don't come in, Dad! She's going to kill you!' but he didn't hear us, and then all of a sudden we hear this *Bang! Bang!* and I figured, 'Oh fuck, Dad is dead.' The next thing I knew, Margaret had jumped out the window to get away."

Barbara's shots hit the coffee table.

After the shooting, John decided that he had to get away from Barbara and his family. He also had to do something about the Soviets, who were increasing the pressure on him to deliver keylists. So John came up with what he considered the perfect solution: he asked to go to sea. He applied specifically for sea duty on a ship deployed off the coast of Vietnam. "People are so stupid," John explained later. "They think no one wanted to go to Vietnam, and that's such bullshit. The Vietnam War was one way to get your ticket punched in the Navy. It was a way to advance your career, and it was a way to get me away from that crazy bitch Barbara."

In the summer of 1971, John received orders to report by November 1 to the U.S.S. *Niagara Falls*, a supply ship based in Oakland but due for an extended Vietnam deployment.

John flew immediately to Washington, D.C., to tell the KGB about his new assignment. "I will be the CMS custodian aboard the ship," John wrote in a note. "CMS stands for CLASSIFIED MATERIAL SYSTEM custodian, which means I will be the officer responsible for ALL of the ship's cryptographic keylists and machines."

No one, not even the commander of the *Niagara Falls*, would have the unlimited access to cryptographic material that John would have as CMS custodian, the new title for the job that had been done by the Registered Publications System custodian in Norfolk. No one! John was confident, as he flew back to San Diego after making a dead drop exchange, that the KGB would soon restore his spy salary to $4,000 per month.

The Navy had, in John's own words, given him "the keys to the kingdom."

# 19

John saw his transfer to San Francisco and the U.S.S. *Niagara Falls* in the fall of 1971 as an opportunity to make a temporary peace with Barbara: patch things up at home and then leave on an extended cruise in the western Pacific. He decided to appease her. "I thought it would add a little vigor to this lump who called herself my wife," he told me, "if I let her choose our next house."

John told Barbara that the price of a house in San Francisco wouldn't be a problem. Location was the important criterion. "I want a house near the Navy base in Oakland so I don't have to do a lot of driving, and I also want to be near a marina and airport," he told her. "Look upon buying this house as an adventure. Take your time and spend all the fucking money you want." Barbara was excited. She bought several maps of San Francisco, and she and John marked every marina and airport on them. They also talked about the different neighborhoods and various styles of homes available. When it was time for Barbara to leave, John gave her a thick wad of $100 bills. "Here's $10,000 in cash for a deposit," he said. "Just remember to find a house near a marina and airport, and stay in the Alameda area. That would be perfect."

Four days later, Barbara returned to San Diego and announced she had put a deposit on a lovely house in Union City. John didn't recognize the name so he consulted a map. He was horrified. Barbara had bought a house that was an hour-and-a-half drive from the naval base and wasn't near either an airport or a marina.

"Why the hell did you buy a house in Union City?" John demanded. "I told you specifically to buy near a marina and airport in the Alameda area. I thought we agreed."

"Well," Barbara responded, "sometimes you can't find a house with everything you want."

"You stupid bitch!" John screamed. "Do you know what you have done? For the next three years of my life I'm going to have to commute for three hours each day. What the fuck is your problem, Barbara? Are you really so stupid?"

The Walkers arrived in Union City in late October 1971, and John reported to work aboard the *Niagara Falls*. The ship was scheduled to remain in port until June 1972 in preparation for its extended cruise to Southeast Asia. Over the next eight months, life at the Walker home degenerated.

"Barbara's drinking really got super bad," John recalled. "I'd come home from work and find that she had spent the entire day in bed with a bottle. The kids were beginning to show signs of a fucked-up family too, particularly Laura, who was running wild."

Margaret was only fourteen, but she was already as tall and as strong as an adult woman. She dominated her two younger sisters and brother, all of whom considered her pushy. Cynthia, at age thirteen, was the exact opposite of Margaret. Quiet, skinny, and mousy, Cynthia was considered to be rather simple-minded by her family. Laura was a sassy and deceptive twelve-year-old, independent and strong-willed. Michael was spoiled. He was Barbara's baby and his father's favorite. Although he was shorter than most nine-year-old boys and thin, Michael was cocky and clever at getting his way.

"Margaret got on dope really early in Union City," John recalled. "She started getting stoned all the time and she began turning my other children on to pot. She was overbearing and bossy. She acted almost like a parent to the others, which wasn't good. One day, I really got angry because she had hit someone, probably Cynthia, whom everyone picked on. I said, 'Margaret, you are not in charge of your sisters and brother, and I swear to Christ that if you hit one of them one more time, I am going to beat the fuck out of you! Now, I am proportionally bigger than you and you are proportionally bigger than them, and my hitting you is just the same as you hitting them.' I tried to explain it to her, but she kept hitting them behind my back, and I couldn't blame her in a way, because if Margaret didn't take control, then nobody was in charge when I was at work."

Cynthia had an especially rough time, John said. "Everyone but Michael picked on Cynthia. She was slow, like the dumb blonde you see in the movies. She was cute, and Barbara and Margaret and Laura totally destroyed Cynthia's self-esteem."

Of all his children, John said he had the hardest time dealing with Laura. "She was the kid who gave us the most trouble. She was totally uncontrollable. She began running away and she really got into a lot of bad shit for her age. The only one who lived a charmed life was Michael. He had all the girls waiting on him. He was the baby of the family."

John and Barbara argued constantly. If he berated her, she would snap, "You made me what I am!" He hated it when she said that. How in the world, he asked years later, could she blame him for her obviously "deep-seated character faults"? John simply began walking out whenever an argument started. "I was a runner. I'd come home and she'd start in on me, so I'd just turn right around and walk out the door and keep going. I refused to argue with her."

John's children remembered their father's actions differently than he claimed. "I remember seeing my father knock my mother across the room," Cynthia Walker told me. "She used to tell people that she was bruised because she had slipped and fallen or had run into a wall or chair, but we knew why she was black and blue.

"I think my mother really started hating my father during this time period," Cynthia added, "but she also loved him. One side of her loved him so much that she couldn't leave him, but the other side hated him so much that she couldn't stand it. The sight of him was repulsive to her."

John certainly wasn't confused about his feelings toward Barbara. "Barbara became nothing to me in Union City," John recalled. "She was a pig who didn't do anything but sit at home, watch television, and drink for hours. She was a weak person and I knew exactly how to punish her for what she was doing to me. What is the opposite of love? It isn't hate, like everyone says. It is total indifference, and that is exactly what she began to see in Union City. I was totally indifferent to her. I couldn't care less what Barbara did. It was really my wish that she would simply dry up and blow away."

The family still went on occasional outings together, usually on *The Dirty Old Man*, but there was always some fear and uncertainty involved in such events. None of the children knew when either of their parents would explode and the beatings would begin. "We all knew something was wrong," Laura Walker said. "My mother loved him, but they never hugged or kissed. We knew they didn't make love either, or at least that is what all of us kids decided. When I got older, my mother told me that when she and my father were sleeping, my father would roll over and become passionate and romantic and get her hot and interested, and then would just roll over and go to sleep without satisfying her. She said he did it on purpose. She said he never had been able to satisfy her sexually.

"The worse my father treated my mother, the worse she treated us," Laura continued. "We paid doubly. We paid for the horrible treatment that my father gave us, and then we paid for the treatment that my mother gave us."

The Walker children gave differing accounts of Union City, but all of them remembered it with particular sadness.

"My mother was totally depressed in Union City," said Laura. "She turned into an alcoholic because of the way my father treated her. It wasn't just the alcohol, though. I think she was having a nervous breakdown."

Even little Michael noticed the change in his mother. "She began drinking straight whiskey and watching television all day long," Michael told me when I asked him about his mother. "Look," he continued, "I really love my mother, but I want to tell you the truth, and the truth is that she got sadistic back then."

One morning, Michael and Cynthia rode a bus into Oakland and bought two mice at a pet store. Michael loved animals and wanted to keep the mice as pets, but Barbara was in no mood for that. "She had been drinking," Michael recalled, "and she wanted to know where we had gotten the mice." Michael and Cynthia lied. "We won them at a pet store," Cynthia said. "Well, you can't keep them," Barbara replied.

Then, according to Michael, "My mother grabbed one of the mice, the one that I had named Little Ben, and she took him into the bathroom and made me and Cynthia stand there and watch while she dropped him in the toilet and flushed it. I saw Little Ben swim like crazy, and then he was gone. I cried and cried, and I pleaded with her to leave the other mouse alone. Now she could have let Little Ben loose outside, but she didn't because she wanted to punish us. A few days later she came into my room and grabbed the other mouse, and with me standing there crying, she tossed him in the toilet and flushed it. I kept asking her to please let him go outside. I kept saying that we could just turn him loose or I could take him somewhere, but she wouldn't let me. It really bummed me out because it was so sick. She got worse. She was really angry inside."

Barbara's outrage at John and frustration at her children always seemed to surface after she began drinking. One night, Barbara ordered Cynthia to wash and dry the dinner dishes. Cynthia cried because the dishes hadn't been washed for several nights and she didn't want to do them by herself. But her mother insisted. Reluctantly, Cynthia filled the sink and began washing while Barbara sat in the living room drinking scotch. An hour later, Cynthia was still in the kitchen and Barbara was getting angry over how long she was taking to finish the job. Finally, Barbara flew into the kitchen.

"My mother grabbed Cynthia by the back of the hair and she pushed Cynthia's face right into the dishwater," Michael told me. "She held her there under the water. I was afraid, really afraid, that she was going to drown her. I remember thinking, 'Not my sister Cynthia, oh God!' I thought my mother was going to kill her right there, but she let her up and then started hitting her."

When I asked Barbara Walker about that incident, she acknowledged that she had done exactly what Michael had described.

Cynthia also was punished by Barbara once for accidentally knocking sand into another girl's face while playing in a sandbox. Barbara wrapped a blindfold around Cynthia's eyes and made her wear it all afternoon. "Now you'll see what it's like to be blind," Barbara told the child as her sisters and friends jeered.

Cynthia Walker broke down and wept when I asked her about these two incidents. She was twenty-eight years old and herself a mother, but the memories still brought back tremendous pain. "There is so much that I have blocked out of my mind," she told me. "I don't want to remember some of these things.

"Both of my sisters were very vivacious and boisterous, and they got what they wanted. I always felt like the ugly duckling. They all told me that I was stupid and retarded, and I believed them. My whole family did that. It wasn't until later and after years of therapy that I began to realize that I wasn't what they said and that I hadn't had a normal childhood."

Even Michael, who was favored as a child, often was afraid when Barbara drank. When he forgot to take out the trash one morning, Barbara lifted him up and stuffed him in the trash can with the garbage.

John was as potentially violent as Barbara, only he used his fists and leather belt when disciplining his children. "My father used to punch Margaret like a man," Laura Walker said. "He'd get mad at her because she did one dumb thing and he'd punch her all over her body, just as if he was in a fist fight with a man.

"I began running away constantly in Union City," Laura remembered. "I just wanted out. I knew something was wrong with my family and I wanted to get away."

Cynthia ran away from home too, but for a different reason. "I didn't want to run away from home, but I didn't want to get hit anymore. I loved my mother and father, but I'd do something dumb like any kid does and I would run away because I knew my mother was going to hurt me."

Barbara Walker told me that she wasn't any happier than her children in Union City. After the Walkers got settled in their new home, she began working at a local hamburger restaurant. "I did it because I had to get out of the house and that environment," Barbara recalled. "It was killing me." The responsibilities of her new job didn't alter her drinking habits. After work, she still drank several large glasses of scotch, often without water. She needed the liquor, she explained later, to get to sleep and ease her guilt about her marriage, children, and John's spying.

Years later, as she sat with a plastic tumbler of scotch in her hand, Barbara told me that her favorite liquor was Johnnie Walker Red, a fact that she considered ironic since John and the espionage are what she claimed had forced her to become dependent on alcohol.

Michael Walker recalled watching his mother get drunk one night in Union City. Barbara collapsed with a loud sigh in front of the family fireplace. "I was sitting in the living room with my dog, and there was a fire going and my mother was drunk," Michael said. "She looked like she was going to barf at any minute. I was either nine or ten years old, and my mom started talking to herself, and then suddenly she opened her purse and *Pow!* out go the credit cards, money, keys, everything right into the fireplace. I was fascinated. She was crying and I knew that she was miserable, but I didn't know what to do. I didn't know how to help her. I was just a little kid and I was in my own little bubble."

By June the *Niagara Falls* was ready to leave Oakland, and John was anxious to get away from Barbara and the kids. He decided to make a final dead drop exchange before the ship left port.

John told Barbara that he was going to Washington "on business," but she knew immediately what he was doing. He was stunned when Barbara asked if she could go with him. She later said, once again, that she asked John to take her because she was trying to please him.

"I was still trying to keep the marriage and my family together, and I thought that if I kept showing him how much I loved him, things would be all right."

They flew to Dulles International Airport and checked into a Holiday Inn in Fairfax, Virginia. The exchange with the KGB went smoothly, and when they returned to the motel, Barbara was startled at the amount of cash that John had received. She began counting the used fifty- and one-hundred-dollar bills, arranging them in neat stacks of $1,000 on the double bed. It took her several minutes, and when she was finished, she had thirty-five stacks in front of her. How were they going to get $35,000 in cash home without arousing suspicion at the airport? she asked. What if airport security decided to open their carry-on bags? John suggested that they hide as much of the money as they could inside the lining of Barbara's coat. They would tape the rest of the cash to their bodies. Barbara tore open the seam and stuffed several stacks of bills inside. When she was finished, John handed her a long piece of gauze and a roll of thick white tape, which she used to attach bills around his waist. He did the same for her, forming a green girdle of somber pictures of Ulysses S. Grant and Benjamin Franklin.

John and Barbara easily slipped past airport security. Once their flight was under way, they took turns going into the lavatory to remove the money, which they stuffed into a bag. "There was no reason to be uncomfortable during the flight," John said. "No one checks a passenger's carryon bag when they deplane."

After they returned home, they went to their bank and opened their safe deposit box. John had brought along ten envelopes, and he put $2,500 into each one, and then put all the envelopes in the box. "You should come to the bank on the first of every month and take out one envelope," John told Barbara. "Each envelope has one thousand dollars in it for our monthly bills. The mortgage, telephone, water, etc. The other fifteen hundred is spending money." Barbara was to buy cashier's checks from a teller before she left the bank and use them to pay the bills by mail. Under no circumstances, John said, was Barbara to deposit any cash in their personal checking account. "There is no way we can justify the cash flow," he told her. Barbara nodded. She assured John that she would take good care of his money while he was at sea.

# 20

On June 16, 1972, the *Niagara Falls* left San Francisco for the naval station at Subic Bay, Republic of the Philippines, its foreign home port. Technically, the three-year-old *Niagara Falls* was a warship, but its most striking features were not its armaments, which included four 3-inch guns, but its cranes. Fourteen different lifting devices rose from the supply ship's deck, like television antennae clustered on the rooftop of a crowded Bronx tenement. The ship also had two twin-jet, turbine-powered helicopters for transporting passengers and cargo.

The *Niagara Falls* actually was a floating shopping mall, 581 feet long, 79 feet across at its widest point, and filled with up to 16,050 tons of such items as uniforms, jet fighter parts, apples, medical supplies, ice cream, and mail. It had a crew of 424, including John.

The radio room was John's empire, where he supervised all message traffic to and from the ship and, for the first time in his naval career, had "officer deck duties," which meant he sometimes got to steer the ship. Because the *Niagara Falls* was scheduled to be gone for ten months, it carried an extraordinary amount of cryptographic materials, including keylists for all of the Navy's most important crypto machines. These included the KWR-37, the NSA's newest cryptographic machine; the KL-47, which was still used as a backup system; the KY-8, a voice scrambling machine that made voice communications sound like chatter by an incoherent Donald Duck; and the KW-7, still the most widely used encoding and deciphering device for the U.S. military.

All keylists aboard the ship were kept inside a special safe located inside a large steel vault protected by a combination lock. But such security was meaningless when the person in charge was a spy. John was the only officer on the ship who had the authority to inspect the keylists and various crypto technical manuals at any time without anyone else present in the vault. Just as he had predicted, this gave him tremendous access. Sometimes he kept his Minox camera locked in his desk inside the crypto vault so he could pull it out whenever he needed to photograph keylists or an interesting classified message. He kept the exposed rolls of film in his camera bag. Safe inside the vault, he would spend hours photographing the NSA-created codes for operating cryptographic machines.

By mid-July, John's ship was busy replenishing U.S. ships in the Gulf of Tonkin off the coast of Vietnam. It was the middle of the monsoon season, and the *Niagara Falls* was frequently caught in turbulent seas and heavy rains. Yet it managed to deliver a record number of supplies to fifty-three warships during a fourteen-day period. It soon developed a routine. It would deliver goods to warships off the Vietnam coast for fifteen days and then return to Subic Bay to restock its shelves, which could take from five to fifteen days.

Because John was the *Niagara Falls* Classified Material System (CMS) custodian, he often was asked to serve as a courier when the ship made its supply run. If a warship needed a fresh batch of keylists, John tucked them into a briefcase chained to his wrist and flew by helicopter to the ship and its waiting CMS custodian. While there, John asked if the ship had any top secret dispatches that needed to be hand-delivered to another warship awaiting replenishment by the *Niagara Falls*. Most of the time, John was given a pouch filled with various classified material to deliver "up the line." Working as a courier gave John access to such a wide range of secrets that after his arrest, the Navy could not determine exactly what John might have stolen or how it might have affected naval operations in Vietnam.

Sometimes John delivered top secret dispatches by helicopter to various officials in Da Nang. He always tried to schedule these trips so he could spend the night in the city and visit the bars and whorehouses. "I usually hid a few beers in my briefcase for the guys on ship when I got back." Flying into a war zone was exhilarating, John said. "I carried a twelve-gauge pump shotgun sometimes, and always had my forty-five automatic with me."

While returning one afternoon from making a delivery in Da Nang, John saw white smoke rising from the brush below the helicopter. "Me and a crew member were leaning out the side door of the helo. The door slides up, and it was open because it was hotter than hell inside the helo. It seemed like 115 degrees at least, so we were leaning out. I didn't have any communication in my helmet, so I couldn't talk to the pilots or the other crew members because of all the noise, but I knew immediately that we were being fired upon and the white smoke was muzzle flashes."

John grabbed the crew member and pointed at the smoke, but he didn't see it.

"We're being fucking shot at!" he yelled. "We're being fucking shot at!" But John's voice couldn't be heard because of the engine noise. John drew his .45 automatic pistol. "I thought, 'I'll show those fucking idiots what's going on!' " He fired the entire clip at the spot where he had seen the white smoke.

When the helicopter landed on the deck of the *Niagara Falls,* John rushed up to speak with the pilot.

"Hey, we were fired at!" John explained, but the pilot was unconvinced. John got mad.

"Look, I saw the muzzle flashes!" he said.

"The smoke could have been something else," the pilot replied. "Besides, if we were fired at, they missed, so there isn't any proof."

"Listen, we were shot at, you dumb shit," John said. "I'm the officer and officers don't lie, and if I said we were shot at and we returned fire, then that's what we did."

The pilot shrugged his shoulders. "Okay, okay, we were shot at."

"Now listen," John continued, "the regulations say that if you are shot at and you return fire, then you should get the combat action ribbon. So we should get it because we saw combat."

The pilot disagreed. "C'mon, they'll think we're nuts if we put in for that!" But John insisted, "I'm the officer and I'm telling you to submit our names for it."

A few days later, John and the helicopter crew were called before the ship's executive officer, who told them that they had no business putting themselves in for the combat ribbon. John was denied the award.

On October 2, the *Niagara Falls* arrived in Hong Kong for "R & R," described in the ship's log as "five glorious and carefree days." John told his commanding officer that he was experiencing severe financial difficulties at a bar he owned in South Carolina and had to return home immediately. "The captain was really pissed because he didn't think officers should take leave. But he let me go." As required, John was thoroughly searched before he left the ship. The shore patrol was trying to stop sailors from smuggling supplies off the ship and selling them in

Hong Kong's black market. No one questioned the dozen rolls of exposed film in John's camera bag, however. There was no reason to suspect that they contained anything other than snapshots of fellow crew members. John was following his golden rule for spying once again. KISS.

John arrived in Union City unannounced because he wanted to check on what Barbara was doing. "She was drunk," he claimed. "All of the money in the safety deposit box was gone. The kids got some of it, I know," John remembered. "They had been getting up early in the morning and sneaking into Barbara's room and going through her purse. They didn't take five or ten dollars. They took hundreds and just spent it."

John flew immediately to Washington, D.C., and delivered his film from the *Niagara Falls* to the KGB. "I had to make an emergency drop to get enough money to pay the bills," John explained. The KGB gave him approximately $30,000 at the drop. When he returned to Union City, he used some of the cash to pay bills. John also prepaid as many monthly bills as he could through April 1973, when the *Niagara Falls* was scheduled to return to Oakland. He wrapped and stashed the remaining cash inside a hollow cinder block. He covered the block with concrete and cemented it to the floor in the back of the garage. Then he flew back to his ship.

On November 28, the radio room in the *Niagara Falls* received an urgent rescue message. An F-4 jet fighter had crashed somewhere in its vicinity, and the ship was ordered to begin an immediate search for the missing pilots. John helped coordinate the rescue mission as the *Niagara Falls*'s crew scanned the water from the deck looking for flares or other signals from the pilots. It was an exciting time for crew members, and they were disappointed when other ships arrived and took charge of the search. John knew at the time that the information he had sold the KGB could have contributed to the downing of U.S. jets. The FBI claimed after his arrest that while on the *Niagara Falls* he took photographs of keylists used in Vietnam by U.S. and South Vietnamese troops. These "in-country keylists" were different from the ones that John had already provided the KGB. They were used *only* in Vietnam and, theoretically, the Soviets could have used them to decipher some U.S. plans about bombing raids and troop movements. In 1972, when John sold the keylists to the KGB, the Nixon administration was dropping more bombs in Indochina than had ever been dropped during any other war. Yet these bombing raids were not as effective as the military had hoped, and the Pentagon never knew exactly why.

The fact that the KGB could have used John's information to ambush U.S. troops and pilots in Vietnam didn't bother him; as usual, he convinced himself the Soviets wouldn't use his information in that manner. He claimed that the KGB never shared any of his secrets with the North Vietnamese. "I was simply too valuable to them as a spy," John explained after his arrest. "If the KGB started giving the North Vietnamese information that I provided, word would have leaked out. The Soviets didn't want anyone to know they were reading our mail, and I am confident that nothing I gave the KGB ever was relayed to the Viet Cong. Getting a steady supply of keylists was much more important to the KGB than helping an ally."

It was this type of reasoning that made it easy for John to participate in a thrilling rescue attempt for downed pilots during the afternoon and later that evening photograph all the classified messages about the incident for the KGB to study.

On December 24, the Secretary of the Navy, John Warner, arrived by helicopter aboard the *Niagara Falls* for a Christmas visit. He was the first high-ranking government official whom John met after he became a KGB spy. The experience, John said later, was stimulating. His spying made him feel just as important as Warner, perhaps even more.

None of John's superiors aboard the *Niagara Falls* had the remotest suspicion he was a spy, as evidenced by his 1972 performance evaluation:

CWO-2 Walker is intensely loyal, taking great pride in himself and the naval service, fiercely supporting its principles and traditions. He possesses a fine sense of personal honor and integrity, coupled with a great sense of humor. He is friendly, intelligent and possesses the ability to work in close harmony with others. He is especially at ease in social situations and has an active self-improvement program which includes enrollment in the commercial instrument flying course and the completion of naval intelligence correspondence course. He is an active sailboat enthusiast and an accomplished aircraft pilot. . . .

When the *Niagara Falls* returned to Oakland on April 12, 1973, John hurried home to reclaim the money that he had hidden in the garage six months before. He found the concrete chipped away and the money inside the cinder block gone. Once again, the Walkers were broke, and John left immediately for Washington and another dead drop. The KGB had restored John's salary to $4,000 per month after he resumed delivering keylists and John anticipated a payment of nearly $50,000 in salary and various bonus payments. When he opened the KGB trash bag, John found a long note, handwritten entirely in capital letters:

PLEASE DESTROY!

DEAR FRIEND,

WELCOME BACK! IT HAS BEEN A LONG TIME! HOW WAS THE *TRIP*? WHAT ARE YOUR IMPRESSIONS AND EXPERIENCES? I HOPE YOU ARE FINE, EVERYTHING IS OKAY AND YOU ARE ENJOYING YOUR VACATION. ENCLOSED ARE $24,500. THIS INCLUDES THE PAYMENT FOR THE PERIOD OF SIX MONTHS . . . PLUS $500 FOR EXPENSES. THE REST OF THE MONEY THAT WE OWE YOU WILL BE ENCLOSED IN

MY NEXT DELIVERY TOGETHER WITH USUAL AMOUNT DUE TO YOU AT THIS TIME. I REALIZE THAT YOU MAY *RESENT* THIS PROCEDURE, BUT WE ARE DOING IT OUT OF CONCERN FOR YOUR OWN SAFETY. MY DELIVERY IS ALREADY MUCH TOO VOLUMINOUS AND DIFFICULT TO HIDE. UNDER THE CIRCUMSTANCES, WE DECIDED TO SPLIT THE AMOUNT IN ORDER TO REDUCE ITS VOLUME AND THUS THE RISK OF AN ACCIDENTAL EXPOSURE DURING THE INSPECTION AT THE AIRPORT IN VIEW OF THE NEW SECURITY REGULATIONS INTRODUCED AT AIR TERMINAL IN JANUARY, THE SECURITY HAD BEEN STEPPED UP TO SUCH A DEGREE THAT I AM SERIOUSLY WORRIED WHETHER YOU WILL BE ABLE TO GET SAFELY THROUGH INSPECTION THE CONTENTS OF THIS DELIVERY....

The note was several pages long and contained instructions for future meetings, but John paused after reading the first page. The KGB, he decided, was "jerking" him around, and he was angry. But there was little he could do about the decision, and he had something more pressing to worry about.

It was almost time for him to undergo a routine background investigation by the FBI. Everyone with a top secret clearance was required to undergo a security check every five years. It was a routine procedure: an FBI agent would review John's credit records and question his friends, neighbors, and relatives to learn if he had any sort of problem that made him a security risk. John wasn't worried about anything that he had done. But he was "scared to death of Barbara's mouth."

"Barbara had been saying stuff to her stupid relatives and even our kids," John recalled. "She'd have a few drinks and then she'd call one of her relatives and say something like, 'You don't know what a son of a bitch John is. He's involved in crime and if you knew what it was, you would urge me to murder the bastard.'"

John decided that he couldn't chance a thorough examination. There was only one thing for him to do—forge his own security clearance. It was risky, but he was confident that he could pull it off.

At that time, a background investigation began when a Navy security officer reviewed the personnel records aboard a ship and flagged the names of all the persons who hadn't had a background check in five years. The easiest way to avoid an investigation, John decided, was by making it appear as if he had already been through one. As an officer, he had access to ship personnel records. One afternoon, he strolled into the records office and removed his own file and the records of another sailor who had recently passed a background review. He compared the files and noticed that the only difference was a salmon-colored background investigation form with an FBI stamp on it. "I think the FBI stamp said something like 'Background Investigation Completed, No Derogatory Information Found,'" John recalled.

John used tracing paper to copy the FBI stamp. The next day, he drove to a print shop and asked the clerk there if he could make a rubber stamp exactly like the FBI's. "I wore my uniform to the print shop and I showed the guy the paper that I had traced. I told him that we had lost the stamp and needed another one exactly like it. He just figured I was getting it for the Navy." The clerk said he could duplicate the stamp, but it would cost $2.97. John grinned.

That same day, John stole the proper salmon-colored form from the ship's supply cabinet. He filled it out on his typewriter and used his fraudulent FBI stamp to authenticate it. He put the forged form in his personnel file and waited. Several weeks later, he thumbed through the personnel records of several sailors. The ship's security officer had tagged them for a five-year review, but had passed over John's file. "I had undermined the Navy's security system and all it cost me was two ninety-seven," he bragged.

The *Niagara Falls* remained in Oakland undergoing various repairs and conducting routine exercises for much of 1973. John found living at home during this period intolerable. He blamed Barbara, of course. "I decided to stop coming home," John told me. "It was as simple as that. I went sailing and I went flying and I stayed on the ship. I just escaped from it all."

Most of the ship's crew slept in three-tier bunks, but because John was an officer, he had his own cabin. He dismantled his favorite reclining chair and reassembled it aboard the ship. He bought a small refrigerator and stocked it with beer, even though having alcohol on the ship was against regulations. He put a portable television on top of the refrigerator. "I'd sit in my chair, drink a cold beer, and watch a program or read. To hell with Barbara and the kids."

# 21

John was more than ready when the *Niagara Falls* began its second extended cruise in the western Pacific on January 3, 1974. The U.S. Navy had been withdrawing from Vietnam since the signing of the Paris Peace Treaty almost exactly one year before, but the Navy still had a fleet of customers waiting for fresh supplies.

One of the ship's first stops was the horseshoe-shaped island of Diego Garcia, a lonely, barren outpost in the Indian Ocean. The Navy was building a communications station on the island, and one of the men assigned there was John's sailing buddy from San Diego, Jerry Whitworth.

The *Niagara Falls* was supposed to deliver its supplies to the island by helicopter, but when both the ship and the helicopter developed engine problems, the supply ship dropped anchor and John was able to go ashore and visit his friend. Jerry gave him a guided tour of the island, but there wasn't much to see. At the time, all of the sailors lived in Quonset huts. There were no women on the island, and there was little except an occasional volleyball or softball game for amusement.

After the tour, John and Jerry sat in metal folding chairs and drank several bottles of beer outside the gray metal hut where Jerry lived. The isolation of the island and lack of women really depressed John. "What in the hell do you do here to amuse yourself?" he asked. Jerry grinned. He kept busy, he explained. He had a girlfriend in Bangkok and he and his friend Cliff went scuba diving nearly every day. John couldn't think of a worse assignment, but Jerry seemed content.

After a few moments, Jerry began asking John about *The Dirty Old Man* and questioning him about various sailors they had worked with at the radio school in San Diego. John didn't even remember some of the men's names, even though he had been their direct supervisor, but Jerry seemed to remember them all and, much to John's surprise, he also seemed to know where most of them were now assigned and what they were doing. "He talked about these people as if they were all his tight friends, but I couldn't see the substance for any friendship between Jerry and these people," John recalled. "I discovered that he would write to dozens of people and then report to every one of them in his letters about what the others were doing. He began doing this to me, sending me letters talking about all of these guys who I didn't give a damn about, but Jerry thought they were his tight buddies. I know many of these guys barely knew Jerry, but that didn't seem to matter to him. It was like everyone he ever met was automatically one of his close friends. Jerry was the sort of guy who might strike up a conversation on an airplane with someone. Later, he would make it sound as if the person he met on the airplane was a longtime friend."

As on previous cruises, the *Niagara Falls* used the naval station in Subic Bay as its foreign home port, and John quickly reacquainted himself with the strip of sordid bars and whorehouses that always spring up near military facilities. Years later, his son Michael recalled finding several color slides in his father's desk at home that showed John lying naked in bed with one or more Filipino women. No sort of sexual escapade between adults seemed off-limits to John. There was no right or wrong, only pleasure and pain, and John was eager to indulge himself in a host of sexual diversions. "A man with cash could buy anything in the Philippines and places like Hong Kong, where life is so cheap."

It was a common practice in the shoddy clubs for young prostitutes to parade naked across the top of the bar. If a customer thought a particular prostitute was attractive, he would tip her with a peso. "The way you tipped one of these girls," John explained, "was by balancing the peso on its edge on top of your bottle of beer." The prostitute would squat down over the bottle and retrieve the peso by picking it up with her vagina. John was fascinated by this, but after seeing several hookers claim the coins, he became bored. One afternoon, John decided to play a prank on one of the prostitutes. He took three pesos from his pocket and used two of them as a pair of tongs to hold the third coin. He heated this coin with a cigarette lighter and then placed it atop his beer bottle. A young prostitute walking along the bar quickly moved over to claim it. She smiled at John seductively as she expertly lowered herself over the peso. When her vagina touched the burning metal, she shrieked and shot up, dropping the hot peso and almost spilling John's beer. The other customers, who had watched John heat the coin, guffawed.

John's pranks often were tainted by cruelty. He recalled an incident involving an old hooker well past her prime. Most bars didn't allow this woman inside because the owners knew sailors liked young, fresh girls, not old, saggy women. One afternoon, the seasoned hustler appeared at a bar where John and some friends were drinking. The woman solicited various sailors, her proposition more a plea for money than a tantalizing offer. She was hungry and hadn't eaten in several days. As the woman was rejected by sailor after sailor, the men began to laugh. None of them would be caught in bed with such an ugly whore. The woman ignored the slurs and continued her rounds. When she reached John, he announced that he wasn't interested in having sex with her, but he was a magnanimous fellow who felt sorry for her and was willing to help her find a suitable sexual mate. Everyone in the bar laughed and began looking for someone or something that the woman could use as a sexual partner. Finally, someone brought in a dog from the street. If the woman could make the dog ejaculate, then she would be paid. The men encircled the old hag and dog. They held the frightened mongrel with its back on the bar and ordered the old prostitute to begin. It took her several minutes, but she was finally able to achieve with her hands and mouth what they demanded. "After she finished, no one wanted to pay her," John recalled, "but I gave her money."

John eventually moved out of the raunchy bars into some of the better clubs. His favorite was The Kangaroo Club and it became his off-duty home. He delighted in sitting at "his" table, surrounded by pretty girls who were fully dressed but were prostitutes. "They used to fight over me, so I would pay to have one girl sit next to me and then have another do things for me. They would polish my shoes and stuff like that, and I remember one time that this girl had done everything she could think of—brought us drinks and polished my shoes—so I removed the clip from my forty-five and had her polish my bullets by hand. I had the shiniest bullets in the Navy."

John became particularly enamored of a young prostitute called

Peaches, and he began to monopolize her time. "My whoring around was not just for sex," John told me one afternoon. "Most sailors would just fuck some girl and then leave, but when I'd run into a girl I liked, I really got to know her and she would tell me things and take me places that no other Americans got to go."

During our discussions in prison, John had bragged about a number of his sexual adventures, but he spoke with surprising gentleness about Peaches. He told me that he badgered her for weeks until she finally agreed to take him to the tiny fishing village where she grew up.

"All of her family came out to meet me, and her father took me inside and pulled out this old box and began showing me his medals from World War II when he was a Kit Carson Scout," John explained. "He didn't speak very good English, but it was really interesting."

John told me that he spent the night in a hammock in the living room of the family hut. "The family was asleep on mats on the floor, all of them in one room," John said. "Mom, dad, grandma, the whole crew was sleeping together just like a pile of gerbils.

"I went outside and I began to think about how fucked up Americans are," John continued. "I mean, we put kids in a room and tell them they have to learn how to sleep alone with the light off. I remember that Michael used to cry and cry because he was scared of the dark, but we wouldn't turn on that damn light, and when I would go to bed, I'd open his door and find him asleep on the floor near the doorway so he could get close to the light that was coming under the door. I mean, who really gives a fuck if your kids sleep with the light on? We are just so fucking wrong!"

Returning to his adventure with Peaches, John told me, "I went out on the beach and after a while, the kids came out and made a bonfire, and they waded out in the water and began throwing nets. They caught about two hundred tiny squid, and they cleaned them and skewered them on sticks and we cooked them right there on the beach over the fire. We drank coconut milk, and the reality of the situation really hit me.

"Hey, these people are poor, really fucking poor, but they had something I didn't have and never had." I asked him what he meant and John Walker, looking a bit unsettled, replied in an angry voice, "They had a fucking family!"

Before the *Niagara Falls* returned to Oakland, it was ordered to participate in an Antisubmarine Warfare Exercise with three other ships. It was one of the first times that a supply ship was used to hunt enemy submarines, and John photographed several classified messages about it because he knew the KGB would want to know how the Navy found Russian subs.

Before the *Niagara Falls* reached Oakland in late July, John made two significant decisions. "I decided to make another go of it with Barbara and the kids rather than divorce her," he said.

John also decided it was time to take on a partner as a spy.

"Spying isn't as easy as it seems. You've got to assemble the stuff and photograph it. Someone could walk in on you at any moment so you tend to do your photographing late at night when people aren't around. This means that you are tired, and it's easy to make a mistake. I used to use a 150-watt bulb when I photographed documents in the crypto vault. What happens if you forget to put the old 50-watt bulb back into the desk lamp and the next day someone notices? Or what if you put the crypto cards back in the wrong order? It's very easy to trip up.

"After the hassle with the background investigation, I knew I was going to have to bring someone in and eventually get out of the service. Otherwise, I was going to have the same problem every five years of my career with the danger of a background check and Barbara shooting off her big mouth. I began thinking about getting out of the service, even though I really loved it, and letting someone photograph the documents while I continued to deliver them.

"I had been thinking about this, I guess for a long, long time and just hadn't realized it, because I knew immediately who I was going to recruit. I had to have someone who was a totally unique individual. He had to be intelligent, trustworthy, and couldn't be a faggot or an alcoholic or into drugs.

"I decided that there was only one person on the entire planet earth that I trusted enough to recruit as a spy."

# 22

Jerry Alfred Whitworth was born on August 10, 1939, in the same bedroom where his mother, Agnes, had been born twenty-five years earlier. It was not a joyous event. Agnes, whom everyone called Bobe, was not married when she discovered that she was pregnant, and her parents, Marion and Cassie Owens, were horrified. The Owenses were a devout, hard-working couple who had come from rural Arkansas to Oklahoma when it was still untamed Indian territory. Cassie Owens could read and write, but her husband could do neither. Even so, Marion Owens possessed a rural shrewdness that came from surviving adversity and working the land. By the time that Jerry Whitworth was born, Papa and Mama Owens had reared six children, buried a seventh, survived the great dust bowl of the 1930s, and established one of the most prosperous vegetable farms in Sequoyah County. The Owenses were one of the most prominent families in the Cookson Hills, and that made Bobe's surprise pregnancy even more humiliating.

The Owens clan arranged a wedding for Bobe before she gave birth. But no one can remember just how long Johnnie Whitworth stayed with his bride. Some claim he left before Jerry was born; others say he waited a few days afterward. "I remember Ike—that's what everyone called Johnnie Whitworth—asking Bobe if she wanted to go to California with him," said Beulah Owens Watts, Bobe's younger sister. "Bobe told Ike no, she wasn't leaving home, and that was the last that most of us ever saw of Jerry's father."

Jerry lived with his mother at his grandparents' farm for the first six years of his life. It was a picturesque place with a pair of cottonwood trees suitable for climbing in the backyard and a deep well that supplied unclouded spring water.

The closest town was Muldrow, a scrawny community of about two thousand residents, some six miles west. Papa Owens liked Muldrow, but he didn't consider it his hometown. He lived in Cottonwood, an unrecognized locale composed of nothing more than a puny cemetery, the old Cottonwood Baptist Church, and three or four houses.

Papa Owens was a man's man—arrow straight and hardy. He spoke few words, was obeyed without question, and showed little outward emotion. Jerry's mother, Bobe, was much the same. She stood almost six feet tall, was reed slender, and was known as the "best basketball player that Muldrow ever produced."

No one knew for certain why Bobe hadn't married after high school or why she found Johnnie Whitworth appealing. But Bobe was unhappy as a single mother, and her son realized this even though he didn't know why. Years later, after Jerry Whitworth had been arrested and found guilty of espionage, his attorneys submitted a presentence personal and mental evaluation of their client to the federal court. In that report, Jerry described his mother as "cold and distant" and complained that Bobe had not spent much time with him as a boy. This lack of affection from his mother haunted him most of his life, the evaluation claimed.

As a child, whenever Jerry wanted attention, he ran to Mama Owens, his grandmother. She comforted Jerry when he got a splinter in his hand. She was the one who hurried to his bed when he cried out petrified by a nightmare. And she massaged his chest with homemade salve when his small body burned with fever.

In early 1947, when Jerry was seven years old, his mother took him to see his Aunt Beulah in El Cajon, California. At the time, Jerry thought the only purpose for the trip was to visit, but while they were there, Beulah introduced Bobe to William "Bill" Henry Morton. Morton's family lived in Muldrow, but he was stationed at an Army base near El Cajon. He was twenty-six years old, seven years younger than Bobe, when they met. After a lightning courtship, Bill and Bobe drove to Yuma, Arizona, and married. No one told Jerry until it was done, and he reacted by running out of the room in tears. When Bill was discharged from the Army in 1948, the family returned to Muldrow, where they lived in a modest house less than one mile from Papa and Mama Owens.

Jerry loathed his stepfather. In the presentence evaluation, Jerry Whitworth described him as an uncaring alcoholic who frequently "physically abused" Bobe. Nearly everyone in Muldrow whom I spoke to agreed that Bill Morton turned nasty when he was drunk. But Jerry's charge that Bill had beaten Bobe just didn't seem to ring true. The charge was more a reflection of how much Jerry abhorred his stepfather, I was told, than of Bill Morton's character.

Less than a year after the family returned to Muldrow, Jerry ran away from home. He went to his grandparents' house and slept in the room that he and his mother had shared before she married Bill Morton. The next evening Bobe came to fetch her son. He was delighted, he told a friend later, that his mother had cared enough to come after him, and he agreed to go home with her. But that night Jerry and his stepfather quarreled. Jerry described the altercation to a childhood friend shortly after it happened.

"I was furious at my stepfather," Jerry said, "so when my mother took me home, I purposely pretended that he wasn't there. I was sitting on the sofa, shining my shoes, when he began talking to me, and I ignored him. It really made him angry and he finally began yelling at me. I just kept ignoring him until he got so angry he yelled, 'Get out of here and don't come back.'

"That's just what I had been waiting for."

Jerry lived with his grandparents after that. More than twenty years later, when Jerry and John Walker, Jr., became friends, Jerry talked about how much he hated his stepfather. One evening, while Jerry and John were sailing aboard *The Dirty Old Man,* Jerry disclosed that he had actually once considered killing Bill Morton.

Jerry's confession, John said later, reminded him of how he too, as a boy, had decided to kill his alcoholic father. But John didn't tell Jerry about that incident. Instead, he listened to Jerry's disclosure and remembered it, knowing it was the sort of insight that might come in handy later.

Jerry was not the only relative to seek sanctuary with his grandparents. Beulah Owens Watts, Bobe's sister, had moved home because of marital problems. Jerry and his cousins, Harold and Arletta, played together constantly during the summer.

Much of the land in southeastern Oklahoma is too hilly and rocky for farming. But the banks of the Arkansas River are tabletop flat and black as fresh-ground coffee. Through the centuries, the Arkansas has flooded with regularity, creating a lush delta along its banks. In Muldrow, this is called the bottoms.

Untold tons of cotton, melons, spinach, peas, and greens had been taken from the bottoms by the Owens family, and Jerry was called upon to do his share of the farm work. Once when his cousin Harold announced impetuously that he hated farming, Papa Owens quietly replied, "Harold, what is there but farming?" It was more a statement than a question.

The only day of the week when Jerry and Harold escaped farm work was on Saturday, when they rode with Beulah to Fort Smith, Arkansas, some ten miles away. While she shopped, they went to the movies. Jerry planned these excursions with precision so he and Harold could see up to four movies in one day by racing from theater to theater. At dusk, the boys would grudgingly retire to the West End Drug Store, where they would wait at the soda fountain for Aunt Beulah. Sipping ten-cent cherry cokes, Jerry and Harold would critique each movie.

"Movies became an escape for me as a child," Jerry told a friend years later. "I learned that there was a much bigger world out there than the farm and Muldrow."

By the time Jerry was a teenager, Bobe and Bill Morton had two young daughters of their own named Regina and Donna Jean. Because Jerry didn't live at home, it was difficult for him to maintain a relationship with his half sisters, but he and Regina became good friends even though she was nine years younger than he. He didn't get along well with Donna Jean, the younger girl, however, and as she grew older, he avoided the house more and more.

Jerry had plenty of money as a teenager. The source wasn't Papa and Mama Owens, or the summer jobs that Jerry held. The money came from his uncle, Willard Owens, who supplied Jerry nearly every Friday night with a twenty-dollar bill. Uncle Willard was fifteen years older than Jerry, but he treated him more like a younger brother. "I don't think anyone loved that boy more than I did," Willard Owens recalled later when I met him. Owens was considered a rogue by Muldrow standards. He was a freethinker—some said "radical"—who argued with nearly everyone, spent his money as quickly as he earned it, and was married three times.

Jerry adored his uncle. In his presentence evaluation he said Uncle Willard had a major influence on him during his childhood. It was his uncle who encouraged Jerry to question, rather than blindly follow, his schoolteachers and the local Baptist preacher. It was Uncle Willard who challenged him to read and get better marks in school. And it was his uncle who convinced Jerry during his senior year in 1957 to give junior college a try after graduation rather than become a farmer as Papa Owens wished.

Jerry didn't want to disappoint his favorite uncle, so after he graduated, he immediately took a summer job on a highway construction crew to earn his college tuition. Several days of heavy rains, however, kept the construction crew idle, and Jerry found himself pacing the floor at the Owenses' farmhouse. The daily downpours also kept Papa Owens housebound, and one afternoon Jerry overheard his grandpa grumbling about Uncle Willard's fast-paced life. The next morning, Papa Owens and Jerry argued.

For the first time in his life, Jerry spoke back to his grandfather. "It's none of your business how I spend my money or how Uncle Willard spends his," the seventeen-year-old boy stammered. A few hours after he and his grandfather argued, Jerry caught a ride into Fort Smith and joined the Navy. The next day, he left for boot camp at Hunters Point, San Francisco. It was only the second time in his life that he had been away from home, but Jerry didn't feel comfortable anymore living at the Owenses'.

# 23

After a few months at sea, most single young sailors have something other than sightseeing tours on their minds when they reach a foreign port. Not Jerry Whitworth. He was a supply clerk on the aircraft carrier U.S.S. *Bon Homme Richard* when he went to sea in 1957 for the first time, and when he heard that the carrier was stopping at Osaka, Japan, for liberty, he rushed to the ship's small library and checked out as many books as he could about the Far East. Working as carefully as when he had planned his Saturday movie outings with cousin Harold, Jerry spent hours scrutinizing the tour guides and mapping a detailed itinerary. Among the books that he read was *The World of Suzie Wong,* a romantic tale about a destitute English painter who falls in love with and marries Suzie, an illiterate Hong Kong prostitute with a heart of gold. Mesmerized by the story, Jerry chattered endlessly about Suzie Wong.

When it was time to go ashore, Jerry's shipmates cajoled him into joining them for a few drinks before he set off on a tour. They whisked Jerry to a bar, got him drunk, and took him to a whorehouse. When Jerry emerged the next afternoon, he told his friends that the illicit experience had been one of the most glorious moments in his life. He had met a wonderful oriental prostitute, just like Suzie Wong, who, he was certain, had felt something special toward him.

It didn't take Jerry long before he realized he was not worldly, so he asked two friends on the carrier to teach him how to dress fashionably, what kind of drinks to order at bars, and how to bargain with hookers. "Jerry was very influenced by other people," recalled Roger Olson, who became Jerry's closest friend in the Navy.

Jerry and Roger had met when assigned to the same barracks at boot camp. It hadn't taken either man long to spill his life story. When Jerry mentioned that his father owned a bar, the Blue Moon Cafe, somewhere in California, Roger pressed him for details. Jerry wasn't certain, but he thought the town's name began with the letter *M*. Roger began reciting names: Madera, Malibu, Maxwell, Mendocino, Monterey, Mendota.

"Wait, I think that last one is it," said Jerry.

"Mendota?" asked Roger.

"I think so."

They dialed information and asked if there was a Blue Moon Cafe listed in Mendota. Yes, the operator replied. A Johnnie Whitworth was also listed in the directory.

"I told Jerry that my parents lived in Dos Palos, which was only twenty-three miles north of Mendota," Roger Olson recalled, "and I suggested that he go home with me that very weekend so we could drive down to find his father."

Jerry telephoned the Blue Moon Cafe when he and Roger arrived in Mendota, just to make certain his father was there. When he and Roger walked through the cafe's door, Juanita Whitworth recognized Jerry instantly.

"You must be Jerry," she said. "I'm Juanita, Johnnie's wife."

Juanita's recognizing Jerry bewildered Roger Olson. "I couldn't figure it out because she had never met Jerry, but when I met Jerry's father, I knew immediately what had happened. Jerry was the absolute spitting image of his father."

Jerry and his father visited for several hours, and on the way back to Dos Palos, Jerry's spirits were high. "I don't think he minded me being around," Jerry told Roger. "Did you notice that he introduced me to several customers as his son?"

Nearly every free weekend after that, Jerry and Roger drove to Dos Palos. Jerry would leave early each Saturday morning for Mendota, where he helped his father run the combination cafe–bar. He would return on Sunday to spend a few hours with Roger and his parents, and then the two sailors would drive back to camp. Roger's mom and dad, Dave and Addie Olson, soon began calling Jerry their "adopted son."

Jerry shocked his Uncle Willard and other members of the Owens clan when he returned to Muldrow for the first time after joining the Navy. Uncle Willard had sent Jerry money for the bus ticket home. What surprised Uncle Willard was Jerry's new attitude toward Johnnie Whitworth, and also Bobe.

"Jerry was really impressed with his daddy," Willard Owens told me, "and he was angry with his mother. No one in Muldrow had told Jerry that Bobe was pregnant before she was married, and when Jerry started spending time with his father, well, he found out. Johnnie told him and it really upset him."

Jerry's best friend in Muldrow, Geneva Green, also recalled that Jerry was upset during his first visit back. "It really bothered him that his mother had been pregnant before they married, and when I asked him why, he said, 'I'm a bastard. Don't you understand, Geneva? *She* didn't want me either!' "

Jerry was discharged from the Navy in August 1960 and moved in with his father. Johnnie was opening another cafe in a nearby town, and he wanted Jerry to manage it, but Jerry couldn't decide. His pal Roger Olson had also been discharged and was going to a California junior college in Coalinga. Roger wanted Jerry to attend school with him. Jerry took several months trying to make up his mind and his father finally had no choice but to withdraw his offer and put one of his wife's cousins in charge of the new cafe. After that, Jerry left for Coalinga.

In the beginning, Jerry said he was going to become an engineer, but he later switched his college major to philosophy. He changed to geology after that, and then finally decided on economics. His latest dream, he told Roger, was to teach college economics in Hong Kong.

Roger graduated from junior college and transferred to a four-year school a few months after Jerry arrived. Once Roger left, Jerry's interest in academics waned, and in June 1963, he abandoned college and reenlisted for two years. This time, the Navy sent him to a supply center in the Los Alamitos Naval Air Station near Long Beach, California. There he met an unorthodox sailor named Windsor Murdock, who both intimidated and intrigued him. "He is one of the most intelligent men that I have ever met," Jerry told Roger Olson in awe. "He can be anything that he wants to be. I mean, he is a totally unique individual."

Shortly after Jerry met Windsor, Uncle Willard telephoned with the tragic news that Jerry's half sister, Regina, was dying of cancer at the age of sixteen.

"Regina had been a star basketball player just like her mother," Geneva Green later told me, "and one day, I think it was her Aunt Beulah who noticed that Regina was limping during a game. Well, they took Regina to the doctor and he found out she had cancer, and in a day or two she took sick and died.

"Jerry came to see me after Regina died," Geneva continued. "I was asleep when he knocked on the door, and when I let him in I could tell that he had been crying because his eyes were all red. He sat down and told me that he had been in the woods, alone, sitting and thinking. He told me that he had prayed and prayed to God to save Regina before she died. He told me he had told God that he would do anything if He would save Regina and not let her die. And then after she died, Jerry said he just couldn't believe in God anymore.

"I remember exactly what he said. 'Geneva,' he said, 'if God can let that happen to a good person like Regina, I just can't believe in Him. Why would He let someone like her be hurt and let her die?' "

Willard Owens recalled a similar conversation with Jerry. "He took Regina's death really hard. Jerry is a sensitive boy, and he told me that after Regina died, he became an atheist."

When Jerry returned to work after the funeral, Windsor Murdock knew that the problem was more than grief.

"Have you ever read *Atlas Shrugged*?" he asked.

"No," said Jerry.

"You should," said Windsor. "It'll change your life."

The next day Jerry bought a copy of the Ayn Rand novel. The book and Ayn Rand's philosophy of objectivism were a revelation to him. He soon had read all of Rand's books and began sending them to Geneva Green and Roger Olson.

Like an evangelical Christian anxious to save souls, Jerry bubbled with Ayn Rand fervor. For him, the murky mysteries of life were now crystal clear. There was no God, Jerry explained to Roger. God was the creation of man, an intellectual brace. Ayn Rand had reached that conclusion, just as he had!

All the weight that Papa and Mama Owens had placed on his shoulders as a child by dragging him to Pentecostal services suddenly was lifted. Logic and reason were the answers, not some primitive belief in a higher authority. Windsor Murdock had shown Jerry the way.

In June 1965, Jerry was honorably discharged from the Navy and went to work as a night manager at a fast food restaurant. He had intended to return to college, but went back to Muldrow instead when a buddy of Uncle Willard's offered him a job.

Jerry lasted three months in Muldrow before deciding that he no longer fit in. He was convinced that the U.S. economic system was about to collapse and the country was about to enter another Great Depression. Townsfolk who had considered Uncle Willard radical now looked upon Jerry as fanatical. He was lonely.

This time, he reenlisted for a six-year tour in order to qualify for vocational training. No one in Muldrow was surprised when he left.

# 24

Jerry wanted to learn electronics, but in May 1967, the Navy sent him to his third choice of schools—the radioman's school in Bainbridge, Maryland, and from there, for advanced training to the Naval Training Center in San Diego, where he would return three years later as an instructor.

Once again, Jerry was lonely. One night, he read a newspaper advertisement that said a lecture about objectivism was being held at a local hall. He arrived just as a petite woman was walking into the building.

"She really turned me on, and I decided I was going to get a date with her," Jerry said later. He sat near her and made a point of speaking with her after the talk. Lynn—Evelyn—Woodhouse, nineteen, was immediately smitten by Jerry. At twenty-eight, he seemed so much more worldly and refined than her teenage friends. He asked her to go with him to another lecture on objectivism that was to take place in Hollywood in a few days. Three weeks later, Jerry asked Lynn to move in with him. She refused but announced that she would marry him if he asked. He proposed, and they were married on September 21, 1967.

"It was a mismatch that no one understood," recalled Geneva Green. "Jerry brought Lynn back to Muldrow to show her off and we were all stunned."

Even Uncle Willard found the marriage between his gangly nephew and his child bride peculiar. "She was a real nut," Willard Owens recalled. "She was skinny and small, and she didn't have much to say. We tried to make her welcome, of course, but she still acted strange. During the night, she got up and just took off. No one knew it until morning, not even Jerry. Imagine, a young girl in a strange town getting out of bed at night and going off on her own without even telling her husband or anyone else that she was leaving. No one knew where she went or what she did. She just came walking in the next morning as if nothing had happened."

Willard Owens wondered if Jerry's new bride hadn't been out during the night seeking male companionship, but when he suggested that, Jerry became enraged.

Later, Jerry told both his Uncle Willard and Roger Olson that he and

Lynn had experienced sexual problems that had left Lynn frustrated and unsatisfied.

In July 1968, Jerry was assigned to the U.S.S. *Arlington*, which was sent to Vietnam. A few weeks after Jerry left California, he received what he later described to friends as a "Dear John" letter from Lynn. She had found someone else and was divorcing him.

"Jerry was very hurt by Lynn. He loved her very, very much," recalled Roger Olson. "It crushed Jerry. Jerry didn't like to lose anyone who was important to him as a friend." Even though they were divorced, Jerry had difficulty letting go when he returned to California. Much to Lynn's surprise, Jerry made friends with her new boyfriend, and when they broke up and she left him, Jerry took the man out drinking. Together, they recalled how much they both loved Lynn. Her next boyfriend didn't like Jerry and told him to stay away from Lynn. Still, Jerry kept corresponding with her and occasionally visited her when she was at work or on evenings when her new lover was gone. This continued off and on for nearly five years after their divorce, until Lynn died in a car accident in 1973.

A close friend of Jerry's and Lynn's wrote a detailed letter to the federal court after Jerry was arrested in June 1985. In the letter, she described Jerry during 1967 to 1970 as being a person who "valued the uncomplicated."

"He used to say that he never wanted to own more possessions than he could fit in a Volkswagen," she wrote.

All that was about to change.

In mid-1970, Jerry reported to his new job as an instructor at the Naval Training Center in San Diego. His commanding officer was John Anthony Walker, Jr.

# 25

John and Jerry were together at the radio training school for only one year before John was transferred to Oakland and the *Niagara Falls*. But during that short period, John gained considerable influence over Jerry. Roger Olson noticed it immediately. Jerry had found another Windsor Murdock, another father figure to admire.

Roger was living in San Francisco aboard a Chinese junk that Jerry was helping him refurbish when John first befriended Jerry. One weekend, Jerry invited John to ride with him from San Diego to San Francisco to meet Roger and see the Chinese junk. The trip was a disaster. John didn't like Roger, and Roger felt the same way about him.

"Your new boss reminds me of an aggressive used car dealer," Roger told Jerry afterward. "The guy is a user. He uses people."

"No, he's not," Jerry replied. "Roger, you just don't know John Walker. He's really a great guy!"

John didn't bad-mouth Roger in front of Jerry, but he quietly worked to break up their friendship.

"When I first met Roger," recalled John, "he had this pained look in his face. I sensed that he was jealous of me and my power to snatch poor little Jerry from him. I mean, here is Roger wanting to have Jerry come up every weekend and help him with this stupid Chinese junk, and I'm keeping him from doing it because we are going out on my boat having fun, drinking, racing, and having girls aboard, and good old Roger is out in the cold. I thought to myself, 'If I can break up their friendship, I would really be doing Jerry a favor because no one needs someone like Roger around.' "

John deliberately entered *The Dirty Old Man* in races on days that he knew would force Jerry to choose between going to visit Roger and staying behind to sail. At first Jerry tried to sustain both obligations. He would compete in a Saturday morning race and then drive 514 miles to San Francisco to help Roger repair his junk. He would race home Sunday night and report to work Monday exhausted. After a while, he didn't drive up to Roger's much.

San Diego became even more inviting after he met Shirley McClanahan. She was ten years younger than he was, and Jerry liked that. "I think Jerry always felt that I was a bit naive," Shirley told me. "The more we dated, the more I decided that he felt comfortable around me because I was younger and he could guide me and kind of help shape how I was."

He gave her books by Ayn Rand and dragged her to lectures on objectivism. He introduced her to jazz and avant garde art shows and foreign film festivals. Shirley didn't care for most of Jerry's preoccupations, but when he took her sailing aboard *The Dirty Old Man,* she was thrilled. After she and Jerry introduced John to Mary Ann Mason, Shirley enjoyed the Wednesday night outings even more, and soon the group became a regular foursome. Each week they raced, had drinks at the yacht club, and then dined at the Brigadeen restaurant. Frequently the meals cost more than $100, and Shirley noticed that John always paid the tab. Always. And John emphasized it after each meal by either mentioning it aloud or by pausing to study the check at length. It was impossible for John to pay for dinner without letting everyone at the table know that the money was coming out of his billfold.

Shirley also noticed that John loved to give Mary Ann flashy presents, particularly when Jerry and Shirley were with them. "I told Jerry that if he bought me something expensive, I'd give it back to him," Shirley recalled. "He was shocked, but I explained to him that all that stuff Johnny bought Mary Ann was like payments for sex as far as I was concerned. I thought John treated Mary Ann like a whore and I told her the same thing. I said, 'My God, Mary Ann, he treats you like a whore. He always buys you gifts after you go someplace for a weekend. It's like a payoff,' but she ignored me. Once, she even thought it was funny. Mary Ann was extremely well endowed, and John was always buying her sweaters that were really low cut. I think he wanted to make her look like a whore too. Mary Ann was having a lot of problems at that point in her life. She was getting involved heavily in drugs and booze and was very promiscuous. She was seeing a psychiatrist, and I thought John was really pulling her down and just using her for his own pleasure, but there wasn't anything I could do."

Despite Shirley's repeated assurances that she didn't expect any presents from Jerry, she still believed he was envious of John's money. "When you listened to Jerry, you could hear the influence that John and his money were having," Shirley recalled. "He was beginning to almost idolize Johnny. I remember when I made third class in the Navy, I was really excited, so I went over to Jerry's room at the barracks. I had never been inside his room before, but when I went in I found all these books that he had bought on how to make investments and make money. He was beginning to get real interested in obtaining wealth, and I knew that was John's influence."

Jerry's view toward marriage and sexual fidelity was also changing, Shirley discovered. She knew Jerry had dated other women after they first met, but when they became serious, she thought he had stopped seeing anyone else. She had been reluctant to engage in sex after a few dates, and when she finally agreed to go to bed with Jerry, it meant something special to her and, she thought, to him.

She later confided in Mary Ann that Jerry was a poor sexual partner. He lacked confidence in bed and had difficulty satisfying her. But she was beginning to fall in love with him, and she wanted their relationship to continue despite the frequent frustration.

Much to Shirley's surprise, Jerry announced one night that it was important for him not to focus on just one woman. "I'm seeing someone else, besides you," he said.

Shirley was crushed and she blamed John, but the truth was that he was only part of the reason for Jerry's attitude. Jerry had seen the movie *Bob & Carol & Ted & Alice*, a 1969 comedy in which two couples swap spouses, and—based on that movie alone—he had decided that it was foolish to limit himself to one sexual partner.

Shirley didn't care for Jerry's view. She and Mary Ann considered themselves rebellious. They smoked marijuana and had psychedelic posters of Janis Joplin and the rock group Santana on the walls of their apartment. But deep down, Shirley still held the same belief in fidelity that her parents had. She loved Jerry. She had taken him home to meet her mother and father. Now she sensed that Jerry was pulling away and was afraid to make a commitment.

A short while later, Shirley discovered that Jerry had gone to bed with another woman who was a mutual friend.

"Jerry was still very important to me at this point. I still was serious about our relationship, and when I found about it, it soured everything because I felt betrayed," Shirley recalled. "It was not something that he should have done. I never confronted him with it, but I felt really hurt."

After that, Shirley saw less of Jerry, although he still called her. She lost track of John, too, after he left San Diego in 1971 for duty aboard the *Niagara Falls*.

Shirley left the Navy and didn't see much of Mary Ann thereafter, but in the fall of 1973, she received a telephone call from John Walker. He had returned to Union City from his first Pacific cruise and was trying to find Mary Ann. Shirley and John spoke for several minutes and she agreed to meet him for dinner. During dessert, John pulled a gift-wrapped box from his coat pocket and handed it to Shirley. Inside was a bracelet made of gold and jade.

"I want you to have this," John said, reaching across the table for Shirley's wrist. "I bought it in Taiwan."

Shirley demurred, but John insisted.

"Okay," she said. "Thank you, but Johnny, if you expect something in return for this, you can forget it. I'm going home alone tonight just like I came."

John laughed. "No problem," he said. But after dinner John announced that he had to retrieve something from his motel room before he drove Shirley home. Once inside the room, John became amorous. "He got real handy and pushy," Shirley recalled, "so I belted him and told him to leave me alone."

Years later, when she told me about her experiences with John Walker and Jerry Whitworth, Shirley wondered aloud—when she first met them, they had seemed so different, but were they really?

She wasn't at all sure they were.

After his Diego Garcia tour ended in June 1974, Jerry Whitworth was discharged from the Navy for a third time. He and Roger Olson had renewed their friendship and they left immediately on a two-month cruise in a twenty-foot sloop that Roger had bought. The 1,500-mile trip took them around Baja California into the Gulf of California and was Jerry's imitation of *Easy Rider*.

It was during a break from sailing, while the men were in a waterfront bar, that they had a discussion very much like the one that Jerry had once had with John Walker aboard *The Dirty Old Man*.

"We were talking about ways to earn money," Roger Olson recalled, "and we talked about hauling a large amount of marijuana back to the United States with us, but the possibilities of getting caught made it just too big of a gamble. Then the idea of selling classified information came up. I knew it was a possibility because Jerry had told me that he had top secret information at his disposal, but we both said that a man shouldn't sell out his country. There was nothing in the world worth selling out your country for. We talked about it for a long time, and we both agreed that it was something we just wouldn't do. No way."

During the voyage, they talked endlessly about their lives, how both had suffered failed marriages and faced uncertain futures. Roger was dating a Jewish woman, and he had become fascinated by Judaism and Israel. The more Roger spoke, the more Jerry became interested in the religion.

"Jerry was not anti-Jew, but now he began to become more and more an advocate of Israel as the trip went on, and he actually began to develop strong feelings about Israel," Roger said. "I knew I influenced him."

Just before the voyage ended, Roger noticed that Jerry had become nervous. He was uncertain about what he should do next with his life, and he was frustrated by his own lack of direction.

"All of my life has been without focus," he complained one night. "I've never been able to find a center in my life, something to concentrate on." As always, Jerry fell back on the teachings of Ayn Rand. "Happiness is the moral purpose of life," Rand had written. Productive achievement is its noblest activity. Logic and reason are the only absolutes. But what were his achievements? Jerry asked. He was thirty-five years old and still a rootless drifter. How had his logic and intellect served him or made him happy? There was no great cause in his life, no passion, no purpose or individualistic fight.

Roger knew his longtime friend was unhappy. "Jerry, more than anything else, I think, wanted attention. He wanted to do something important. He wanted to be someone and amount to something in someone's eyes other than his own."

# 26

San Diego International Airport, also known as Lindbergh Field, lies slightly northeast of the Naval Training Center where John and Jerry had originally met. Since both men were pilots, they knew the airfield well, particularly a colorful restaurant called Boom Trenchard's Flare Path Cafe near the main runway.

Jerry had just returned from his two-month voyage with Roger when John telephoned from Oakland and said he wanted to fly down and take him to lunch. Jerry was eager to tell John about his sailing adventure and his new job—spotting swordfish for sports fishermen from a low-flying Piper Cub airplane. They sat upstairs at Boom Trenchard's in a corner table out of earshot of the bar. John let Jerry chatter on, listening patiently to his account of the Baja cruise, theories about national politics, and talk about his latest interest—Israel. After lunch and a few gin and tonics, John's voice dropped to a whisper and he got to the point.

"Jerry, I want to talk to you about something that is highly confidential and sensitive and extremely delicate," John said. "It involves crime, so if you don't want to discuss it, tell me right now and we will drink these drinks and leave here friends and I will never bring it up again."

Jerry told John to continue.

"Okay, the next thing that you got to understand is that if we even talk about this, if I tell you what I am doing, you will be violating the law because you will be part of a conspiracy, and you could be put in prison even though you haven't done anything at all. This is how important this is. We are talking about something here that is extremely dangerous!" John explained. "So do you want to hear more or should we finish our drinks and discontinue this conversation?"

By now Jerry was totally absorbed and pushed John to hurry up and tell him.

"Okay, Jerry, but if I tell you anything further, you've got to promise me that you are not going to go to the authorities and turn me in. You have got to give me your word as a gentleman and as my best friend that it will never go any further than here, this table, even if you decide that you don't want to get involved," John said. "This is very, very important because I have never told anyone else what I am doing," John added, lying. "No one but you, and you are the only person that I trust."

"Okay," Jerry replied. "What is it?"

"You promise not to turn me in?" asked John.

"Yeah."

"You sure?"

"Sure. I promise forgodsakes!"

"Okay," said John. "I trust you. I want you to know that you are the only person I've told this to, and the only reason that I am telling you now is because what I am doing is very safe and very, very profitable, and I want you to get involved. I want a partner and you are the only person that I would ever trust. I'm really putting my balls in your hands with this."

John sounded so sincere that day. But years later he recalled how he had continued to "bait the hook" that afternoon. "Bringing Jerry into the ring was a very difficult thing to do and extremely dangerous because all Jerry had to do was say, 'Yes,' to me and then pick up the telephone and turn me in. If Jerry had really played his cards right, he could have become a national hero. The Navy would have given him meritorious promotions, allowed him his choice of duty stations, and given him anything he would have asked for if he had turned me in. I knew this. It wasn't a little thing, it was a big thing. Jerry had a lot to gain by turning me in. So I had to make certain that the money I discussed with him had to outweigh the money that he could get by turning me in. I had thought about how to do this for a long time, and I wanted to touch all of the right spots, so I took my time and I dragged my pitch out. There were at least twenty different times when he could have said, 'Okay, John, I've heard enough. Let's drop the subject,' but he didn't. Particularly after I mentioned the big drawing card. I told him that he could make from one thousand to four thousand dollars per month if he helped me. I kept emphasizing that it was safe. 'There is no chance at all that you will be caught,' I said, and then the icing on the cake was that I tailored my pitch to fit what I knew Jerry wanted to hear. He had told me enough about his cruise with Roger that I knew he wanted to do something with his life. I made it sound as if I was doing something that was really important. Admirable, in fact."

After several minutes of evasive talk, John finally described what he was doing—sort of.

"Okay, Jerry, you promised not to rat on me, so I'm going to tell you what I do. I'm going to trust you. I gather intelligence in the international arena. I buy it and sell it."

"You mean you sell classified information?" Jerry asked.

"Exactly. I've been doing it for years!"

"Holy shit!" Jerry replied. "Who's the buyer?"

"I had anticipated this question," John said later, "and I knew that my answer was critical. This could turn him on me. So I said, 'Jerry, I can't tell you that, but I will say that you should understand there is a large population of people who buy this type of information. It is not necessarily the bad guys. It could be publications like *Jane's Fighting Ships* [a private publication that specializes in providing information about U.S. and foreign military equipment] or it could be an ally, for example, Israel.'

"Israel had been having a tough time and Jerry had told me all this bullshit about Israel and the Jews, so I purposely led him in that direction. 'There are lots of reasons why an ally, like Israel, would want to buy classified material, Jerry. You know that. You know what NOFORN [no foreign distribution] means,' I said.

"I suggested Israel to soften the blow and I kept hammering on the point that Israel was our best friend, almost our fifty-first state, for godsakes. It had always been my intention to claim I was passing information to Israel if I was ever captured. I figured that all the Jews in this country would see me as some sort of misguided patriot and they'd get me out of trouble since they own all the newspapers and television networks.

"But the point about Israel was really irrelevant. He was part of the conspiracy now. We were talking about theft and transportation to a foreign government. He knew that classified information wasn't supposed to go to anyone, allies included.

"But Jerry agreed on the spot to do it, to become my partner, just as I figured he would. The next step was talking about his future. How to get him back in the service and where he should go to get the best documents."

Every few minutes, Jerry interrupted their conversation by simply leaning back and shaking his head, John recalled later. "He just couldn't believe that I had been a spy for years without him figuring it out. He kept asking me questions."

"Does Barbara know what you are doing?" Jerry asked.

"I got to be truthful with you," John said. Then he lied. "Yeah, I have to admit that she knows I am into something illegal, but she doesn't know what it is."

"Does anyone else know what you do?"

"No," said John. "No one. You are the only one who knows that."

"Can Barbara be trusted?"

"C'mon Jerry," John replied. "You know what a fucking dunce Barbara is. But she won't blow the whistle as long as I keep her in booze and money. Besides, she doesn't know enough to really do anything, and who's going to believe a drunk?"

"Were you doing this at school when we met?" Jerry asked.

"Yes," John replied. "Sure was."

"Damn!" said Jerry. "While we were at radio school, you were spying for the Israelis?"

"Yes," John said again.

"Damn, how long before that?"

"I'm not going to tell you," John replied. "Look, Jerry, in this type of operation it is better if you don't know too much. All you really need to know is that it is completely safe, there are really no major risks, what I do really doesn't hurt anyone—it's just information sharing—and you can earn a lot of money by doing it. One hell of a lot of money. More money than you could ever make flying over the goddamn ocean trying to find a bunch of fucking swordfish for some fat-ass fisherman."

"Why," asked Jerry, "did you pick me? How did you know that I would say 'Yes'?"

"You're my best friend Jerry. I trust you," John replied. "I also talked to you long enough to know that you would do it with me. You probably didn't even realize it, but I have been making queries over a long time."

Jerry looked surprised, so John mentioned their conversation aboard *The Dirty Old Man* about the movie *Easy Rider*. Jerry didn't even remember it.

"Jerry, we are the very best at what we do," said John. "We are intelligent, and what I am doing is not hurting one person or any government. Believe me, this is safe and easy money—really easy money, just there for the taking, and we are helping our friends the Jews."

All profits would be split fifty–fifty, John explained. Jerry would steal the documents, John would be the courier. He would meet Jerry "anywhere on the planet earth" to pick up material and would deliver his share.

"Cryptographic material is the best. You can get up to four thousand dollars per month for it, but you'll get at least a grand for routine message traffic," John explained. "Of course, some crypto is worth more. The KY-8 system [an older, voice broadcast system] isn't going to get that much 'cause it's been out there a long time and, believe me, we aren't the only sellers in the market. But the KW-7, now, that's a gold mine, baby! If you can get me good KW-7 crypto, you'll be getting four thousand a month no sweat, as long as you live."

Jerry suddenly interrupted John's explanation. When John had first begun his recruitment pitch, he had talked about message traffic. Now he was talking about something more serious—cryptographic material. John felt a sudden panic. "I thought, 'Oh shit, it's finally dawned on this dummy who the buyers really are and he's getting scared.'"

Jerry looked at John for several seconds and then said, "Under no circumstances can you tell anyone that I am involved, and that includes your buyers. I must remain anonymous."

"Of course," John replied quickly. "You will be a silent partner. No one will ever know. I swear it. I absolutely swear it. It will be our secret."

Like a salesman who had just closed a lucrative deal, John thought about his meeting with Jerry on the flight home to Oakland from San Diego. He marveled at Jerry's eagerness to join him. "I felt very comfortable. I knew Jerry would not turn me in. He was simply too excited about the money and being part of a spy ring. I really thought he was going to change his name to James Bond!"

Jerry Whitworth refused to testify years later at his trial on espionage charges. But he admitted to being a spy after his conviction, when interviewed by Dayle C. Carlson, Jr., a correctional consultant, who prepared the presentence report about him:

> During interviews, Whitworth admitted that he had passed classified information to John Walker.... Whitworth stated that it was a period of his life during which he was somewhat disillusioned with circumstances in the world, including the Watergate experience, the takeover of South Vietnam and Cambodia by the Communists and other unsettling political events. He was particularly interested in the survival of Israel and felt that its struggle was worth supporting. He stated that he was also attracted to the mystique and what he described as "heroics" of being involved with passing classified information to Israel. He agreed to assist Walker. Although there was an agreement for Whitworth to receive approximately $1,000 a month in the beginning, Whitworth stated that he was not particularly interested in the money at first.

Jerry Whitworth had been taught as a child the difference between right and wrong. But he also had learned something else growing up in the Cookson Hills of southeastern Oklahoma, something that was honed by Ayn Rand's call for each individual to become more than merely a cog in some vast bureaucratic machine.

Perhaps John Steinbeck described this independent attitude best in his classic novel, *The Grapes of Wrath,* a book that Jerry admired. At one point in the book, Pa Joad tells his family that "sometimes a fella got to sift the law" if he wants to survive. A man has to take a few risks now and then if he wants to amount to something.

After he was convicted, Jerry Whitworth told his Uncle Willard during an emotional prison visit, "Don't believe all the things they are saying about me. I thought what I was doing was heroic when I did it. My conscience is clear, completely clear."

# 27

$B$ack in Oakland, John received bad news. He was being transferred from the *Niagara Falls* to a staff job at the naval base in Norfolk. He didn't want to go. Neither did Barbara. When he broke the news to her, Barbara jolted John with some news of her own. She wanted a divorce.

Barbara had done just fine while John was at sea. The owners of Tilly's Restaurant were so pleased with her work as assistant manager that they had offered to put her in charge of the entire eatery. The extra pay plus child support from John would be enough, Barbara thought, for the family to survive without him.

Barbara had told the children about her decision before John got home from the Philippines. "One night, when she was sitting at the bar at the house in Union City, my mother told all of us that she was going to divorce Dad when he got back," recalled Michael Walker. "I was really upset. I didn't want them to get a divorce. I didn't want to lose my father."

Laura Walker's reaction was just the opposite. "I felt great," she recalled. "We would have been set. . . . I was thrilled that she was going to finally get rid of him."

Barbara's sudden backbone surprised John. He asked her to step into the master bedroom to discuss her decision. The children waited outside.

"None of us really knew what my dad would do or how he would react," recalled Laura. "Everyone was afraid. When they came out, all four of us kids were in the family room waiting. My mother came up to us and she said, 'We are all going to Norfolk. We are going with your father!'

"I just couldn't believe it, that she would do this to us," said Laura. "I said to myself, 'Hey, this is it. I'm getting out.' "

Barbara told me later that John had fallen on his knees in the bedroom and begged her not to leave him. He had talked about his grandfather and the great times the Scaramuzzos had as a large Italian family. He reminded her of their early years together, how much in love they had been. Barbara knew that there wasn't much of a chance that their marriage could be repaired. Too much had happened. But she was willing to try once again. She still loved John and, if he would only make an effort, maybe they could get along. It was a thin hope, but she grasped at it anyway. The truth was that despite her intentions, Barbara couldn't imagine life without John and, in his own strange way, he couldn't imagine life without her.

"I really hadn't been thinking straight when I talked Barbara out of her decision," John told me later. "I'd been away from home for two long tours and my experiences in the Philippines had really stuck with me. I had begun to romanticize having a family like my grandpa. You know, a good old Italian family with everyone fat and happy. I just wasn't in touch with reality, but it hit fast."

Laura ran away from home that night. She was fourteen, and when she came home on her own the next day, John directed her into the master bedroom for punishment.

"If you want to run away," John said, "then do it and don't ever come back home again! If you run away again, we don't want to hear from you! Don't come back and don't ask us for any money. Just get the hell out of here if you want to go!"

John walked to the closet and removed a leather belt.

"Now bend your ass over that bed," he said.

Laura obliged and John began hitting her with the strap.

Laura was determined not to cry so she clenched her teeth and refused to shed any tears as John struck her. When she thought he had finished, she stood up and started to turn. She intended to show him that despite the pain, she hadn't cried. He hadn't broken her pride.

John was not finished, however, and as Laura turned, the belt caught her on the arm and broke the skin. The sight of her own blood panicked the girl.

"You don't even know me!" she screamed, holding back tears. "You don't understand me!"

"You're right," John replied, lowering the belt. "I don't."

"My father never hit me again after that," Laura told me.

After a five-day drive across the country with the family, and with *The Dirty Old Man* in tow, John reached a suburban D.C. motel. He left the kids splashing in the pool and Barbara drinking in their rented room while he drove to a dead drop exchange with the KGB. He had several rolls of film from the *Niagara Falls* to deliver, and he also wanted to tell the Russians about his new assignment in Norfolk and, most importantly, his new partner.

As a staff officer in the Amphibious Force, Atlantic Fleet in Norfolk, John knew that he would have limited access to cryptographic equipment.

"I believe I will only have access to the KG-13 keylists," John explained in his dead drop note to the KGB. "No access to KW-7."

But, the note continued, there was still a very good chance that he could keep a steady flow of KW-7 keylists coming. His closest friend, Jerry Whitworth, had agreed to become a spy and reenlist in the Navy.

"I never had any intention of keeping Jerry's identity a secret from the Soviets," John recalled, "despite my promise to him. It just wasn't realistic. The Russians weren't going to play ball unless they knew all the characters."

John knew the Russians would be upset because he had recruited someone without their permission, but he also knew that the KGB wasn't going to utter a single complaint about Jerry when it realized how valuable he was going to become to them.

"Whitworth is an expert in communications satellites," John explained in his note.

"I knew," John said later, "that mentioning satellites was all it would take to get the KGB excited."

# 28

Jerry Whitworth reenlisted and was sent to the Navy's satellite communications school at Fort Monmouth, New Jersey, just as he and John planned. Only the Navy's most competent radiomen, known by their peers as hot runners, were accepted by the school, and Jerry's record was so good that he fell into that group. The Pentagon was in the midst of redesigning its entire military communications network, and the Navy was leading the other services in technology. It would have been difficult for the KGB to choose a better time to infiltrate naval communications. The service was on the verge of launching the first of four telecommunication satellites that were to be placed above the earth at precise "geosynchronous altitudes." This meant that each satellite would travel around the globe at the same speed as the earth's rotation, causing it, in effect, to always be in the same spot. From their locations, the four satellites would be able to cover the entire globe, each casting a giant "satellite footprint" over the earth. Once the satellites were in place, any Navy ship traveling anywhere in the world could broadcast an ultrahigh-frequency radio transmission upward and bounce it off a satellite back to the proper Navy communication station below.

Besides improved communications, the satellites would also solve one of the Navy's most vexing problems. Since 1914, when the first ship-to-shore radio broadcast was made, the Navy had been looking for a way for its ships to send messages without revealing their locations. The problem was that though high-frequency radio broadcasts could travel three thousand miles without becoming too weak to transcribe, they could be traced. Like a lighthouse beam, the ultrahigh-frequency radio transmissions left a path behind that could be followed to its source. If an enemy ship intercepted a broadcast, it could follow the radio waves back to the transmitting ship. This was extremely dangerous during war, particularly for submarines, whose domination of the seas depended upon surprise. Several attempts were made to make ships' transmissions difficult to trace, but none worked. During the cold war, worry about the "traceability problem" increased, especially after Soviet intelligence ships began operating routinely off the East and West Coasts, where they could intercept ship-to-shore transmissions. Finally, the Navy had a way to circumvent the Russians. What no one suspected was that Jerry Whitworth, one of the first radio operators to be trained in satellite communications, had become a KGB spy.

The use of satellites was leading to other massive revisions in U.S. military communication. The Navy had already created the Common User Digital Information Exchange System, known as CUDIXS, to control access to the twenty-channel communication satellites that were to be used jointly by the Navy and other service branches. Other communication systems had to be revamped or created because of the sudden revolution that technology was bringing to communication. Among the most important communication systems were AUTOVON, or Automatic Voice Network, a worldwide defense department telephone system; AUTOSEVOCOM, Automatic Secure Voice Communications System, a worldwide defense department telephone system with security devices installed on it to protect its transmissions; and AUTODIN, Automatic Digital Information Network, the message system that routes messages from military installations to the proper destination. Jerry Whitworth worked hard to develop an expertise in every one of these communication systems.

Thus, just as John Walker had entered the submarine force when it was being transformed from the diesel age to the nuclear age, Jerry Whitworth was at the edge of a communications revolution in the Navy.

Through no effort of its own, the KGB was getting a look inside the Navy as it developed the most sophisticated military communications network in the world.

Years later, William O. Studeman, a rear admiral and top naval intelligence expert, claimed that Jerry Whitworth's "misuse of a position of trust in naval communications jeopardized the backbone of this country's entire national defense."

Back in February 1975, after he completed five weeks of training at satellite school, Jerry's mind was only focused on one thing. Anxious to brief his new spymaster, he flew directly from the school to Norfolk and telephoned John's home. Barbara answered. No, she explained, John wasn't home and she didn't know where he was or when he would be back. But Barbara agreed to come to the airport, pick up Jerry, and put him up for the night in the three-bedroom brick-and-frame house at 8524 Old Ocean View Road that she and John had bought. During the ride from the airport, Jerry began to sense that John either had left Barbara permanently or was only occasionally staying with her and the children.

The next morning the two men got together and Jerry immediately brought up Barbara's stability. How much did she know about John's spying, and was she a risk? he asked.

"Barbara doesn't have enough guts to be a risk," John replied. Those words marked the start of a five-minute discourse about Barbara that was filled with profanity and hatred. John made it clear to Jerry that he viewed Barbara as nothing but a piece of "useless flesh" who was absolutely worthless to him.

Then the conversation turned to espionage and John discovered that Jerry's technical training was so sophisticated that despite his years in the Navy, John frequently had to stop Jerry in mid-sentence and ask him to explain. Finally, Jerry resorted to drawing crude diagrams on John's notepad that explained how messages were relayed via satellite.

John had received $35,000 from the KGB at his last dead drop exchange, and even though the money was all for him, he wisely decided to reward his partner. John counted out $4,000 in fifties and hundreds for Jerry, and explained that the sum represented his apprentice salary of $1,000 per month.

"I'm paying you for January and February, while you were in school," John explained. "The remaining two grand is an advance for March, and this is just the beginning."

Jerry had even more good news.

"I've requested duty at Diego Garcia," he explained. The island had become an important link in the Navy's satellite chain and had been outfitted with the Navy's most important cryptographic machines. Jerry began rattling off the various machines: KW-26, KG-14, KG-13, KW-37, and, of course, the ever-faithful KW-7.

"In other words," John said, looking up from the notes he was taking, "everything that's fucking important when it comes to crypto is on the rock."

Jerry grinned.

"We are going to have to have a code," John explained, "some way to communicate by mail so I can know where to meet you and can tell my buyers what to expect."

John suggested referring to stolen documents and keylists as pictures because of Jerry's interest in photography. But Jerry thought this idea was too transparent. He suggested they use scuba diving as a code. Jerry would write that the diving was great if he was able to steal keylists. If not, he would complain about his underwater treks.

Patiently John went over the crude diagrams on his notepad, slowly repeating the crucial points in the satellite communication network. At last satisfied that he had it right, he tucked the pad in his pocket.

"Jerry, there's something else we need to discuss," he explained. "If either of us ever gets caught, which there isn't much chance of, but just the same, if one of us gets caught, he doesn't squeal on the other. There is nothing worse in the entire goddamn world than a snitch."

"Right," Jerry replied.

"We got to swear to it," said John. "We got to swear that we will never rat on each other."

John had a flair for the melodramatic, and he wanted Jerry to feel as if they were entering into a sacred "blood oath," similar to the dramatic ceremonies that he had seen in movies about the Mafia, in which young gangsters cut their own fingers and then pressed their bleeding hands against each other's as a symbolic brotherly bond. They were going to be like that. Brothers in silence.

Jerry joined John in swearing fidelity to each other and then, like a father handing down a valued family heirloom, John offered Jerry the battered Minox that the KGB had given him seven years earlier.

Jerry laughed. He had already bought his own Minox, he explained. He was anxious to get to work.

Three months later, John received a letter from Jerry, who by that time was settled in Diego Garcia.

"Hi, Johnny," it said. "I finally made my first dive. It was real good."

# 29

Shortly after Jerry's visit to Norfolk, John moved into the Beachcomber Motel and Apartments a few miles down the street from his house. Barbara was furious. She now realized that being persuaded out of a divorce in Union City had been a major mistake. The children were also unhappy.

Margaret, now seventeen, did whatever she pleased, Cynthia, sixteen, and Laura, fifteen, had become chronic runaways, and Michael, thirteen, was unruly and rebellious.

"My mother had me arrested twice by the police and declared incorrigible," recalled Laura. "Not once, but twice she had me put in a juvenile home. She had Cynthia arrested too! She simply couldn't control us, and we hated home. Quite frankly, I wished at the time that I could have stayed in the detention home because it was better than my own home."

Michael had gotten into minor scrapes in San Diego and Union City, but those problems had been the typical things that small boys do, such as stealing a model car from a toy store or accidentally starting a fire while playing with matches. In Norfolk, however, he became a self-described "hellion."

Recalling his childhood, Michael Walker told me with pride about his sexual adventures as a boy. "I got my first piece of ass when I was nine or ten years old. I had been looking at *Playboy* books that my dad had for some time and I knew what sex was about. There was this neighborhood girl and we both were curious, so we began petting and finally we went into the woods and I achieved penetration, although I was too young to climax. This was in Union City, and by the time I hit Norfolk, I was a sex fool. I mean, I was only thirteen years old, but I was going out with girls who were sixteen and eighteen and having sex regularly.

"I thought I was really cool. I never really attended junior high school in Norfolk because I didn't like it. Once I skipped school forty-three days in a row. I'd be out on my own or go to one of my buddies' houses and watch television all day. We began smoking Marlboros and drinking Pabst Blue Ribbon, and I tried to grow a mustache.

"I remember coming home one day and my mom asked me, 'Hey, Michael, did you go to school today?' and I wasn't going to lie to her so I said, 'No, I didn't go today. I didn't go yesterday. In fact, I haven't gone all week! So what are you going to do about it?' And she wouldn't do anything. I thought I was one tough kid."

Barbara called John at the motel whenever there was trouble with the kids. Each time, his reply was the same. "My attitude at that point," John said, "was that there was no problem so big that it couldn't be run away from. I really didn't want to be hassled and I really didn't want any part of Barbara or the kids, any of them, even Michael."

He was busy with his girlfriends, both old and new. After moving into the motel, John had used his contacts in the Navy to locate Mary Ann Mason. She had left the Navy and was living with a man in San Diego, but when John invited her to fly with him to the Bahamas, Mary Ann told her boyfriend that she had to rush to the East Coast to visit a relative. Reunited, John and Mary Ann took a week-long vacation and John proved to be as generous as ever.

"I knew that he and his wife weren't living together," Mary Ann recalled, "but it didn't seem to bother him. He was the same old Johnny and, as usual, he had plenty of money to spend."

John soon found a new girlfriend in Norfolk. Patsy G. Marsee was an employee at the Armed Forces Staff College. John met her through a mutual acquaintance and he described her a few days afterward in a conversation with Arthur as a "woman of the 1970s."

"She doesn't need to hang on to some man all the time," he explained. "She isn't a nag."

John didn't hide his girlfriends from Barbara or his children. When Barbara left town one weekend and asked John to supervise the kids, he arrived at the house arm-in-arm with a girlfriend.

Cynthia Walker also bumped into her father at the restaurant where her boyfriend worked.

"My boyfriend took me into the kitchen to introduce me to his friends," she recalled, "and as we were getting ready to leave the kitchen, he opened the door and then yanked me back."

"What in the world is wrong?" Cynthia asked.

"Your father's in the lounge," the boy replied.

"So what's the big deal?"

"Well, he's with a girl and it's not your mom."

"I was only sixteen years old then," Cynthia Walker remembered, "and I didn't know what to do. Should we leave or what? I finally decided just to go in and eat and act like nothing was wrong. We walked right past his table and he looked at me and didn't even acknowledge me, like I didn't even exist, and it got me really upset."

Such escapades outraged Barbara. One afternoon, she ordered Michael and his cousin, Curt Christopher Walker, the youngest child of Arthur and Rita, to get into the car. Barbara drove the boys to the Beachcomber Motel and made them sit outside John's apartment until they spotted John walking with a girl.

"Look, Michael," Barbara Walker said, "there's your father with one of his whores!"

Another time, Barbara woke up Michael after midnight, and ordered him downstairs to the den.

"She had done this sort of thing before when she was drunk," Michael explained to me later, "and she was drunk on this night. She had a bottle of beer and I sat as far away from her as I could when we got downstairs. I smelled trouble coming. I was, maybe, yeah, I was fourteen at this point. She says, 'Michael, I know you are fooling around with women,' and I said, 'No way, Mom.' She says, 'Don't lie to me. I know you are having intercourse with girls, aren't you?' And I said, 'Intercourse, uh, what's that, Mom?'

"Well, she got really angry and she says, 'You know your father fools around with women, don't you?' and then, just like that, she says, 'Did you know your father is a spy?' I couldn't believe it. I didn't believe it. She went from his fucking around to him being a spy, just like that. I stood up and I said, 'Okay, Mom, I'm going to bed now,' and I started to walk to the door when she suddenly throws this bottle of beer at me and comes close to hitting me in the face with it.

"My mother began screaming at me. 'You are just like your father! Just like Johnny Walker!'

"That was the first time she ever mentioned to me that my dad was a spy, and it tore me apart. I didn't believe it. I figured she was lying because of what he was doing to her."

Barbara soon began complaining to Arthur and Rita about John. Arthur had retired from the Navy in 1973 in Norfolk after reaching the rank of lieutenant commander, and he and Rita still lived in the same modest brick house that they had bought back in 1968. Rita became a sympathetic listener, and Barbara was soon telling her about not only John's womanizing, but other wrongdoing.

"John is doing something so horrible, I can't even tell you," Barbara told Rita one day. "But it is just so horrible and illegal that you would hate him if you knew."

Rita didn't doubt it. She already disliked John.

The two women's friendship seemed odd because they had nothing in common except being sisters-in-law. Rita spent all of her time fussing over her children; was strict, stubborn, and spoke her mind. Occasionally, Arthur tried to defend his brother. John's womanizing was harmless, he said. To which Rita responded, "Adultery is one sin that no spouse ever forgives."

The fact that Arthur and John decided to form a business at the same time that Barbara was crying on Rita's shoulder didn't help either couple's marriage. On June 23, 1975, the two brothers incorporated Walker Enterprises, a small company that installed radios and stereo equipment in new cars. It was really Arthur's business. All John provided was the much-needed capital. But Rita didn't want Arthur and John to associate.

Rita recalled her feelings toward John during an interview one Sunday afternoon while we sat in her kitchen. "John treated Barbara lousy and Barbara was in a lot of pain. She would come over and I would know that she had been drinking. Oftentimes, I would make her spend the nights in our den on the couch because I didn't want her driving home. She needed someone to lean on, she needed help. Don't ask me to explain it, but Barbara still loved John despite all the things that he did to her. She still loved him! It was amazing. I couldn't stand watching him use her and the kids. It made me sick. But she still loved him."

One night, Barbara invited Arthur and Rita over for one of her notable Italian dinners. John wasn't there. Afterward, while everyone was clearing the table, Barbara suddenly collapsed.

"I can't feel anything in my arm," she screamed.

Rita and Arthur rushed to help her.

"Art, call an ambulance!" Rita ordered.

But before Arthur reached the telephone, Barbara called him off.

"It's okay," she said. "Don't call anyone. I'm going to be okay and John will just get angry if he finds out."

They helped Barbara onto the couch.

During the next hour, Barbara would claim to be suffering nearly intolerable pain one instant and then recover magically, only to have a relapse whenever Rita and Arthur mentioned that it was time for them to go home.

When Rita and Arthur finally got away that night, Rita turned to her husband and said, "Barbara is falling apart. We've got to do something."

"It's okay if you want to help," Arthur replied. "I think you should. But I've got to stay out of this. John's my brother."

The next day, Rita telephoned Barbara.

"Barbara, you've got to make up your mind. You either stay with John or leave him! You can't go on like this. Whatever you decide to do, I'll help you through it, but you've got to decide. You've got to do something."

Rita was not the only person urging Barbara to act. After John moved out, Barbara had gotten back in touch with her older sister, Annie Crowley Nelson. Annie was also pushing her to abandon her failed marriage. Annie and her husband, Bob, lived on a farm near Anson, Maine, and one night, Bob Nelson got on the phone and told Barbara that she and her children were welcome to move in with them "until you can get on your feet."

With Annie and Rita encouraging her, Barbara contacted Albert Teich, Jr., a Norfolk lawyer, and instigated divorce proceedings. John was indignant. Over the years, he had physically beaten and humiliated Barbara. He had driven her to alcoholism, destroyed her feelings of self-worth, and openly flaunted his sexual affairs with other women in front of her. But the fact that she had decided to divorce him without warning, to John, was unthinkable.

"She didn't even have the decency to call me on the phone and tell me she had filed for a divorce," he seethed to me later. "I didn't know until the guy served me with court papers. She was a real pig."

As soon as John was served, he rushed to see Barbara and tried to talk her out of it.

"You are going to lose all your medical benefits," he argued. "What's wrong with how we are living now?" At one point, he even argued that getting a divorce might damage the children emotionally.

John later admitted that his motives for trying to stop the divorce were based solely on self-interest. "Barbara was a loose cannon," he told me, "and I didn't want her blabbing things to her relatives and having them call the FBI."

But Barbara Walker told me that she believed John's behavior was part of the confused "love–hate" relationship that they shared.

"In his own way, John still loved me and he still does," Barbara Walker explained to me one day. "You see, what really had happened was that I had become a mother to John. It wasn't his father who had messed him up. It was Peggy, and I had become his second mother. He would play around with his girlfriends—once he telephoned me and told me that he was waiting for some young girlfriend of his to get out of the shower so they could go to bed together—but then he always wanted me there to run home to."

This time, however, Barbara decided firmly to abandon her "fifth child."

"Okay, you fucking bitch," John yelled when she stayed adamant about the divorce. "But I'm not only getting a divorce from you, but from the kids, every one. You just go do your thing. I don't want visitation and I don't want to hear about your problems or theirs. Just go! I want all of you to get the fuck out of my life!"

No, Barbara told him. The divorce wasn't going to be that easy. She wanted $10,000 in cash, $500 per month in child support, and $1,000 per month in alimony. John was flabbergasted. He had no choice but to agree, but, afraid that she would turn him in, he asked her not to mention alimony in writing. At the time, he was earning $18,000 per year from the Navy. "There's no way I can explain paying you that much money each month on my salary," he warned her.

Barbara agreed. John could pay her the $1,000 per month under the table. The divorce became final on June 22, 1976. In addition to the cash and child support, Barbara got the deed to three lots in Florida that John had bought over the years for $40,000 as investments.

Barbara told John that she and the children were moving to Maine to live with Annie and Bob. They would leave Norfolk on a Friday, she said. Actually, the moving truck came on a Wednesday and she and the children left that night. She had lied to John because she hadn't wanted to face him again. All she wanted was to get as far away as possible.

"Barbara just couldn't hack it anymore," recalled her sister, Annie, who came down to help Barbara move.

"I'll never forget that move," said Michael. "My mother, my Aunt Annie, and my sisters and I were all packed into my mom's car. It was a brand new Monte Carlo, which she had bought, I guess, with some of the divorce money. We were in there with our dog and two gerbils and off we went for Maine. It was crazy! We didn't know anything about Maine and I didn't even know for sure where it was. I wanted to stay in Norfolk with my dad, but my mom wouldn't let me."

As promised, John sent Barbara an envelope of cash during the first week of July 1976. It included the $1,000 alimony that he had promised. But on July 31, 1976, John retired from the Navy and immediately stopped sending Barbara alimony.

"I considered it nothing but blackmail," he recalled. John told Barbara that he would help her out financially if and when he could. But now that he was out of the Navy, he claimed his spy income had stopped.

"I was trying to wean her from the spy money by convincing her that

I wasn't getting anything more from the Soviets," he said. "I had made up my mind before the divorce was signed that I wasn't going to support that bitch any longer, and I thought if I could convince her that I had stopped spying, then she really would be out of my life for good."

Barbara felt betrayed. "He'd promised to pay me and I'd agreed to keep the alimony out of the court document," she told me. "I had protected him once again, and he had lied to me."

John hadn't wanted to retire, especially from the job that he had in Norfolk. As a member of the staff of the commander of the Atlantic surface forces, John had both an impressive title and a cushy job. In truth, John was a mailman. He supervised the delivery of classified messages to offices across the sprawling naval base with a staff of six, including four young women whom he dubbed "Johnny Walker's girls."

"It was the best job I had in the Navy for getting pussy," he said.

But after he and Barbara were divorced, John felt he had no choice but to retire because he knew that he couldn't survive a background investigation and he was afraid to chance forging another one. "It was just too risky with Barbara shooting off her mouth."

Once out of the Navy, John began spending time in the offices of the American Association of Professional Salespersons, a company that he had founded and incorporated in February 1975. The AAPS was not really John's idea, but rather that of a group of entrepreneurs who decided that independent salesmen and saleswomen were the only professionals in the country not represented by some sort of national association. John didn't know anything about sales or national associations, but the business seemed like a "sure money-maker." Besides, even if it didn't make a profit, as long as it didn't become a financial drain, it provided John with a convenient method for laundering his spy income.

John had already rented an office, hired a secretary, and placed advertisements in several magazines. In return for yearly dues of about $150, a member received a pretentious-looking membership card and was promised discounts on the price of hotel rooms and car rentals. The majority of the money went directly into John's pocket.

One of the first persons whom John asked for help with his new business was his father, Johnny Walker. John had only recently learned where his father lived.

Johnny Walker had deserted Peggy and his sons back in Scranton in 1961. John had just finished submarine school and had reported aboard the U.S.S. *Razorback* in San Diego when Peggy telephoned him, sobbing. Johnny had left a typewritten note on the kitchen table for her. In it, he explained that he no longer loved her and had decided, now that their sons were grown, to leave Scranton with another woman. Johnny's new romantic interest was Dorothy Dobson, one of Peggy's co-workers at Prestwood's Photo Studio.

Peggy was both furious and heartbroken. She had stuck with Johnny

Walker through his bouts with alcoholism and his roller coaster careers, and had even turned her head the other way to his philandering.

"Your father swore to me that he wouldn't do it again," she told John. "He promised and I believed him." The idea that she might also bear some blame for the dissolution of the marriage never entered Peggy's mind.

The family lost contact with Johnny until November 1964, when he resurfaced and asked Peggy for a divorce so that he and Dorothy could marry. At the time, John was bitter about his father's actions. John called his father a "goddamn bum" in a sympathetic letter to his mother that Peggy saved. "I'm thoroughly ashamed of him, and if he was to walk in here right now, I'd punch him," John wrote.

But John's anger mellowed over the years, and when Peggy told him one day that an uncle had heard Johnny Walker's voice on the radio while driving through southeastern Maryland, John decided to track down his father. He found him living in a tiny town on the eastern peninsula of Virginia. John got Johnny's address by telephoning the radio station where he worked. A secretary there also gave him the telephone number, but John didn't want to risk calling the old man and having him hang up or refuse to meet with him. John telephoned Arthur, but he wasn't interested in getting reacquainted with his father. So John drove alone to Temperanceville, the tiny hamlet where Johnny and his second family lived in a rented house.

John tapped on the door. A frail, bespectacled man answered.

"Hello, Dad," John said.

"Hello, Jack," Johnny Walker replied, using the name that John had gone by in Scranton. "Coffee?"

Their reunion lasted into the evening. John met Dorothy and his half sisters and brothers. He and his father were uncomfortable at first, but that feeling passed.

Like most sons, John had always seen his father, even when he was drunk, as an imposing figure. But after that session, John realized Johnny was, in John's own words, a "beaten and sickly old man." His father still had a magical speaking voice though, and John was certain that Johnny could find a dozen or more recruits for the association of salespersons.

"I told him that he could be the manager for the eastern Virginia region," John recalled. Johnny would get a finder's fee for every salesperson who became a member.

"I'd always hated my old man," John said later. "But after that, I decided, 'What the hell? He really wasn't a bad guy after all.'

"We didn't have that much in common anymore, and we were total opposites, but, so what, I didn't see nothing wrong with us being friends."

# 30

The "diving" at Diego Garcia turned out to be better than either John Walker or Jerry Whitworth had ever imagined, particularly after Jerry maneuvered himself into the position of Classified Material System [CMS] custodian. He remained there for one year and didn't return to the States until March 1976, when he took a sixty-day leave. He immediately flew to Norfolk and gave John eight rolls of film that contained, John said later, the keylists for three cipher systems and hundreds of classified messages. It was an impressive cache, but when Jerry handed it over, he told John that he just didn't feel quite right about what they were doing.

John immediately paid Jerry $12,000, which represented his salary for the past twelve months, and then counted out another $6,000 bonus and announced that he was raising Jerry's monthly salary to $2,000.

"Jerry, there's nothing to feel bad about," John said. "Remember, there are a lot of buyers out there, including our allies. Don't worry so much."

Jerry apparently believed the ruse. Before flying to Norfolk, he had stopped in California and had dinner with Mary Ann Mason. During their conversation, Mary Ann told Jerry about her recent vacation with John.

"He's still spending money like crazy," she told Jerry. "He's bought a couple of airplanes and still has a boat. Tell me, Jerry, where in the world does John get his money?"

"He's a spy," Jerry blurted.

"I couldn't believe it," Mary Ann Mason told me later. "Jerry told me that Johnny had been selling classified information to an ally country for years and that was why he was so well off. When I asked who the ally was, Jerry told me, 'Israel,' and I thought, 'Wow, what a novel idea, selling information to Israel.' "

At the time, Mary Ann didn't think Jerry was lying. "I really think Jerry believed what he was telling me," she said, "because he was as taken with the idea as much as I was. He really thought it was exciting and neat, and he told me that John was really doing something significant."

With $18,000 in cash now in his pockets, Jerry left Norfolk for the Caribbean, where he planned to visit with his former flight instructor from San Diego, who had opened a charter airline service on one of the islands. A few days after Jerry left, John received a telephone call from him. Jerry's former teacher hadn't shown up as promised, and Jerry was furious about being stood up.

"That was so like Jerry," John said, recalling the incident. "He had always talked like this guy was his best friend, and this guy probably looked at Jerry as just one of some twenty-six students in a class."

Disappointed, Jerry flew to North Dakota, where he visited Brenda Reis, with whom he had been corresponding since her high school tour at the Naval Training Center. Brenda agreed to return to San Diego with Jerry and live with him while she attended the state university there. They hadn't planned on marrying, but Jerry soon found that Brenda's tuition was a strain on his income, so he suggested that they get married in order to qualify for a Navy allotment. They were wed on May 24, 1976. Jerry insisted that the marriage remain a secret. "Jerry told me later," said John, "that he didn't want all his friends to know that he had screwed up again if the marriage didn't work out."

In June, Jerry reported to the U.S.S. *Constellation,* an aircraft carrier, where he once again had excellent access to cryptographic material. The timing of the assignment gave John a chuckle. On July 4, 1976, one of the national television networks used the flight deck of the U.S.S. *Constellation* as the anchor spot for a part of the bicentennial celebration. When John turned on his television and spotted the U.S.S. *Constellation,* he started laughing. John could just picture Jerry in the ship's crypto vault snapping photographs of the KW-7 keylist with his spy camera while the rest of the crew was outside watching some Hollywood movie star sing about the two hundredth birthday of the red-white-and-blue. What made the situation even more hilarious was that Jerry actually seemed to believe he was helping Israel, and John had long disliked Jews.

"I was surrounded by some dumb shits," he told me.

Now that John had retired from the Navy, the Soviets sent word that they wanted to meet him face-to-face overseas. They suggested three possible sites, only one of which John was able to remember later. Appropriately enough he chose Casablanca and suggested the meeting take place in early August 1977. That was when the U.S.S. *Constellation* was scheduled to arrive in Hong Kong for liberty, and John figured he could meet Jerry there, pick up his film, and then fly to the meeting in Morocco.

John wrote the Soviets a message agreeing to the meet and stuck it in the package that he was preparing to deliver to the KGB in April 1977.

A few days before the scheduled exchange, John made a frightening discovery. He came downstairs from his bedroom one morning and noticed that the door to his study was open. His first thought was that Sherrie, his half sister and Johnny and Dorothy's child, had been in there. Sherrie had leukemia and was undergoing treatment at a Richmond hospital. Because the six-hour drive from her home to the hospital exhausted her and Johnny, the two frequently stopped at John's house for the night in order to break up the trip from Temperanceville.

Sherrie, who later succumbed to the disease, was an inquisitive child, and she and Johnny Walker had stayed with John the night before. "I figured she had wandered into my study," John said. But when John went inside, he became concerned. A window was open and several items on his desk had been moved. He quickly checked the bottom drawer of his desk where he kept his instructions from the KGB, the KL-47 rotor reader, and other spy-related paraphernalia. He had made it a practice to place a small piece of clear adhesive tape inconspicuously along one side of the drawer. If the drawer was opened, the tape would be torn in half and John would know instantly that someone had been looking inside. John checked the tape. It was torn. He jerked open the drawer and did a quick inventory. Nothing was missing.

"I began to suspect the FBI. I decided they had broken into my room and looked for information about the next drop. It really wasn't that crazy an idea. I mean, if the FBI had broken into Daniel Ellsberg's psychiatrist's office over the Pentagon Papers, then what would keep them from going after me?" John explained. He decided to use someone else to make the dead drop delivery.

John drove to an old Victorian house at 617 West Ocean View Avenue, which he owned, and knocked on the door of an apartment rented by Roberta Kiriluk Puma, a six-foot, 140-pound, twenty-seven-year-old blonde with green eyes. John had met Roberta, who was a freelance writer, artist, and bartender, one year earlier when she had applied to be the resident manager of the six apartments in the house.

John's pitch was simple: if Roberta went to Washington with him on a business trip, he would forgive a $500 debt that he claimed she owed him. He'd also give her a few bucks for herself. John showed Roberta four photographs of the drop site and explained that she would have to help him make a delivery there.

Roberta Puma later recalled her response to John in a story published in *The Virginian-Pilot and The Ledger-Star* after John's arrest. In that story, which she helped write, Roberta said she considered John's offer to be "one of the goofiest come-ons" that she had heard. She did not suspect that he was doing anything illegal, she said. Rather, Roberta thought John was trying to get her into bed.

She agreed to go with John after discussing the matter with a friend who urged her to "see how far the charade will go." A few days later, John and Roberta drove in his car to Dulles International Airport, where John rented a car for himself. They drove both vehicles to the Ramada Inn in Rockville, where John parked the rental car and slipped into the front seat of his own car with Roberta. Following his directions, Roberta drove through the drop area on a trial run.

"He didn't act like there was any particular urgency, and he was not any more nervous than usual," the newspaper quoted Roberta Puma as saying. John told Roberta that they would keep in contact that night by talking on Channel 9 of a Citizens Band radio in his car. They would pose as members of an ambulance crew responding to an accident.

A short while after they returned to the hotel, John announced that he was "going out in the field." As instructed, Roberta left the hotel later that night and drove to the drop area. When she spotted the signal can beside the road, she picked up the CB mike and repeated the message that John had told her to use. "This is mobile one, proceeding to accident scene." Roberta waited a few seconds, but John didn't reply, so she drove through the drop area without stopping and then returned to the Ramada Inn as she had been told to do.

Unbeknownst to Roberta, John had been watching her at the drop area. He had put on military camouflage, smeared his face with black and green greasepaint, and crawled along a drainage ditch until he was a few hundred feet from the road.

"I had my 12-gauge shotgun and my .38 revolver with me," John later told me, clearly enjoying the recounting of this adventure. "I had arrived near the drop point just when it turned dark, around seven-thirty P.M., and worked my way into the area. I was hoping to come in behind the FBI. I didn't think they would expect anyone to come at them from behind and I thought I might be able to sneak up on them and see one of them lighting a cigarette, whispering, or maybe overhear them when they received a radio transmission.

"I was hidden in the grass and bushes when Roberta drove into the area and I listened to her transmission through an earphone on my portable radio."

If the FBI were hiding, John figured they'd make their move and arrest Roberta during her first trip through the drop site.

"No one moved or did anything when she came by, so I figured it was safe, but right after she left, I heard these damn dirt bikes and I saw two lights on the road."

John buried his face in the dirt.

"Those damn FBI agents got dirt bikes!"

The motorcycles, however, swept past the drop site without stopping.

Hurrying from his hiding place to a pay phone, John called Roberta at the Ramada Inn and told her to make another drive through the area. This time, he told her to toss out the garbage bag that he had brought with him from Norfolk.

John crept back into position in the woods and soon saw the beams from an approaching car. It stopped, and John watched as the murky outline of Roberta stepped out, opened the car trunk, and removed a bag of trash. He half expected searchlights to flood the area and a battery of FBI agents to rush Roberta and handcuff her. But as she walked toward the telephone pole and put the bag next to it, nothing out of the ordinary happened.

A few minutes later, another car pulled up and a man leaped from the car and grabbed the trash bag. John wasn't close enough to see the license plate, but he assumed it was a KGB courier. The car sped away.

"I immediately figured out that Sherrie must have gotten into my desk drawer and opened the window," John said later. "I shouldn't have been worried at all about the FBI. But afterwards, I began to wonder how I would have reacted if I'd come up on some agents in the dark with my shotgun. It might have been an interesting scene—me, heavily armed, sneaking up behind the FBI."

In the newspaper account, Roberta Puma said John had suggested they spend the night together at the Ramada Inn after she finished making the drop, but she said she refused. So John drove Roberta home and gave her an envelope filled with cash.

"I opened up the envelope and was stunned," Roberta Puma said in the news article. "There was fifteen hundred dollars in the envelope, I think. And money hadn't really been discussed in depth. I wondered if he was testing me, my honesty. . . ." She telephoned John and told him that he had overpaid her. The next morning, he took back about $1,000.

Sometime after the drop, John took Roberta to lunch at Knickerbocker's Restaurant in Norfolk and began asking her a series of hypothetical questions. Would she spend a month in jail for, say, $10,000? He kept increasing the jail time and the money it would be worth, ending at half a million dollars.

"I told him I wouldn't spend a weekend in jail for any amount of money, any amount," Roberta Puma said.

John was disappointed. He had been toying with the idea of hiring Roberta to make his dead drops, thus taking one more step to protect himself from arrest.

# 31

John had always thought of himself as unique, but after his experiences crawling through the woods while Roberta Puma made the dead drop, he began to see himself as something more. He was an historical figure. No one he'd ever read about had spied as long for the Russians without getting caught. He was certain of that. So John decided to keep a journal that would memorialize his adventures. He couldn't write anything incriminating, but he could keep notes to prompt his own memory about his spy escapades in later years. He wasn't certain whether he would ever make his journals public. He toyed with the idea of sealing them until after his death. Whether or not the journals ever became public really wasn't the point. What was important was to document his experiences in some form. Even if he was the only person who knew what he was doing, he still felt a need to put it in writing. It made it all more real, he said later, and that helped him feel important.

Before John left for his meeting with Jerry Whitworth in Hong Kong and the face-to-face rendezvous in Morocco with the KGB, John purchased a stenographer's pad and a new ballpoint pen and began his journal with the trivia of flight times and departures notes that he had come to believe were the stuff of legend.

John had written Jerry and suggested that they meet at the Hong Kong airport so he could pay Jerry the $8,000 owed him, pick up Jerry's film, and catch his next flight. But Jerry had rejected the idea. If John was going to fly halfway across the world, he might as well take enough time to visit and have dinner. Besides, Jerry wanted John to spend a little time getting to know Brenda, who also was flying to Hong Kong to meet Jerry's ship.

"I thought he was nuts," John recalled. "I mean, what was I going to say? 'Oh, hi, Brenda. My name is John Walker and I was just in this part of the world and so I thought I'd drop by to see my old pal Jerry?' How could I explain being in Hong Kong?"

Despite his misgivings, John acquiesced.

The U.S.S. *Constellation* was delayed and arrived later than scheduled, which further irritated John. When the aircraft carrier finally dropped anchor, John was waiting with several hundred wives and sweethearts on the pier.

John and Brenda had rented rooms at the Holiday Inn, and after Jerry spent a few hours with his bride, he hurried into John's room. He had hidden his film in the bottoms of Q-tips boxes, a move that he considered clever but that immediately alarmed John.

"What the hell did you do that for?" John demanded. "Why didn't you just carry them off the ship in your camera case?" If someone had discovered them hidden in the Q-tips boxes, they would have been suspicious.

Jerry shrugged. It just seemed like a good idea at the time, he said. The spies he had read about and seen in the movies always hid their film.

"Jesus, Jerry, this isn't some second-rate spy movie," John complained. But his anger cooled when Jerry told him what was on those photographs from the carrier.

Jerry had taken snapshots of technical manuals for the KW-7, KWR-37, and the KY-36, three of the most heavily used cipher systems in the Navy. If the Russians had any brains at all, they would be able to use the schematics in the technical manuals to recreate the three cryptographic machines in Moscow. Jerry's photographs were almost as good as giving the KGB actual, working machines!

Jerry's delivery put John in a festive mood, and he joined Jerry and Brenda that night for an exotic dinner at an Indian restaurant. "Only Jerry would eat Indian food in Hong Kong," John joked later.

He left Hong Kong for Bangkok the next morning. He had planned to go sightseeing during his trip, and even though he was behind schedule because of the Constellation's lateness, he didn't alter his plans. He checked into his Bangkok hotel and he went directly to a whorehouse. Rising early the next day, he decided, on a whim, to join a tour that was departing from the hotel lobby. On the bus, he met a schoolteacher from New York City. According to notes in his journal, they spent the day together and that night he had sex with her. He listed her name and hotel room number in his chronicle, and years later, after John's arrest, the teacher was appalled when the FBI knocked on her door and began questioning her about her one-night encounter with a spy.

"I was always cautious on these trips when I met strangers," John recalled. "Anyone I met could have been a secret agent, either CIA or KGB, but none of them ever said anything remotely connected with espionage, so I felt safe."

When John was actually traveling, he kept the Minox film for the Russians in his shoulder camera bag. But when he was leaving a hotel room to go sightseeing or to a whorehouse, he usually taped the small metal film canisters along the back of the bottom of the curtains. That seemed the safest place to hide something.

Always one to mix business and pleasure, John had invited his Norfolk girlfriend, Patsy Marsee, to meet him in Casablanca. He had planned to meet the Russians before Pat arrived, but because the *Constellation* was late, John missed his first scheduled meeting with the KGB. As a result, Patsy Marsee arrived in Casablanca at about the same time as John's meeting with his KGB contact.

"It was hard to explain to Pat, but I told her that I had business and that she couldn't come with me to the meeting. It was difficult because who the hell did I know in Casablanca, especially at night, and what kind of business would I be having there?" John recalled. "I mean, you usually don't go to Casablanca to recruit salespersons for an association."

Still, Patsy Marsee didn't question John's behavior. He left her at the hotel and took a taxi to the city's public aquarium. The building was dark and the streets were empty. John began walking along an avenue as he had been instructed. The KGB had given him a code to use. His KGB handler was supposed to approach him and ask, "Didn't we meet in Berlin in 1976?" John's response was, "No, I was in Norfolk, Virginia, during that hectic year."

John didn't want to screw it up so he kept thinking about the code words as he walked along the narrow path. The street began to wind and get even narrower, until it became so constricted that only one car could pass. It was becoming darker and John felt uneasy. He couldn't see anyone on the street, and he began to wonder if the KGB had given up on him after he missed the first meeting.

"Hello, Mr. Harper," said a deep voice behind him.

John spun around. The man must have stepped from the doorway of one of the buildings. John couldn't tell whether he was the same KGB agent that he had met nine years earlier outside the Zayre department store or someone new. He wasn't even certain this man was a KGB agent. Why hadn't he used the agreed upon code?

"Let's continue walking, shall we?" the man said.

John looked through the growing darkness. The man was close to six feet tall, weighed about 190 pounds, and was about the same age as John.

"Uh, what about the signal?" John asked.

"I don't think it will be necessary," the man replied. Perhaps sensing John's uneasiness, he added, "But if you wish to talk about how you were in Norfolk during the hectic year of 1976, you may."

He began asking John questions in the same manner as that agent he'd met almost a decade ago outside Zayre's. How did you get here? Where are you staying? What was your route of travel? Did you notice anything suspicious around you during this trip? Did you meet anyone suspicious? Are any new people coming into your life? Okay, what's on the film?

That answered and the film turned over, the KGB agent talked about specific items that the Soviets wanted procured: more KW-7 keylists, technical manuals for cipher systems whenever possible, information about communications satellites. Once the agent had finished giving John a shopping list, both men began to relax and the conversation turned personal.

"How is Barbara? Is she still drinking heavily?"

"Yes," John replied, "but she is not a threat. She will keep quiet as long as she is paid."

"I'm sorry about the divorce," the KGB agent said, in a tone of voice that John felt was sincere.

"Then you obviously don't know my wife," John replied, chuckling. The agent didn't understand at first, but then he laughed. As they walked, he said that his superiors wanted him to meet John face-to-face at least once a year. He gave John a sheet of paper with the words *The Vienna Procedure* typed at the top. It was an elaborate set of directions for a face-to-face meeting in Vienna, Austria in January 1978.

"Have you been to Vienna?" he asked.

"No," John replied.

"Oh, it is a lovely city, but it is cold. Almost as bad as my country in the winter. You must dress warmly."

The agent suggested that John shave off his beard before the face-to-face encounter and that he not wear his hairpiece while he was in Vienna.

"It would be very difficult to recognize you with such a disguise," he said.

"Yeah, I guess it would," replied John, who thought the idea stupid.

"Have you read the book, *The French Connection?*" the KGB agent asked, referring to the Robin Moore book about two New York police detectives' year-long investigation of a narcotics kingpin.

"No," said John.

"You should, it will give you excellent tips about avoiding surveillance. It really is useful."

Later, John said he was astounded that a trained KGB agent was recommending an American crime book as the best source of advice on security precautions.

"When you fly to Europe," the KGB agent continued, "do not fly into Germany under any circumstances. The Germans are much too thorough at airports. It is too dangerous to go through their security. You should fly to a country like Italy because the Italians, they are corrupt and a backwards people. You can fly into any city you like in Italy and it will not be a problem."

"Okay," John responded.

"Also you should take a train to Vienna," the agent continued. "It is called Wien in Europe. A train is good because there is no security check. Customs will not be a problem for you. But do not bring any narcotics. The customs look for narcotics. They have trained dogs to smell them."

"No sweat."

"You must also be extremely cautious about people you meet and never, never, come to any of our embassies or telephone them. It is simply too dangerous."

Having finished with his lecture, the agent turned his attention to Jerry Whitworth. Does he drink excessively? Have a drug problem? Is he a homosexual? Why has he been in and out of the Navy so many times?

John described Jerry in detail. "I was always scrupulously honest with the KGB. I might not volunteer some information, but what I told them was usually always the truth," said John. "I didn't want to risk being caught in a lie because I felt these people were dangerous."

At one point, John even told the Russian about Jerry's intellectual fixation with Ayn Rand. The agent interrupted.

"Who?"

The KGB agent knew *The French Connection,* but he knew nothing about Rand, much more famous and influential than Moore. Obviously, books by Rand, a Russian emigrée and staunch anticommunist, weren't on the agent's reading list.

After a few minutes of chatter, the agent asked John, "Are you still doing this only for the money?"

"Yes," John answered.

The agent paused and John figured that a lecture about the joys of communism would follow. But it didn't.

"We will talk about this further, perhaps in Vienna."

Then the agent handed John an envelope of cash and asked him, as usual, to sign a receipt for it.

As John was writing his name, the agent said, "My country appreciates greatly what you are doing for all humanity. This is important for you to know. This is a great thing you are doing for peace."

John nodded.

"If something ever happened to detain you," the agent continued, "would you send Jerry to Vienna?"

The question caught John completely off guard. What could possibly happen? And why had the KGB asked if Jerry could come to Vienna? Were they considering dealing directly with Jerry and cutting John out since he was no longer in the Navy? Was the agent trying to give him some kind of hidden message—that if he didn't play along, he could be eliminated?

"I'm not certain he would have the balls to do it," John said. "This is definitely a two-man operation. He gets the material and I deliver it."

"Of course," the agent replied. "What do you mean, 'balls'?"

John explained. It would be foolhardy for Jerry to come to Vienna since he still was in the Navy, John added.

"Of course," the agent responded.

"Good-bye, dear friend," he said, before turning to leave. "And remember," he added, "to be careful."

The KGB agent's words kept buzzing through John's head.
"If something ever happened to detain you, would you send Jerry to Vienna?"

John couldn't stop thinking about that question as he and Patsy returned home from Casablanca. "I knew that I was only valuable to the KGB as long as no one knew what I had given them," he explained later to me during an interview. "You see," he said, quite seriously, "if I were dead, then the CIA and FBI could really never be certain what I had stolen. I am the only person who really knows what the KGB got from me.

"So I am certain that the KGB seriously considered killing me at some point. The Russians had to think about it. It didn't have anything to do with my loyalty or service to them. It had to be a logical decision on their part. Here was a guy who had given them valuable information for several years. Now, he no longer was directly producing information, although he was still delivering what Jerry produced. The truth was that I had become Jerry's handler and the question that had to be in the KGB's mind was, Should we execute this guy and cut our own deal with Jerry or wait? If they did a .22 caliber slug-behind-the-ears number on me, how would Jerry react? In some ways, killing me might have been an incentive to Jerry."

The more John thought about it, the more paranoid he became.

"I didn't know what the Russians were thinking and I decided that I needed some insurance. I needed to convince them that I was invaluable as a spy even though I wasn't directly producing material. This is when the idea of recruiting others besides Jerry began to form in my mind."

Before his return flight landed in New York City, John outlined a letter on the back pages of his journal. It was a letter that he intended to send to his brother, Arthur, a letter that was not only going to make Arthur angry, but also bring their joint business, Walker Enterprises, closer to financial ruin. John was tightening the noose on Arthur, and while he would later deny in interviews that he intended to put pressure on him, this was exactly the effect of the letter.

SUBJ: Position of Jaws in WE [Walker Enterprises]

1. This is not a "Dear John" letter. I have put my thoughts, recommendations and basic position in writing for three reasons:
   a. I wrote it during my Far East trip.
   b. We seldom have the opportunity to talk.
   c. You are difficult to talk to anyway since you become strongly argumentative when I bring up *my* problems.

2. At the risk of boring you with the obvious, the following facts should be recapped:

FINANCIAL

a. I have invested considerable direct cash into the formation of WE.
b. I have invested a large sum of invisible cash into WE in the form of a vehicle, office furniture, typewriter, copy machine, bldg rent, utilities, secretarial pay, personal vehicle expenses . . .

John's letter continued in this cool and calculated manner. He demanded the repayment of more than $10,000 [spy money] that he had pumped into Walker Enterprises, along with back wages and compensation for time lost. John knew Arthur couldn't afford to pay, but he didn't care.

"Arthur had never missed taking home a paycheck from Walker Enterprises, but the company was losing money like crazy," John told me later. "Now who in the hell do you think was making that possible? Me! That's who! I was financing his kids' college education for christsakes! I just kept pumping more and more spy money into the business."

John had decided it was time for old Uncle Art to feel reality.

# 32

Four months passed quickly, and in mid-January 1978, John boarded a flight for Italy. Jerry had delivered another promising cache of cryptographic material and collected another $6,000 in salary. This time, Jerry hadn't complained about what they were doing, nor had he brought up the subject of Israel. He was beginning to get used to the extra income.

"In the Wild West days, the bad guys had to wade down streams to cover their tracks," John recalled, "but today's criminals worry about keeping their names out of computers and that was my big worry about going to Europe."

John used an alias when he bought his ticket from Norfolk to New York City. But traveling under a fictitious name was a bit trickier on out-of-the-country flights. Airlines compare the names on each passenger's passport with their ticket. With the KGB's help, however, John came up with a way to beat the system.

"Having a fake passport or two would have been stupid because if anyone saw them, they would know you were doing something illegal," John explained to me. "So I did something much simpler. I misspelled my name."

When John bought his ticket to Milan, he told the ticket agent that his name was John A. Waller, Jr. It was such a minor oversight that the harried airline ticket agent at John F. Kennedy International Airport didn't even notice the difference when she glanced at John's ticket and passport. As a result, there was no record in the airline's computer of anyone named John A. Walker, Jr., ever leaving the country.

The KGB had been correct, John discovered, when it told him that security at Italian airports was virtually nonexistent. "The place was a madhouse!" John hustled through Italian customs without ever having to open his suitcase or get his passport stamped.

The KGB had told John to board a train for Vienna next, but he decided to make a side trip on his own. He had realized when he met the KGB in Casablanca that he was totally defenseless. "The KGB always wanted to meet me at night in out-of-the-way places where I could be robbed or even murdered," John recalled. He also remained paranoid about the Russians. "I still didn't know if they were going to kill me."

So John asked a taxi driver in Milan where he could buy a small, cheap handgun, and within a few minutes he was taken to a cramped apartment where he paid $100 for a .25 caliber automatic with twenty-five bullets. He also paid the cabbie a $25 finder's fee. "The gun was a piece of crap, but it was small enough to fit in my coat pocket."

The train ride to Vienna was long and tiring. Just as the KGB agent had said, the only time John had to show his passport was when the train reached the Austrian border. At that point, the doors to the train were locked and the Austrian customs officials came aboard with German shepherd dogs. While the dogs sniffed each passenger and piece of luggage for narcotics, the snappily dressed customs agents glanced at—but did not record—the names on each passenger's passport.

The lax security wasn't the only thing that the KGB had been correct about. It was teeth-chattering cold in Vienna on the night of January 20, 1978, when John checked into the Hotel Regina, one of the city's moderately priced hotels. The KGB had told John to stay there but he immediately felt uncomfortable because most of the guests were Austrian and the only language he heard was German. "I really felt out of place. In the middle of January, there aren't many American tourists in Vienna."

The city has a population of 1.6 million and is divided into twenty-three sprawling, crazy-quilt districts, but it didn't take a skilled ship's navigator like John long to get his bearings. The Hotel Regina was only one block away from the U-Bahn, the city's efficient and heavily used subway system. Just as he had done when making dead drops in the

United States, John decided to familiarize himself with his route on the morning of the face-to-face meeting. He boarded the U-2 subway line, which rings the ancient inner city, and rode it five stops until he reached the U-4 line that carried him away from the old city to the Schönbrunn Palace, the summer home and favorite residence of the former ruling family of Austria, the Hapsburgs.

With schoolboy awe, he noted in his journal that the trains operated on an "honor" system, with passengers buying small orange tickets that they later punched themselves in machines near the tracks.

While riding toward the 1,400-room Schönbrunn Palace, John read the sheet of instructions that the KGB agent had given him in Casablanca. The Vienna Procedure was written on a single sheet of white typing paper, and the first time that John saw it, he thought it had been typed. But when he looked carefully at the document, he realized each letter had been printed by hand across the page in incredibly small and neat lines:

### THE VIENNA PROCEDURE

AT 18:15 P.M. COME UP TO THE "KOMET KÜCHEN" STORE (KITCHEN CABINETS AND APPLIANCES) ON THE CORNER OF SCHÖNBRUNNER STRASSE AND RUCKERGASSE. TO GET THERE WALK FROM SCHÖNBRUNN PALACE AND PARK GROUNDS; ON SCHÖNBRUNNER SCHLOSSSTRASSE AND ITS CONTINUATION SCHÖNBRUNNER STRASSE TO RUCKERGASSE. TURN LEFT ON THE LATTER AND STOP AT THE WINDOW OF THE "KOMET KÜCHEN" STORE, WHICH IS LOOKING ON RUCKERGASSE, JUST A COUPLE OF YARDS AWAY FROM THE CORNER. FOR EASY IDENTIFICATION PLEASE CARRY YOUR CAMERA BAG ON YOUR LEFT SHOULDER AND HOLD A SMALL PAPER BAG IN YOUR RIGHT HAND. PAUSE BY THAT WINDOW FOR ABOUT TWO MINUTES FROM 18:15 P.M. TO 18:17 P.M., DRIFTING SLOWLY ALONG IT AWAY FROM SCHÖNBRUNNER STRASSE TOWARD THE OTHER CORNER OF THE BUILDING . . .

Finding the Komet Küchen store was easy. It had four large red, white, yellow, and blue neon signs extending from it, and two stories of brilliant silver aluminum siding above its store windows. When John reached it, he gazed through the display windows at the washers and dryers, color televisions, and stereos inside. He walked around the corner of the store as instructed, paused, and then returned to the front of the building. As he was walking back, John noticed that there was a public park diagonally across the street from the store. A KGB agent could easily and unobtrusively watch him from the park benches there and also tell if he was being followed.

Following the instructions, John crossed the street and stood in front of another display window. He was now standing parallel to the park. He walked down the sidewalk and turned right at the next corner into a narrow side street lined with cars. The instructions called for him to walk one block and turn left, then walk another block and turn left again. This brought him back to the main thoroughfare, and he found himself once again facing the public park. Had anyone been following John, he would have been easily apparent to a watcher sitting in the park. There would be no reason for someone to take such an indirect route unless he was shadowing someone. John was having fun despite the bitter cold. He was getting caught up in the James Bond-type procedures and the drama of clandestine meetings.

John continued his trek and was led by the instructions up and down a number of streets that always brought him back to a major street, Meidlinger Hauptstrasse. A bird's-eye view of the course would show that John had walked in a series of circles all near city parks or small plazas where a KGB agent could sit unnoticed and see both the beginning and end of his jaunts.

The last stop was outside a clothing store called Bazala, a four-story building on the corner of Meidlinger Hauptstrasse near a small plaza. As he stood in front of the store's two glass doors, John realized that despite an hour of walking, he was less than four blocks away from the Komet Küchen where he had started!

By the time he got back to his hotel, it was time for him to turn around and return for the actual meeting. A light snow was falling when he arrived at the Komet Küchen at 6:15 P.M. The wind was stronger too.

John had placed Jerry's delivery in his camera bag and he was carrying the .25 caliber automatic in his hand inside the right pocket of his coat. By the time he reached the Bazala clothing store, he couldn't feel his toes because they were numb.

"Hello, dear friend," a familiar voice said. It was the same KGB agent he'd met in Casablanca. "Do you have something for me?" The men exchanged camera cases and the KGB agent excused himself. He walked away, but returned a few minutes later.

John gripped the automatic pistol tightly in his hand. If someone was going to arrest him or if the KGB intended to kill him, now was the perfect time. Bundled pedestrians hurried past, their shoes making a slight crunching sound in the snow.

"Dear friend, let us walk this way please."

John removed his finger from the trigger, but left his hand in his pocket with the weapon.

"I assumed that we would go to a safe house or at least inside a coffeehouse because it was freezing outside," John recalled later. "But he motioned me to begin walking and told me that it would be too dangerous for us to go inside anywhere. I couldn't believe it! I was freezing and we were going to walk the streets for at least another fucking hour or two."

Once again, the KGB agent followed the same script. He questioned John about his trip and then asked questions about the acquisition of specific "merchandise" and possible future "acquisitions." These were followed by inquiries of a more personal nature about John's family and, as always, Barbara's drinking habits.

At some point during the conversation, John decided to bring up a topic of his own. He reminded the KGB agent about his comment in Casablanca, when the agent had asked whom John would send in his place if he was ever detained.

"There is only one person I would trust to make such a trip," John said. "My brother Arthur. He is the only person that I would ever consider to replace me. His is intelligent enough to do it, and he has the balls to do it. He is an international traveler and he looks so much like me that even you might have trouble telling the difference."

The KGB agent already knew about Arthur because John had told the Russians about the various members of his family.

"Does he know what you do?" the agent asked.

"He knows I'm doing something illegal, but not what."

"Would he do it?"

"He's having tremendous financial difficulties," said John. "Has been ever since he got out of the Navy. He owes me. I think Art can be turned."

"Do nothing," the agent advised, "until I speak to my superiors."

By now the two men had been walking for more than an hour in the wind and John was exhausted. But the agent had not completed his agenda.

"My friend, why do you Americans wish to destroy us?"

John was surprised by the question. The last thing that he wanted to hear was a propaganda speech. "We don't," he mumbled. "You guys are the aggressors."

"My friend, this is so untrue," the KGB agent said. "In Siberia, we have more minerals than any other nation. We have enough oil for our country and we have a nation twice the size of the United States. We don't need anyone else. We don't need the extra problems. All we wish is to be left alone. It is the United States who is the aggressor."

The agent spoke about the decadence of the West. Why capitalism was doomed to fail. How oppressed peoples across the globe were taking up arms and endorsing communism. John couldn't believe it. It was simply crazy. He was freezing!

"The first time that he discussed his country—he never said Russia when we were together—I was really snickering under my breath," John recalled. "I was thinking, 'Oh God, this is typical propaganda bullshit.' Here he is telling me about the beauty of socialism. I really scoffed at it."

After an agonizing forty-five-minute indoctrination, the agent finally finished talking. Once again, he thanked John for his contributions to world peace.

"Just keep the money coming," John replied. He thought the KGB agent looked pained by the remark. He hoped so!

By the time that John got back to his hotel, he felt physically and mentally drained. But after he warmed up, he found that he was too excited to sleep. He decided to spend some of the money that the KGB agent had given him. He caught a taxi outside the Hotel Regina and asked the driver to take him to a brothel. Having sex with a big-busted Austrian fräulein would be the perfect end to his high-strung day. He was sure that James Bond would have done the same thing himself.

# PART FOUR

---

# *FAMILY*

*He that loves not his wife and children, feeds a lioness at home, and broods a nest of sorrow.*

**JEREMY TAYLOR**
*Sermons*, Vol. I

# 33

John kept in sporadic touch with his children after the divorce, not because he particularly missed them, but because they were his kids and they might be useful someday. He was still paranoid about the Soviets, and felt vulnerable because he was acting as Jerry's handler and not producing any classified material himself. John also knew that Jerry was not the most reliable long-term partner. Jerry's naval career was a revolving door of discharges and reenlistments, and his life was full of vacillation and bursts of interest and then disinterest in fads. Like a pimp without a working stable of whores, John knew that he would lose his spy income and possibly his life if Jerry ever quit.

"The material we were giving the KGB was just too valuable to chance letting us live if we ever stopped producing," John explained once again. "Jerry and I were really victims of our own success. I knew that. But I also knew that if I could recruit one of my own children, then the KGB could never lay a hand on me. That is why I went after them. That's the real reason. They were my only ticket out."

Whether or not the KGB ever intended to harm John is impossible to tell. But in John's mind, that threat was always there, and recruiting one of his children was the best insurance policy that he could think of.

"It's a parent's job to protect the children. Even if they are adults, it's your obligation as a parent to protect them," John told me. "I mean, they are your kids. I understood that. I knew that if I recruited any of my kids, I would be putting them in harm's way. There is no way that I can justify that, but I began to consider the risks and the profits. My kids just didn't have it. They weren't going to make anything out of their lives—especially Cynthia, whom everyone had picked on. She didn't have any self-esteem. This made me start to think of spying in a different way. I had been doing it for a long time, and it was a safe way to make a lot of money. Why not let them in on the gravy train? You see, I was actually helping them. They sure as hell weren't going to amount to anything on their own."

By late 1977, Barbara and the children had outstayed their welcome at the farm owned by Annie and Bob Nelson and had moved to

Skowhegan, a small Maine town. Barbara had spent all of her money from the divorce. Now broke, she was forced to take a job at the Dexter Shoe Company, cementing shoes together on a piecework basis to support herself, her children, and her mother, who had moved in with her.

Margaret was the first to flee Maine. She moved to Boston, where she lived with family friends and worked in a factory making plastic cups and bowls. John telephoned her first.

"Margaret had been a feminist since she was five years old," John recalled. "You couldn't tell that child anything, and I didn't think there was much chance of convincing her to go into the service. But I decided to try anyway."

John convinced Margaret to move to Norfolk and stay with him until she could find her own apartment. He offered to pay for her ticket and expenses until she found work. Once she arrived, John began urging her to join the military. "As I predicted," John said, "Margaret wasn't interested at all in enlisting. 'I don't think I could put up with all that discipline—the "yes, sirs" and other crap,' she told me."

Instead, Margaret enrolled in a junior college and decided to become a graphic artist.

"I couldn't believe that dummy," said John. "I went to the library and checked out a census that showed salaries that different professions earned. I said, 'Look here, Margaret, graphic artists aren't even listed on this because they don't make squat.' But she didn't care. She was a complete zero brain."

In fact, John's effort to recruit Margaret had been half-hearted; her strong personality made it unlikely she would join the service. His next target was exactly the opposite.

When John told me about his attempt to recruit Cynthia, he couched it in the most sympathetic terms possible. "I talked to Laura and Cynthia on the telephone and I really got pissed about the situation up there in Maine," John said. "Cynthia was just going to rot away up there, so I decided to fly up and rescue her."

Of all his children, John had shown the least attention to Cynthia, whom he constantly belittled and referred to as "a retard." But suddenly, he was concerned about her—enough so that he left immediately for Skowhegan to convince Cynthia to return with him to Norfolk. She would be easy, he felt, to push into the military and recruit as a spy. In his own strained logic, John saw his plan as a reflection of his love for Cynthia.

"This wasn't all for me. The Navy had been good for me and I really believed that the military would have been good for all of my kids, even if they didn't become spies. Particularly Cynthia, who I had to get away from her mother."

Before Barbara and the kids moved to Maine, Cynthia had fallen in love with a young Marine in Norfolk and become pregnant. Now, at nineteen, she was unmarried and single-handedly raising her small son, while struggling to attend classes at a vocational school. She was surviving financially on welfare and having a tough time emotionally.

John planned his trip so that he would arrive while Barbara was working. He found the house and knocked. Cynthia answered, dressed in a bathrobe. She was sick, but still thrilled to see her father.

"Pack your shit," John commanded. "You and the baby are going back home to Norfolk. I want you to live with me."

"But Daddy," Cynthia replied, "we have the flu."

"Forget the flu," John said. "It only lasts seven days. Now is the time to make your escape and get out of here. Now where's your stuff?"

John helped Cynthia pack a suitcase and the three of them rode to the airport. John left Cynthia and the baby inside the terminal while he went out to refuel his airplane. When he returned, he found Cynthia near tears and the baby crying.

"Cynthia couldn't decide what to do. I mean, it was ridiculous. Her mother had picked on her all her life and she still didn't know what to do," John recalled.

"You got fifteen minutes to decide," John said to Cynthia. "This is your last chance because I'm leaving in fifteen minutes with or without you and the baby. I've turned in the rental car, you know, so there's no way for you to get home unless you call a taxi, and I'm not paying for that!"

Cynthia was confused.

"I didn't know what to do," she told me later, her voice filled with emotion. "I *love* my dad, but I was afraid."

As John's deadline approached, he turned more insistent.

"You are going to be a fucking welfare mother all your life if you don't get out of this environment! Is that what you want?" he demanded. "Cynthia, you got to build some self-esteem. Look, come to Norfolk with me. We'll find someone to take care of the kid and you can join the service. I didn't have any confidence once and look what the Navy did for me. It can do the same for you, and it will get you away from your mother, who is a goddamn lazy alcoholic. Look, Cynthia, my dad was an alcoholic too. I know what you are facing. This is your big chance. Your only chance. You got to take it just like I did."

Cynthia couldn't decide and John finally gave her an ultimatum. Go or stay? Decide now! This instant!

"We're staying," Cynthia said, clutching her son in her arms.

Enraged, John turned around to leave.

"Daddy," Cynthia said, beginning to cry. "How are we going to get home?"

John didn't answer. He stormed out of the small terminal and returned to Norfolk alone.

"I had done my best to help that girl," John said later. "But she didn't have the guts to go with me."

Remembering the incident, Cynthia Walker later told me amid tears why she hadn't gone with John. "I wanted to have a good relationship with my father, but I was afraid to move back to Norfolk. All of my family considered me dumb. But I listened and watched them, and they really didn't know anything about me because they were so busy talking. I was afraid to go back with my father to Norfolk because I knew what he wanted me to do. He never said anything specific, but my mother had told all of us that he was a spy, and I was afraid to go back with him because I knew he would try to get me involved. I just felt it."

# 34

The Russians sent word that they were extremely pleased with the materials Jerry had collected aboard the U.S.S. *Constellation,* so much so, that they were doubling Jerry's pay to $4,000 per month, the same amount that John was receiving.

In a meeting in San Diego on July 7, 1978, John told Jerry about the raise and gave him $24,000 in cash. Jerry had some splendid news himself to report. In order to aid Brenda's graduate studies in nutrition, he had requested a transfer to a ship based in northern California and, much to his delight, he had been ordered to report on August 10 to the U.S.S. *Niagara Falls,* the same supply ship that John had served on between 1972 and 1974. In fact, he was going to have John's old job as CMS custodian, which would give him easy access to cryptographic machines and keylists. John, Jerry suggested, could even give him tips on where to photograph materials aboard the ship!

"Fantastic!" John replied. "We're making all the right moves!"

Eight days later, John told his KGB contact during another face-to-face meeting in Vienna about Jerry's new assignment. John's handler didn't have to be reminded of what a prime source the U.S.S. *Niagara Falls* was for crypto.

"This is just excellent," the KGB agent said.

Unlike the weather during their January meeting, it was perfect in June 1978, and the temperate summer evening put both men in festive spirits as they strolled along Meidlinger Hauptstrasse.

"Vienna in the winter—oohhoo," the KGB agent said, shaking his shoulders as if he were dislodging snow, "It's nearly as terrible as my country. This is much nicer." John laughed with him.

Again, the agent lectured John about the faults of capitalism, but this time John challenged him and discovered the agent eager for debate.

"I kept wondering what KGB regulation required him to give me an indoctrination speech every time we met," John said. "When we first talked, I thought he was just going through some routine of bullshit that the KGB required, but after a while, when I got to know him, I came to believe he honestly was sincere about what he was saying. He usually began by asking me why the United States wanted to destroy his country, and I always replied that his country was the aggressor.

"I told him, 'The United States doesn't want to blow you dummies up. We don't want your country. Christ, every American in the United States including those on welfare, has a higher standard of living than people in your country.'

"But after listening to him speak, some of what he said began to make sense, and I could see why he actually believed the Soviet Union was in dire danger from the United States I mean, Russia didn't fly over us after World War II in U-2 spy planes taking photographs like we did of them. Imagine the frustration of knowing that those airplanes are up there flying over you every day, and you don't have sophisticated enough weapons to shoot them down.

"And after the war, you know, there were some generals in the Pentagon who wanted to drop 'a big one' on Red Square. I began to think, 'Yeah, I can see where this guy is coming from. I can see why he's worried.'

"I liked some of the things he told me about the Soviet Union too, although I don't know if they are really true. For example, he asked me a lot about Watergate and the press. He said he couldn't understand why Nixon had to resign. He just didn't understand the press in our country at all. I mean, the Soviet press follows the party line because of principle. It believes what it says is best for the country, but the press in America doesn't give a damn about anything but making money. A reporter will print anything to get ahead and get his promotion. He doesn't have to prove anything, he just prints it. In the Soviet Union, the press can't print a story unless it is true. I mean, if someone is arrested, the Soviet press can't splash their names in the newspaper and ruin their lives until after they are convicted of the crime. Our media runs a tiny retraction if a guy is found not guilty and says, 'Oh, we're sorry,' after they've printed a zillion stories tearing the guy's life to shreds! I agreed with him on that one. I hate the fucking press.

"He made some other interesting points. We got into an argument, for instance, about church and state, and he told me there really wasn't any real separation between church and state in the United States. The Soviet Union is the only country in the world, he explained, where there isn't a state-backed religion and that's really why we want to destroy it. He told me this—now this is a KGB agent talking—he told me that the state of Rhode Island required all candidates for governor to sign a statement which said they believed in the Holy Trinity! That's outrageous— if it's true. I never checked it, but it sounds like something we'd do. I mean, the Boy Scouts of America requires its members to believe in a deity, doesn't it? I know it does! I think that really sucks. I mean, he was right, we have a government-sponsored religion. We force people to believe that there is a God.

"So the truth was that this KGB agent and I really began to develop a genuine friendship, I honestly believe that. I really think this guy liked me and it bothered him that I was doing this only for the money. He really wanted to win me over, so I listened to him and sometimes agreed with him. I think it made him feel better."

A short time after he returned from Vienna to Norfolk, John called Jerry to ask for his help. John had been sued by a Norfolk investor who claimed that John owed him money because of a business deal that involved John's professional sales association. John had decided to scare the investor into dropping his $10,000 lawsuit by threatening him with violence.

"Jerry, we're going to run a little scam on this guy," John explained over the telephone. "I need you to come out here and pose as a Mafia goon."

Jerry loved it and flew to Norfolk. Together, he and John paid a visit to the investor, and with Jerry standing silently behind him as a "Mafia enforcer," John threatened to kill the investor if he didn't drop the lawsuit. The ruse apparently worked because Norfolk court records show the case was dismissed at the plaintiff's request.

Jerry returned to California and duty aboard the U.S.S. *Niagara Falls,* which soon left on an extended Pacific cruise. On December 14, 1978, John flew to Manila to meet with Jerry at the Philippine Plaza Hotel. The *Niagara Falls* was anchored at Subic Bay to replenish its supplies, just as it had done when John was aboard.

Jerry's delivery was impressive. Working diligently during a four-month period, Jerry had copied the technical manuals for five more cryptographic machines, along with keylists for them. This delivery, when added to all previous ones, gave the Soviets the internal diagrams of nearly all U.S. cryptographic machines and was later described by federal prosecutors as the most damaging disclosure that Jerry Whitworth made as a spy. In effect, Jerry passed John sufficient information in Manila for the Soviets to reconstruct *all* of the United States's most widely used cryptographic machines. Intelligence experts would later claim that the military would have to spend several million dollars to alter the machines and hurry newer types of machines into place.

John had toyed with the idea of mixing business and pleasure in the Philippines. He had thought about trying to find his former Filipino girlfriend, Peaches, and returning to her picturesque home. But after he saw what Jerry had collected for him, he was simply too nervous to take any chances. John knew how important the documents were that Jerry had photographed. Even one technical manual by itself would have been sufficient to thrill the KGB, but Jerry had far surpassed that.

John flew home the day after the meeting with Jerry.

On January 27, 1979, in what now had become an almost routine procedure, John delivered the film to his KGB handler in Vienna outside the Bazala store. It was another painfully frosty night, but this time John wore electric socks to keep his feet warm. Both men were elated by what Jerry had photographed.

At one point, the KGB agent broke his self-imposed rule against their leaving the freezing city sidewalks. He motioned John inside a modest coffeehouse. It reminded John of some dank and dreary bars that he had frequented in Norfolk, but the temperature was much warmer than in the street. The KGB agent ordered for both of them in fluent German. The coffee shop was filled with men and only one or two women. John had been ordered by his handler not to speak while inside for fear he would draw attention to himself, so John simply nodded when the pudgy waitress brought them two steaming cups of what John thought was black coffee and two bowls of soup. The drink tasted bitter, and John could manage only a few swallows. His companion drank the brew easily and noisily sucked the soup from a large spoon.

When they went outside, John asked if the KGB had just tried to poison him by buying him such a poor cup of coffee. The KGB agent explained that the drink was Mokka, an after-dinner coffee favored by Austrians. "You especially should like it," the agent said. He explained that in the late 1600s, the Austrians repelled an invasion by the Turks. One of the items left behind by the fleeing Turkish army was a bag filled with mysterious brown beans. No one knew what to do with them until an Austrian spy, who had operated inside a Turkish camp, came forward and taught his fellow countrymen how to brew the beans into coffee. "Mokka," the KGB handler said, "is a good drink for spies."

This was a common story in Austria, one told routinely by tour guides and tour hosts, but John didn't know it. He was impressed with his handler's seeming "intelligence and wit."

John returned to Norfolk delighted after the exchange. Everything seemed to be going right in the spring of 1979. The money that he was earning as a spy was enabling him, as he put it, to "live every fantasy that I ever had."

On February 17, John and Patsy Marsee boarded John's Grumman American AA-5B single-engine aircraft in Norfolk and left on a daring month-long South American escapade that John chronicled faithfully in his journal. "2/17 Fly low, we observe island chain running east–west. That's impossible! Is our compass wrong? Has 'Devil's Triangle' got us?" The trip took them to Mexico, Guatemala, Costa Rica, Panama, Ecuador, and Peru, and when they returned home, John telephoned Jerry to brag. "We virtually pushed my small plane to the limit of its endurance," he said. "Just a small change in the weather could have killed us."

Jerry was also enjoying his spy money. On May 12, he gave a lavish party at the Hotel Del Coronado in San Diego, one of the world's oldest and most impressive hotels. After an elaborate sit-down dinner in a private dining room, Jerry stood and told the forty or more guests he wished to make an announcement. Everyone assumed he was going to announce his engagement to Brenda. Instead, he revealed that they had already been married for three years.

"Everyone was stunned," John told me later with a chuckle. "Particularly old Roger Olson. He couldn't believe that Jerry, his best buddy, had kept a secret from him. I loved it. Old Roger really didn't have any idea about the kind of secrets that Jerry was keeping!"

Jerry paid for the entire evening, and, in some cases, for the transportation and lodging of his special guests, including John. Jerry had even invited two attractive women to the party because he thought John might find them appealing. He was right.

"I had a really excellent sexual experience with both of them," John bragged later. "In fact, one of the girls, I think she was nineteen, wanted me to take the train with her up to Coalinga, but I had to turn her down."

John had other commitments. He and another Norfolk pilot, Mickey Baker, had agreed to ferry two small airplanes from Norfolk to Reykjavik, Iceland, in late May and early June. Each pilot was to be paid $1,000, plus expenses, for delivering the airplanes. But John wasn't doing it for the cash. The Icelandic flight in the Cessna 177 airplane was extremely dangerous. It was another adventure, another chance for John to prove he was better than his peers.

As soon as he returned, he flew to Europe for a June 30 meeting with the KGB in Vienna. This trip was particularly important because John had invited his mother, Peggy, to accompany him. Peggy had dreamed about visiting Italy. She still remembered most of the fairy tales that her father, Arthur Scaramuzzo, had told her about the old country.

"My Johnny had always told me that someday he was going to take me home to Italy," Peggy told me later. "I never really believed him though, 'cause kids, they say lots of things, and when he told me that he had bought the tickets and we really were going, why, I almost had cardiac arrest."

Peggy was sixty-six years old when she and John left New York City, but by the time the airplane landed at Leonardo da Vinci International Airport, a few miles outside Rome, she felt like a teenager.

Peggy took dozens of photographs, which she carefully pasted in a scrapbook. Just as she and her husband had kept a scrapbook of their achievements when they were first married, now Peggy and her favorite son would keep a record.

"I was just so excited," Peggy recalled. "I thought I was going to die and John, he says to me, 'Mama, you're embarrassing me,' because I was just so excited about being there and seeing everything. But I didn't care. It was just so wonderful. Oh, it was just so wonderful!"

After several days of frantic sightseeing, Peggy and John caught a seven A.M. train from Rome to Vienna, a seventeen-hour trip.

Vienna was disappointing after Rome. Peggy went on a few tours while John was out "conducting some sort of business," but she was ready to return to Scranton when it was time to leave Europe. Before she and John left their Viennese hotel, her son asked her to wear a money belt through U.S. Customs for him.

"It has some important papers in it that I don't want stolen," he told her. Peggy attached the bulky belt that John had sewn himself around her waist over her slip. It was not noticeable under her loose dress. Despite the discomfort, she obediently wore it throughout the long transatlantic flight to New York City.

"There's no one like my Johnny," Peggy said lovingly when we spoke later about the trip. "How many sons do you know who would take their mother on such an extraordinary trip?"

I didn't have the heart to tell her that John had used her. The money belt contained $24,000 from the KGB in fifty- and one-hundred-dollar bills. Federal laws prohibit U.S. citizens from bringing more than $5,000 in currency into the country without reporting it. I had been told about John's scheme by Arthur, who also had mentioned it to the FBI.

"John told me that he had used our mother as a pack mule to bring his spy money into the country," Arthur said during an interview. "He hid the money in a money belt and had her wear it, because he didn't think anyone would search a little old grandmother. 'Who's gonna search a sweet little old lady?' he asked me. And John was right. No one did."

# 35

The good times never last long enough. Two months after John's trip to Europe, Jerry arrived in Norfolk with troubling news. The *Niagara Falls* was being put into dry dock for overhaul, and the repairs would keep the ship out of commission for one year. Obviously, there was no need for the ship to use its cryptographic machines or to receive keylists when it was being worked on. So Jerry was losing his access.

Something else was bothering Jerry too. He and Brenda were having marital problems, in part because of his extended tours at sea aboard the supply ship. They'd been married nearly four years, but Jerry had been at sea much of that time.

"It's become a problem," Jerry explained.

John wasn't surprised, nor did he believe that Jerry's absences were the real root of Jerry's marital strife. Brenda was changing. In the beginning, when she was a teenager, she had depended upon Jerry for everything, and he had molded her. He had tried to do the same earlier to Shirley McClanahan and before that to his first wife, Lynn. John recognized what was happening. Brenda was changing, growing up. Jerry began to feel insecure around her, particularly since she was about to finish her education. He was being forced to accept the threat of being married to an equal partner, and it obviously scared him.

"Okay, Jerry," John said sympathetically, "why not request a transfer—shore duty?"

Jerry promised to try and after returning to California telephoned John with good news. He had been assigned to the Naval Telecommunications Center at Alameda, California, where he would not only be CMS custodian, but also chief of the message center and manager of the AUTODIN Center, which routed messages between the various services. John congratulated him. It was another perfect assignment for a spy. But during their conversations, John felt that Jerry was hiding something from him.

"Jerry was as easy to read as a book sometimes," John recalled. "The guy didn't have much imagination."

John pushed Jerry for an answer. What was bothering him? And Jerry finally confessed. He was thinking about retiring from the Navy!

"That asshole didn't realize the risk that he was going to put us in if he retired!" John recalled later. It was time, he decided, to have a "heart-to-heart" talk with Jerry. It was also time for John to get himself some of that personal insurance he needed. It was time once again for him to approach another one of his children.

John always learned from his mistakes. He had tried to recruit Margaret and Cynthia too suddenly. So he was much more cautious with his youngest daughter, Laura. He began wooing her in early 1978 when he first learned that she had decided to join the Army after her graduation. In June, two weeks before Laura was to report to basic training, John flew to Maine and brought her back to Norfolk for a vacation.

"Of all my children, Laura was the one that I knew the least and the one that caused me the most trouble as a parent," John said. "At this point in my life, I considered Margaret a total loser. Cynthia was destroyed. But Laura was sharp. She seemed to be intelligent and she seemed to be doing something with her life. She would beat up somebody if they picked on her, unlike the other two girls. She was tough. She was screwed up, of course. All my kids were, but she was doing something with her life. I knew too that Laura craved attention; she always wanted to be in the center of the spotlight.

"She had joined the Army because a neighbor was an Army recruiter, and I considered the Army the least attractive branch of the service. There was not a hell of a lot to learn in the Army, but still I was impressed and I told her that I was impressed with her over the telephone. Then I suggested that we get together before she went into the Army. So she came down to stay with me and, I mean, she was a total stranger to me. When I left home, she was a little girl, but now I got this attractive, adult woman visiting. I told her that I wanted to get to know her and that she really didn't know me. I took her out on the boat, and we went to bars together and went to dinner. I bought her several hundred dollars' worth of clothes, and I told her a lot about myself and my conduct during the marriage and why I hadn't been home much. I didn't have a chance to really find out what was on her mind, but I did develop some rapport with her, and that is what I wanted to do."

Laura considered the visit magical. For the first time in her life, her father paid attention to her. He showered her with affection and gifts. He spoke to her as an adult, almost an equal, and was very polite and complimentary. Her father was just plain "charming."

Laura was hearing John's side of the marriage story for the first time, she said later. It was a twisted version filled with self-justification, but for a young girl eager to win her father's approval, it was a convincing spiel. John didn't really have a choice when it came to abandoning his family, he explained. Whenever he came home, he and Barbara would fight.

"I honestly thought it was better for me to stay away," he told his daughter.

Laura was confused by this new side of her father. "I was his daughter," she explained to me later. "I was his child and I looked to this man as a daughter would look to a father. I wanted him so desperately to love me, and suddenly he was paying attention to me," Laura recalled. "We were going out together as father and daughter. He was buying me clothes. He was talking to me and asking me for my opinions."

By the time John took Laura to the bus station for her trip to Fort Gordon, Georgia, and basic training, Laura was a convert. "He was just wonderful," she said, "and I felt for the first time a closeness to him."

John continued to lavish his daughter with attention, and just before she finished basic training, he surprised her with a visit.

"It was really wild because the Army usually doesn't let soldiers who are in basic training go off base for special liberty, but my dad talked my commanding officer into giving me special permission to have dinner with him," Laura later recalled. "I had done extremely well, and I got to go out with my dad, and I was really excited and proud."

John had brought Laura a small bag of marijuana because he knew that she enjoyed getting high. After dinner, they smoked several joints together while seated in the car he had rented.

Laura was enthralled. "I remember thinking, 'Wow, here I am getting stoned with my father!' "

After a while, John began asking Laura about her training. Simple questions at first, about what she did and the type of equipment that she used. Laura had been assigned to communications and had just learned about cryptographic equipment and clearances.

"Well, how does all that stuff work in the Army?" John asked. "What do the machines look like?"

Laura told John everything he wanted to know.

"After that he wrote to me frequently," she recalled. "He kept saying that he wanted to make up for all the lost years when I was a child. No one but my dad was writing to me. No one. I really began to appreciate what I considered was his love and to accept it."

As a member of the Signal Corps, Laura was trained to operate the KG-27 cipher machine. She was sent to Fort Polk near Leesville, Louisiana, but she didn't fit in. At the time, Laura was a racist.

"I really hated blacks," she explained. "All they ever had been to me was trouble. I hated them and I have to tell you now that it was stupid and I am really sorry for it, but I was having trouble with blacks and I shared my problems with my dad."

It was during this period that Laura met Philip Mark Snyder. Her father would later claim that Laura dated him because "she wanted a nice white boy to protect her"—a charge that Laura didn't deny.

Mark had grown up in Lanham, a Maryland suburb of Washington,

D.C., where his father worked for the National Aeronautics and Space Administration. He had a medium build, sandy brown hair, and a quiet manner that hid a rebellious nature. As a teenager, Mark had carved a tattoo on his right arm, carefully filling the torn flesh with ink. He had dropped out of high school and worked as an electrician's apprentice until he was old enough to join the Army. He arrived in Fort Polk in February 1978, four months before Laura. They met when she was assigned to the Fifth Signal Battalion, which was his unit, but they didn't begin dating seriously until Laura moved into the same trailer park as Mark.

"We used to get together at night in the trailer park," Mark recalled. They would share a beer or smoke a joint and talk about how lousy the Army was. A short time after they began dating, the two set up housekeeping, and in August 1979, Laura discovered she was pregnant.

"Marrying Mark was an escape for me," Laura told me later. "I was looking for someone to love me and take care of me."

"We decided to get married because of the baby," Mark recalled. "To me it was really an esteem thing. I mean, we were in love and everything, but the fact that she was going to have my baby really influenced me to go ahead and do it."

They wed on September 17 in Simpson, a small community near Fort Polk, in a simple ceremony conducted by a justice of the peace. No member from either family was present. After the ceremony, Mark and Laura left immediately on a trip to Virginia and Maryland to break the news to Mark's parents and John. The newlyweds arrived in Norfolk a few weeks after Jerry Whitworth told John that he was thinking about retiring. For John, the timing of Laura's surprise visit was perfect.

One afternoon Laura accompanied her father to watch Patsy Marsee play softball. Afterward, they stopped at Knickerbocker's.

"We need money," Laura said. Mark had put them several thousand dollars in debt, she claimed, because he was hooked on marijuana.

"He doesn't sell it though," she told John. "Instead, he's been smoking it himself, which means he doesn't have any money to pay the dealer when he comes around, so we have to pay with money from our paychecks. Dad, we're broke and need money for this baby."

"In other words, you want some cash from me," John replied. He then began asking Laura the exact same questions that he had once asked Roberta Puma.

"Laura, would you spend two years in jail if, at the end of it, someone promised to give you, say, ten thousand dollars for your trouble?"

"Sure," Laura said. "I'd do two years for ten thousand."

"You know, Laura," John continued, "the Army is an awful lot like prison. In a sense, you already are in prison. You have to do your time. But there is more than one way to get compensated for it. A way to get ten thousand dollars or more. The same was true for me when I was in the Navy. I was doing my time, but there was a way for me to make extra money so we could afford things like nice apartments and sailboats. Your mother understood these things and I think you might too. What I am trying to tell you, Laura, is that I have been involved in something for a long time that involves crime and if you don't want to hear about it, then tell me now, because otherwise I intend to tell you how I got my money for things like my boat and my airplane, and how you can make a lot of money for yourself and Mark so the two of you can live very comfortably and afford the really nice things in life that you deserve, without too much trouble and totally without any danger."

Laura urged her father to continue.

"It was exactly the same bait that I used with Whitworth," John confided to me. "I mean, why would I change it since it worked with him? I began telling her about what I did, piece by piece, pulling in the line."

The only difference between John's pitch to Laura and his recruitment of Jerry was emphasis. He didn't bother mentioning allies like Israel. "I really talked about how much money she and Mark could make," John said. "It was something which they could do together, I said."

Just as he had done with Jerry, John declined to tell Laura whom he sold classified information to. Instead, he said that he had willing buyers.

"But Daddy, I'm pregnant," Laura said. "I'm going to get out of the Army, so there is no way I could get stuff for you."

"There are ways to deal with that problem," John remarked. "You don't have to get out of the service just because you are pregnant. Besides, what are you and Mark going to do if you get out of the service and have a baby? How are you going to make enough money to support a child? The Army is your job, Laura, and you can't just quit your job because you are going to have a baby. You guys aren't going to be able to afford a pot to piss in once you quit your job."

Laura was confused. "But I'm pregnant," she repeated.

John was quick with a solution: "Jeez, Laura, why don't you just get an abortion? I mean, you can always have more kids later."

"I told him that I could never do that," Laura explained to me later, "never kill my child, and my father said, 'Okay, then don't get an abortion. There still are other ways that we can get you back into the service.' I couldn't believe that he wanted me to abort my own child."

Laura told John that she would think about his proposition. Later that night, when she and Mark were alone, she told Mark that her father had suggested she get an abortion so she could stay in the Army. Mark was irritated. What kind of grandfather suggests aborting his grandchild? he demanded.

"It was just an option," Laura said.

"Well, I don't think it is an option," Mark replied.

Before Laura and Mark left Norfolk, John took them to a new car dealership and put a $500 down payment on a brand new Mazda GLC. It was a wedding present, he said. Laura was exuberant, even though she had no idea how she and Mark would make the payments. She was smart enough to know that John was putting them deeper in debt, but she still wanted that car.

A short time after Laura and Mark left Norfolk, Jerry finally made up his mind. He submitted the required forms in October 1979 to retire from the Navy.

Now that Jerry was definitely bailing out, John began turning up the heat on Laura. In October, he flew to the small Louisiana home town of Bill Wilkinson, his old Navy pal from the U.S.S. *Simon Bolivar*. By this time, Wilkinson was Imperial Wizard of the KKK and was delighted when John stopped to see him.

While there, John donned the white pointed hat and robe of the white supremacy group and posed for snapshots in the living room of Bill's home in front of the fireplace. Afterward, John asked Bill to appoint him kleagle of Virginia, which meant that he was the Klan's organizer in the state.

The next day, John flew to Leesville to see Laura, but he couldn't find her at the Army base.

"I finally located Mark and discovered that Laura had quit the Army and that she and Mark were living in this really shitty trailer away from the base," John recalled. "I went over there and let her have it. Here she was pregnant, married to a pothead. Her car isn't working, she's quit her job, she's living in a pigsty, and she's got no future, no prospects, nothing."

John quickly unleashed his anger: "Laura, you are worse than some nigger bitch," he said. "At least niggers have their babies and stay in the Army, and you are so fucking stupid that you didn't even get that right."

For the next several hours, John admonished his daughter. Her life was "totally fucked up," he said. The more he talked, the angrier and more vulgar he became. He called his daughter a "nigger welfare cunt." Even her unborn child was berated by John. "I can just imagine what an asshole this baby is going to be," he told her.

John slept on the couch in the living room of his daughter's trailer that night, but rose early the next morning. "I'll never forget what happened that morning," he recalled later. "Laura was pouring herself some corn flakes while Mark was getting dressed in his uniform. It is probably 5:30 A.M., and I came in and I sat down next to Laura at the kitchen table, and Mark comes walking in with a water pipe and a bowl of marijuana and he breaks out an ounce and starts smoking it. He is sitting there getting stoned, and Laura is looking at him with this hatred in her eyes. My God, it's a wonder she didn't draw blood."

Laura Walker recalled that breakfast encounter as a breaking point for her. She had been through a day of verbal abuse from her father, and now her husband was sitting before her, smoking pot for breakfast. She had made a terrible mistake. The honeymoon between them came to a screeching halt. After Mark left for work, Laura broke down. She told her father that her marriage was a disaster.

"If I hadn't gotten pregnant, I would have never married him. I know that," she said.

"Look, honey," John replied, "Mark isn't really that bad a guy. I like him. He's probably okay. The problem is that you two have to get back in the mainstream of life. You've got to get back in the Army and make some money. You guys could make about fourteen hundred a month if you go back in and, like I told you before, I can help you make a lot more than that." Once again, John offered to pay her to spy, only this time he was gentle, understanding.

"Okay, look, I can get you five hundred dollars, maybe even one thousand dollars each month, just as a retainer," John explained. "You don't have to do anything right now, except go back in the Army. Later, once you're back in and things are going smooth, when your career is good, then you can start getting stuff. I can give you five hundred now. Today! I brought it with me, but you have to get back in the Army."

Years later when I interviewed Laura, she told me that her father had developed a system for breaking her down. "His approach was almost like brainwashing, a brainwashing technique, although I didn't realize it at the time. First, he'd break you down and make you feel like the lowest form of life. He'd say you are never going to be successful. You are not very bright. You're just not anybody special. He'd break your spirit down and just devastate you. Then he'd come to your rescue. 'Why don't you let me help you make a lot of money?'"

The pressure that he put on her, Laura said, almost made her shake. She was willing to say almost anything to get him to ease up, back off, and tell her that he cared about her. Yet, Laura Walker insisted during her talks with me that she consistently declined to join her father as a spy.

In her testimony at Jerry Whitworth's trial, she was not that firm.

QUESTION: You refused each and every time?
ANSWER: Each and every time.
Q: And your refusal, I take it, was firm?
A: Sometimes it was; sometimes it wasn't.
Q: Now, when you say 'Sometimes it wasn't,' what was the basis for you not being firm?

A: Sometimes I would just be in an emotional low, and because he was so persistent. There were times when I felt broken and he really worked on that. So there were times when it was difficult for me to be firm.

Q: But in your mind you never were going to provide him with any classified information.

A: That's correct.

Q: And you never have?

A: That's correct.

John Walker was outraged when he read accounts of his daughter's testimony in a newspaper. "No matter what Laura says now, that morning she left me no doubt she'd do it. She agreed to be a spy, and the fact that she said that she would be a spy and took the five-hundred-dollar retainer I gave her and then never got back into the Army and never gave me any classified documents just shows what kind of unscrupulous cunt she really is."

John Walker vehemently defended his attempt to recruit his daughter to me. "She was pitched," he said, "not to enrich me in any way. The only reason that she was pitched was because I was her father and I wanted to help her out of the mess she was in. I merely did what any father would do. I helped my daughter out of a tight spot the best way that I could."

# 36

John and Laura were not the only Walkers who found the fall of 1979 a stressful time. Arthur Walker also faced what he later described as a "desperate" situation. His dream company, Walker Enterprises, was bankrupt and his marriage was souring. On an unseasonably warm afternoon in early December 1979, Arthur sat down in his office at Walker Enterprises and totaled his company's debits and credits on a yellow legal pad. The numbers almost made him break into tears.

How had his company fallen into such a bad financial condition? Where had he gone wrong? Everything had happened so fast.

"I was physically ill," Arthur recalled. "I was embarrassed and I was scared. I honestly thought that I was on the verge of losing my house, my cars, everything that Rita and I had worked for."

Arthur had one other thought as he looked over the numbers on the legal pad before him: "Why can't people stay in the Navy forever? Why had I ever gotten out?"

Arthur had done well in the Navy. From the time he enlisted in 1953, he had seen the Navy as a safe harbor where he could "feel comfortable and secure without having to worry about setting the world on fire."

Shortly after he and Rita married in May 1956, Arthur had announced, "I've decided to make the Navy my career. Why, if I put in twenty years and make chief petty officer—which shouldn't be too difficult—I could retire at age thirty-eight and receive one hundred and seventy-five dollars per month for the rest of my life. Can you imagine that, Rita? The Navy would pay us one hundred and seventy-five dollars per month! Why, we'd be in fat city!"

Rita considered the comment significant. Neither of them, she told me later, ever "dreamed big." Money wasn't going to be the driving force in their lives. A decent job, a decent home, a decent income, and decent kids. That's what life was all about.

In the Navy, Arthur's motto was "Go along, get along." Promotions came slowly, but they came. And when they did, Arthur recognized they were often based on luck and longevity as well as work. "I never looked upon myself as unique or anything like that," Arthur told me during a prison interview. "I always saw myself as just a run-of-the-mill sort of guy and that really never bothered me."

In the 1960s, when other sailors clamored for duty on a nuclear-powered sub, Arthur stayed behind on diesel-powered boats. It took him seven years to rise to the petty officer rank of sonarman first class. By comparison, John rose to a similar rank in less than five years. The Navy did commission Arthur as an ensign, but he was chosen during the post-Korean War period when there was a shortage of naval officers and the Navy decided to lower its qualifications. Even after he became an officer, Arthur's career was not glamorous. His best assignment was his last, when he was named an instructor of antisubmarine warfare techniques at the Atlantic Fleet Tactical School in Norfolk. He taught there from 1968 until his retirement in July 1973, and during that assignment, he rose slowly through the ranks to lieutenant commander.

Arthur's personal life was as ordinary as his career. Rita had stayed home and raised their three children. He had been active in a few neighborhood projects, but nothing outstanding. They lived on a tight budget. Their only real financial asset was their red-brick home, which had cost them $27,500 in 1968.

As long as Arthur was in the Navy, his life was orderly, routine, and satisfying. His kids did well in school and avoided the drug and truancy problems that John's encountered.

But in July 1973 the Navy nudged Arthur out, and his life slowly began to fall apart. At first, things looked promising. Arthur went into business with some sailor pals and earned about $1,000 per month peddling frozen chickens, playing cards, and candles to military exchanges. The sales commissions were enough, with his Navy pension, to pay the bills.

Arthur wasn't happy though; he didn't like sales and there were problems with his partners. So he went out on his own, selling car radios. Military communities were filled with young sailors anxious to upgrade the radio systems in their cars.

Arthur got a $10,000 second mortgage on the house, filled the garage with inventory, and went to work. His pitch was simple. Why pay several hundred dollars for a mundane radio manufactured by an auto maker in Detroit when you could buy a superior unit from him at half the price? His best customers turned out to be car dealers who were dissatisfied with what Detroit had to offer.

Within a few months, Arthur was being pressured by several dealers to install the radios that he sold. He was on a roll, but no bank in town would give him another loan. So Arthur turned to John for help, and the two brothers formed Walker Enterprises, incorporating it in June 1975—one year before John and Barbara divorced.

As usual, John thought big, and from the start, he pushed Arthur to expand. At first, cash wasn't a problem. John just dug into his pockets and advanced Arthur a series of personal loans. By 1976, Walker Enterprises had moved into a large rented building and Arthur had hired a receptionist and four mechanics to install radios and air conditioning units. But the company began to flounder in 1977, at about the same time John began withdrawing his financial support. By the next year, Arthur had lost all of his big customers. Detroit auto makers had gotten tough and had begun pressuring dealers to buy accessories directly from them, not from local outfits like Arthur's. By late 1979, Arthur's dream company had become a horror show of debts.

"Things at home really deteriorated too," Arthur Walker recalled. After Barbara and John were divorced, Rita severed all ties with her brother-in-law, and she urged Arthur to do the same.

"Art's friendship with John really got to be a bone of contention between us," Rita acknowledged later. "I didn't like John, never did. Also, Arthur was killing himself. He was working round the clock at the business, and John didn't do a damn thing. I really resented it."

On that December 1979 afternoon—when he totaled up the company's debits and credits on a legal pad—Arthur finally stopped fooling himself. He called John to ask for advice.

"Goddamn Arthur, this is a nightmare," John said after examining the company's books. "Arthur, we got to shut this baby down right now before everything gets flushed down the drain. Let's shut the doors and say the hell with it."

That night, John typed a "kiss off" letter for Arthur to mail to all of Walker Enterprises's creditors. The company had gone bust.

Shutting down Walker Enterprises wasn't as simple as John had naively promised. Several companies sued, and the IRS called Arthur to task for not withholding his employees' payroll taxes. Arthur was hounded by feelings of guilt and failure.

One afternoon, Rita found him in their bedroom laying out his old Navy uniform.

"What are you doing, Art?" she asked.

"Oh, I don't know," he replied. "Just making certain I got everything, I guess. You know, with all the trouble going on in Iran with the hostages, you never know when the Navy might call me back."

Rita began worrying about Arthur's mental stability.

"He was really acting strange," she recalled.

John recognized his brother's despondency, too, but in it, he also saw an opportunity. Shortly after New Year's Day in 1980, John invited Arthur to lunch. He picked him up and drove north about two miles from Arthur's house to a tiny restaurant at the end of a small shopping center. Along the way, John tried to cheer up his older brother.

"Life can really be a bitch," John said. "But, hey, we're the Walker boys, remember? Everything is going to work out."

Arthur didn't think so. During lunch, all he could talk about was how terrible his life had become.

"I feel almost helpless for the first time in my life," he told John. "I don't seem to have any control over anything. What's happening here? I mean, I was trying to do the right thing at work, but we just kept getting deeper and deeper in debt. Now I got to get a job and feed the family and come up with some way to pay off all these debts."

After lunch, the two men returned to John's truck.

"Damn it," Arthur said, "I could just cry."

"C'mon, let's walk," John said. He put his arm around Arthur's shoulder. As the two brothers stepped down the sidewalk, John said, "I think I know a way for you to get out of this mess."

# 37

John was scheduled to meet his KGB contact in Vienna on January 26, 1980. Having in his own mind safely recruited both Laura and Arthur, he left for Oakland on January 19 with a dual purpose: pick up whatever film Jerry had for him and convince Jerry to change his mind about retiring.

Jerry needed both a kick and a carrot. The carrot was easy. John intended to offer Jerry more money if he stayed in the Navy and kept producing as a spy. He was certain the KGB would back him up. But the kick would come first. Jerry's access at Alameda was excellent, but Jerry wasn't producing. Knowing that he was about to retire, he had begun to lose interest in spying.

"It's just too difficult to get anything good, Johnny," Jerry complained when they got together. The communications center at Alameda was much too crowded, and Jerry was worried about being discovered. Just before he had left the U.S.S. *Niagara Falls,* he had been caught by his boss, Terry Cliffton Pierce, looking at schematics of cryptographic equipment.

Pierce had demanded an immediate explanation, but Jerry, keeping his cool, had wiggled out of the situation by claiming that he was having a problem with one of the cryptographic machines and was trying to repair it. The answer had satisfied Pierce, but just the same, the incident scared Jerry.

"Do you honestly believe you can just quit?" John finally asked, after listening patiently to Jerry's complaints. "Don't you understand the danger you're putting us in, not to mention Brenda? Who do you think we're dealing with, some dipshit in western New York?"

Jerry seemed amused. Why should he or John have anything to worry about? Hadn't John been assuring him that the stolen cryptographic material was going to ally nations? Why would they wish to hurt either of them? John was overreacting in an attempt to keep him from quitting.

"You've been reading too many spy novels," Jerry said.

"Jerry, this is not some two-bit spy book," John replied. "What I'm trying to make you understand is that you could be putting us both in danger by retiring. The people I have been dealing with are very dangerous people. The items that we have given them are *only* good as long as no one knows they have been compromised. Now do you understand what I'm trying to tell you?"

Jerry continued to brush John's warnings aside. Once again, he accused John of exaggerating.

John exploded. "You dumb asshole!" he snapped. "You could get us both killed! This is not some stupid game! Haven't you ever heard of the fucking umbrella trick? Don't you read the goddamn newspapers? This shit really happens!

"The people we are dealing with," John added, his voice intense, "can reach anywhere in the world—anywhere! You can't hide from them. They are that powerful!"

Jerry's demeanor changed. John's comment about the "umbrella trick" was a direct reference to the sensational September 1978 murder of Georgi Markov, a Bulgarian defector, who had died mysteriously in a London hospital. Before his death, Markov told the police that he had been poked in the leg with the tip of an umbrella. Surgeons discovered a minute hollow metal ball in Markov's thigh containing traces of ricin, one of the five most toxic substances in the world. Police theorized that the murderer jabbed the ball into Markov's leg with the umbrella tip, and the poison escaped after the heat of Markov's body melted wax used to seal two tiny holes in the ball. Because Markov was a persuasive anticommunist commentator for the British Broadcasting Corporation, intelligence officials immediately claimed the KGB had executed Markov. John had read all the news stories he could find about Markov's death, and he and Jerry had discussed the daring murder shortly after it occurred.

"Jerry's face got white, and I realized that he had finally figured out what I was saying," John said. "I think he had actually convinced himself through the years that we were helping the fucking Israelis! I think he was genuinely surprised when it dawned on him who I was selling the information to. Not that it mattered. After all, I told him at the start that the buyers could have been the Mafia or an enemy as well as an ally. He knew that from the start."

The next morning, John had a chat with Brenda about Jerry's request for retirement. The discussion was held after Jerry left for work. "We were sitting in the living room having coffee and Brenda was all excited about her school work, bubbling on with joy about how Jerry was getting out and she was going to become a doctor of nutrition and also a doctor of medicine so she could do research or whatever, and as I'm sitting there listening to her ramble on and on, I thought, 'Jeez, she had been married to Jerry for five or six years by now, and he has gotten about one hundred and fifty thousand dollars in spy money, and they have been living this good life, and she doesn't have any fucking idea about what is going on!' I mean, here is a person with an IQ of God only knows, one hundred and eighty or more, and she thinks Jerry is going to be able to support her schooling if he gets out of the Navy."

John decided to burst Brenda's bubble. "Brenda, you realize, don't you, that Jerry and I have income on the side through an interest that we invested in together?" John asked.

Yes, she understood that.

John was blunt. "That money is contingent on Jerry having a certain type of job and being in a certain geographic area, and the scenario that you just have spelled out to me makes it clear that Jerry isn't going to be getting any more money from our investments."

Brenda seemed unconcerned. They could manage without the extra money, she said.

"Brenda, I'm not sure that you have any conception of what kind of income Jerry really has," John said. "I think you should talk to him about it." *

After Jerry got home from work, he and John talked again about his decision to retire. It was time for the carrot.

"I think we should ask for more money," John told Jerry. Five or six thousand dollars per month. Jerry liked the idea. John went on to explain that he'd come up with a way for Jerry to photograph documents at Alameda without being caught.

"What you need is a van to photograph this shit in," John explained. "Look, I'll try to get you, say, ten thousand for a new van. You drive it to work and at lunch time you tell folks that you have to take a nap or whatever. You stick stuff in your briefcase, take it with you, and photograph stuff, then you simply take the stuff back in your office."

It sounded like a workable plan to Jerry.

"By the time I left," John recalled, "I felt confident that Jerry was going to pull his request for retirement and buy a van."

John received some unexpected help in scaring Jerry back into line from an unusual source. Christopher John Boyce, a twenty-seven-year-old Californian convicted of being a KGB spy, had escaped from the federal correction institution at Lompoc, California.

Jerry had followed Boyce's trial and discussed it with John, who also had developed an interest in Boyce and his partner, Daulton Lee, the subjects of the 1979 best-selling book, *The Falcon and the Snowman: A True Story of Friendship and Espionage* by *New York Times* reporter Robert Lindsey.

Several members of the media speculated after Boyce escaped that he had been broken out of a federal prison by specially trained agents of the KGB, who had smuggled him out of the country and into Russia.

Jerry followed the story closely. Imagine, the KGB breaking a spy out

---

*Brenda Reis Whitworth declined to be interviewed. This conversation is based on John Walker's statements to the author and the FBI, and various polygraph examinations that John took.

of prison! Sweet Jesus, if that was true, Russian agents really did have a long reach.

John barely had time to unpack on his return to Norfolk before he headed for Vienna. The wind was blowing and it was snowing when John met with his KGB contact on January 26. John had told the Russians in a dead drop note delivered a month earlier that Jerry had been transferred to Alameda, but he had not mentioned that Jerry had put in for retirement. Now that he had recruited Laura and Arthur, and also convinced Jerry to stay in, John felt the meeting with the KGB would go smoothly. But he found his KGB contact in a foul mood.

"Why did Jerry move? What's wrong with him?" the agent asked.

"He had to move," John explained. "His ship was put in dry dock and all his equipment was shut down."

"He was supposed to be aboard the ship for three years," the agent said. "You promised us three years."

"Jesus Christ!" John responded, "I don't run the fucking Navy! Look, Jerry found out that his ship was going into dry dock for repairs, so he got himself reassigned to Alameda, and that's one hell of a good spot."

John named the cryptographic systems that Jerry was working with. They included the KW-36 and the KGB's much beloved KW-7. He also had access to some technical manuals and lots of message traffic. The problem, John explained, was that Jerry didn't have anywhere safe to photograph documents. The communications center was much too busy to risk Jerry smuggling in his Minox for photographs.

"But I've come up with a solution," John explained. "You need to buy Jerry a van so that he can photograph documents in it during his noon lunch break."

John expected the KGB agent to be impressed by his solution, but instead, the agent looked confused and asked John to explain his idea once again. The problem, John discovered during the second explanation, was that the agent didn't realize what John was talking about when he used the word *van*. The KGB agent thought he meant a large truck used by companies for deliveries. How, the agent asked John at one point, could Jerry drive such a vehicle to work without appearing suspicious?

"Listen," John said, after explaining what a van looked like, "everyone in California rides around in vans. It ain't going to be a problem." John couldn't believe how stupid his handler seemed to be.

Once again, the KGB agent broke one of his own rules and hustled John into a Vienna coffeehouse so that the two of them could get warm. They sat, as before, at a back corner table, and as they drank their hot drinks in silence, John noticed that his KGB handler seemed nervous. Outside on the sidewalk again, the agent and John struck a deal. The Russians were willing to give Jerry $10,000 for a van, and they would also pay John and Jerry as much as $12,000 per month for good crypto, the agent said. But that was not all. "Tell Jerry we will pay him a ten-thousand-dollar bonus if he can get unbroken crypto for three straight months. This is important."

The agent also told John that the KGB couldn't get their replica of a KWR-37 cryptographic machine, which they had built according to the technical manuals that Jerry had stolen, to decipher Navy messages. John immediately volunteered to get Jerry to look into the problem.

"There is one other thing you should know," John said. "I've recruited Laura and talked with Arthur."

The KGB agent was so shocked by John's announcement that he stopped in his tracks for a moment.

Why, he demanded hotly, had John taken such a dangerous step without permission? "He was really pissed off about Laura," John recalled. "He told me that she would never give us anything and that she was a big risk. I don't know how he knew that, but he did. He told me she was nothing but trouble."

John did his best to cool the agent's anger. He explained that Barbara knew he was a spy and that she had told all of his kids that he was a spy. Recruiting Laura and Arthur might have been foolish, but John didn't consider either of them a real danger. "Laura is too weak a person to ever turn me in," he said, "and Arthur would never turn on me because we are of the same blood."

The agent was unconvinced. "There are people in your country who have come to us before. You aren't the first," he snapped, "and some of these people have helped the cause of peace for years and retired, yes, actually retired and died in their beds of old age without anyone ever knowing they were our friends.

"But," the agent said, "there have been those who have come to us through the years who have been foolish. They have been exposed. The chances of being captured expand each time another person is added to the circle."

John listened closely, but his natural cockiness kept him from revealing any outward anxiety. Suddenly, the agent became silent. He stopped and faced John.

"People can get hurt in this business," he said. After several silent seconds, he added, "You must realize that you are not the only person at risk here."

John was confused. His first thought, he said later, was that the KGB agent was suggesting John's family could be in danger. But he later decided that the agent was talking about himself. "It suddenly hit me that this guy had his ass on the line too! I mean, he had to explain to someone in Moscow why Whitworth had been transferred, and he had to get us raises and tell his bosses back in Red Square how I had recruited Laura and Art without his permission. I think he was a bit worried too. I mean, who wants to be sent to Siberia?"

The two men spoke for a long time, and eventually they both began to relax. Before their meeting ended, the KGB agent asked John for a favor.

"Tell me, my friend," he said, "how is my English?"

John nearly burst out laughing, but he knew the agent was serious. Perhaps the misunderstanding about vans had made him question his grasp of the language.

"Your English is okay," John replied.

"Is that all?" the KGB agent responded.

"It's fine, really, although it is somewhat outdated sometimes."

"What do you mean?" the agent asked.

"Well, we don't use words like *dough* or *bread* for money anymore."

"What do you call it?"

"Money or cash."

Both men laughed.

"It wouldn't hurt if you threw in a bit of profanity," John continued. "You see, most American men cuss a lot." There was nothing wrong, John explained, enjoying the role of teacher, in occasionally sprinkling a conversation with obscenities. "Of course, if you really want to fit in around sailors, there is only one word you need to know." John told the agent that military veterans loved to use a four-letter word that was slang for intercourse. The agent seemed offended by such language. He said that only the uneducated used such vulgarities, but he had read and heard stories about American leaders such as Richard Nixon using such words in private.

Before the two men parted, the agent promised to deliver $200,000 to John on May 18 at a dead drop outside Washington. This would include raises in pay and also money for the van. "From now on, no more recruitment without talking to me first," he added. "We must be careful."

The Russian began to walk away, but stopped, turned, and said something that John couldn't quite make out because of the wind. As John made his way back to the U-Bahn and his hotel, he realized what the agent had said.

John's KGB handler had taken John's advice seriously. He had told John to "get fucked."

"He really had a great sense of humor for a Russian," John said later. "I was beginning to like him a lot."

John telephoned Jerry after returning from Vienna to Norfolk. "Have you seen Mary Ann recently?" he asked during a brief conversation. It was a prearranged signal. Exactly one hour after Jerry received that telephone call, he drove to a pay telephone several miles from his house. When it rang, he answered. John was on the line calling from a pay phone in Norfolk.

"Jerry, you should go ahead and buy the van," John said. "We can get ten thousand dollars for it. Also, there's a bonus for you if you can get three months of unbroken yellow [yellow crypto keylist cards]."

"I've canceled my retirement request," Jerry said. "Everything is a go!"

# *38*

---

Had John Walker, Jr., not been a spy, he would have liked to have joined the FBI after retiring from the Navy. This is what he said, with all seriousness, during one of our prison interviews. The idea of exposing people, catching them doing something wrong, really turned John on.

As it was, he became a private detective after his sales association folded. His first job was with Wackenhut, an international security company.

John simply appeared at the Wackenhut office one afternoon and asked to speak to Philip Prince, the manager of investigations. Prince had been in charge of Wackenhut's office in Norfolk for only one month and had been a private detective for only four months, but his inexperience didn't show. He was a highly decorated retired Marine who had served three tours of duty in Vietnam. His military experience gave Prince a self-assured style that impressed John.

John's proposition was simple. He was willing to work dirt cheap in return for on-the-job training.

"Money really isn't a problem," he told Prince. "I've got my pension and I've made some really hot investments. I don't want to earn more than five thousand a year or I'll get Uncle Sam peeking into my knickers."

John's timing proved to be perfect. Wackenhut had been much more interested in promoting its security guard services in Norfolk than in investigating cases. As a result, Prince's office was poorly staffed, poorly equipped, and poorly budgeted.

"He was very up front about what he wanted," Prince told me later, "and quite frankly, I was impressed. John spoke intelligently and at the same time admitted that he had a lot to learn. The biggest thing was he was dying to go to work. I mean immediately!"

Prince sent John to Thomas Nelson Community College, where he whizzed through several special courses on arrest procedures and suspects' rights that the state required before granting a private investigator a license.

At the time, Wackenhut handled mostly messy divorce cases. Virginia didn't have a no-fault divorce law, so angry spouses often hired Wackenhut to find evidence of adultery. Prince was trying to move the agency away from such piddling cases into investigations of insurance fraud, a more interesting and lucrative area.

Because of its shipyards and large blue-collar work force, the Tidewater area was a hotbed for workmen's compensation claims, and it was not unusual for an insurance company to find itself being ordered to pay benefits to a disabled worker for the rest of his life. However, if an insurer could prove the worker hadn't been seriously injured while on the job or had exaggerated those injuries, it could either cancel or reduce its liability payments.

John soon became Wackenhut's star investigator of insurance fraud. While other Wackenhut employees were content to punch a time clock, he worked nonstop. Each case John was assigned seemed bigger and more important to him than the last. And he refused to give up until he obtained a "kill"—his terminology for catching a disabled worker doing some physical task that he shouldn't have been able to accomplish because of a work-related injury.

John hated to waste time and rather than waiting for a "suspect" to do something wrong, he began "setting them up."

His first so-called sting operation involved a suspect with a back injury. John let the air out of one of the man's car tires and then took photographs of him lifting the spare tire out of his car trunk.

"John had a theory about being a private investigator," a fellow detective, Lonzo Thompson, told *The Washington Post* later. "His theory was: Always set the person up. Just don't sit there. Tempt them. Play on a person's greed. He felt everybody was basically greedy and you always get them through greed."

John's sting operations soon took on the elaborateness of a *Mission: Impossible* operation. He even gave each sting its own name. He was proudest of the "Great Grocery Giveaway," a scam that involved no less than four or five fellow detectives.

The grocery giveaway sting was created to catch a woman who had suffered a back injury. John had a special circular printed that said the woman had won $50 worth of free groceries at a neighborhood store. But she had to collect them within five minutes. The woman raced to the store without putting on her neck and back braces. In the parking lot was a cart filled with the heaviest groceries that John could find. As the woman lifted the bags out of the cart, John hid in his van and took pictures.

John remained the master of the sting. "I really saw myself as the producer," John told me later. "I would use secretaries, professional actors, just about anyone I wanted to hire to produce a perfect scam. I could pull one on anyone and make it believable.

"The things I did as a private detective," John continued, "were much more exciting and imaginative than what I did as a spy."

Tempting people and catching them seemed to prove to John that his view of mankind as basically corrupt was accurate.

John always posed as someone else on a case, even when he didn't need to. It was all part of the drama and intrigue. His favorite disguise was that of a Roman Catholic priest. He was accused of posing at various times as a Boy Scout leader looking for a campsite, a surveyor purporting to survey the land in the vicinity and a bird-watcher attempting to take photographs of wildlife.

Besides disguises, John became an expert in other phases of private detective work. He spent more than $25,000 on various video cameras, pinhole lenses, and electronic bugging devices. He also bought several trick canes: one contained a short sword, another had a stiff spring inside it that could be used as a club, a third was a black-powder rifle, and the last had a secret vial inside that could be used to hide poison or alcohol.

"Most investigators only wore a gun when they were going on an assignment which was obviously dangerous," Prince recalled later, "but John was married to his gun." Whenever Prince and John went out to lunch, John removed his sports jacket. "I really think he wanted people to see that he was carrying a gun," Prince said.

Sometimes John carried three guns at a time. "Look, I'm not a weight lifter, I have poor eyesight and I'm vulnerable because of that," John told a co-worker one day. "A guy like me has to make sure that he has superior firepower."

Wackenhut was hired to provide security at a wedding reception one afternoon, and John was assigned to help check invitations at the front gate of the posh estate. The night before, he startled a fellow detective by telephoning to ask what kind of "firepower" the man was bringing with him.

"Here's what I'm packing," John volunteered. "My first three rounds will be armor-piercing bullets so I can take out a car if it crashes the gate by shooting its engine. The next two rounds will be hollow-point bullets for maximum stopping power when the suspects exit the car. I'm also bringing my rifle with the banana clips, which can carry up to ninety rounds."

His fellow detectives never knew when John was telling the truth or exaggerating, in part because he so frequently mixed the two. One of John's co-workers recalled, for example, that John had taught him how to investigate burglaries.

"Do you know how you can tell if a professional burglar or some kid ransacked a house?" John asked him one day. "A kid will go through a chest of drawers from the top down, which means he has to open and close each drawer as he works his way down the chest. But a pro starts at the bottom and works up so all he has to do is open each drawer. He never has to close a drawer."

John was right, the co-worker said, but he couldn't leave well enough alone. "After he told me that, he started telling me how he had solved more burglaries than the entire police department. It was just nonsense."

Prince liked John, but Michael Bell, the manager of investigations for Wackenhut's Richmond office, didn't. He thought John was a dangerous "windbag." When singer John Denver arrived in Norfolk to perform, Wackenhut was hired to provide security. John was anxious to help, but Bell convinced Prince to give him the plum assignment.

"John was furious that he wasn't involved," Bell recalled later, "but there wasn't anything he could do about it."

That didn't stop John from telling people that he had helped. "John Denver never gives anyone autographs," he bragged after the concert to a girlfriend, "but I did manage to get him to sign a few things for me."

It was conversations like this that made some detectives at Wackenhut wonder about John's credibility. One night, Prince took John to the UDT Seal Club, a watering hole for retired Seals, the elite special forces in the Navy.

"Most of the guys who hung out there were rough boys who had been through a lot of combat and training, and weren't afraid of getting into a good fight," Prince recalled later.

John's usual swagger disappeared when the two men entered the bar, and his chatter about scams and gun battles never surfaced. After a few quick drinks, John excused himself and left.

The next morning when John came to work, he shrugged off his obvious discomfort in the Seal Club. "The kind of shit we are doing is just as dangerous as anything those guys ever did," he told Prince, but Prince disagreed. He told John that anyone could talk a good game, but few could deliver in a combat situation.

Prince asked John how he would have reacted if someone in the bar had picked a fight with him. Without any sign of embarrassment, John said that he would have talked his way out of a fight. "It would have been the only smart thing for me to do because of my size and age," John explained. "I'm not into macho bullshit." But, John added, that didn't mean he wouldn't have gotten even.

"Phil, it might take three years or even longer," John said, "but I'm a Sicilian, and we Sicilians always get revenge."

To illustrate his point, John recalled how he had gotten even one night with a woman friend who had irritated him. The two of them were in a bar when the woman decided that John should drive her from Norfolk to the seashore nearby. John was drunk and didn't want to go, but ultimately gave in. He said the woman undid the zipper on his trousers while he was driving and engaged in oral sex with him as he drove. A few seconds after the woman began, John reached the toll booths on the Virginia Beach Expressway. He had a quarter and could have driven through the automatic toll gate, but instead, he aimed his car at a toll booth with a female attendant in it and gradually brought the car to a stop. The woman engaged in sex with John looked up into the face of a startled attendant, John said, laughing.

"If you fuck with me," John explained, "you'll pay a price."

# 39

Working as a private detective dovetailed perfectly with John's spying. It gave him an instant justification for a quick trip to Washington and frequent excursions to California.

On May 18, 1980, John retrieved $200,000 from the KGB at a dead drop. Twelve days later, he and Patsy Marsee flew to Oakland where Jerry and Brenda were waiting. Jerry led the group outside the airport terminal to see his silver and blue Dodge Ram van. Inside was a chilled bottle of champagne and an assortment of cheeses, which the foursome savored on the ride to Jerry and Brenda's new condominium in San Leandro. When they were alone the next morning, John counted out Jerry's share: $100,000 in fifty- and one-hundred-dollar bills. Jerry was excited. "I've never held one hundred thousand dollars before!"

The new van was working flawlessly at Alameda, Jerry reported. He had told his subordinates that his physician had placed him on a rigorous program of morning exercises that required him to take a noontime nap. This gave him the freedom to photograph documents whenever he wished by simply slipping them into his briefcase and going out to his van to rest. Once inside, with the curtains pulled tight, Jerry could photograph without fear of interruption. He merely returned the documents after he finished. He was confident that he could earn the $10,000 bonus that John's "buyers" had offered for three months' worth of consecutive keylists.

A few days after John returned from California, he received an unexpected visit from Laura and his new grandson, Christopher, less than a month old. Laura was going to show Christopher to Mark's parents. Then she would continue north to Maine to show Barbara the baby.

John made a fuss over Christopher and Laura, and then, after dinner that night, once again pressured her to become a spy. John's offer apparently remained on Laura's mind when she arrived in Skowhegan, because she told her mother about it. Laura's visit and revelation that spring came at a dramatic time in Barbara Walker's life. Her beloved son, Michael, had decided to leave her.

In June 1980 Michael went to Norfolk to be with John. He was seventeen years old, and Barbara had not been able to control him for some time. Michael never liked Maine and had resented his mother's decision to move there after the divorce. Barbara's sister and her husband lived in an old farmhouse near the tiny Maine hamlet of Anson. Michael described the farm, years later, as being "in the boondocks—the real sticks."

"It was five miles to the nearest store," Michael said. "Annie and Bob and their kids had ninety cats and old dogs. I just wasn't used to anything like it. I had to learn how to milk cows and I didn't like that. They had chickens running everywhere, and they were mean and chased me. When it was time for dinner, Bob would grab a chicken and twist off its head. After seeing that, I stopped eating chicken and still won't. They are the lowest, mangiest creatures on earth. I was miserable on that farm. We didn't like our cousins, and they hated us. They called us city slickers and we called them country bumpkins."

Michael talked to his father only twice during the first year after the divorce. He pleaded with him during both conversations: "Please let me come live with you, Dad! I hate it here." But Barbara and John both said no. John didn't want to be bothered and Barbara wanted Michael to make a fresh start. He had failed seventh grade in Norfolk, so Barbara enrolled him in the seventh grade in Anson in the fall of 1976. The fourteen-year-old newcomer didn't fit in. Michael's language was as filthy as his father's, he was a chain smoker—"I only smoke filterless Camels, a man's cigarette"—and he was impossible to discipline. His goal as a student was to be so disruptive that he would be suspended from school. He succeeded.

Barbara's decision to move to Skowhegan in 1977 had been prompted, in part, by Michael. The Walkers had been living with Annie and Bob for about one year when Michael hit his twelve-year-old cousin, Jennifer, in the face several times with his fists. Both families decided it was time for Barbara to find her own place.

"My mom had gone through all the money that she got from the divorce," Michael recalled. "She had paid to have plumbing added to Annie and Bob's house and she had taken everyone out for lobster dinners several times. She was still drinking a lot too. The money just slipped through her hands."

Once settled in Skowhegan, Barbara again enrolled Michael in the seventh grade. "School had started about three days before my mom took me in, and when I went into the classroom everyone was watching me," Michael remembered. "I was really scoping out the women, and I was blowing it with the teacher but making it with the chicks."

Michael's teacher asked him to take a seat and open his textbook.

"What page, man?" he replied.

The woman teacher corrected him. "Don't call me 'man.'"

"Okay, man, now what page was that?"

"I remember that everyone started howling," Michael recalled. "That was the beginning of the end, because the teacher gave me detention, which meant I had to stay and work after school, and I wasn't going to stand for that. I knew I was on the way out of there."

There was one teacher who tried to work with Michael. Years later, Michael could only remember his last name: Nixon. Each morning when Michael arrived at school, William Nixon would give him a pep talk. "We're going to work hard today, right, Mr. Walker?" But despite Nixon's encouragement and personal interest, Michael stayed in trouble.

"I would come to school stoned as hell on marijuana," he recalled. "I mean really blown away. I was just stoned out of my mind. Someone would say, 'Hey, Mike, wanta try some coke?' and I'd say, 'Sure, man, why not?' Or someone would say, 'Hey, Mike, got some great speed here,' and I'd say, 'Hey man, give me some!' I let my hair grow down to my waist and I didn't care about nothing but having a good time and getting high."

Michael began mimicking the Hollywood stereotype of a marijuana-crazed, fun-loving teenager. Even when he wasn't stoned, he acted as if he were by always taking on the appearance of someone without any cares, worries, or thoughts.

"I was seeing the principal every day, and when I was in class I was acting like an idiot. I spent my time drawing pictures of marijuana leaves on the desks. I remember once we had to take this test, so I drew little pictures in all those tiny squares you were supposed to black in for answers, and the principal called me in and he said the test showed I had an IQ of two."

Once again Michael dropped out of the seventh grade. He and two other Skowhegan boys spent their days smoking pot in a shed. They called themselves the "Barn Rats," and they installed an old carpet, lounge chairs, and an elaborate stereo system. They began stealing to make enough money to buy marijuana.

"We would stake out a house and watch it so we knew when the people left for work," recalled Michael. "We'd break in by just kicking in a door or a window with our boots. I got real good at rummaging through drawers with my knuckles so I wouldn't leave any fingerprints."

Barbara knew that her son was smoking marijuana and running wild, but she had been unable to control Cynthia and Laura as teenagers, and Michael was more stubborn and had been spoiled more as a child than either of them. She simply didn't know what to do.

According to his own account, Michael successfully burglarized five houses in Skowhegan before the police closed in on the Barn Rats. A juvenile court judge gave Michael a blistering lecture, but because it was his first offense, he was put on probation for six months. At the time, Michael didn't know his father had been arrested on burglary charges as a teenager in Scranton in 1955 and had gone through an almost identical process. When I later told him about his father's criminal past as a juvenile, Michael considered the similarities more than mere coincidence. It was another example to him of how father and son were inexplicably bound, how fate was leading him along the same path as his father.

Barbara was embarrassed and alarmed by her son's arrest and decided that Michael needed professional help. She telephoned Marti Stevens, a trained counselor and schoolteacher with a good reputation for helping kids in trouble. Stevens agreed to accept Michael as one of six special students she was tutoring. She taught Michael basic courses for half a day; the other hours, he was required to work at the farm because Barbara couldn't afford to pay tuition.

"I had forty cows to handle and chickens to feed," Michael recalled. "I hated it, but I wanted to make it. I didn't want to be stuck in seventh grade all my life. I was still getting stoned every day, but I was trying, really trying. I remember being out in a field shoveling frozen cow shit on a freezing February day. Finally, I said, 'Screw this, I can't handle this teacher and I quit,' but three days later, she called me up and got me back out there. She told me that she was going to make me pass my tests and get me into high school and she helped me. On the day of the tests, I went to school straight and I passed 'em, and that fall, I was back in school with kids my age and they all said, 'Hey Mike, how'd you do this?' and I said, 'Hey, I got my ways.' "

Much to Barbara's surprise, Michael did well in school. Off came his shoulder-length hair. Gone was the small plastic bag of marijuana that he used to carry boldly in his shirt pocket. Michael even began bringing school books home. The reason for the change was simple: Michael was in love.

"It was the first time I really was in love with a girl, even though I had been having sex with this other chick in Skowhegan quite a long time," he recalled. "I wanted to keep this relationship strong and healthy." Michael was sixteen, his girlfriend was eighteen. She had a car, money, and came from a well-respected family.

But after nearly two years, Michael's girlfriend told him that she wanted to date other men. Without missing a beat, Michael returned to hanging out, smoking dope, and making trouble.

During the summers of 1978 and 1979, Michael spent several weeks with his father in Norfolk. They developed a relationship during these sessions that Michael later had trouble describing. Most of the time, John was more of a "best buddy" to Michael than a father. But John still made it clear that he was in charge.

"We had a really neat friendship, but my dad still projected his military training with me. Like I wouldn't just walk into his den. I'd walk up to the door to the den and I would stand there until he looked up and recognized me. Then I'd ask, 'Can I come in?' and he'd say, 'You can enter.' I'd go over to his desk and stand there until he was ready to speak to me. That didn't bother me though. I liked my dad a lot. He was really a cool dude and he was the most . . . I don't know exactly what the word is that I'm looking for, but I guess charismatic, yeah, charismatic, and most versatile, flexible person that I knew.

"Why, he could be a dirty, low-down biker one day and be wearing a tuxedo the next. He could do anything or be anyone he wished, it seemed.

"My dad lived alone and I liked to do things for him. I would clean the house and make it really pretty. I'd wash all the windows and vacuum every room and mow the grass. I would do everything I could to please him and make him like me," Michael recalled. "I could hardly wait until I could move to Norfolk and be with him and go out on his boat and party with him."

On the June morning in 1980 that Michael was scheduled to leave Skowhegan for Norfolk, his mother walked into his room and sat on the end of his bed. She wanted to speak to him before she left for her job at the shoe factory.

This is how Michael remembered their exchange: "I was in bed sleeping when she came in around eight o'clock. She was really sad. She sat down on my bed and I felt terrible because she was crying, and she said, 'Michael, I have to go to work, but before you go I got to tell you something,' and then she told me that she wanted me to stay in Skowhegan with her and not move in with my father in Norfolk. I said, 'Mom, I love you, but I have to go. It's time for me to make a break and I want to live with Dad.' My mother began crying and left the room.

"I honestly think that she knew what was going to happen to me and she wanted to warn me or keep it from happening," Michael said. "She knew what my dad had tried with Laura and that my father was going to do the same with me, but I don't think she knew how to keep it from happening. Maybe she thought I'd just tell him no. I don't know, but when she left that morning, I really believe that she knew what lay in store for me in Norfolk."

# 40

The first thing that John did when Michael arrived in Norfolk was give him a $100 bill. "This is your allowance," John said. "One hundred bucks a week." Then John took Michael outside and pointed to a small truck. "This is my truck, but it's also yours. You can use it any time you want." There were few rules in John's house. Michael was responsible for keeping the house clean. That was all. Anything else was okay.

Within a few days, Michael had located a marijuana connection and fallen back into the habit of being stoned constantly. At first, his father didn't mind.

"My dad was a moderate to high pot smoker back then, and he'd tell me, 'Hey Michael, here's a couple hundred bucks. Go buy me a quarter pound of Hawaiian,' and I'd go do it and I'd break it up and take the seeds out of it, so he wouldn't have to, and I'd put it in this little stash box that he had on his desk. He'd dip his pipe in there and he really liked that. We had a unique relationship for a father and son."

But as the summer continued, John tired of Michael's constant smoking. He had plans for his son, and Michael couldn't do the things that John wanted if he were stoned all the time.

"When Michael joined me in Norfolk, he was addicted to marijuana," John recalled, "and the beautiful thing about pot, of course, is that it makes you not care about anything. I knew that his mother had sent him to a work farm of some sort in Maine where he had to shovel cow shit, and that was exactly what I'd expected from her. Barbara was always trying to get someone else to solve her problems. It might have worked for a while, but I knew the kid wasn't going to stop until he wanted to. So I didn't badger him or hassle him about it at first. I let him get stoned all the time. And then one day, I went up to his bedroom because I wanted him to do some painting on the boat, and he is zoned out, totally zoned out. His eyes were red and it looked like he was ready to pass out, and I said to him, 'Fuck Michael, why am I even talking to you? You ain't even here! I don't need this,' and I left the room.

"Later, he told me that my reaction had really scared him because I hadn't been beating him to death with lectures. He knew that he had really disappointed me and pissed me off, and that upset him. He told me that he was going to stop smoking pot, which, of course, was just a ridiculous statement.

"I told him, 'Look, Michael, there is nothing wrong with smoking marijuana. Nothing. There is nothing wrong with alcohol. There is nothing wrong with riding a Ferris wheel, but goddamn it, if you do it twenty-four hours a day, you are fucked up! If you go overboard and get addicted to something, anything, then it stops being fun and takes control of your life. What you kids don't understand is the joy of moderation.'

"I explained to him that something is only fun if you do it in moderation, and it seemed to make sense to him."

John suggested that Michael cut down on his marijuana use gradually. If he did, Michael could begin helping John on various insurance investigations at Wackenhut. Michael got excited. Working with his dad as a private eye was something that he really wanted to do. He promised to try, and John sent him to take the same private investigator courses that Philip Prince had sent John to.

A number of changes occurred at Wackenhut that fall before Michael finished his training and turned eighteen, the minimum age required by Virginia to obtain a private investigator's license. Prince had built up an impressive investigative unit by then and successfully weaned the office from the nickel-and-dime divorce cases. But Prince was dissatisfied with his salary. It hadn't grown as fast as the office's case load, nor had he received a promotion. He resigned to start his own private detective agency, which he called Confidential Reports.

John figured Wackenhut would tap him for Prince's job, but instead the company transferred Michael Bell from its Richmond office and put him in charge of investigations. John was outraged, with good reason. Michael Bell did not bend his ethics to meet John Walker's standards.

"I didn't care for his methods," Bell recalled. "I told him, 'John, not everyone is guilty. When an insurance company hires us, it wants us to find out the truth,' but John thought everyone was guilty and he kept dreaming up all these scams to prove it."

John suddenly found himself being constantly reeled in and second-guessed on the few cases that Bell assigned to him. Even when John pulled off a good scam, his new boss was critical.

"What if a person with a legitimate injury gets hurt during one of your scams?" Bell asked. "You know someone might try to pick up groceries from a cart and actually hurt themselves. You're going to open us up to a lawsuit!"

John ignored Bell as much as possible, but Bell didn't let up. One afternoon, Bell called John into his office. An attorney had called and complained that John had offered to lie on the witness stand in order to win an insurance case. John denied the charge, but Bell didn't believe him. John left Wackenhut that afternoon and drove to Phil Prince's house.

"How about a job?" John asked.

Philip Prince knew that no one in Norfolk had as good equipment as John did. They quickly struck a deal and became partners in October 1980. The two men opened an office in the Kempsville Professional Building, only a few miles from where Art and Rita lived and where Walker Enterprises had been located. Because John owned most of the physical assets—guns, video equipment, electronic bugging devices, and his surveillance van—he was named corporate president.

Confidential Reports had a meager beginning. During the first two months of 1981, it handled only fifteen cases, the biggest one paying $348. In all, Prince and John billed $1,341.95. Even though both men received military pensions, their case load was barely enough to pay office expenses, so John agreed not to draw a salary. Instead, Prince would just keep tabs on how much John was owed, and when the company got into better financial shape, John could collect his back pay. There was only one problem with the arrangement. John needed some way to account for the extra money that he made as a spy. So he told Prince that he was forming his own company on the side for tax reasons. It was incorporated January 30, 1981, with John listed as president and Arthur as secretary–treasurer. Technically, the company specialized in helping companies guard against industrial espionage, but it was really set up as a way for John to conceal his spy money. His cockiness was reflected in the company's name—Counter-Spy. "I didn't feel the FBI was ever going to catch me at this point. That's why I called the company Counter-Spy, rather than making it one word. I thought it was rather funny," John told me. "Here I was advertising the fact that I was a spy, and that is what I was using this business for—laundering my spy money."

Invoices from Counter-Spy show that John billed a number of fictional and actual persons for "technical countermeasures." Nearly all of the billings were fake.

Meanwhile, business at Confidential Reports picked up. Prince, refined and smooth, spent his time sweet-talking clients and charming local attorneys and insurance company representatives. John stayed behind the scenes and did most of the actual investigations.

In May, Prince was able to convince three national insurance companies to hire Confidential Reports to perform investigations of suspected fraud. None of the cases amounted to much individually, but in June, one of these insurance companies hired Prince and John to investigate ten suspected cases of insurance fraud, and in July, Confidential Reports collected $5,390.68 from its clients. Soon another major insurance company began sending Confidential Reports work.

Word was getting around the insurance industry—Confidential Reports got results. John and his roughshod tactics were the reason. And, as he had promised, John always included Michael as his willing apprentice.

Michael had always been small for his age, and when he filed an application with the Virginia Department of Commerce for a private investigator's license, he could easily have passed for a boy much younger than eighteen. He had a baby face, weighed only 120 pounds, and stood only five feet, five inches tall. But Michael was a tremendous private investigator because he wasn't afraid of anything.

Because of his size, Michael could perform surveillance jobs that his father couldn't. Once Confidential Reports was hired to watch a suspect, but each time John drove to the man's neighborhood, he had to abort the surveillance because the suspect lived in an area with a neighborhood watch program, and whenever John parked near the suspect's house, a concerned neighbor called the police. Frustrated, John put Michael on the job. The next morning, Michael donned a pair of short pants and a tee-shirt and rode his bike into the neighborhood. He stopped near the suspect's house and sat on the curb "fixing" his bike. No one paid any attention. The next day, Michael tried a bolder approach by knocking on the door of the suspect's house and offering to mow his lawn for a ridiculously low price. While Michael was mowing the grass, the suspect came outside with two glasses of lemonade. He and Michael began talking, and the novice investigator soon discovered enough for his father to set up a successful scam. Michael began dreaming up his own schemes, following his dad's guidance. "I was patterning my life after his," Michael recalled. "I wanted to be just as good as he was."

John wanted Michael to finish high school and had intended to enroll him in Frederick Military Academy in Norfolk when he first arrived, but after John read his son's high school transcript, he knew the military academy wouldn't accept the teenager. He telephoned officials at Ryan Upper School, one of the better nonmilitary private schools in Norfolk, and convinced them to give Michael a chance despite his dismal performance in the Skowhegan school system.

Classes were difficult for Michael. He wasn't as well prepared academically as most students. But he was smart enough to get a passing grade, and what he lacked in academic skills, he made up for socially. By the end of his first year, the class voted Michael "Mr. Personality." Like his father, Michael seemed to have a talent for getting people to do what he wanted. The fact that he was almost two years older than most of his classmates helped. Michael was the only person in the junior class old enough to purchase beer legally, and that won him friends. Michael's home life also impressed his classmates because he seemed to be able to do what he wanted and could throw a party whenever he wished.

Michael's parties soon became legendary at school. No one wanted to miss the free food, beer, and bedrooms that Michael made available. The parties also were "safe," because Michael always hired bouncers. He also bragged that because his father was a private eye with contacts at the police department, no one had to worry about being busted. The marijuana growing in ceramic pots in Michael's room only added to his classmates' awe.

An incident during the summer of 1981 showed how carefree life with Father could be. Michael was cleaning his dad's houseboat (he had traded in *The Dirty Old Man* for a houseboat after the divorce) when John arrived home with two women he had met at a local bar. Both women were in their thirties, and John had promised them a cruise. Once underway, the two women paired off with John and Michael. Everyone began drinking heavily and after an hour of drifting under the hot sun, one woman announced she was going swimming. She took off her clothes and jumped into the water. John stripped and jumped in too, carefully holding his can of beer up over his head in an unsuccessful attempt to keep it from going under water. The woman with Michael giggled and began peeling off her clothing.

Everyone was naked and in the water except for Michael, and when they yelled at him to join them, he refused.

"I had a hard-on and didn't want them to see me," Michael recalled. "I was only eighteen and I was embarrassed. Of course, they all knew what was going on. I was standing on the boat like an idiot and everyone was laughing at me, so I thought. 'What the hell?' and I went to the other side of the boat and pulled down my pants and lowered myself off the side into the water. But then I thought, 'Hey, this really sucks,' so I climbed out of the water really quick, and I was drying off with this towel when the woman I'd been talking to climbs into the boat and comes up to me and rips off my towel.

"I said, 'What are you doing?' because I was standing there naked, and she grabbed me and starts to kiss me and I pushed her away. 'I can't fuck you in front of my dad,' I said, and everyone, including my father, just started roaring."

The woman persisted, but Michael just couldn't do it with his father watching.

Despite their closeness, Michael still knew that his father was keeping a secret from him. John made sure of it. He would drop hints periodically, usually when they were in some bar—Bob's Runway, for instance.

"Michael, you're getting pretty old," John said once.

"Yeah, so what?"

"You're almost old enough for me to tell you how I make my extra money."

"Okay, how?"

"Later. Maybe in a little while I'll tell you."

John was clearer when he spoke to Michael about what he had planned for his son. From the moment Michael moved in, John began pestering him about the Navy, constantly talking about how great the service was. In the summer of 1981, before Michael's final year in high school, John pushed even harder. He brought Michael brochures about various Navy programs and even had recruiters telephone Michael at home and chat with him.

"Michael, you've got to do something with your life after school," John said one evening while they were grilling hamburgers in the backyard.

"I'm going to be a private investigator with you," Michael replied.

"No way," John answered. "Look, Michael, there is no retirement program for PIs, no nothing. Being a PI is a career that someone starts after they retire."

"Okay," Michael replied, "I'll join the Navy."

"That would be great, son," John replied. "You would really make your old man happy if you did that."

Years later, Michael looked back on that casual conversation and saw more importance in it than he had at the time. "I had always thought about going into the Navy because my dad was in the Navy. I liked the uniform and status that the Navy had. Besides, my dad was such a neat guy and I wanted to be like that. I really wanted to be like him. What I didn't realize until later was that he had been grooming me to be a spy with all this private investigator stuff and talk about the Navy and being a radioman. I just didn't see what was happening."

# 41

Jerry Whitworth flew to Norfolk on November 6, 1980, to deliver John another magnificent haul of documents. The NSA had started distributing a new cipher system known as the KG-36, and Jerry had copied a keylist for it and portions of its technical manual. He had photographed a keylist and updated schematics for the KWR-37 too, which the KGB had been having trouble getting to function. More importantly, he had collected ninety straight days of keylists for the KW-7 machine.

On June 6, 1981, the KGB left $100,000 for John at a dead drop outside Washington. Inside was a note commending Jerry for his work. Using their prearranged code, John telephoned Jerry and told him that "the buyers" had paid $50,000 for his last delivery.

Hoping to increase his earnings, Jerry had started dabbling in the stock market and real estate. His first purchases were high-risk, high-gain stocks, and he did poorly. Ultimately, he lost $30,000 in the stock market. But those losses didn't seem to depress him. There was always plenty more money to spend.

Like most radio operators, Jerry enjoyed electronic gadgets. He spent $1,218.90 at Mohmad Edid Abdallah's television store during one shopping spree and eventually bought more than $20,000 worth of personal computer equipment.

Jerry and Brenda had started living better too. They spent money for a painting and two sculptures. They began dining at San Francisco's better restaurants. Jerry bought a Fiat convertible, a Mazda sports car, and "his and her" motorcycles. Jerry had moved a long way from Ayn Rand's theory of objectivism.

On July 12, Jerry and Brenda arrived in Norfolk for a short vacation. John paid Jerry the $60,000 in spy money and couldn't help but marvel at the change in his friend.

"He kept wanting me to push for more and more cash," John claimed later. "Jerry kept complaining. He said we were being underpaid for the risks that we were taking, particularly since he was providing such good information. Jerry would ask me, 'John, do you know how much one nuclear missile costs? Or one little communication satellite? Those things cost millions of dollars each, but we are providing information that is more important than a missile or a satellite and what are we getting out of it?' "

Then Jerry made a suggestion that John later claimed astounded him. Jerry had found someone else to bring into the spy ring! *He* wanted to recruit another spy!

The candidate was a disgruntled Navy lieutenant assigned to the U.S.S. *Independence,* an aircraft carrier. The lieutenant and Jerry had met and talked endlessly about world politics. Jerry was confident that his newly made friend could be turned.

John quizzed Jerry about the lieutenant and then cautioned Jerry against approaching the man until "our foreign buyers" approved the plan.

"Doesn't it bother you," Jerry asked John after telling him about the lieutenant, "that we are so good at this and no one will ever know it?"

John nodded.

Privately, however, Jerry's transformation was beginning to worry him. If the KGB approved Jerry's plan, then Jerry would become the new spy's handler.* John wasn't sure he liked that.

There was one thing, however, that John was certain about. Jerry Whitworth had found a new fad to follow: greed.

# *42*

After Walker Enterprises collapsed, Arthur Walker found himself needing a job. This time, he fell back on his Navy experience and went to work at VSE Corporation, one of the largest publicly held defense contractors. With more than 1,700 employees in twenty-six offices around the country, VSE handles thousands of classified documents each day. Arthur helped identify what kind of repairs were needed during ship overhauls in Norfolk.

Arthur told me that he hadn't really fully understood what John meant in January 1980 when the two of them had taken a walk outside the restaurant. "John didn't say, 'Hey, Art, you want to be a spy?' He just planted a few seeds."

But after that initial conversation, John got more specific, and by the fall of 1980, John was pestering Arthur about getting documents for him.

Arthur knew better. He had been thoroughly familiar with espionage laws while in the Navy, and in February 1980, shortly after going to work for VSE, he had signed a statement that said, "I shall not knowingly and willfully communicate, deliver, or transmit, in any manner, classified information to an unauthorized person or agency. I am informed that such improper disclosure may be punishable under federal criminal statutes . . ."

In retrospect, the FBI would decide that John used a textbook KGB method to entrap Arthur. He began by asking Arthur to let him look at *unclassified* materials, and when Arthur brought some samples one afternoon to John's van in the parking lot outside VSE, John gave him an envelope filled with cash.

---

*Confidential FBI records show that John acknowledged during questioning after his arrest that he had given the KGB the name of the Navy lieutenant. John also admitted during a lie detector test that he had given the KGB the name of a young Navy seaman in Norfolk for possible recruitment. John insisted during FBI interviews, however, that he couldn't remember the name of either man and he said he was totally unaware of what action, if any, the KGB took once they had the men's names.

"Consider it up-front money," John said. Inside was $6,000, an intentionally extravagant payment for seemingly worthless material.

"John, don't give me any money for this," Arthur protested. "Besides, you're paying all the debts from Walker Enterprises."

John agreed to take back $2,000 from the envelope, but he insisted that Arthur keep the rest.

"Keep it to play with," John said, "and for godsakes, don't tell Rita about it."

Arthur tucked the money in his briefcase.

A few days later, John asked Arthur for more documents.

"The only thing that I have that anyone would be remotely interested in would be some general ship plans which are unclassified," Arthur replied. "Do you want something like that?"

"Yeah, if it can make us some money, then do it."

"Okay, how do you want to do it?" asked Arthur, assuming that John intended to photograph the documents. John laughed, and gave his brother the news: "Hell no, you do it."

"He showed me a Minox and a Kodak 110 camera," Arthur later told me, "and I felt more comfortable with the Kodak, so I took some general plans that were unclassified out of the office and drove down one night to his detective agency, and I photographed them. It was challenging work because the plans were large and difficult to photograph."

Arthur called John the next day.

"Hey John, the photos of the general plans are in your drawer."

"Hey, great, thanks for helping me out."

Arthur figured he'd gotten off easy. "I didn't feel bad at all because the general plans weren't classified and I had helped him out and, remember, he was footing all the debts from Walker Enterprises."

But Arthur had given John more than he realized. The plans that Arthur photographed were of an amphibious assault ship, and while Arthur thought they were worthless, the KGB apparently did not. Captain Edward D. Sheafer, a senior intelligence officer for the Atlantic Fleet, testified at Arthur's trial that the Soviet Union was building an amphibious assault fleet in the late 1970s and had directed its agents to locate technical information about such ships. John had hoodwinked Arthur once again.

Arthur was not as naïve about what was happening as he later appeared to be. "I got to be honest here," he told me during one candid conversation. "John was mentioning money, big money. I have to admit that there was a temptation there. Maybe that's not the right word, but if someone says, 'Hey, I'll pay you fifty thousand a year to do this,' you are going to stop and think about this for a minute or an hour or whatever and say, 'Huh? Fifty thousand! What will I do for fifty thousand bucks a year tax free?' I mean, there might be things that I would do for money, but other things that I wouldn't. Like I wouldn't kill anybody, but if a bookie asked me to deliver money for him, well, that's a crime, but it doesn't seem too bad. At least it doesn't at the time, but you've already made that first step, you know.

"That's what I'm talking about. I'd already taken the first step, you know. I had given him unclassified documents. I had photographed documents in his office and nothing bad had happened to me. Nothing. In return, John had given me money. I hadn't done anything illegal up to that point, but it was a step in that direction. A big step."

In the fall of 1981, John finally pressed Arthur for classified material.

"Arthur, you've got to get me something that says classified on it," John said. "I'm hurting bad. I really need something to please them. Anything that even looks classified. Anything."

"At this point," Arthur told me later, "I had a lot of mixed emotions. I love this country and I began thinking about it, about what John had already done. . . . I began convincing myself that John couldn't have given away anything that was that important. I mean, Little Artie Walker really should be talking to the feds at this point, but instead, I'm getting ready to steal some shit and take pictures of it."

Arthur asked John for instructions.

"If I'm going to do this shit, I need some methodology," Arthur said. "I need to know how this stuff is done. Mostly photographs?"

"Primary method is photographs. Film. Find something of value and photograph it," John replied.

"What's worth the most?"

"The best? Crypto, especially keycards; after that, top secret/crypto, secret, confidential, and technical manuals."

"I ain't got no crypto or even know what it looks like anymore. Best I could even hope to see might be some secret. How am I going to judge whether something's valuable?"

"By the classification."

"Classified tech manuals?"

"Yeah, they're good."

On September 1, 1981, Arthur went to the security office at VSE, where classified documents were locked in a safe. He requested the "damage control book" for the U.S.S. *Blue Ridge,* the flagship for the Pacific Fleet, which carried the fleet commander and his staff. It was one of the most important ships in the Navy.

Arthur said he needed the book because he was working on the ship's overhaul schedule. The book was classified confidential, the lowest possible classification in the government, but Arthur thought that it might still contain information that John could sell because the U.S.S. *Blue Ridge* was the flagship.

The book contained a list of all the ship's vulnerabilities, its schematics, and information about its equipment and its capabilities. Arthur took the book to his desk and removed several pages that were clearly marked "CONFIDENTIAL." He then returned the book to the safe at VSE without anyone noticing that the pages were missing. Tucking the classified documents in his briefcase, Arthur drove home, and after eating dinner with Rita, announced that he was going to John's office to help him with a case.

For the first time, Arthur was terrified, having finally acknowledged to himself that he was in too deep now to get out.

"I felt like Jell-O when I was doing it. The fact that I even considered it bothered me more than the documents themselves. I'm not even sure how to explain it. . . . I was trying to help him at this point, okay? He is the man, I mean, he needed something that said 'classified' on it. He was trying to prove his value to someone else. . . . I don't want to sound naive. I knew what I was doing was wrong. But I just couldn't turn him in."

Arthur took photographs of the pages that dealt with the number of troops the U.S.S. *Blue Ridge* could carry, its fuel-carrying capacity, and its stability system. He left the film in the top drawer of John's desk with a note. The next morning, Arthur returned the confidential pages that he had taken from the book.

John gave Arthur $6,000 for photographing the U.S.S. *Blue Ridge* book, but once again, John took back some cash—$3,000 this time—as reimbursement for the debts he was paying for Walker Enterprises.

"Go out and have some fun," John told Arthur. "Live a little. You never have any fun."

"What do I tell Rita?" asked Arthur.

"Tell her the money is from the detective agency. For helping me with my cases."

Arthur hid the money. The only purchases that he could remember later besides cocktails were a new toupee, new brakes for his car, and a gas grill that cost $300.

John didn't stay away from Arthur once he had—as Arthur later put it—"hooked 'im." Soon, John was pressuring Arthur for more classified documents and was urging him to quit VSE and find a job where he would have better access.

Arthur felt trapped, he told me later. He loved his brother and he felt obligated to him because of the business debts. But he also felt guilty.

"I don't know how to put this, maybe, except to put it in religious terms. Once you start sinning, you either stop sinning or you just keep going and going and you carry this guilt around, subconscious perhaps, but there is always a bit of tenseness. It's one of those things that you push back inside, you know, that makes you worse for it. It eats on you, and it would be nice to go tell someone, but who can you tell? Who? Who? Things with Rita were not good," Arthur told me. "We were together, but we were separate. Our sex life had ended. We weren't

fighting and there wasn't any screaming or yelling. We were just growing apart."

When I spoke with her later, Rita agreed with Arthur's assessment. "I
was withdrawing from Arthur physically and it was because of John.
Maybe I was punishing him for befriending John. But I was beginning to
see a change in Arthur, something different about him. He was beginning to be influenced by John. I could feel it."

Arthur was confused. He wasn't unhappy with his life, he told me
later, but he was bitter about what had happened to him and his
bitterness became his rationale. John was always throwing it up in his
face. Arthur had played it straight all of his life, worked hard, and no
one seemed to care. What had he gotten in return? Now he knew John's
secret. John was a spy, a traitor, but he had a nice house, a houseboat,
an airplane, his own business, young girlfriends, and an exciting life.
What did Arthur have?

John was offering him a chance to walk on the wild side and put some
adventure in his life and Arthur, with prodding from John, decided that
he deserved it.

After his arrest, I asked Arthur if he blamed John. It was John, after
all, who baited and recruited him, and turned him against Rita.

"I could blame John," he replied, "but it was still my choice. I could
have said no, but I couldn't say no. Let me rephrase that—what I mean
is, well, I should have said no to him, but I couldn't really. I just
couldn't. He was my brother."

# 43

The Navy called it "dropping guard," and this turned out to be a
painfully apt description when Jerry Whitworth was on duty. Whenever
a ship arrived in port in San Francisco, the commander could elect to
"drop guard" by asking the Naval Telecommunications Center at Alameda to handle all its message traffic during the months it was in port.
About two thirds of the ships that came to port dropped guard and
relied on Alameda, and Jerry Whitworth, to collect all communications
about its future assignments, operational plans, ship modifications, and
anything else that happened to be addressed to it. The first person in
Alameda to receive such messages was the "in-router," who was respon-

sible for making certain the message was delivered to the right box so that it ultimately could be delivered to the ship's commander.

It was not a sophisticated system in 1981. Aaron Darnell Brown, a Navy in-router during 1981 in Alameda, recalled years later how he hand-carried messages from teletype machines to various wire baskets in the center for routing. During an average twenty-four-hour work period, the message center received 1,300 messages ranging from confidential to top secret. Brown usually put them in the wire baskets and, he noticed, Jerry Whitworth then examined each message. Brown figured Jerry was just doing his job.

Jerry was not well liked by many of the Navy radio operators at the center, according to Karen Margaret Barnett, a "watch stander" at Alameda responsible for making certain that messages from the center got to their final destinations. "He thought he was just better than the rest of us," she complained.

Shortly after Jerry and Brenda returned from visiting John in the fall of 1981, an incident occurred that caused Jerry to lose his arrogance.

When he reported to work one day, Jerry discovered that a breach in security had been uncovered and swarms of naval investigators were examining the records at Alameda. He was petrified. Apparently, one of the younger sailors who worked at the center had destroyed a crypto-graphic keylist without having another sailor present, as required.

"Jerry called me and told me about the security breach and how the Navy was making it into a federal case, you know, as big as the crucifixion of Jesus Christ," John recalled. "Anyway, Jerry told me that he was being assigned temporary duty at Stockton.

"I really didn't think much of it until I asked him what his access there would be like, and Jerry says he's not going to have any access in Stockton. He was going to have a desk job there."

John urged Jerry to apply for the CMS custodian at Stockton so he could continue getting keylists, but Jerry sounded uninterested. What Jerry didn't have the guts to tell John was that he had engineered his own transfer to Stockton, because he wanted to stop spying.

The Alameda security breach was only part of the problem. Jerry was flip-flopping again. Less than two months earlier, he had complained to John about how no one would ever know how great they were as spies. Now Jerry was running scared. He had had enough.

Jerry knew that he had become addicted to the money, but he thought he could beat that. What he had trouble figuring out was how to deal with John. Like the other people in John Walker's life, Jerry felt a Svengali-like attraction and loyalty to his mentor. John was counting on him. John was his very best friend, even better than Roger Olson.

It had been an adventure at first, like the two free spirits in *Easy Rider*—who refused to play by the rules. But the incident at Alameda had brought the spying into focus. Hey, the Navy wasn't messing around. This was serious stuff. Sooner or later, he was going to be caught. Jerry knew it and he was scared.

When federal agents arrested Christopher Boyce (of *The Falcon and the Snowman*) that August it was revealed the KGB hadn't broken Boyce out of prison. No one had. He'd simply escaped on his own. Jerry thought: so much for romance and intrigue.

The question was: What to do? And Jerry wasn't sure.

John sensed that Jerry was withdrawing, but he didn't react immediately. "I just didn't need this shit. I was busy as hell at the detective agency and I didn't have time to fly out to California and hold Jerry's hand every time he got frightened."

John had problems of his own in late 1981. He was tired of Patsy Marsee and was trying to break off their relationship. Meanwhile, he had taken up with Pamela "P.K." Carroll, a twenty-two-year-old woman with emerald eyes and light brown hair, who had applied for a job at the agency. John not only hired her, but pursued her, even though she was about the same age as his own daughters.

Just as he had done with all of the other women whom he courted, John had promised to take P.K. to the Bahamas. He was scheduled to leave on New Year's Day. John decided to fly out to see Jerry after the Bahamas trip.

Jerry seemed to be in good spirits when John arrived. He was enjoying his new job at Stockton and his break from spying. He was thinking about retiring again. John wasn't surprised. "Whenever Jerry faced a problem, he ran away," John said.

"Your transfer is really going to cause me some problems," John complained. "And it's going to hurt you financially. I thought you liked getting those ten-thousand-dollar bonuses."

Jerry announced that he no longer needed any spy money. Brenda was going to have her degree in a few years and her income, along with his pension, would be more than enough for them to make it financially. Besides, Jerry had decided to become a stockbroker, and a successful broker could make $100,000 per year easy. That was more per year than the sporadic payments that he had received from John, and there was no risk of going to prison.

"Shit, Jerry, what risk?" John asked. "There is no threat of us being caught. The FBI isn't a threat at all, really. Unless some catastrophic accident happens, like a tree dropping on my car or something like that, we are completely safe."

Jerry wasn't so sure. What about Barbara? he asked. Didn't she know what was going on?

"She doesn't know anything," John said, "and she's not going to talk. Listen, there are things about Barbara you don't know. She can't go to the FBI about me without hurting herself and besides, I'm sending her money. Don't worry about Barbara."

John turned the tables. "What about Brenda?" Did she know?

"Jerry told me Brenda didn't have a clue to what he was doing," John recalled. "Jerry said he had convinced Brenda that he was working for the United States in a secret sort of way. He never fully explained what he told her, but he convinced me that she didn't know."

After hearing Jerry's explanation, John said, "Hey, that's a good idea, telling her that you are working for the government. I wish I'd thought of it first. At least it explains some of the extra money around the house."

Jerry asked John if he had a plan in case he ever was captured.

"Look, if either of us are ever arrested, we hang tough," John said. "Neither of us will say a word until we get lawyers, and for godsakes don't believe the FBI if they come in and tell you that I've squealed, 'cause it won't be true. They will simply be trying to turn us against each other. Certainly don't admit anything and don't incriminate yourself, and if we are ever caught red-handed, then we claim the material was being sold to a friendly nation like Israel."

John paused and then grinned. "I mean, you believed that once, didn't you?"

Jerry didn't react. He was angry.

"I've been thinking about the money," John continued, "and I've been wondering whether we could get you a one-shot, lump payment in return, say, for a promise to deliver keylists for the next ten years."

Jerry appeared surprised. He was talking about getting out of espionage and John was talking about locking him into it for another decade.

"One million dollars," John continued, "works out to be the same one hundred thousand per year that you think you can make as a stockbroker, only this is tax free. Think it over."

# 44

Despite his persistent reminders, John had been unable to get Laura to follow through with what he thought was her promise to reenlist in the Army and become a spy. Instead, after Mark was discharged from the Army in the fall of 1980, they and the baby moved in with Barbara in Skowhegan.

Laura's marriage was a shambles. She was tired of Mark, but he still wanted to make it work. He had gotten a job in Skowhegan with the federal CETA program and later found work at a company making fire alarms. But his salary still was not enough for them to afford their own place. Mark and Laura weren't the only persons living with Barbara. Cynthia and her little boy lived there, and so did Barbara's mother, Annie. Although Annie was receiving Social Security and Cynthia was receiving welfare, Barbara remained the main breadwinner.

John would occasionally send Barbara a few hundred dollars for emergencies, but he wasn't paying her anything regularly and Barbara really didn't care. Over the years, John had earned nearly $1 million from the KGB, but his family had seen very little of it.

"It was a strange situation in Maine," Mark Snyder told me later. "Barbara was working hard, no doubt about it. She was gluing shoes together and making four or five dollars per hour tearing her hands apart. But I remember she wouldn't take any money from John. She said she didn't want his money or anything to do with him."

In April 1981, Laura decided that she wanted out of Skowhegan and her marriage. "Laura went to this wedding of a friend of hers in California, and she liked it out there and wanted to move back there," Mark said. "I said, 'Okay, whatever,' and she went out to get established and Chris stayed with me in Skowhegan."

What Mark said he didn't realize until later was that Laura wanted only Christopher to join her in California, not him.

Laura's decision to leave Skowhegan irritated Barbara. She accused Laura of abandoning her son. But Laura felt she had no choice. She settled in Hayward, near San Francisco, and went to work at a home construction company. About a month after she left Skowhegan, Laura telephoned Mark and asked him to bring Christopher to her. When Mark arrived, he announced that both of them were staying.

"The agreement was that Mark would stay with me until he got his own place," Laura said. "Then he was supposed to move out. Eight months later, he was still there. He never moved. I would beg him. I gave him money. I tried everything. I gave him half of my five-hundred-dollar income tax refund to go, but he still wouldn't. I'll never forget that morning after I gave him the money. It was his day off and I said, 'What do you plan to do? Are you moving this afternoon or later or what?' He said, 'I am not leaving.' I remember I just began to cry and to sob right there because I knew that I could not get rid of this guy. I was bound to this man because he was my husband, and I had become a born-again Christian and I was trying to understand what it meant to live my life for the Lord. I knew that divorce was wrong, but I could not understand why I had to be with this creep any longer. It was a total nightmare."

When John arrived in California on January 29, 1982, Mark was still living with Laura, although they rarely spoke to each other. "My father always seemed to arrive at my most vulnerable moments," Laura recalled. "I don't know how he planned it, but he always had that knack for coming when I was desperate."

John telephoned Laura after he finished talking business with Jerry and invited her to join Jerry, Brenda, and him for dinner. Mark wasn't invited and Laura was happy to get away from him for an evening. John and Laura got along extremely well that night, so John suggested that they spend the next day together.

"I want to see my grandson," John explained, "buy a camera and take some pictures of him."

The next morning, they drove to San Leandro with two-year-old Christopher. John bought a camera and they drove to a park where Christopher could play.

"Okay, what are you going to do?" John asked Laura as both watched Christopher making roads in a sandbox.

"I don't know."

"Well, do you want to get into the espionage or not?"

Laura said she couldn't reenlist in the Army because of Christopher.

"I've talked to a recruiter for you," John replied quickly. "All you have to do is sign over custody of Christopher to your mother or me and then go back into the Army. Your mother would love to get custody of Christopher because then she could get a welfare check for him, and you'd have a job again."

How long would she have to give up Christopher? Laura asked.

"Just fill out the custody agreement, then go back in the Army for training, and once you get a decent apartment you can get Christopher," John said. "Besides your Army pay, I can give you up to five hundred dollars per month as a retainer, and once you start giving me documents, that amount will increase. But you've got to make up your mind, Laura, because my man in Europe is getting worried about you. You're going to be too old soon.

"So tell me," John continued, "are you going to join the Army and take the money, or what?"

In interviews after his arrest, John claimed once again that Laura agreed to do it. "She said, 'Okay, I'll do it, if you'll give me money for a divorce from Mark.' So I agreed to help her get her bills cleared up and pay her enough to get a divorce and get back to Maine, where she could reenlist."

When Laura Walker recalled her conversation with her father, she denied she had ever agreed to be a spy. But again her court testimony revealed some ambiguity.

QUESTION: Please tell us what was discussed.

ANSWER: He started by saying that his man in Europe was concerned because I was getting older, and that—I can't remember how, but he somehow indicated that I was reaching an age limit of some sort. And then he said again that the offer still stood for me to—if I was willing to agree to do what he had proposed. And we talked about my going back in.

Q: What did he say about the kind of information that would be desired, if anything?

A: He said that anything was valuable. And he mentioned journals, manuals, repair manuals. But the most desirable was codes, any kind of codes that I could get my hands on. No matter how old, they were still valuable.

Q: Now, how was your position, if you accepted, described by your father if you had gone forward with a plan where you were supplying information? Did he have any word that he used to describe the relationship between you in the business?

A: Partners.

Q: At that time, in this park in 1982 in San Leandro, did you give him a firm answer as to whether you were going to participate or not?

A: I didn't come right out and say "No," but I tried to explain that I wouldn't—that I couldn't do it.

Q: Did you say anything or do anything that would encourage him to think that it was still an open possibility or that your participation might be forthcoming?

A: I think I was a little wishy-washy in my refusal.

Q: Did he give you any money that day?

A: No.

Q: Later on did he send you any money?

A: Yes.

Q: And that was in connection with what event?

A: The divorce.

Laura told me that her chat in the park with her father had scared her. "When he said, 'I was talking to my man in Europe,' it was the first time I had ever heard a reference to a foreign country," Laura explained. "It really stunned me because the reality of the fact that he was transmitting secrets to a foreign country hit me. But what surprised me and shocked me even more was the fact that he discussed me with some foreigner, and it freaked me out! I suddenly became afraid. People knew my name and they may have a whole dossier on me, and all of a sudden I was feeling really afraid for myself and my son. 'Am I being watched?' I wondered. This whole spy thing began to mount on me. . . ."

Once again, when John left Laura in California, he was convinced that she was going to help him. A few days later, he sent her $500 and a charge card. When the money arrived, Laura had intended, she said later, to pack up and move back East. But she didn't carry through with her plan.

"I had changed my mind. When you are twenty-one years old, your marriage is a disaster and has been from the beginning, and you have a two-year-old child and, to be perfectly honest with you, I could not get my act together and I'll admit it—I was a doe head and I made so many expensive mistakes—so I decided that I was not going to go and I called my dad and said, 'I am not going to go,' and he said, 'Well, I hope you send the credit card back,' because he knew he would never see the money. I sent the credit card back, but I gave Mark the money and here again, I made the same mistake twice, can you believe it? I gave him five hundred dollars again to move out, and he did not move."

John later recalled his exchange with Laura that day over the telephone: "I asked her if she had gotten the money and credit card. 'Yes,' she said, 'the money was gone. I need you to send me five hundred more.' I told her that I wasn't sending her any more money. Maybe an airline ticket, but that is it, and then I asked her if she was going to help me or what? And she says, 'It depends on whether you send me another five hundred dollars.' "

In February 1982, John left for Vienna to meet his KGB handler. During the long flight, he thought about Laura and how his Russian handler had predicted that she would never provide any material to him. His handler had warned John that recruiting Laura was a mistake. All Laura would be was a threat. "I remember thinking that Laura was running a scam on me. Her own father!" John told me later. "How could I have been so stupid? But it was finally hitting me. She never intended to spy, really. All she was doing was simply using me for the money. She was stringing me along." John paused, and then he said, with little emotion in his voice, "At that point there were two people I should have killed: Barbara and Laura."

# 45

John was startled when he spotted his KGB handler approaching him on February 13 outside the Bazala men's clothing store in Vienna. There was another man with him. He was much bigger. He towered over John, standing well over six feet, with an immense head and bulky shoulders.

"Hello, dear friend," John's handler said. "Do you have something for me?"

John handed him a package that contained several rolls of film, including the photographs that Arthur had taken of the damage control book for the U.S.S. *Blue Ridge*. The KGB agent turned and disappeared around the corner, leaving his comrade and John alone for several minutes in front of the store. Neither spoke. John kept his right hand in his coat pocket the entire time, his finger wrapped around the trigger of a .32 caliber automatic.

When the handler returned, the threesome began walking down Meidlinger Hauptstrasse. "John," the handler said, "I want to introduce you to a new friend. He will be meeting you from now on."

John was amazed. Not because he was being turned over to a new handler, although he certainly hadn't expected such a move, but because his first handler had called him by his first name. He had never called him anything other than "friend" during the years that they had been meeting, and John couldn't decide whether he was trying to impress his replacement or whether he had intentionally wanted to show John some affection.

"Okay," John replied. What did he care?

After the brief introduction, his handler fell back into the usual routine, first asking John about his trip and security precautions. Then he asked about Jerry.

John decided to break the bad news. Jerry, he reported, had been transferred because of a security problem at Alameda. He had temporarily lost all access to cryptographic keylists. As soon as John finished his sentence, the new KGB agent said something in German. John could tell from his gruffness that he wasn't pleased, but John didn't have the foggiest idea what he had said. Suddenly, John found himself being chastised by his new handler while his old KGB friend walked quietly along his side.

Why had Jerry been transferred? the second KGB agent demanded in English. Was it possible that Jerry had been moved because the FBI suspected he was doing something wrong? How long would Jerry be at his new job? Would he be able to return to his last job and continue delivering KW-7 keylists?

John's first handler had always been thorough in his questioning, but he had always taken time to phrase them in such a way that John felt comfortable. They spoke as equals. This KGB agent was different. He spoke to John like a superior officer speaking to an underling or a boss directing an employee. John snapped back one- or two-syllable responses interspersed with profanity. This, in turn, irritated his new KGB master, who began quizzing John not only about Jerry's latest transfer, but about Jerry's aborted tour aboard the U.S.S. *Niagara Falls*. Within minutes, John found *himself* being reproached because he had missed his first face-to-face meeting in Casablanca in August 1977.

"I don't need this shit!" John finally announced, his hand still in his pocket with the automatic pistol. "Listen, I don't run the fucking Navy. If you want to find out why Jerry's fucking ship was late and why the fucking *Niagara Falls* went into dry dock and why he was fucking transferred from Alameda, then why the fuck don't you call up the fucking president of the fucking United States and ask him what the fuck is going on?

"You assholes tell me that security is what is important," John continued. " 'Don't do anything that is dangerous,' you tell me, but then you fucking complain that we aren't aggressive enough and you claim Jerry isn't doing enough. Why don't you get your fucking act together?' "

On a soapbox now, John released a long series of complaints. He was tired of always walking the streets of Vienna in the cold. He was tired of having to stay in the Hotel Regina instead of American hotels where he felt more comfortable and didn't stick out. He was tired of the KGB never being satisfied with his deliveries.

John complained about real and imagined transgressions. He had learned more about security from reading spy novels by Robert Ludlum than from the real thing—KGB agents. Why hadn't they taught him more tricks?

"You guys are supposed to be the best! Hah!"

The new KGB handler was obviously not used to such insubordination or such obscenities. John's first handler quickly intervened. Such outbursts by both sides were counterproductive, he said.

"My friend, you have been very helpful in the past, and I am certain you will be doing your best," he said. "Perhaps you should tell us what you have brought us."

John outlined the materials that Jerry had taken before he left Alameda, which pleased the two agents, and then he mentioned the photographs that Arthur had taken. The documents, he explained, were only marked confidential, but they were pictures of a flagship and, more importantly, they signified that Arthur had stepped across the line and become a full member of John's ring.

"Can we expect future deliveries?" the new KGB handler asked, in a voice that was considerably more respectful.

"Yes," John replied, "Arthur is a good hand."

John made Arthur's position at VSE sound much more impressive than it was, and he explained that someone with Arthur's experience would move quickly into a position of importance with even better access. John also told the Soviets about his second encounter with Laura and said that while she was still wavering, there was a chance that she might reenlist and begin supplying documents.

Like a door-to-door salesman, John put his comments about Arthur and Laura in enthusiastic terms, but his testimonials apparently had little impact.

"Jerry is important," his first handler said. "He must get back to a job with better access. This is crucial. Is there something wrong?"

John didn't attempt to cover up Jerry's vacillation. "I didn't want them to think I was playing games," John told me later. "I wanted them to know that Jerry was prone to flip-flops."

John's new KGB handler abruptly asked him about Barbara. John was unsure, he explained later, if the agent was truly interested in hearing about Barbara or was simply trying to demonstrate that he had done his homework and was smart enough to realize that Barbara posed a threat to John.

John repeated his standard line about his ex-wife: Barbara was an alcoholic and alcoholics are unpredictable, but as long as he occasionally sent her money, he didn't believe she would harm him. "Basically, she is an extremely weak person and doesn't have the guts to turn me in," he said. "She doesn't want to go to jail either, and Barbara is intelligent enough to know that she would go to jail if I go to jail."

John himself didn't understand why he said what he did next. Perhaps he was still smarting from the berating that his new handler had given him. Perhaps he said it because deep down he realized that Barbara *was* actually a very real threat to him and he wanted the KGB to do something about that. He wasn't certain, but years later, he recalled that he had tossed the problem of Barbara "back in the Russians' faces." If the KGB considered Barbara a threat, John asked, then why didn't it do something about her?

"Why not simply eliminate Barbara?" he asked. "Why not kill her?"

Neither agent reacted.

"The KGB is supposed to be the biggest and most dangerous organization in the world, and I was clearly providing the Russians with information they considered vitally important," John told me later. "They knew Barbara was a problem, so I wondered why they didn't do it. I mean, all it would have taken was one little accident, and with Barbara's drinking, how hard could that have been? Anyone in their right mind would have gotten rid of her, but I told them I couldn't do it because she was the mother of my children. I just couldn't do something like that. But that shouldn't keep them from doing it. I told them I was surprised they hadn't taken some action before, and I made it clear: If they thought Barbara was a threat, then it was up to them to handle her. It turned out, of course, that they were as weak as everyone else around me."

Without commenting about Barbara, the KGB agents brought up the subject of money. It was becoming too dangerous for the KGB to pay John in Vienna. Now that his spy ring was expanding, the amount of cash he was due was simply too much to be safely carried in Europe and through U.S. Customs. It would be much safer for everyone if all cash payments were made during a dead drop from now on. The only problem was that John and the KGB had limited themselves to one dead drop per year. Obviously, John and his fellow spies would have to wait six months longer if the KGB stopped paying John in Vienna. John knew that Jerry wasn't going to like the idea, but John figured neither of them had a choice. Carrying stacks of money the size of two lunch boxes was just too risky. He reluctantly agreed with the Russians' suggestion.

John didn't feel comfortable bringing up his idea of a one-time, $1 million payment to Jerry even though he and the KGB agents were now discussing finances. The timing just didn't seem right. But he did drop a hint. Jerry, he told the KGB, had reacted well when he was paid the $10,000 bonus for providing three months of unbroken crypto. It might be necessary to increase such bonus payments in the future, John explained, to keep Jerry interested.

"He is not as aggressive as you were," John's first KGB handler said, smiling broadly.

The mood among the three men had improved, but John still was irritated over his clash with his new handler and, he recalled later, he was angry that the KGB was assigning him such an abrasive contact. "I really liked my first contact," John said, "and now I was being stuck with a guy with no sense of humor."

John decided to bring up Christopher Boyce to see if the Russians would comment on his arrest, subsequent escape from prison, and capture. Neither KGB agent reacted when John mentioned Boyce's name. They acted as if they had never heard of him. But John didn't drop the subject. Years later, in discussions with me, John made it clear that he considered himself a much better spy than Boyce, and he admitted that all of the attention that Boyce had received in the media had irritated him. "I was selling the Russians tech manuals for the KW-7 when Boyce was still in diapers," John bragged to me.

One of the things that had fascinated John in *The Falcon and the Snowman* was a description of Mikhail Vasilyevich Muzankov, identified in the book as a KGB senior official. John thought it odd because the KGB agent obviously had told his name to the two American spies. John had never asked his handler what his name was and the man hadn't volunteered it. Muzankov also stuck out in John's memory because the book said his front teeth were made of stainless steel, earning him the nickname "Steely Teeth."

Without reason, John turned to his new handler and rather mockingly asked, "You aren't Steely Teeth, are you?"

The KGB agent didn't respond, but John's first handler did.

"He knew exactly what I was talking about," John said later. "He said the KGB hadn't realized until after that book came out that only Russia and a few countries like Mexico still used steel and gold for replacing teeth. He told me the KGB wouldn't allow any agent to have steel teeth anymore, and if they had 'em, they had 'em pulled. Once again I was amazed! These guys were reading books about themselves to find out what they had done wrong."

As usual, John's original KGB handler gave him a short lecture about the superiority of communism during the face-to-face meeting. After that lecture, the three men stopped and John's first handler unbuttoned his heavy coat and removed a red Paper Mate pen.

"I had worked with this guy a long time," John recalled, "and we had developed a genuine interest in each other, I believe. When it was time to say good-bye, I, honest to God, thought I saw tears in his eyes, and he gave me this red Paper Mate pen that he said he had bought at a canteen in Moscow, so he figured it was safe for me to have it because he knew they were made in the United States. Actually, I'd never seen one like it because it had a ring calendar around it, a continuous calendar, and it was really nifty. I didn't say anything about not seeing it though. I just took it."

John began digging through his pockets.

"What are you doing?" the handler asked.

"Shit, I've got to find something for you," John replied.

"No," he said. "No matter what you give me, it would be bad because it would be from an American."

"I tried to get him to tell me if he was being promoted or what," John recalled, " 'cause I was really curious, and he wouldn't say too much but I think he was getting a promotion and that made me feel good."

Before the KGB agents left, John's original handler paid him a final compliment.

"He told me that spying wasn't easy," John said, "but he said his bosses were extremely pleased with my work. They were so pleased they wanted to make me an admiral in the goddamn Russian Navy or something, which I considered utter bullshit and laughable."

But something his handler said pleased John.

"Of all the spies in America," he said, "you, John, are the best!"

# 46

John's detective business gave Arthur a great cover. Whenever Arthur wanted to get away from Rita, he announced that he was going out to work with John on a case. Generally, he drove to his favorite country-western bar for a few nightcaps. Sometimes, Arthur really did volunteer to help John on investigations. After a while, Rita quit asking Arthur where he went at night.

After twenty-six years of marriage and three children, Arthur still cared for Rita. He didn't wish to hurt her, but he also didn't want to spend his life feeling as if she were holding him back. Why, he asked John one afternoon, should he have to sit home watching television at night just because Rita didn't like to go out?

John, of course, pushed Arthur to party and included him in as many outings as he could. Even though they both wore toupees and there was a similarity in their looks, speech, and mannerisms, John and Arthur were two different personalities and were treated much differently by John's crowd.

It wasn't uncommon for John to get drunk and write obscene suggestions on cocktail napkins that he would ask a waitress to deliver to some young woman sitting alone at the bar. The raciest Arthur ever got was to demand that an attractive cocktail hostess give him a hug before he paid his bar bill.

P.K. Carroll noticed the dissimilarity. One night she told Arthur that from then on she was going to call him "Uncle Art" because he seemed to be everyone's favorite uncle. The tag stuck. Pretty soon, everyone called him Uncle Art. John, on the other hand, was either called Johnny or JAWS—his initials. No one ever thought of him as someone's uncle.

John recognized the differences. "My God Arthur, no one feels comfortable smoking dope around you," John complained one afternoon. "Everyone waits for you to go home before they light up."

In early April 1982, John telephoned Arthur and told him that he desperately needed more classified documents. "I'm really in a bind this time, Arthur. My back is against the wall. Isn't there anything you can get for me? It would really be a good time if you can find something else."

Arthur assured John that he'd try.

On April 28, Arthur called John with some good news. VSE had been hired to study the LHA class of amphibious assault ships. These Navy ships were used to carry as many as two thousand Marines and 150 officers to shore during an assault. Arthur knew that the Russian Navy was far behind in building attack craft such as the LHA class ships, and he thought John might be interested in some of the research material that VSE had been given. In particular, VSE had access to a large volume of magnetic tapes that contained millions of tidbits of information about the assault ships. One item had caught Arthur's interest. It was a computer printout of all the malfunctions and breakdowns aboard the assault ships during a five-year period. The printout, known as a casualty report extract, also contained information about where the ship was located when the malfunction occurred, what the ship's mission was, and how the mishap had affected the ship's ability to perform in combat.

John didn't quite understand why a computerized list of mechanical breakdowns was so important, but Arthur explained that a veteran engineer could use the data in a variety of ways. He could figure out how many U.S. assault ships at any given time were "combat ready." He could determine how long the ships could be expected to operate before breaking down. He could determine the most common problem with assault ships and use that information to design a better vessel.

The new computer format intrigued Arthur.

"It's in a wild, new format," he explained. "It's totally different than the casualty reports that you've seen in the past!"

"Sounds interesting," said John. "What's it classified?"

"Either confidential or secret, not sure," said Arthur.

"Okay, I'll come by for lunch tomorrow. Meet me in the parking lot for lunch and bring some pages."

When Arthur got to work that morning, he walked to the VSE security office to check out the casualty reports file, but the security supervisor didn't want to give it to him. Even though its classification was only confidential, the security officer felt squeamish about releasing it from the security office. He suggested that Arthur simply look through the book at a nearby table. The normally genteel Arthur became incensed. "I need this at my desk," he insisted. "What's the big problem, I've got a clearance!" The security supervisor backed down.

Just before noon, Arthur rolled up a section of the file, tucked it under his arm with some other papers, and walked outside where John was waiting in his van. They rode to a nearby shopping center and parked outside a K mart store.

Arthur was nervous. The confrontation with the security supervisor had upset him. "I'm going to get a soft drink," he announced. John was used to Arthur's squeamishness. He looked over the computer printout while Arthur was gone, but he waited until Arthur returned to snap pictures.

"What the hell are you doing?" asked Arthur.

"I'm showing you how easy this all is," replied John. "You don't need to do this in my office, you can do it anywhere. Believe me, I used to do it aboard ships."

John was using his Kodak 110 camera to take pictures of the computer printout as it rested on a seat of the van. "No special lighting or nothing. See how simple this is? You could do this at work if you didn't mind pushing your balls to the wall. My man on the West Coast has a van just for this purpose."

John had mentioned his "man on the West Coast" before. He was always telling Arthur how much money his partner was earning. Arthur assumed that John was talking about Jerry Whitworth because he knew that John and Jerry were close friends.

After John had taken about seven photographs, he told Arthur, "I'll let you know if these are worth anything."

Later that afternoon, John telephoned Arthur and suggested that he remove the remaining portions of the casualty report and photograph them that night.

Arthur objected. "I thought you were going to see if those pictures were worth the trouble?"

"No sense in returning the book and then checking it out again and again. That would look suspicious."

Once again, John had forced Arthur to participate more deeply than he intended. Obediently, Arthur removed several more pages before he turned the book back to the security officer.

That night, Arthur drove to John's detective office to photograph the pages he had stolen.

"I thought I was going to have a heart attack," he recalled. "I was so paranoid and scared. I knew I was going to get caught this time. Any moment, a gang of G-men were going to come bursting through John's office door. I couldn't believe that I was photographing this stupid report for him, and I promised myself that this was going to be the last time. I just couldn't take it anymore—the pressure and the fear of getting caught. It was crazy. I mean, this report wasn't worth all that tension and danger. I literally thought I was going to die while I was taking pictures."

As he had done with the photographs of the U.S.S. *Blue Ridge,* Arthur left the film in John's desk with a note. The next morning, Arthur returned the missing pages to the casualty report.

When Arthur talked with John a few days later, he said, "Hey, John, no more photographing for me. I can't do it. I can't do, Bubba. If we find anything, you are going to find a way to do the snapping."

But Arthur didn't have the courage to say he was finished as a spy. John was just too important to him.

That July, Arthur met Sheila Woods while working on a private detective case for John. A friend of Sheila's had hired Confidential Reports and Arthur interviewed her as part of his investigation. She was recently divorced, the mother of two grown children, and close to Arthur in age. They liked each other from the start.

"I think the reason that Arthur and I became good friends," Sheila told me later, "was because I honestly felt that I had walked in his footsteps and he in mine. We were the oldest children in our families and both of our fathers were alcoholics. . . ."

In Sheila, Arthur found a sympathetic friend and listener. Before long, they were lovers. Arthur was careful to keep his affair secret from Rita, but John soon figured out what was going on and encouraged Arthur.

John was happy, he told me later, that Arthur was finally having a "little fun in his boring life."

"Old Uncle Art was finally loosening up!"

# 47

By the summer of 1982, Laura Walker was desperate. She and Mark were fighting incessantly, she wanted out of the marriage, but couldn't leave without Christopher. The problem was money. It always was. She didn't know whom she could borrow money from. Her father was still furious at her for not reenlisting and her mother was surviving from paycheck to paycheck. Laura began thinking of people she knew with cash. Jerry Whitworth! When John, Jerry, Brenda, and Laura had gone to dinner together in February, Jerry seemed to be flaunting as much money as John. Laura began to wonder. Could he be a spy? Laura didn't know the old Jerry, only the new Jerry Whitworth, John's creation.

"Jerry was very much like my father," she told me later. "In fact, he was so much like my father I could not tell who was copying who that night at dinner."

Laura telephoned Jerry and he sounded excited to hear from her. Within a few minutes, he had invited her to dinner. When they met, she noticed that he had come alone, without Brenda. Laura assumed this was because Jerry didn't want Brenda to know he was meeting with her, and Laura took this as a good sign. But Jerry had another reason for not bringing along his wife. He knew that John had attempted to recruit Laura, and he didn't want her bringing up espionage in front of Brenda.

Jerry and Laura had a good time that night. Jerry told great stories and was a good listener. He called her a short time after that dinner and they got together two more times, Laura told me later. It was during their last rendezvous that Laura asked Jerry to lend her $600. He wrote her a personal check.

"Jerry Whitworth flipped for me," Laura Walker told me. "I knew it and understood it, but he didn't make a pass until after I borrowed the money. That is when he made his overt sexual pass. He made his pass and when he found that he was going to be unsuccessful, he stopped."

With Jerry's money, Laura had a way out and she took it. She and Christopher moved into another apartment, leaving Mark behind. Before long, Laura began dating someone else—much to Mark's irritation. He still hoped they could reconcile their problems.

About one month after Laura moved out, Mark went to her new apartment while she was at work and took Christopher. They left on a bus bound for Lanham, Maryland. After the Greyhound crossed into Nevada, Mark telephoned Laura and told her what he had done.

Up to this point, the marital strife between them had been limited to a husband–wife problem. But Mark's decision to take Christopher made it into a Walker family problem.

Laura Walker and Philip Mark Snyder both vehemently disagreed over what happened next. Both have testified under oath before a federal grand jury to exactly opposite stories.

"Mark reminded me during one of his phone calls," Laura Walker told me, "that he knew my dad was a spy. I had told Mark about him earlier. . . . Mark told me, 'I don't want you to raise Chris anyway, especially with your family.' Then he reminded me that he remembered what my dad was involved in. I understood completely what he was saying to me. He was blackmailing me, and I got on the phone and called my mom and said 'You better call Dad and you better tell him that Mark knows!' "

Barbara Walker was furious when Laura told her what had happened. Why had Laura told Mark? She called Laura selfish and disloyal. But Barbara did as Laura had asked. After talking with Barbara, John placed an angry call to Laura.

Laura later was questioned at Jerry Whitworth's trial about that conversation. Under oath, she said her father had suggested that Mark might be killed.

> LAURA: He [John] asked me how much I cared about my husband and how I would feel if he suddenly no longer existed.
> Q: And what did you say?
> A: I said I didn't care.

Later, under examination by Whitworth's defense attorney, Laura Walker expounded on her answer:

> Q: What else did he [John] say to you?
> A: He said that he couldn't believe that I would tell my junkie husband about his private life. And then he asked me if I still loved him, and I said, "No." Obviously, I wasn't feeling very much love for him at that time. He just took my two-year-old son. And then he asked me how I would feel if he was not around anymore, and it was very clear to me what he was saying.
> Q: What was he saying?
> A: I felt that he was asking me how I would feel if my husband was dead by unnatural causes.

Philip Mark Snyder denied to me and in testimony to the grand jury that he ever blackmailed Laura. "Laura never told me about her father," Mark Snyder said. "I never knew John Walker was a spy. Never! I swear it. It was a total lie on her part."

Mark Snyder accused Laura of "concocting" the blackmail story in an unsuccessful effort to get John to go after Christopher.

"Laura is a very manipulative person," Mark Snyder said. "I think she was trying to get her father to harm me. I think Laura was so angry that *she* wanted me dead."

Whatever the truth, in the summer of 1982, John Walker believed Mark Snyder posed a threat to him and his ring. John was angry, but not enough to kill. Instead, John figured that Mark would keep his mouth shut as long as he had Christopher.

"I couldn't believe that cunt daughter of mine would do what she did," John told me later. "And then when I talked to her she wants me to go get her son for her. I said, 'Laura, you are a bitch, a cunt bitch. If you want your son, then go to Maryland and get him yourself. I am not going to get involved.'

"I didn't think Laura was making any sense," John continued. "I mean, she said Mark was going to turn me in if she went after Christopher. But then she wanted me to go after Christopher. Why would that make a difference? I mean, if I went after Christopher, what would keep Mark from turning me in? She was acting crazy."

The message to Laura was clear. She became convinced that neither John nor Barbara was going to help her regain custody of her son if it meant putting the spy ring in jeopardy.

# PART FIVE

# MICHAEL

*Train up a child in the way he
should go, and when he is old he will
not depart from it.*

**Proverbs 22:4**

*Few fathers care much for
their sons, or at least, most of them care
more for their money.*

**LORD CHESTERFIELD**
*Letters, 27 May 1752*

# 48

Michael Walker loved to surf and John gave him plenty of money to spend on gear. Surfing was more than a hobby to Michael. It signified a way of life.

"Riding waves was almost orgasmic," Michael told me after his arrest. "You could put the most beautiful woman in the world naked on the beach and have an eight-foot perfect wave coming in, and a true male surfer would have to think twice about which he would choose."

Surfing was carefree, exciting, sexy. "It was what I wanted to do."

Just before his high school graduation, Michael enlisted in the Navy. His surfer friends were stunned, and his closest surfing pal felt betrayed. Joining the Navy was for nerds, not carefree surfers.

Michael didn't care. He had done this for his father as he had promised, a reverse graduation present of sorts.

Michael hadn't told John what he was doing. He just did it, and at first, he wasn't certain that the Navy would take him. When the recruiter asked if Michael had ever used any narcotics or had smoked marijuana, Michael answered truthfully. As a result, he was sent to the district recruitment command in Richmond, where he was issued a special drug waiver. At that time, the Navy told Michael that he probably wouldn't be allowed to handle classified documents because of his self-acknowledged use of drugs. But apparently no one made such a notation in his Navy personnel file.

John beamed when Michael announced that he had enlisted. "You've really made your old man proud," he said.

Because Michael was still a senior in high school, his entry date was delayed until December 1982, eight months away. Michael planned to surf as much as possible that summer and fall, but John had other ideas. He insisted that Michael enroll in typing and math courses at Tidewater Community College. "These are skills you'll need to get a job with access to classified information," John explained. "Those are the best types of jobs."

Michael wasn't thrilled, but he did as he was told. The classes weren't difficult, and he still could surf in the mornings.

One spring night, Michael stopped by The Lone Pine, a Virginia Beach restaurant, to talk to his dad.

"P.K. and I started going over to The Lone Pine every night," John recalled later, "because a lot of lawyers and insurance agents used to hang out there." It was important for John to mingle with potential clients because his business partner, Phil Prince, had pulled out. After nearly two years together, the two men couldn't get along anymore, so Prince had signed over his share of the company to John.

Michael found his father, P.K., and Uncle Arthur all drunk. Someone was celebrating a birthday and John had ordered a special cake shaped like a nude woman. When the guest of honor went to the bathroom, one of the men at the party unzipped his pants and stuck his penis in the absent person's drink.

"When the guy got back from the bathroom and took a drink, everyone cracked up," Michael told me later. "My dad knew how to throw some great parties."

Michael, soon as drunk as his father, accidentally crashed into the front desk where a young cashier, Rachel Sara Allen, worked. Neither of them paid any attention to the other.

A few days later, John asked Rachel if she would like to spend Father's Day with him, P.K., and Michael on the houseboat. Rachel politely declined, but John persisted. Rachel was suspicious. She thought John might be attempting to get her alone on the boat. John wouldn't give up. He called her that weekend. "Michael is really excited about you coming over," John said. "You can't let him down."

As she drove to John's house that afternoon, Rachel reviewed what she knew about her host. He had been one of the first regular customers she had met working that spring at The Lone Pine. With his "plastic hair," girlfriend half his age, and his endless supply of cash, John stuck out.

She and John became friends by accident when she chastised him one night for playing the bar's video game.

"You waste too much money on that," she told him. The nineteen-year-old's impertinence surprised John.

"From now on," Rachel continued, "every time you bring me a dollar, I'm going to give you seventy-five cents and I'll keep a quarter up here so you'll have some money when you go home."

John liked that.

Soon, Rachel had met all of John's crew: Uncle Art, P.K., and the other investigators from Confidential Reports.

Now she was about to meet Michael.

Rachel wasn't eager to fall in love. The five-foot two-inch blonde was on the rebound from her first serious love affair, and she didn't have a very good impression of men.

Rachel had had a difficult childhood. Her parents divorced when she was five years old, and she had hated her stepfather. As a child, she developed into a bookworm and spent much of her days alone. Her only date during high school was to the junior prom, which she attended with her chemistry lab partner, a boy who, like her, hadn't dated before. "We never even kissed good night when he brought me home," she told a friend afterward. There was only one man whom Rachel was close to as a child. Her father, a veteran Navy officer, showered her with attention and affection, but was away much of the time.

After high school, Rachel enrolled at Old Dominion University, where she took a full schedule of science courses. She also worked at a Hallmark card shop to help pay her tuition. During her first semester, Rachel had a 3.7 grade point average, but she had paid a price. Her weight had dropped from its normal 128 pounds to eighty pounds. She was fatigued, lonely, and depressed.

During her second semester Rachel fell in love with a sailor eight years her senior. His name was David and he treated her as if she were the "most beautiful person in the world." In truth, Rachel had blossomed into a beauty, but she didn't realize it. Then, after a whirlwind romance, Rachel discovered that David was seeing other women. She was crushed and vowed not to be so trusting of men.

When she pulled up to John's houseboat on Father's Day, Rachel made up her mind: if John was there without P.K., she would turn around and leave immediately. She was walking toward the boat when John appeared with P.K. at his side.

"You've got to meet Michael," John said. "C'mon."

Michael was already on the boat. When he saw her, he was tongue-tied.

"I could barely talk," recalled Michael. "I thought, 'Oh shit! My dad's hit the jackpot for once!'"

Rachel and Michael sat on the deck as John steered the houseboat out into the bay. Both were uncomfortable, not knowing what to say to each other. Then Rachel asked Michael the name of the high school he had attended.

"You've never heard of it," he replied. "It's a small private school."

"Try me," responded Rachel. "I've lived here all my life."

"Ryan," answered Michael.

"You got to be kidding," beamed Rachel. "My stepsister goes there. Do you know . . ."

For the next hour, the two compared notes. Rachel couldn't stand Michael's best friend, but she approved of some of his other pals. By the time the foursome returned to the pier, Rachel was no longer in a hurry to go home.

John fixed lasagna for dinner and at a quarter to ten, P.K. announced she was going to bed.

"You know, John, you don't get *any* if you're not in bed by ten," P.K. proclaimed.

John jumped to his feet like a schoolboy. "Good seeing you Rachel. Glad you could make it out today," he said, racing upstairs.

Michael and Rachel both laughed. A few minutes later, Michael began getting romantic with Rachel. She didn't mind a few kisses, but when he made it clear that he was interested in more, she stopped him.

"I'm a biology major," Rachel said, "and I know you are probably getting uncomfortable. I don't want you to have any problems getting to sleep tonight, so I'm going to leave now."

Michael couldn't believe it. She was serious. She got up and left.

When Rachel got home that night, she woke up her stepsister. "Tell me everything you know about Michael Walker," Rachel demanded. "He's such a nice guy!"

The next night, Michael stopped at The Lone Pine to say hello. When Rachel left work that night, there was a note under the wiper on her car. "Let's go to the beach tomorrow. Please!!!! Love, Michael." Rachel put the note in her purse, and when she got home she tucked it into a scrapbook. She was confident that Michael Walker was going to be someone special.

Michael had a single rose with him when he arrived in the morning to take Rachel to the beach. He had bought it from a street vendor at the corner. From that day on, Michael always brought Rachel a rose when they had a date.

Michael and Rachel drove to the beach and tossed a Frisbee around. Later that night, he stopped at The Lone Pine and left another note on her car. They went to the beach each morning that week, and Michael stopped by every night when Rachel was at work. On Saturday, Rachel invited Michael to go scuba diving and that night, Michael once again attempted to have sex with Rachel. As soon as he tried to slip his hand up into the top of her bikini, she stopped him. Michael got angry this time and the next day, he didn't call Rachel or stop by The Lone Pine. She telephoned him the next morning.

"What's the problem?" she asked.

"What's your problem?" Michael responded.

Rachel didn't understand, so Michael spelled it out. "This isn't my style," he said, "to go out and just play around. I want to get serious."

They talked for nearly an hour, and Rachel agreed to go with Michael on the Fourth of July to Cape Hatteras, even though it meant lying to her father about the overnight trip.

The combination of the beach, sunset, fireworks, campfire, and Michael proved to be too much for Rachel to resist. They made love that night in the back of Michael's truck under a sky filled with fireworks. Afterward, Rachel told Michael about David and how much she had loved him and how he had hurt her.

"You aren't going to do that to me, are you?" she asked. "You're different, aren't you?"

Michael assured her that he was.

After that weekend, Michael and Rachel were together constantly. Rachel desperately wanted Michael to love her, and she was willing to do just about anything to please him. When they went to a nightclub favored by punk rockers, Michael paraded Rachel through the crowd.

"Rachel, everyone thinks you are one hot chick," he told her proudly. They found a table and ordered a pitcher of beer. The waitress asked if they wanted glasses, and Michael quickly said no. Rachel didn't understand, but when the pitcher arrived, Michael took a big drink from it and passed it to her. "This is how we do it here."

Rachel loved it!

When her college classes started, Rachel had a difficult time studying, and her grades began to fall. One night, after she got off work, Michael told her that he had something serious to tell her. They parked near the beach.

"Rachel, I'm going into the Navy. I have to report in December."

"How long have you known?" she asked.

"Since March."

"That's before we started dating!" Rachel said, starting to cry. "Why didn't you tell me? Have you just been taking me for a ride? Is this some little game you were playing? Get a good screw or two in before you get sent off?"

"No, it's not like that, I love you," he said. "You've got to believe me. I love you more than anything."

Michael had bought Rachel a scuba-diving air regulator on her birthday. It was the most expensive present she had ever received. When his birthday arrived, Rachel gave Michael an expensive diver's watch. It was much more than she could afford, but she had gotten a line of credit from the jewelers and planned to pay it off each month. "The watch was just a token," she said, handing him a card. "Here's my real present." Michael didn't pay much attention to what it said on the outside. It was the note that Rachel had scribbled inside that mattered.

Your birthday present is ME! No matter where you are sent in the Navy, I will go with you. I love you and will stand by you.

They hugged and that night Michael told Rachel that if he could find a way out of his obligation to the Navy, he would. He planned to talk to his dad about it. Surely an old seadog like John would know a way.

After Rachel left that night, Michael told John that he'd made a mistake by enlisting. John listened intently and then went to work. He told Michael that going to boot camp would be good for him and Rachel. They could have some time apart to put their relationship in perspective. If Michael really loved Rachel, then joining the Navy was exactly what he should do. After all, it was a job and Michael would need a job if he wanted to marry Rachel someday. They spoke a long time and when John finished, Michael was confident that his father was correct.

The next day, Rachel noticed a change in John. From that day on, he was never very friendly toward her.

The night before Michael left for boot camp, Rachel spent the night with him at John's house. She couldn't sleep, so she got up and went downstairs. Michael found her sitting in a chair, crying softly. Michael had promised her that he would find a way out, but he hadn't. He began repeating all the reasons that John had cited to him. But in those early morning hours, those reasons didn't make as much sense to Michael as they had before. He suddenly found himself repeating to Rachel, again and again: "I don't want to let my dad down. I can't let my dad down."

# 49

In September 1982, John flew to California to deliver $60,000 to Jerry from the Russians. He also needed to pick up whatever film Jerry had.

Jerry's performance at Stockton had been highly praised by his Navy superiors. He had not done as well, however, as a spy. He had photographed only a few keylists for John, and it was clear that his enthusiasm for copying documents had waned.

"All Jerry talked about during my visit was how he wasn't being paid enough and how the risk just wasn't worth the money," John recalled. "My suspicions were confirmed. Jerry was going weak on me once again. He was getting scared, and I sensed that he was pulling back."

John reminded Jerry of the danger, but this time Jerry didn't seem afraid. So John switched tactics and talked about the $1 million payment.

"Jerry, imagine going back to Muldrow and telling your relatives you earned one hundred thousand a year just by playing the stock market," John said. "Jesus, they'd be impressed. Not to mention the things you could buy for Brenda."

"Jerry vacillated," John told me. "One minute, he'd be complaining about the money and hinting that he wanted out. A minute later, he'd be figuring out some new way to photograph documents. It was crazy."

When Jerry's tour ended, he was assigned to the U.S.S. *Enterprise,* an aircraft carrier that had just left on an extended eight-month cruise.

Jerry was scheduled to fly to Subic Bay in the Philippines on October 11 to join it as a technical control chief. As such, Jerry would have access to cipher systems for the KW-7, KG-14, KG-36, KWR-37, and KY-57, as well as hundreds of operational plans, orders, and other messages.

"This is really great news," John exulted. "This can be a real gold mine. I'm sure we can get them to go along with the million-dollar deal! Just be certain to take along plenty of film."

Jerry took John seriously. He drove to the Pacific Camera Shop in San Francisco and bought a new Minox and the store's complete stock of film—twenty rolls.

When Jerry arrived aboard the U.S.S. *Enterprise,* he discovered the carrier was going to participate in several unusual war games, including an exercise four hundred miles off the Soviet coast with two other aircraft carriers. It was the first three-carrier exercise ever planned in the Pacific, and the Pentagon was anxious to see how the Russians would react to more than thirty warships appearing off their shore. The U.S.S. *Enterprise*'s presence had already been noted by the Soviet Union. On September 23, while Jerry was buying his camera and film, the carrier was "the subject of extensive Soviet air, surface, and subsurface surveillance," according to the carrier's manifest. "Of note was the unprecedented Soviet use of backfire aircraft on 30 September and 2 October to reconnoiter the *Enterprise* battle group," the book noted.

Obviously, the KGB was going to be interested in learning everything it could about the *Enterprise*'s mission and the upcoming three-aircraft-carrier war exercise. John had been correct. There was a lot of money to be made by Jerry—if he had the guts to go through with it.

Laura Walker was still having a difficult time during the winter of 1982. She had lost her job, and her car had been repossessed. She hadn't heard from Mark Snyder about Christopher, and she had broken up with her boyfriend. She was broke, so as always she called John. All she needed was a few hundred bucks to get back on her feet, she explained. John was surprised to hear her voice. They hadn't spoken since he criticized her for breaking their "blood oath of silence" by telling Mark about the spying.

John didn't make it easy for his daughter to ask for a loan.

"What about our deal?" he asked.

"What deal?"

"C'mon, Laura," John said. "Don't be a cunt. You promised to help me by going back into the Army. Do you want to do it or not?"

Laura dodged the question, but this time, John knew better than to give Laura cash without some proof that she was going to help him. No money unless she reenlisted.

"I don't know if I can reenlist," she said.

John began castigating her: Why not? The Army was the only real job she had ever held! Now that she wasn't stuck with her son, she didn't have any more excuses.

Laura lashed back. If John really cared about her and her son, he'd help her get Christopher back.

"You're a private eye. You've got an airplane. All you'd have to do is fly to Maryland and grab him for me," she said. "You do it all the time for people who hire you."

"No way," John said.

Like two snarling alley cats, father and daughter slashed at each other. Finally, Laura told John that she had never intended to spy. She was simply leading him on for the money.

"I don't see why I should get into espionage just to make you rich!" she snapped.

"Fuck you, Laura!" John told his daughter. He slammed down the telephone receiver.

Just before Christmas, Laura received an envelope in the mail with John's return address in the corner. She thought John might have changed his mind and mailed her a check. But there was no cash inside. "He sent me a bill, itemized, and typed out," Laura told me later. John listed every dollar of money that he had spent on Laura since her high school graduation: the costs of the clothes that he had bought her, the spy money he had paid her, the $500 that he had put down for the now repossessed Mazda. The total was more than $3,000 and at the bottom of the typed statement, John had written a message: "This is what you OWE me and I expect to be paid!"

Laura tore the paper into pieces and responded with a letter of her own.

"You have some nerve, you adulterous pig," she wrote.

"I used foul language," Laura said later, "and wrote about the things that he had done to my mother."

At that instant, it was as if all the years that had passed didn't matter. Once again, Laura felt like the teenage runaway John had beaten with his belt. She hated him.

John telephoned Laura a week later. "I got your letter," he said. "I'm glad to see that you got things off your chest." He wasn't angry. It was as if nothing had ever happened.

"I hope you're still thinking about my offer," he said. "We could really make some good money together."

Michael did exceptionally well during his indoctrination at the Great Lakes Naval Training Center, but the knowledge that he gained wasn't quite what the Navy intended.

"The Navy is just like everything else in life," Michael told me. "You have to play by their rules. But once you learn the rules, you can move around them. After the first week in boot camp, I was making money— lots of it."

When a new class of recruits arrived each week, Michael was eager to make life easier for them—for a price. "I'd say, 'Hey man, you want to learn how to iron your clothes the proper way so you can pass inspection? Okay, that'll be five bucks.' "

New recruits were not allowed to shop at the military store or leave the training center. "If anyone needed cigarettes, *Playboy*, or even stamps, they knew who to come to—me," Michael recalled proudly. "I was Mr. Fix-it."

Each chance he got, Michael telephoned Rachel. He always called collect, but her father was happy to pay the tab. Her father also agreed to buy an airline ticket so Rachel could fly to Chicago for Michael's graduation. Barbara Walker wanted to attend too, but she didn't have enough money. She could have called John for the cash, but instead she telephoned Rita and borrowed $200. Rita knew Barbara was good for it. "When they lived in Norfolk, she used to borrow money when her kids ran away from home. We'd let her use our American Express card and then she'd pay the bill." At that point in her life, Barbara was doing everything that she could to avoid John.

Barbara and Rachel were supposed to meet when they both arrived in Chicago at O'Hare Airport, but they couldn't find each other, and when they finally got together, Rachel was in tears. "She had made arrangements in Norfolk to rent a car, but the company had screwed things up," Barbara Walker recalled. Barbara rented one and drove while Rachel gave directions. Within minutes, they were lost.

When it became clear that neither Barbara nor Rachel knew where they were going, Barbara pulled into a gas station and told Rachel to ask the attendant for directions. As she stepped from the car, Rachel slipped in the snow and fell down. She had spent her entire week's paycheck on a long-sleeved silk dress with matching shoes, and she had her long hair styled fashionably atop her head.

A few seconds later, Barbara and Rachel were following one of the attendants, who had offered to lead them in his car to their hotel.

"I don't know what that guy saw when I fell," Rachel told Barbara, "but he sure volunteered fast to take us where we are going."

Barbara and Rachel giggled like best friends.

While Rachel put on fresh makeup in her room at the Holiday Inn, Barbara opened her suitcase and removed a bottle of Johnnie Walker Red scotch. They hurried to Michael's graduation after Barbara had several drinks. It seemed to take forever, and when it finally ended, Michael threw his arms around his mother first and then hugged and kissed Rachel. The three of them went to dinner with one of Michael's boot camp buddies and his girlfriend. Afterward, Michael and Rachel left Barbara alone in her room and went into Rachel's room. "I knew they were having sex," Barbara told me later, "and I didn't want to disturb them. The kids needed some time to themselves."

The next morning, they visited Chicago's aquarium and then drove to a bar in Milwaukee, where the minimum drinking age was lower than in Illinois. All three got drunk. "We had an incredibly great time," Michael recalled, "and my mother was really running the party, buying drinks and taking care of everything."

Back at the Holiday Inn, Michael knocked on his mother's door late that night sometime after he and Rachel had retired. He wanted to visit. "We talked until three or four in the morning," Barbara said. "Michael told me he had decided that God had a purpose for him. He wanted him to become a teacher, and I was so proud of Michael." The story, Michael said later, was "bullshit." He had simply wanted to make her happy.

Rachel was not impressed when Michael returned to bed early that morning.

"Why don't you go get in bed with your mother?" she complained.

"I'm sorry, bunny," he replied. "We just needed to talk."

He kissed her gently on the cheek.

"It's okay bugger-bear," she said, using her nickname for Michael. As a child, Rachel had had a teddy bear she carried everywhere. It was her bugger-bear. She pulled Michael close.

Because Michael still didn't have a specific job, he remained at the Great Lakes center for several more weeks of what the Navy called A-School.

"I was alone but I got to move into this dorm, and now all the recruits had to salute me, and I really enjoyed that," Michael recalled. "I'd go on walks and when someone forgot to salute me, I'd get into their face. 'Oh, I'm sorry, sir. I forgot to salute you.' 'That's okay, but don't let it happen again. Now get your ass moving.'"

Michael claimed he received special treatment at A-School.

"This chief comes in to class and he says, 'Okay, which of you is the private eye?' and I thought, 'Wow, that's me,' so I raised my hand and he says, 'I want you to be my yeoman. Come with me.' Then he says, 'You've just passed this school 'cause it's a school for idiots and you aren't an idiot. Now, it's up to you to help get the guys who are idiots through.'"

Michael's job as the chief's yeoman was similar to that of a teacher's assistant. He bought himself dark glasses, a briefcase, and a pointer. When he came into class, he spoke with authority. "Okay, gentlemen, this is what we are going to do today."

"This is where I really learned how to manipulate people," Michael said later. "I really began to refine the skills that I was going to use as a spy and use the Navy rules and regulations to my own advantage. The class I was working with was really bad—they were all fuckups—and I didn't think any of them were smart enough to pass one of the final exams. So I went into the chief's office, and I found the answers to the test, and I made fifty copies. I went to the barracks that night before the test and said, 'Attention on deck.' Well, all these idiots stumbled out of bed and I told them: 'You guys are a bunch of fuckups, and no one is going to pass the test, but I'll tell you what I'm willing to do. If you can raise fifty dollars between all of you, I'll show you a way to pass.' Well, these dummies pooled their money and gave me the fifty bucks. 'Okay,' I said, 'here's the answers to the test, but if any of you get into trouble, it's your ass not mine. I'm the yeoman and the Navy is going to believe me.' No one ever got caught, and I knew they wouldn't. Like I said, I was learning how to manipulate the system and make money. I'm sorry, but that's how it was. That's how I was. I was nineteen and street wise. I knew how the game was played and I loved beating it.

"My old company commander came up to me after these guys had all passed the test, and he says, 'Congratulations, Walker. I don't know how you did it, getting these dummies to pass, but the Navy is glad you did.' "

# 50

While Michael was undergoing his Navy training, John was frantically calling his congressman. His passport had expired and he was scheduled to meet his KGB handler on January 15, 1983, in Vienna. A helpful aide in the Norfolk office of Republican Representative G. William Whitehurst assured John that if he hand delivered his expired passport to the congressman's office, someone there would make certain he got his new passport in time. He did, and the congressman's office came through.

"I thought it was neat that a congressman helped me get to my KGB meeting on time," John told me later, breaking into a grin.

On January 10, John boarded Eastern flight 508 from Norfolk to New York City flying under the alias of John Williams, then used his actual name on a Swissair flight to Zurich. The next day, John took the train to Vienna, checking into the luxury Vienna Intercontinental on the eleventh. The hotel was filled with Americans, even in the middle of winter.

The morning of his meeting, John walked to the white marble U-Bahn station less than one block away from his hotel. As usual, he wanted to walk through the area on the day of his face-to-face meeting to make certain that nothing had altered his KGB-approved route. The U-Bahn runs above ground at this location, and as John stood on the concrete landing, he felt strange, as if someone were watching him.

John surveyed the dozen or so persons waiting for a southbound U-4 train. Only one looked suspicious. Dressed in a heavy pea green overcoat and black hat, he turned his head as soon as John looked at him. The man was in his mid-thirties, was larger than John, and had a gaunt look.

John was worried that he was being followed, so he decided to perform a small test. He boarded the next southbound train, but stepped back onto the platform just before the doors closed, and then hurried up the stairs leading to the subway entrance. He heard the sound of someone else climbing the steps behind him. Resisting the urge to look, he crossed to the other side of the tracks and went down the stairs leading to the northbound platform.

When he reached it, John turned around to see. No one was following him. He began to relax.

"I figured I was just nervous," John recalled later. "I always had butterflies before a dead drop or face-to-face."

When the next silver-colored train arrived, John stepped through its double doors and found a seat in the rear of the car. As the doors closed, John noticed a man dash past the window . . . wearing a pea green coat and black hat.

Now John was alarmed. Was he being followed? Had Mark Snyder tipped off the FBI or CIA? John didn't think that either had authority to arrest him in Vienna, but he wasn't sure. Perhaps his imagination was getting the best of him.

There was another possibility. Less than four blocks from the Intercontinental Hotel was the Soviet embassy, a large, square, muddy brown building with radio antennae on the roof and police with machine guns standing guard near the heavy iron gate that surrounded the complex. Could the man in the pea green coat be a KGB agent?

John decided to remain on the northbound train as it circled the old city. When it reached its second stop, he got off and looked up and down the ramp for the man in the pea green coat. He didn't see him. Just to be certain that he wasn't being followed, John boarded another northbound train, this time on the U-1 line, whose tracks went northeast. A gaggle of small girls and boys dressed in colorful blue-and-green uniforms entered John's car. Several women were apparently taking the noisy group ice skating. Just as the train's doors were about to close, the man in the pea green coat burst into the car. When he saw John, he quickly turned away.

"At that point, I knew I was being followed," John recalled. He had seen the man too often for it to be a coincidence.

Because John had flown to Zurich, he had not been able to buy a small handgun, as was his routine in Italy, but he did have a hardwood cane with a firm brass handle. He also was carrying Jerry's film from Alameda because he had been afraid to leave it at the hotel. It was sealed in a plastic bag and was tucked into his coat pocket. If he was arrested, the film would be difficult to explain.

At the first stop after the U-Bahn crossed the Danube River, the children exited. John jumped up and dashed out the door. He walked down the stairs and followed the schoolchildren.

John had exited at the Vienna International Centre, nicknamed UNO-City because it houses the United Nations Industrial Development Organization and other U.N. agencies. He followed the children about a hundred yards to an ice rink and entered it behind them.

"I looked out the door and, sure enough, I spot this guy. This damn dude is still following me," John recalled. He left the rink, again turning to his right. He continued walking, crossed a concrete pedestrian bridge, and entered a large park. "The park had a lot of turns in it and I didn't know what to do," John said. "I started down this path and then realized that it was a loop and that I was heading back in the same direction where I had been."

John looked around. The only figure he could see in the snow-covered park was the man in the pea green coat.

"Just as I was about to exit the loop, I saw him entering it. We were both on the same path," John said. "Everyone always says to watch someone's eyes and you can tell if they are going to hit you. Bullshit. You watch his hands because that is where things are going to happen. He had gloves on and his hands were outside his pockets. I could feel him staring at my face. If he would have had his hands in his pockets, I would have been afraid because he might have had a weapon.

"The second that I passed by him, I turned and I whacked that mother fucker with my cane on the back of his head. He was wearing a hat that must have softened the blow, but he fell to his knees and I whacked him one more time on the head. Then I got the fuck out of there. I didn't run, I just walked toward the rink at faster than normal pace. I was worried because I didn't have any idea who the hell this guy was. Whether he was a mugger, a CIA agent, a KGB agent, or some poor son of a bitch out for a stroll. People do a lot of walking around over there. I was really worried though."

After the assault, John returned to the hotel and stayed in his room until the time of his meeting. As usual, he began his walk at the Komet Küchen store, but a few minutes after John left the display window and began his route down Ruckergasse, his KGB handler appeared.

"Hello, dear friend," he said. "Do you have something for me?"

John was surprised that his second KGB handler had approached him so quickly. "He seemed to scoff at the elaborateness of the Vienna

Procedure. I had barely begun my walk and after the first couple turns, he showed up."

Impatience, John noticed, was not the only personality trait that made his new handler different from his first. The KGB agent was humorless, abrupt, and unfriendly. But he followed exactly the same script as the first agent. He began with questions about security, followed by specific questions that he had memorized about various cipher machines and keylists that the KGB wanted.

John explained that Jerry had been transferred to the U.S.S. *Enterprise,* but before John could explain what a good post it was, the agent interrupted. What had Jerry done wrong? he asked. Why was he being moved around so much? Perhaps he had been caught and the Navy was moving him somewhere it could watch him. Was John certain that the FBI hadn't caught Jerry? Could Jerry be trusted?

The Soviets had always been suspicious and anytime there was an anomaly, they stopped all payments until they could verify John's delivery and make sure it had not been doctored. "I honestly believe that whenever Jerry changed jobs, the KGB considered the next delivery an FBI plant and had to revalidate it," John told me.

As the two men walked through the snow, John tired of the questions. He exploded with a chain of profanity. The problem with Jerry wasn't his past, John explained, it was his future.

"Jerry's talking about retiring once again," John explained. "You need to give him more money."

John told the KGB agent that Jerry needed $1 million. In return, he would spy for ten more years.

"Imagine how this dummy feels," John recalled, referring to his second KGB handler. "He is assigned to be the handler of one of the most important American espionage operations in the KGB's history, and during his very first meeting alone with me, I tell him that Whitworth might retire. And then I told this shithead that the only way to make certain that Jerry didn't get out was by giving him one million dollars. He couldn't believe it. I'm certain he saw his entire KGB career going down the toilet."

The KGB agent didn't give John an answer about the $1 million. Instead, he asked about Jerry's access. He also asked about Arthur and Laura.

John played up Arthur's importance but not Laura's. He also decided, he said later, not to tell his KGB handler about his encounter with the man in the pea green coat.

Two days after their meeting, John went to Munich, before returning to New York City. During the trip he again sensed he was being followed, but he couldn't prove it.

Back in Norfolk, John felt safe again. He decided that the man in the pea green coat wasn't from the FBI. If anything, he was a KGB agent sent to watch him. His new handler had put a tail on him. But why? Maybe the KGB's decision to change his handlers wasn't a fluke, as he had believed earlier. Maybe his first handler hadn't been promoted. Maybe the KGB had chosen a gruff handler to deal with him because it wanted someone who hadn't befriended him in charge of the case. Thoughts like these hounded John, he said later. Like the Russians, he was becoming suspicious whenever there was a change. His natural paranoia preyed on him too. As far as he was concerned, there was only one explanation for the man in the pea green coat and his new, gruff KGB handler.

"If necessary," he recalled later, "the Soviets were setting the stage to eliminate me."

# 51

Jerry Whitworth didn't have to wait long during October 1982 for some tantalizing top secret messages to cross his desk aboard the U.S.S. Enterprise. The carrier and the twelve ships and submarines that traveled as part of its battle group entered the South China Sea on October 19 and intentionally crossed into what the government of Vietnam considers its territorial waters. The United States did not recognize Vietnam's claim and said the carrier was merely sailing through the area as part of a "freedom of navigation" exercise to keep the waterway open.

The trip was not reported in the carrier's unclassified ship history that year, but it was confirmed later in court testimony by Captain Charles Reed Jones, Jr., commanding officer of the Navy's Fleet Intelligence Center in the Pacific. "The Enterprise battle group was asked to conduct a challenge to the Vietnamese-claimed territorial waters in the South China Sea," Jones testified. "That claim is not recognized by the United States. It's not recognized in international law because it's considered to be excessive."

The battle group was doing more than simply establishing the right of U.S. naval ships to cruise wherever they wished. The U.S.S. Enterprise was engaged in electronic surveillance, which is part of a rarely mentioned but almost routine cat-and-mouse game played by the superpowers.

The Vietnamese had no way of knowing on October 19 if the arrival of an aircraft carrier off their shoreline was part of a training exercise or actual attack. So the military there took immediate defensive action. It cranked up its radar, prepared whatever surface missiles it had, and launched aircraft to monitor and, if necessary, encounter the intruder.

The entire time that Vietnam was taking such steps, the U.S.S. *Enterprise* was busy monitoring the country's military preparedness. Using the latest electronic surveillance devices, the ship attempted to identify Vietnamese missile sites and isolate the frequencies that the Vietnamese used for emergency communications.

Sometimes, these war games are even more sophisticated. A carrier, such as the U.S.S. *Enterprise,* might jam the enemy's radar to see how it reacts. This form of intelligence-gathering is extremely effective, but it is also dangerous. For instance, on March 23, 1986, the U.S. Sixth Fleet conducted a "freedom of navigation" exercise in the disputed waters of the Gulf of Sidra off the coast of Libya. For two days, Libya fired surface missiles at U.S. aircraft and ships. The United States responded by attacking several Libyan airplanes and missile installations on the Libyan mainland. Libyan leader Colonel Muammar el-Qaddafi had warned the United States against crossing what he described as a "line of death" across the gulf, but U.S. officials claimed Libya had no territorial right to control the area.

The U.S.S. *Enterprise*'s cruise into waters claimed by Vietnam elicited the response that Navy intelligence officials had hoped for. Messages from reconnaissance aircraft and other members of the battle group streamed into the radio room where Jerry worked. As Navy analysts collected electronic data about Vietnam's air, land, and sea defenses, Jerry quietly copied the messages that he wanted to keep for delivery to the Russians.

Monitoring Vietnam was just the start. Sometime during November and December, the carrier battle group conducted "real world surveillance of the Soviet naval units operating in the Indian Ocean," according to the *Enterprise*'s manifest. Details of the operation remain classified, but intelligence officer Jones disclosed during testimony that the U.S.S. *Enterprise* battle group happened upon a Russian aircraft carrier in the Indian Ocean. The *Enterprise*'s skipper decided to take advantage of the presence of the *Kiev* and conduct war games, including "a practice long-range strike against the surface force." The *Enterprise* did this by sending several aircraft on a mock attack of the Russian carrier. The aircraft, Jones later testified, flew "seven hundred nautical miles toward the *Kiev*, made contact, visual contact, with the *Kiev* and then came back."

Once again, U.S. intelligence personnel aboard the *Enterprise* used sophisticated electronic monitoring devices to record the Russians' every move during the mock attack, and Jerry Whitworth carefully put aside copies of the messages that he figured would bring the highest price.

The biggest intelligence-gathering operation and most dangerous cat-and-mouse game still awaited the carrier. Records show that on April 9, 1983, the *Enterprise* rendezvoused with the aircraft carriers the U.S.S.

*Midway* and the U.S.S. *Coral Sea* for the first-ever exercise in the Pacific conducted by three aircraft carriers. Within days, the three battle groups traveled to within four hundred miles of the Soviet-controlled Kamchatka peninsula. Officially, the operation was purely a training exercise, an attempt "to demonstrate effective joint and combined theater operations with a three-carrier battle force . . . in a high threat environment." But the Navy had an ulterior motive. Just as the *Enterprise* had gathered intelligence about Vietnam, the three carriers were eager to observe how the Soviet Union intended to react to the sudden appearance of three carriers and nearly thirty support warships at the lip of its border. Using sophisticated electronic snooping and jamming devices, intelligence officials aboard the carriers diligently recorded the Soviets' military reaction. The number of Russian aircraft launched, locations of Soviet missiles, frequencies of emergency broadcasts, all were monitored.

During testimony later, Lieutenant Commander James Dale Jeeter explained that the three carriers operated exactly the "way they intended to fight." This was important because the Pentagon, which had spent more than one year preparing for the exercise, assumed the Russians would respond under similar "real life battle conditions." The three-carrier exercise was also important because if the United States ever had to "successfully carry a war to the shores of the Soviets" it would most likely use a three-carrier formation.

During the seventeen-day exercise, the three carriers simulated dozens of wartime maneuvers in response to a series of possible scenarios. The 255 airplanes aboard the three ships were constantly engaged in mock attacks and reconnaissance missions, while U.S. submarines attempted to penetrate the carriers' defenses without being detected by antisubmarine ships. The communications center aboard the *Enterprise* was swamped with messages.

When the Navy conducts most of its operations, especially large ones like this, it carefully lists all of its objectives in a thick instruction booklet, which it gives to the various participants. Such books existed for the three-carrier operation, but the Navy wanted to try something new with this exercise. So nearly all of the day-to-day operational orders that were issued during the exercise were sent or received by the *Enterprise*'s radio room, just as they would have been had the United States actually been at war. This gave the Pentagon a chance to review the performance of its ship's various radio crews. It also gave Jerry Whitworth access to a step-by-step narrative of what the three carriers would do during an attack.

At one point during the operation, the Soviet Union claimed an F-14 aircraft from the *Enterprise* violated Russian airspace. Whether or not this incident occurred, and, if it did, whether it was part of some intelligence-gathering ploy or an accident, is classified information. The Pentagon will acknowledge only that the Russians protested. But Jerry later told John about the F-14 intrusion and gave John some of the one hundred classified messages that the Pentagon later acknowledged were transmitted after the F-14 flight.

When the three-carrier operation ended, the Pentagon tried to determine whether it was successful. Its immediate reaction was mixed. While the exercise had given the Navy a chance to train its commanders, the Pacific Fleet headquarters was dissatisfied and frustrated because, strangely, the three carriers had not generated as much intelligence information about the Russians' response to a three-carrier threat as the Pentagon had anticipated. Pentagon analysts couldn't figure out why the Soviets hadn't done more to monitor the fleet exercise. It seemed somewhat odd, especially since the Russians had paid close attention to smaller exercises in the past that were less important.

Years later, Pentagon officials wondered if Jerry Whitworth hadn't been the reason for the Russians' lack of interest. "Jerry copied everything he could about the operation," John confided after his arrest.

If a full-scale war ever erupted between the Soviet Union and United States, the twelve-inch stack of messages that Jerry had photographed would provide the Russians with a blow-by-blow chronology of how the U.S. Navy intended to form an off-shore flotilla and attack the Soviets' borders. What's more, the three-carrier operation had been done in cooperation with Canadian naval forces, so the Russians could identify what our northern neighbor would do during a war.

Selling the KGB messages from the three-carrier operation was akin to giving one football team its opponent's playbook a few days before the Super Bowl. Only the consequences were much, much higher.

Years later, federal prosecutors asked Lieutenant Commander Jeeter and intelligence specialist Captain Jones to put a dollar value on the messages that Jerry had copied while aboard the *Enterprise*. Both said that would be impossible.

"Basically, what you have here is a cookbook of how we do business," Jeeter explained. "It's a recipe. You know, it's kind of like Coca-Cola. Once you have the recipe, you may do it a little bit different way, but you always come back to the cookbook."

Added Jones, "It would be hard to put a price tag on it. . . . If, for example, you had your forces arrayed so that you could look at the exercise and follow it and watch it, you could develop an awful lot of insight, but if, on top of that, you had all the boilerplate of that exercise, the purpose, the tactics, and the wrap-up of how the opposing force thinks they've done, well, you've got to save just an incalculable amount of manpower, and the value you have to put on that is tremendous because the insight that it provides you into that Navy's capabilities and, more importantly, I think, that Navy's senior management's thinking and insights into that thought process and what they think is awfully important . . . and . . . of tremendous value."

As the *Enterprise* returned to the United States, Jerry recognized the messages he had stolen as a golden opportunity. They could easily earn him enough money from the KGB to retire. Just as important, they could provide him with a way out from under the thumb of John Walker.

Jerry had a plan.

# 52

John was angry when he telephoned Arthur after returning from Vienna. Arthur immediately drove over to John's house.

"My buyers said the stuff you gave me from VSE was so utterly useless that they don't want me even to risk carrying it around," John told Arthur. "Isn't there anything at VSE besides this low-level confidential shit that you could get me?"

"Not really, John. We just don't have much there."

John had a suggestion: Could Arthur tell by looking at various ship overhaul schedules when the Navy was changing the DEFCON level, the numerical system that reflects the defense readiness condition of the military on a scale of 1 to 5.

Arthur wasn't certain. "What would I see that would be a clue?"

"An increased ammunition order," John replied. "Or maybe a change in a ship's overhaul schedule."

"That's good, but I'm not going to see or hear that kind of stuff."

"Will you see a sudden pull back of a ship for fixing?"

"Sure, but there might be other reasons besides a change in the DEFCON. If I think of something that would be indicative, I will let you know."

John wasn't letting Arthur off the hook that easily. "Okay, you work on overhaul planning, so you know when a ship is going to overhaul, right?"

"Yes," Arthur replied, "but this type of planning goes on approximately one year prior to repair. I don't have any information on ship movements during that year, only when the ship is going into the shipyard. Is someone really going to pay to know when a ship is going into overhaul?"

"They might," John replied. "They might pay for something like that."

"I got a definite impression," Arthur told me later, "that at this point, John was scratching for anything that would help him deliver. He was going to pitch this ship overhaul information to somebody."

The two brothers spoke about other information that might interest the KGB, and then John became pensive.

"Wouldn't it be nice," he said to Arthur, "if we could raise our kids like the Mafia does, where you are born into a family operation and there isn't anything to worry about? Imagine, you wouldn't have to sweat about your kids getting a good job or having financial problems. They'd just do what they were supposed to do and inherit your family operation."

"Listen, John, that's a bunch of bullshit. I know my kids wouldn't ever do it, especially now. You'd have to start them from birth, and even then I'm not sure you could achieve that with them 'cause there would be so many other influences. I mean, my kids wouldn't break the law even for me."

John disagreed. "Your kids will do anything for you," he said. "Trust me. A kid can never say no to a parent."

"I began to become suspicious," Arthur told me later, "because I knew Mike had enlisted in the Navy. I wondered if John had pushed him into spying. John had told me that his man on the West Coast was getting out of the business, and I knew John was really under a lot of pressure to come up with something. I didn't want to say anything though. I figured it was between Mike and his dad and besides, what could I say? I had done it too. I'd spied for John, so what in the hell would I tell Michael?"

# 53

Jerry Whitworth received an enticing letter from Brenda shortly before the U.S.S. *Enterprise* arrived home in San Francisco Bay on April 28, 1983.

"I long to have you home," she wrote him, promising delights. "Look for the white 1957 Rolls-Royce, a chauffeur, and me, the lady in red."

The boys in the radio room were jealous. Jerry seemed to have it all. Indeed, Brenda had ridden to the dock in a rented Rolls-Royce and was waiting for him in high heels, dark stockings, and a fetching bright red dress with a white linen jacket. But as the aircraft carrier neared the pier, it ran aground on a sand bar and remained stuck for five hours until the incoming tide could free it. By the time Jerry came ashore, the bill for the Rolls had risen to $470. It didn't matter. Brenda tipped the chauffeur two twenty-dollar bills and thanked him for sticking around for nine hours.

Jerry had a surprise for Brenda too. He had bought two of the most expensive seats at the San Francisco Opera for the 1983 summer season. The box seats cost $500 but Jerry added another $200 as a donation so that Brenda's name would be listed in the program as a contributor.

Jerry had followed John's advice and always used cashier's checks for large purchases. But Jerry was no longer a mere puppet. He had devised his own scheme to hide his income by using as many as forty-two different bank accounts and forty-four credit cards.

It was going to be difficult to give up such luxuries, but Jerry had definitely decided to end his spying. He would do it slowly though, giving John only a few documents from the *Enterprise* at a time, in order to keep the spy money coming as long as possible. Jerry also had a trick in mind. He had intentionally fogged the rolls of film (photos of about a third of the *Enterprise* documents he stole) that he was going to give to John. As a result, none of these pictures of the classified messages would be usable.

After his arrest, Jerry Whitworth claimed he had fogged the film because he had decided that he no longer wanted to spy and was also feeling pangs of patriotism and guilt over what he had done.

But John Walker saw Jerry's actions as much more devious. He believed that Jerry had fogged the film in order to get the KGB angry at John. He also believed that Jerry was trying to extort more money from the KGB.

John was anxious to find out what sort of material Jerry had when he arrived on June 3, 1983, in California. When the two men were alone, Jerry gave John the fogged film and a large envelope filled with a dozen classified messages. John scribbled notes on the back of the envelope as Jerry briefed him about his delivery. "All messages . . . secret and one top secret," John wrote.

John was clearly impressed as Jerry explained how the carrier had sailed into waters claimed by Vietnam, and participated in a three-carrier war game, and how an F-14 had intruded Soviet airspace.

"Jesus Christ!" John remarked. "This is fucking great shit, Jerry."

Years later, John remembered that he was also a bit confused during Jerry's briefing that day. "I didn't know why Jerry gave me both film and copies of documents, but when I asked, he said he wanted me to have the copies so I could read them because they were so interesting. They were about the F-14 intrusion into Soviet airspace. What I didn't realize until later was that Jerry obviously wanted the KGB to know that he had valuable messages. The copies were just a sample."

The film that Jerry gave John represented only about one third of the classified messages that Jerry had stolen. The rest, he said, were still hidden on the ship and it was much too dangerous to move them now.

"That didn't strike me as odd at the time," John recalled later, "because the stuff he had showed me was really great and I wasn't worried about getting any more. Of course, now I realize I should have been suspicious of Jerry."

John asked Jerry whether he had been able to get any cryptographic keylists, but Jerry said he hadn't. Jerry had been promoted to senior chief and lost his access. "It would seem odd if a senior chief was the classified materials custodian," Jerry explained. "That's a junior radio-man's job."

Jerry didn't have access to any technical manuals either, he added. But he could keep giving John messages that would interest his buyers.

On June 12, 1983, John delivered Jerry's film and stolen messages to the KGB at a dead drop outside Washington. Even though Jerry hadn't been able to steal any keylists, John figured the KGB would be thrilled by the classified messages. John still didn't have any idea, at this point, that Jerry's film had been intentionally fogged. The only items that the KGB were actually going to get were the copies of messages about the F-14 intrusion.

John also picked up a package from the KGB at the dead drop. He assumed it contained cash, but when he opened it, he discovered there wasn't any. During the drive back to Norfolk, John decided the Soviets were simply playing it straight. "I figured the Soviets were worried because they didn't understand why Jerry was being trans-ferred, and they always assumed the worst—that the FBI had figured us out. So they weren't going to pay us until they were certain Jerry was legitimate."

There was another reason for the Russians to be cautious on June 12, 1983—a reason that had nothing to do with either John Walker or Jerry Whitworth.

Less than two months earlier, the FBI had surprised the KGB by nabbing Lieutenant Colonel Yevgeny Barmyantsev, a high-ranking So-viet military attaché, during a fake dead drop that had taken place amazingly close to John's dead drop site.

Barmyantsev had fallen into a trap set by the FBI counterintelligence office in Washington. Special agent Bill O'Keefe had dreamed up the scam and spent nearly one year putting it into action.

Following logic that would have pleased John Walker, O'Keefe de-cided that the FBI should entrap the Russians rather than always waiting for them to make the first move. O'Keefe got approval to teach John Stine, a forty-five-year-old security officer at a defense contracting firm, how to play the role of a dissatisfied American anxious to betray his country for cash.

The FBI scheme, code-named Operation Jagwire, turned out to be amazingly similar to John's real-life experiences with the KGB.

Stine approached the Russians on Thanksgiving Day in 1982 by simply walking into the Soviet Military Office in Washington and offering his services. After he gave them several documents marked SECRET, he was paid $500 and hustled into a basement garage and car trunk for a zigzag trip through Washington. Later, Stine met his KGB handler face-to-face and was given $4,800 stuffed into a soda can along with detailed instructions for future dead drops. The instructions were written in exactly the same way as those John had received.

When Barmyantsev showed up to pick up Stine's delivery, the FBI rushed in. Barmyantsev was so alarmed that he wet his pants, according to an account of Operation Jagwire written by journalists David Friend and Vance Muse. The entire sting operation remained a secret until Friend and Muse wrote about it in *Life* magazine.

It is likely, intelligence officials now believe, that operation may have inadvertently spooked the KGB before John's dead drop and cost John and Jerry their KGB paychecks. The Russians were already nervous about Jerry when Operation Jagwire occurred.

Neither John nor Jerry knew about the FBI's sting operation on July 28, 1983, when Jerry flew to Norfolk and asked for his spy salary.

"There isn't any," John replied.

Jerry wanted to know why.

"Because you fucked things up," John replied, "with all your stupid transfers and inability to decide whether or not you are going to keep doing this!"

John asked Jerry if he had brought the other two thirds of the messages from the U.S.S. *Enterprise* with him and was irritated when Jerry told him no. Jerry and Brenda had sold their condominium in San Leandro and were moving to Davis, California, Jerry explained. The movers had accidentally packed the messages with his household effects, which were in storage.

John didn't believe Jerry, but he didn't say so. He wasn't certain what Jerry was up to. John also thought it was odd that Jerry had raced out to Norfolk to get his spy salary. Why was he in such a rush?

A few weeks after Jerry left Norfolk, John received a formal invitation in the mail.

Master Chief Lloyd Long requests the pleasure of your company for the retirement ceremony for Senior Chief Jerry A. Whitworth. Please join us in celebrating Jerry's last hurrah . . .

So that was it. Jerry had decided to retire without telling John. "That son of a bitch was too scared to tell me that he was getting out," John recalled. "He did it behind my back. He was going to get us both killed."

Back in California, Jerry considered himself safe. He didn't have anything to worry about because he still had one year's worth of classified messages from the U.S.S. *Enterprise* as bargaining chips. That was why he had given John *copies* of the messages about the F-14 intrusion as well as the fogged film. Jerry had to make certain that the KGB understood what he had to offer.

Jerry knew the KGB would be tantalized by those messages, and it wasn't going to go after him as long as he had something it wanted. He also felt confident the KGB would give him all of the back pay it owed him even though he had retired. Once again, the KGB wasn't going to risk losing the messages from the *Enterprise*. They were his "insurance."

Of course, John was about to unknowingly walk into a precarious situation when he flew to Vienna and met his handler. By that time, the KGB would have developed Jerry's worthless film and would want to know why Jerry had ruined it.

John had always said that the KGB was ruthless and that he was always on the verge of being assassinated by KGB agents. Jerry Whitworth, either intentionally or unintentionally, was about to put John's theory to the test.

# 54

Marie Hammond was horrified when she met Laura Walker at the airport in Buffalo, New York, in July of 1983. Laura looked emaciated, fatigued, and disheveled. Marie wondered if she hadn't made a mistake inviting Laura to stay with her at a farm south of Buffalo on the edge of Lake Erie, where Marie's grandmother lived.

Marie and Laura had become good friends in 1980 when both of their husbands were stationed at Fort Polk, but Marie hadn't seen Laura since then and she said later that she might not have recognized Laura that day had she not been expecting her.

"Laura had hit rock bottom," Marie told me. All she owned were two pair of blue jeans, two blouses, one dress, and some underwear. Marie was afraid to let Laura sleep alone that night because she was so depressed. So she put a cot in her bedroom for Laura to use.

"She was so fragile," Marie recalled. "She was at the breaking point. I sat on the edge of the cot that night and held her and she just sobbed and sobbed."

Five years older and a born-again Christian, Marie was a safe port in

Laura's turbulent life. Marie herself was no stranger to heartache. At age nine, her father drowned. She hated her stepfather. When she was fourteen years old, she had a nervous breakdown. But she had repaired her life thanks to religion and by marrying, at age sixteen, Bill Hammond, her childhood sweetheart. Now she felt that God had called her to help Laura Walker. He had sent her to Marie, like the lost sheep who is found.

The next day, Laura said she wasn't certain that moving in with Marie had been such a good idea. Laura wanted to telephone her mother, so Marie agreed to pay for the call.

"Mother," Laura said when she reached Barbara, "I need money. I want to go get Chris, but I need money to do it."

Barbara was broke and in no mood to make a loan to Laura.

"I don't have any money to loan you," Barbara replied.

"Well, you can get it from Dad," Laura insisted. "All you have to do is ask him."

Barbara became angry. If Laura wanted money from John, why didn't she simply call her dad and ask him for it? Why did everyone expect Barbara to run to John when they needed his help?

"I'm tired of being fucked!" Barbara snapped. "Go find someone else to fucking use!" She slammed down the telephone.

Years later, Barbara Walker recalled that conversation to me with sorrow. "Normally, I wouldn't have said that to her. I usually would do anything for my children, but I was hurting and so tired of hearing Laura whine about Christopher. I was tired of bailing her out all the time."

Laura was outraged. "Whenever my mother asked me for money, I always sent it to her," Laura told me later. "Hundreds of dollars. Sometimes I did not have it. But if I did, I sent it. . . . She knew I was desperate. All she had to do was say, 'No.' But she was angry because she knew I was on my way to get Chris and she was not happy about that. And do you know why? Because she thought that once I got Chris that the espionage would be brought up and my dad would go to jail, and my brother might be dragged into it because at that time Michael was in the Navy, and, of course, she might go to jail too!

"All anybody was interested in was covering their own butt," Laura said.

Laura tried to call her mother back that day, but all she got was a busy signal. She assumed incorrectly that Barbara had taken the telephone off the hook. Actually, Barbara was telephoning Mark Snyder to warn him that Laura was in Buffalo and might be coming after Christopher.

"This is when I decided in my mind that I was going to cut off all ties to my family," Laura explained later. "That call was it. It was probably not a wise thing to do, but when your own mother tells you to fuck off, you have really hit the bottom."

Marie was just as angry when Laura told her what Barbara had said. "What kind of family does this to each other?" she asked.

"You don't know the half of it, Marie," Laura replied. "My family has worse secrets than this one!"

The two women talked for several minutes and then Laura said, "Marie, I'm going to fix my family. My mother doesn't know what it's like to lose a child, but I'm going to teach her what it's like. I'm never going to speak to her again. As far as I am concerned, she can just think that I'm dead."

Marie agreed—it was a good idea.

A few days later, Laura and Marie came up with another way for Laura to get enough money to go after Christopher. Marie was an avid follower of the televised ministry of Virginia Beach evangelist M. G. (Pat) Robertson, host of *The 700 Club,* a "prayer and praise" program. They decided to telephone Robertson and ask his ministry for the money.

They phoned several times, but their request for money was turned down. After listening to Laura's story, however, one counselor offered to pray for her over the telephone and during that prayer, the counselor began speaking in tongues. Marie was on the line. "I thought, 'Oh great, this is going to do a lot of good,' but then the counselor started interpreting the tongues for me," Marie Hammond told me later. "She said, 'Thus sayeth the Lord, your friend shall not return to Stephen [Laura's boyfriend in California] and live in sin.' She outlined about seven things that Laura was required to do to have the Lord walk with her, and then she said that if Laura did those seven things, God would return Christopher to her. He would deliver her son back to her. I'd never told this counselor about Stephen, but she mentioned him by name. It truly was a miracle."

Laura took the message seriously. She joined a charismatic church and was later baptized in a swimming pool. One Sunday, while Laura was at church, Barbara telephoned the farm and asked to speak with her.

"She's not here," Marie told Barbara. Then Marie added, "I put her on a bus to Maine about a week ago. She was coming to see you. Hasn't she arrived there yet?"

"No! She's not here!" Barbara replied.

"I wonder what's happened to her?" Marie said. "I hope nothing is wrong!"

Barbara was worried. She telephoned John.

"Something's happened to Laura!" she told him. "She's disappeared! We've got to find her."

John thought Barbara was drunk and exaggerating, but after they talked for a few minutes, he decided that she was serious. He promised to call the state police in New York and have his pals in the Norfolk police department put out a missing persons bulletin.

When Laura returned from church, Marie told her what she had done. "I just couldn't let your family continue treating you the way it has," Marie said. "Besides, you said you didn't ever want to talk to any of them again."

Laura agreed. Now Barbara would know what it was like to lose a child.

That fall, Laura began working as a waitress in a diner and earned enough money to buy a truck and some clothes. She also began talking to Marie again about going after Christopher, but she was scared.

One night Marie found Laura crying. This is how Marie later recalled the conversation.

"I heard Laura sobbing in her bedroom and I went in and asked her what was wrong. She said, 'Oh Marie, everything is so screwed up.' Laura had been praying, but she still didn't know what to do and I said to her, 'Well, I'm sure the Lord has—' and, I remember Laura cut me off in mid-sentence. She said, 'Marie, you don't understand. My father has committed treason!' I was confused and really didn't understand what Laura was telling me, and she saw that and I think it made her angry. She said, 'Marie, my dad is a spy! He was a spy in the Navy and he's spying now, and Mark knows it and if I try to get Christopher, Mark will turn us all in. He'll claim that I was a spy too.' She was afraid."

The two women prayed together for several hours and then Marie went back to her own bedroom. She couldn't sleep.

"I got out of bed and I sat near the window and looked outside," Marie said later. "I was scared too. I said, 'God, there has to be a solution.' . . . I must have prayed for another two hours and then finally I said, 'Okay, God, I'm leaving this up to you. Show me the way.' "

# 55

On March 27, 1983, as soon as Michael returned to Norfolk from boot camp, he asked Rachel to dinner at a posh restaurant.

"I want you to marry me," he said. "Will you be my wife?"

Rachel began crying. "Yes!" she said. "Oh Michael, I love you!"

They agreed to wait for one year before marrying, in order to save some money. Michael didn't tell his plans to John. "The last thing my dad wanted was for me to get married."

During the next few weeks, he divided his time between Rachel and surfing with his pals. John didn't seem to mind, but he continually lectured Michael about becoming too serious with Rachel.

"You're about to go overseas," John told Michael one afternoon, "and you don't want to be tied down to a woman here. There's no sense in missing all the fun you can have in those ports."

John thought marriage was an outdated and unworkable tradition.

"You know, Mike," John explained, "I don't hate your mother. The woman is intelligent, she can be a hard worker and a good wife. But I fell out of love with her. I didn't love her anymore. It happens. Marriage isn't for everyone. It's not for me and it may not be for you.

"Half the marriages in America end in divorce and most of the others aren't truly happy. If you don't love a person, it's better to get out. Why stay in there, because after a while you begin to hurt each other? That's why I don't understand your mother. Why does she want to bury me? We're divorced, but she can't let me go."

Michael agreed. "We tried to get Mom to date when we lived in Maine, but she wouldn't," he told John. "She still acts like you guys are married."

"That's so fucking crazy," John said. "Your mother hates my guts because I dated other women. But what the hell. It's part of the game of life in America. I'm telling you that every sailor does it. Every one of them!"

Remembering their conversation later, Michael told me, "My dad told me it was better if I didn't get married. He said I should have fun with Rachel but definitely not get married. I thought about it, and I began to think of the domestic cases that I'd worked as a private detective, and I have to admit, I was becoming skeptical. Rarely had I seen a happy marriage, but I was convinced that Rachel and me were going to be different. I didn't tell him that, but I felt that way."

On April 13, Michael kissed a teary-eyed Rachel good-bye and boarded a plane en route to the aircraft carrier, U.S.S. *America*. More than 5,500 men were assigned to the carrier. Michael reported to Fighter Squadron 102, nicknamed the Diamondbacks. It was an elite unit, part of the eighty-five aircraft on board. At the time, the squadron operated a dozen F-14 Tomcat fighter jets, the Navy's most sophisticated supersonic tactical warplanes. Because of Michael's secretarial skills, which he had learned at night school, he was assigned to the administration office for the fighter squadron.

One of the carrier's first stops was Diego Garcia, the same island his father had visited, and on which Jerry had served. Any free moment, Michael headed for the beach with his surfboard. "I really felt," he said later, "I'd made the right choice by joining." Michael took so many pictures of the beach, waves, sunsets, carrier, and his newly made surfing friends that he filled three photo albums. He wrote to Rachel every day, but she was busy and didn't respond as regularly. Michael wrote John too, and in May 1983, he received a cassette tape from his dad. It started like any other letter written by a father to his absent son. John compared his Navy experiences to Michael's and talked about how he missed him, but John's manipulative nature and self-interest quickly surfaced.

Howdy Mike, this is Dad.

Let me see, it's the um, fourth of May 1983. . . . I just got your letter. . . . I'm a real shit for not having written to ya but I'm not gonna tell ya why cause you're about as busy as I am and I don't have to explain, right?

Okay, I see that they have told you that you have to put two years in on your squadron before you can be transferred. Well, that's usually the kind of bullshit they tell everybody. You'd be amazed at how easy it is to beat that so-called two-year rule. You know you could take a test for another rating and pass it, and if you made third class and your squadron had no billing for it, they would be obligated to transfer ya anyway. But all in all, it doesn't look that bad for ya. . . . yeoman is by far the better of the ratings. A PN really handles nothing but enlisted pay records and enlisted problems, but yeomen, on the other hand, are more like secretaries.

A yeoman handles a wide range of things from officers' records to classified control. They could handle the intelligence library and, and jobs such as that. I mean, it's definitely a racket. . . . Advancement is quick. I'm sure it is. Your typing will help you. . . . Christ, just get down there and practice. And you're already talking about reenlistment. Man! that is all right.

Okay, um, what you are allowed to do is pass on the ship's operating, squadron operating schedule to your immediate family even if it's ah, restricted or classified. You'll find there's an anomaly there that doesn't seem quite understandable, ah, that is to say, the movement of a ship could be classified information, confidential or even secret, and yet the Navy acknowledges the fact that you're gonna go home and tell your wife what your sailing date is. And you are saying how come I am allowed to reveal classified material to my wife who is not cleared. Well there really is no answer for that. There's probably some stupid instruction somewhere that says, ah, it is permissible to ah, tell your immediate family the ship's movements . . . Anyway, let me know your schedule and what you mean when you say three more eight-month cruises. What ships and what are, what is your squadron's deployment schedule? Ah, I would really be curious to know what that is. . . .

Okay, I hope you haven't forgotten Mother's Day. . . . Your mom did call and P.K. talked to her. I was somewhere and she was looking for your address and I didn't call her back. I haven't heard anything from Margaret. I'm too busy, and Laura, of course, fell off the fucking planet. . . . Mother's Day, I almost feel obligated to try to get up to Scranton with or without P.K. Maybe I can get Uncle Art to go, but basically, I haven't much opportunity to have any contact with the family. . . . Work, work, work, same old shit, right?

"Just like my father, I loved being on the ocean," Michael recalled. "It was in my blood, I guess. There was something about being at sea that I loved."

The U.S.S. *America* returned to Norfolk in June, and Michael discovered his father had converted his room into an office. Michael was upset because his father hadn't even asked him. He also was angry because P.K. had moved back into the house and acted like she had more of a right to be there than Michael did.

John detected Michael's anger and offered a half-hearted apology to Michael about taking over his room. After a few days, Michael moved out of the house and into a room at the naval station barracks.

"I was getting tired of my dad," Michael said. "He was doing stupid things, and P.K. was really pissing me off. She was using my dad. It was black and white and I saw it, but he didn't, and when I tried to tell him about it, it made him mad. I mean, he was on this real ego kick about his age and being young."

John didn't try to stop Michael from leaving. "I figured it was time for him to get out on his own," John recalled. Besides, John's indifference only seemed to make Michael more intent on pleasing him.

"I knew my father was a spy," Michael recalled. "My mother had told me and he had dropped hints when we'd gone to bars. He kept saying that he'd tell me someday how he made his money. But the truth is that I got tired of waiting for him to ask me. I mean, here's how I felt, what's the deal, doesn't he think he can trust me?"

While the U.S.S. *America* was in port, Fighter Squadron 102 worked out of the Oceana Naval Air Station in Virginia Beach. Michael continued his secretarial duties in the administration office, where one job included signing and opening all registered mail. Often he received low-level classified reports during such deliveries.

One night when P.K. was gone, John invited Michael over for grilled hamburgers in the backyard. During dinner, John quizzed his son about his job at the air station.

"What'ya do out there?"

"I type orders and other things, do some filing, and also open up the registered mail," Michael said.

"And then I told my dad on purpose," Michael recalled, " 'It's real neat, Dad, every once in a while, secret documents come through there and I get to look at them and they have all kinds of information in them.' "

Michael watched to see his father's reaction, but all John said was, "Oh really? Sounds interesting."

"He didn't approach me," Michael said, "and I didn't understand why. It really pissed me off."

A few days later, John asked Michael to come by the house. He took Michael into the den and closed the door.

"Michael, you may know this already," John said, "because your mother might have said something about it to you, but if you make copies of those documents that you work with, the classified ones, and you give them to me, I can get you some money. Some big money."

"How much?"

"Five thousand a month if it's good stuff."

"I wasn't shocked when he told me," Michael said to me later. "I thought it was really cool. I mean, he finally trusted me enough to tell me what he did. He thought I was man enough to handle what he was saying."

Michael asked John, "How do I know when to take something?"

"Mike, when the time comes, you will know it is right."

"Okay, cut me in."

Remembering that conversation, Michael told me later, "I was proud, really proud, and I felt so cool. I mean, this was just like a story out of some book, a spy novel, really! I could hardly wait to meet some beautiful blonde Russian agent."

Michael didn't keep John's secret well. He told a surfing buddy that John was a spy, but Michael made it sound like John worked for the CIA. "It was like I was the first kid on the block to have a spy for a father," Michael recalled. "We were going to be spies together, man.

"I didn't have any ideological concerns," Michael explained. "I was in it because my dad was in it. He was a PI, I was a PI. He was in the Navy, I'm in the Navy. He's a spy, I wanted to be a spy."

Michael told Rachel while they were riding in Michael's truck to a party.

"Hey Rachel, there's something you should know," Michael said. "Look, my father's a spy and I'm a spy too."

"Wow! Really!" Rachel said.

"Yeah, I'm going to make us a lot of money."

Michael stole his first classified document a few days after John recruited him. It was amazingly simple. The document was a report that came in the registered mail. Michael signed for it, looked through it, and thought it was something his father might want to see. So he simply stuffed it into a small backpack that he kept his personal items in and took it to John's house. He walked into the den and tossed the report on John's desk.

John looked through it. "This is very good, Michael," he said. "See if you can bring me more."

Michael didn't have access to cryptographic materials. In fact, Michael wasn't supposed to have access to any classified documents because he hadn't undergone a background investigation by the Navy and didn't have even a minimum security clearance. But no one in the Navy had taken the time to question Michael's assignment. Instead, they simply believed him when he said he had the necessary clearances.

Even though Michael couldn't get cryptographic materials, he had access to information about the F-14 fighter jet and to some classified messages about various operations. One exercise, in particular, interested John.

The U.S.S. *America* was scheduled to go on a Caribbean cruise in late October 1983, but Michael received an emergency telephone call from the ship and was told to report early. Michael called John.

"Something big is happening, we're pulling out tonight!"

"Get what you can, but be careful," John warned.

At 5:30 A.M. on October 25, the United States invaded the tiny Caribbean island of Grenada, where a sixteen-member military council had taken control of the government only a few days earlier.

Michael was part of the Navy force that participated in the invasion, and he claimed later that during it he saw dozens of sensitive messages about how it was coordinated and planned. "I didn't understand most of the sensitive stuff that came in because it was in code, but I was able to read a few things," he recalled. Michael had not become sophisticated enough as a spy to know how to steal the messages and copy them. But each night he wrote down as much information as he could remember, and after the carrier returned home, he shared this information with his father.

"The United States played a much larger role than it admitted in the coup in Grenada," Michael claimed later, "and when I told my dad about what I had seen, he got really excited. I was on a roll."

Michael was beginning to realize that he had been "groomed" for the spy business. Why else had his father pushed him to become a private investigator, to study typing at night school, and to join the Navy?

One day, Michael confronted his father. "Dad, did you groom me to be a spy?"

John didn't reply, so Michael asked him again. "Is this some sort of planned thing or what?"

"What's your Social Security number, Mike?" John answered.

"What?"

"Tell me the first three numbers of your Social Security number," John repeated.

"Zero, zero, seven," Michael replied.

"Right," said John, "only that's oh-oh-seven, just like James Bond, ya dummy. You've got a license to kill, baby!"

Michael was startled.

"How did he do that?" Michael asked me later. "How'd he arrange for me to get those numbers? My dad really had planned it all out. He knew all along."

This is what John told me when I asked him about his recruitment of Michael:

"I knew in my heart that Mike couldn't refuse me. . . . He had always wanted to please me. It's natural for a son to want to please his father, and Michael always had. Ever since he was a small boy, he and I had a special relationship. He was clearly my favorite so I knew that he would do what I asked him to.

"I had planned to wait until Mike was a little older and better established in the Navy, but Jerry had forced me to move. I was losing Jerry and that meant I didn't have anyone else to produce. Art couldn't deliver shit and I knew that without Mike, I was running a real risk. See, that is what recruiting Michael was all about. I had to get him into the ring before I could get out of it. That was the only way for me to get out without getting a .22 slug behind the ear. I realized that right after I became a spy. Mike was my ticket. He was my way out. No one was going to mess with *me* if Mike took over my organization. I could retire with P.K. and get some chickens and move to the hills of Virginia and relax because the KGB would be afraid to move on me.

"I don't know how else to justify what I did except to give an analogy. I began thinking of Joseph Kennedy, okay. I mean, here was a guy who had done things when he was younger that he shouldn't have done, but he didn't get caught and he made enough money to send his kid to Harvard. I thought about Joe Bonanno [Joseph Bonanno, the alleged "Father of Fathers" in the Mafia]. He was the real godfather, but he made enough money that he ultimately became legitimate and even wrote a book.

"You see, money is the key. It always is. If you make enough money, then it doesn't matter what you've done. You automatically become respectable. It was too late for me to ever become respectable, but I could still be the godfather. My family could come to me and I would give them money. I could turn the business over to my son some day. Only I was going to tell him, 'Michael, put money aside. Don't do what I did. You can make millions as a spy if you handle yourself right.' I was going to tell him that his kid was the one who could go to Harvard. He could be legitimate. It was an honorable thing that I was doing. It really was."

Like most young girls, Rachel had dreamed about having a big wedding, but when Michael returned from the Caribbean cruise, she agreed to elope in December 1983. "We were getting a lot of static from our parents," Michael told me. "My dad was against it and so was hers, so we just went to Virginia Beach, got the license and blood tests, and had a justice of the peace do it one afternoon."

Michael bought two bottles of champagne and they went back to their new apartment after the quick ceremony. Michael didn't tell his father, and he didn't wear his wedding ring whenever they got together. But John knew.

"Mike, are you married?"

"Yeah."

"Why didn't you tell me about it?"

" 'Cause I knew you didn't want me to do it."

"That's true, but it's the father's duty to help pay for the wedding and buy things."

The day after that conversation, John gave Michael and Rachel a popcorn popper and $50. Now that Michael was his business partner, John saw no need to keep him well supplied with $100 bills as he had done before.

"I was really pissed," Michael told me. "I needed to come up with a seven-hundred-dollar tuition payment for Rachel's college, and she is working her butt off as a waitress, and my dad gives me a popcorn popper. What the fuck did he think I was, some nerd who watched television and ate popcorn all the time?"

Michael decided that his relationship with his dad was going to be purely business, but John didn't seem to notice.

"I don't think he even realized our relationship had changed," Michael recalled. "I didn't want to have anything to do with him, and he didn't even seem to know."

Michael had developed his own game plan, and spying was an important part of it. "I don't want to give the impression that I was greedy," Michael told me later. "I didn't become a spy for the money, but I wanted to make something of myself and I wanted to be comfortable. I had a dream. I was beginning to see myself a lot like Jerry Whitworth. Here was a very intelligent man who was really a man of the world, and he was married to a woman who was going to be a doctor. I liked that idea. Me, an old sea dog who's been everywhere and learned about life the hard way, and my wife, Rachel, being a doctor learning things from school. We could teach each other. I didn't need my dad messing up my life anymore, but I did need the spy money. That didn't change. I wanted that money."

# 56

Michael was not the only person John tried to recruit in the fall of 1983, after he discovered Jerry had retired. He said he also approached his half brother, Gary Richard Walker, the oldest of three children born to Johnny Walker, Sr., and Dorothy Dobson Walker after they left Scranton and settled in Virginia.

John had first met Gary back in 1976 when their father began commuting to Richmond to obtain medical treatment for Sherrie, John's half sister who died of leukemia after fighting the disease for five years.

Gary had joined the Navy in July of 1979 and had been stationed in Norfolk with a helicopter squadron responsible for finding and destroying underwater and surface mines.

"Gary was really a nice kid," John recalled, "and I invited him over to the house and out on the boat a few times when he came to Norfolk. He didn't have anything, of course. In fact, he was sending most of his money home to my alcoholic father. I could see it happening all over again.

"My father had used me as a kid, and now he was using Gary the exact same way. He was sponging off him, taking his money and spending it on booze.

"So I decided to recruit him, again, not to enrich me in any way, but to help him out. We were driving in my car one day and I began the same way that I had with Whitworth. 'Gary, I know a way you can make some money,' I said. 'It's something I've been doing for a long time and it's completely safe, but it's also illegal. Even my telling you about it will be enough for you to get into trouble because you will be part of the conspiracy. Now, do you want to hear more or not?'

"I couldn't believe it," John recalled, "but Gary said he'd have to think about it and he said that he didn't want me to tell him any more at that point. I figured I'd wait for a while and then try again. I was really amazed 'cause he was the first one who told me 'No.' "

Gary Walker testified in 1986 that he had no recollection of John's proposition.

In the fall of 1983, John was still expecting Jerry Whitworth to deliver the remaining two thirds of the documents he had taken off the U.S.S. *Enterprise,* even though he had retired from the Navy. John wanted the film of those documents before he met his handler in Vienna in February 1984, so he flew to California on January 27 to visit with Jerry at his new trailer in Davis.

At this point, John still didn't realize that the last film delivery had been fogged.

"In California, Jerry tells me that he's been too busy to photograph the remaining two thirds of the documents that he had stolen," John said. "I was furious."

"What the fuck is wrong with you, Jerry?" he demanded. "Do you want to die? Are you trying to get us both killed?"

For the first time in their friendship, Jerry got angry. He didn't need John telling him what to do. The risks were just too great to continue spying, he complained, and besides, with Brenda about to finish her education, he didn't need to spy any longer.

Much to John's surprise, Jerry also didn't want to give him the remaining two thirds of messages from the *Enterprise*. But Jerry was no match for John when it came to pressure.

"We argued and finally I told him that I was going to photograph the remaining two thirds of documents in his house," John said. "I wasn't going to Vienna without them. That scared him because he didn't want Brenda to come home and find out what we were doing. So we drove to this motel, and when we got there, I was so pissed, I said, 'Jerry, this is your fault, you go in there and register us.' I figured the motel owner thought we were both queers 'cause we went into the room for two hours and then came out. We photographed the hell out of his material in that room, and then I left town. The last thing Jerry asked me was when was he getting paid."

John's KGB contact was irritated when they met on February 4 in Vienna. What was going on with Jerry? he demanded. John was surprised. He hadn't yet told the Russian that Jerry had quit the Navy.

"What do you mean?" John replied. The KGB agent quickly explained that the film that John had delivered at the last dead drop had been fogged. It had been photographed under a light that was too intense. The only items that were any good were the copies of messages that John had included in the dead drop—the ones that dealt with the F-14 intrusion into Soviet airspace. Obviously, the KGB agent explained, his country was anxious to learn all it could about the war games that the U.S.S. *Enterprise* had participated in off the Soviet coastline. But the KGB was confused. Why had Jerry overexposed the photographs?

"Are you positive that the film was fogged?" John asked. "Your people didn't mess it up developing it?"

The KGB agent didn't bother to respond.

"I thought to myself," John recalled later, " 'Thanks a lot Jerry, how in the hell am I going to explain this one?' This is Jerry Whitworth, who considers himself a professional photographer, who hasn't taken a bad photo in his life, and suddenly, he has messed up several rolls of film. Jerry was obviously jerking me around, but at that point I still didn't understand what he was up to."

John told his KGB handler he had no idea why Jerry might have overexposed the photographs. He also told him that Jerry had quit the Navy and had also been complaining about how little money the Soviets had paid them in comparison to the price of building a nuclear missile or launching a spy satellite. The KGB agent looked visibly shaken, John claimed later. The real problem with Jerry was money, John said. It had been fifteen months since Jerry had been paid. Why, he asked, had the Soviets not paid them anything at the last dead drop? The KGB agent didn't offer a lengthy explanation.

"He simply told me," John said later, "that the Soviet embassy in Washington didn't have enough cash on hand for the dead drop. Someone had screwed up. It was fucking unbelievable. Here we are, supposedly the world's most important spies, and the Soviets can't raise enough cash to pay us."

During his talk with the KGB handler, John attempted to begin to deemphasize Jerry's importance to the spy ring. John wanted, he said later, to disassociate himself from Jerry in case the KGB decided to kill him.

Still, he made one last shot at getting a $1 million payment for a guarantee from Jerry to continue spying ten more years. In the back of his mind, John explained later, was the thought that even if the KGB didn't bite this time, it might the next, when he asked for $1 million for himself.

"He didn't seem to like the idea of paying Jerry more money," John told me. "He felt that Jerry was trying to pressure him and take advantage of him."

John tried to reassure the KGB agent. He explained that he had personally photographed the remaining two thirds of the messages from the U.S.S. *Enterprise* and was certain that the photographs were good. He also promised to check with Jerry to see if he still had copies of the first batch of messages to compensate for the fogged film.

Then John changed subject. Michael had been successfully recruited and had been aboard the U.S.S. *America* during the invasion of Grenada, he announced. Better yet, Michael had been transferred on January 31, 1984, from his air squadron to the U.S.S. *Nimitz,* the largest aircraft carrier in the U.S. fleet. Michael was working hard, John assured the KGB agent, to get into the ship's administration center, where he would have access to classified documents.

Arthur also was scouring VSE for worthwhile information, John added, possibly a method for alerting the Soviets if the DEFCON was changed by the Pentagon.

John had several other potential recruits in mind too. His half brother, Gary, might be turned because he was financially assisting his parents. John knew other persons in Norfolk who might be recruited, and there was a chance that John could goad Laura back into the Army or maybe John's other daughters, Margaret and Cynthia, could be turned. Obviously, John was attempting to prove his continued worth to the KGB.

The agent stopped John's sales pitch. He was mentioning so many potential recruits that the KGB agent was having trouble keeping track of them. "He didn't like me using all of their names, saying them out loud," John recalled.

The agent suggested that each recruit be given a single-letter designation so their actual names wouldn't be overheard, but, he added, there wasn't any point to assigning letters to persons who weren't already in the military. John agreed.

From now on, the KGB agent explained, the letter S would stand for Michael, and K for Arthur. Jerry would be called D, and Gary F. John didn't ask why, he simply noted the letters on a small card that he was carrying.

The Russian agent turned the conversation back to Jerry and his irrational behavior. Jerry was becoming a problem, the KGB agent said. His sudden retirement could be a signal that he had become worried about being captured.

"He could become a risk," the KGB agent said. "You must watch him closely."

After the meeting, John returned to his hotel and found that he couldn't think about anything but Jerry and the fogged film.

"It was clear that Jerry had fogged the film intentionally," John said later, "but why? What purpose could he possibly have for fogging film and then sending me to the KGB with it?"

John telephoned Jerry as soon as he returned to Norfolk. "I told that son of a bitch about the fogged film and he told me not to worry about that because he still had the original one third of the messages and he would photograph them again for me," John recalled. "That's when I knew that Jerry had fogged the film. Why else had he kept those messages around?"

John decided that Jerry had tried to pull off a "rather simple and stupid scam." Jerry had fogged the film because he wanted to make certain he could collect his back pay and also sell the material in installments, John concluded, and he hadn't cared whether the Russians killed John in the process.

"It wasn't going to work," John recalled. "I told Jerry that it was his ass if he didn't take pictures of the first one third of the messages and bring them to me."

Jerry brought the film to Norfolk in April 1984. He came on the same weekend that John was to make his dead drop outside Washington and, once again, Jerry was hoping to be paid on the spot all of the back salary money that the KGB owed him. But the KGB had other ideas. The Russians weren't going to pay anyone who gave them fogged film.

John and P.K. met Jerry, and when the two men were alone, John got right to the point.

"I know why you are here," John said. "You want your money. But you're too early. You are going to have to wait a few days."

That weekend, John made a dead drop delivery and picked up a package of cash. The Soviets had listed each member of John's spy ring by his letter code name and marked a dollar amount next to each letter. John took his Swiss Army knife and cut out all of the letter designations and amounts except for Jerry's, and then he called Jerry into his den and showed him the paper. He wanted Jerry to realize that the spy ring had other suppliers and John wasn't dependent on him.

"Okay, I'm going to let you read this because I don't want to get caught in any argument between you and those motherfuckers," John said. He handed Jerry the piece of paper.

It said: "*D* gets ZERO."

"Jerry's face turned white," John Walker recalled, "and I said to him, 'It's your own goddamn fault because you are playing these stupid games and they are disciplining you. You are going to get us all killed.' "

The two men sat for several minutes without talking. Then John said, "Jerry, we have been friends for a long time, and if you think you are going to pull this off with the people we are dealing with, you are nuts. I don't need this type of aggravation. You're going to take the heat on this alone. I've got other suppliers besides you."

Jerry left the next day. A few days later, John received a letter from him. Jerry said he was resigning from the spy business.

"I'm out of it," Jerry wrote, and then he added a sentence that really infuriated John. "I suggest that you hire someone with cheaper labor costs."

"That was such an insult," John told me. "It really pissed me off and I thought to myself, 'Screw this guy. He'll come crawling back eventually,' because I knew Jerry couldn't cut it on the outside. He was a loser."

A few days after Jerry wrote his resignation letter, he typed another letter, but this one was addressed to the resident agent of the FBI in San Francisco:

Dear Sir:
I have been involved in espionage for several years, specifically I've passed along Top Secret Cryptographic Keylists for military communications, Tech Manuals for same, Intelligence Messages, and etc.

I didn't know that the info was being passed to the USSR until after I had been involved a few years and since then I've been remoreseful

[sic] and wished to be free. Finally I've decided to stop supplying material—my contact doesn't know of my decision. Originally I was told I couldn't get out without approval, this was accompanied with threats. Since then I believe the threats were a bluff.

At any rate the reason for this letter is to give you—FBI—an opportunity to break what brobably [sic] is a significant espionage system. (I know that my contact has recuried [sic] at least three other members that are actively supplying highly classified material). (I have the confidence of my contact).

I pass the material to my contact (a US citizen) who in turn passes the material to a contact overseas (his actual status—KGB or whatever—I don't know). That is not always the case tho, sometimes US locations are used. A US location is always used to receive instructions and money.

If you are interested in this matter you can signal me with an Ad in the *Los Angeles Times* Classified Section under "Personal Messages (1225)". What I would expect to cooperate is *complete immunity* from prosecution and absolutely no public disclosure of me or my idenity [sic]. I will look for an Ad in *Monday editions only* for the next four weeks. Also, I would desire some expense funds depending on the degree that my livelihood is interupted [sic].

*The Ad*: Start with "RUS:", followed by whatever message you desire to pass. If your message is not clear I'll send another letter. If I decide to cooperate you will hear from me via an attorney. Otherwise nothing further will happen.

Jerry signed the letter: RUS. He wanted to make certain it was difficult to trace, so he made a copy of the letter and sent the copy to the FBI. If the price was right, he was ready to squeal. It was the one surefire way to get out of John's clutches.

# 57

Michael had hoped his transfer to the U.S.S. *Nimitz* would give him better access to secret material than he had as a clerk for the fighter squadron. But when he reported aboard the carrier in January 1984, he found himself assigned to the recreational department, where he was put in charge of handing out and collecting basketballs.

John was irritated. He telephoned Michael the weekend of April 15 and asked him to come over. By this time, John had already had his angry exchange with Jerry. Now John was going to turn up the heat on Michael.

John formed several stacks of bills, $1,000 each, on his desk, and when Michael arrived, John made certain that he got a good look at all the money. Then John picked up one of the stacks and gave it to Michael.

"This is all you're getting this time," he said.

"But I thought I was going to make a thousand a week doing this," Michael complained. "Not a thousand every six months."

"You want more money, you've got to earn it," John replied. "You're a big married man now, off on your own. No one is going to give you spending cash for nothing."

Now it was Michael's turn to get angry.

John didn't care. He explained to Michael that Jerry had quit the Navy, leaving him in "deep shit."

"I'm counting on you to produce some heavy-duty shit, otherwise neither of us is going to make any money," John told Michael.

Michael returned to work determined to get promoted. He took an advancement test for his next promotion three times. He also worked hard to befriend as many sailors as he could who worked in the operations administration office of the carrier.

"I was really busting my ass," Michael recalled later, "and my dad was helping me by filling out all the right forms and putting just the right words on them to get me that promotion."

Still, promotions take time, and neither Michael nor John was patient. They both were becoming frustrated and irritable. Michael began to avoid his father, and John began to feel that Michael wasn't trying hard enough.

Michael also was having problems at home. When he first told Rachel about the spying, she had been fascinated. She had assumed that Michael was spying *for* the Navy with his dad. But after they were married, Rachel discovered that Michael was stealing secrets for another country, and she immediately assumed it was the Russians.

Rachel knew what Michael was doing because he brought home several classified reports from the Oceana Naval Air Station that he had tucked into his backpack. Being curious, Rachel had looked through the reports, unwittingly leaving her fingerprints on them for the FBI to find later. Since her father had been a twenty-year Navy man, she knew that Michael was breaking the law and she warned him.

"Michael, you're playing with fire," she said, shortly after they were married. "This is dangerous."

"Hey, it's okay," he replied. "My dad and I got everything under control. I can handle this."

The spying was not the only issue causing Michael and Rachel problems. Michael didn't seem to understand why Rachel needed to work so hard to get her college degree. Never a scholar himself, Michael saw little value in good grades.

"So you get a C instead of an A. What's the big deal?" he complained. He began to pressure her about the time she spent studying, particularly when she refused to be with him because of homework. She either was at school, studying, or at work as a waitress at Chi-Chi's restaurant. "Rachel didn't have any time for me after we got married," he complained later.

Rachel, meanwhile, felt Michael was immature. All he ever wanted to do was surf and party with his punk rock friends. Every time she managed to earn a few extra bucks at the restaurant, he spent it.

John contributed to the growing tension between the two newlyweds. He had always told Michael that the pickup truck he had driven since high school was his. But one morning, Michael was hit from behind while driving his truck and it was demolished. When it was time for the insurance company to pay for the damages, Michael discovered that John had never signed the truck's title over to him, so John received and pocketed the insurance claim payment.

Without the pickup truck, Michael and Rachel had to depend on her 1974 Dodge Dart. Their days began at five A.M., when Rachel drove Michael to the Norfolk Naval Base. Then she would return home, shower, dress, study, and hurry to her eight A.M. class. Michael got off work at three P.M., the same time that Rachel's classes ended. She would hurry to the base to pick him up, fix dinner, and then leave for the restaurant, where she waited on tables until one A.M. Bored without his wife at home, Michael began dropping by the restaurant late at night to wait for Rachel. His drinks came out of her tips.

Because Rachel could make better tips by working on Saturday nights, she often chose work instead of going out to party with Michael.

The $1,000 that Michael collected from John in April 1984 went fast. Michael said later that he gave $700 of it to Rachel so she could pay for summer school. But their money problems weren't because Michael and Rachel were poor. He earned $11,000 per year from the Navy and also received extra pay for housing. Rachel's father also gave her $150 per month to help with her schooling. On a good week, she earned $200 to $300 in salary and tips as a waitress. The money never seemed to be enough, though, and the main reason was Michael. John had given Michael everything he desired as a teenager, and Michael was completely without financial discipline. He spent money as soon as he received it.

Besides arguments about Michael's spying and finances, the couple also had troubles because of their relatives. A few weeks after Michael and Rachel were married, John decided it was time for him and P.K. to meet Rachel's parents. He suggested that everyone get together for dinner at a Norfolk restaurant. It sounded like a great idea but quickly turned into a disaster. John chose an expensive restaurant that Michael and Rachel simply couldn't afford. Don't worry, John told Michael when they met in the lobby, he would pick up the tab.

Even though Rachel's father had been in the Navy, it soon became clear that he and John had nothing in common. Worse, John showed up a bit tipsy and quickly began drinking heavily. Rachel's side of the family didn't drink at all. They sipped iced tea and coffee while John began telling bawdy stories about his adventures as a private investigator.

When the bill finally arrived, John handed it to Michael and asked, "What's your share?"

John laughed and announced that he would bail out the newlyweds since it was clear that they didn't earn enough between them to pay their own way.

Rachel was embarrassed and Michael was humiliated. As they left the restaurant, Rachel's father whispered to her. Never again, he said, did he want to go anywhere with John Walker.

After that, Michael and Rachel didn't see much of John. If Michael wanted to talk to his father, he drove over to his house. Yet Michael still had an intense loyalty, not only to John, but also to Barbara.

For instance, as soon as Rachel married, her father had signed over to her all of her insurance policies and the title and registration for her car. She, in turn, listed Michael as her beneficiary on the insurance policies and as the co-owner of the car. But Rachel discovered Michael had listed two beneficiaries on his life insurance policy. If he died, the money would be split equally between her and Barbara.

In July 1984, Michael announced that he had agreed to pay half of the cost of an airline ticket to bring his mother to Norfolk for a vacation. His sister, Margaret, paid the other half. Rachel was irritated because she knew that she would have to work extra shifts to pay the cost of Barbara's ticket. Why, she wondered, should they have to pay for his mother's vacation? If anything, Barbara's money should be paying for them to have a vacation.

By the time that Barbara arrived in Norfolk, Rachel was steamed, but Michael didn't care. Michael and Margaret insisted on taking their mother out to celebrate, even though neither could afford it. After dinner they stopped at Chi-Chi's to say hello to Rachel, who was working. The three of them were having such a good time that they decided to go barhopping, and Michael borrowed some money from Rachel.

Barbara spent the first week of her visit with Margaret, and then, during the first week of August, moved in with Michael and Rachel.

Barbara began unloading her problems on the couple. Her mother, Annie, had died, and she had been forced to ask John for $500 to help cover the cost of the funeral. He expected to be repaid, but Barbara had quit her job at the shoe company in Skowhegan and didn't have any other job lined up. She was thinking about moving to Hyannis, where Cynthia lived. Perhaps she could find something there.

One afternoon, Rachel arrived home from her classes to find Barbara sitting on the couch, drinking the only liquor that Michael and Rachel had in their apartment—a bottle of Triple Sec.

"I want to go see John," Barbara announced. "Will you drive me to his office?"

Rachel agreed. On the way, Barbara said she didn't want Rachel to come inside. Rachel was glad not to be caught in a family squabble.

Barbara marched into John's office without acknowledging his secretary.

"I need ten thousand dollars," she said. "I want to go to school."

Barbara's demand caught John off guard. "I looked up and here's Barbara demanding money," he recalled later. "She said if I didn't give it to her, she was going to tell. I tried to calm her down, but she had been drinking. She tells me that she is moving to Hyannis to be with Cynthia because she [Barbara] doesn't have a job and she can't pay her rent or the telephone bill or the utilities."

John said he stalled. It was clear to him, although Barbara denies it, that she was implying she would turn him in if he didn't give her the money.

"I don't have any money right now," he told Barbara.

"The truth was," John recalled later, "I really didn't have any money because Whitworth had screwed everything up. If I'd had ten thousand in cash I would have given it to her."

"Look, Barbara," John said. "My head ain't the only one that is going to roll here if you start shooting off your mouth."

Barbara told him that she didn't care.

"You promised to pay alimony and you never did," she said. "You owe me ten thousand dollars and I want it now!"

Barbara was furious when she returned to the car and Rachel. She began chain-smoking, smashing her cigarettes out before they were half finished.

"I'm going to fix him," Barbara said. "He owes me. He can't do this."

Barbara began drinking large glasses of Triple Sec without ice at the apartment. Rachel excused herself, explaining that she had to get ready for work. Hurrying to the telephone, Rachel called Michael.

"Your mother went to see your father today," she said, speaking softly so Barbara wouldn't hear, "and they fought. She's going crazy!"

"Oh my God!" Michael responded. "What happened?"

"I didn't go in, but she keeps saying that he owes her and she is going to get him."

Rachel worked late that night, but the next morning when she drove Michael to work, she asked him what had happened.

"I think everything is going to be okay," he assured her. "We talked."

That afternoon when Rachel finished her classes, she found Barbara waiting for her. Barbara wanted to know how to catch a bus that would take her to downtown Norfolk.

"Oh, I'll drive you downtown," Rachel volunteered.

"No, no, I don't want you to get involved," Barbara said.

"Where do you want to go?"

"The FBI," Barbara said.

Rachel tried to act nonchalant. "Why would you want to go there?" she asked.

"I'm going to turn John in, but I can't say for what, only that he's doing something illegal."

Rachel pressed Barbara.

"You've got to tell me. Is Michael going to be hurt by all this? What are you going to say?"

Barbara dodged the questions but finally blurted out her reason: "John's a spy!"

Rachel faked shock.

"Oh my God, no!" she said. She called Michael immediately.

"Michael, I'm here with your mother," Rachel said. "She wants me to take her downtown. Do you understand what I'm trying to say?"

"Are you talking about a federal agency?"

"That's right."

Rachel gave the telephone to Barbara, who had a brief exchange with her son. He was coming home immediately, he said. They needed to talk.

Barbara was drinking when Michael arrived. She was so upset that she was shaking, Michael recalled later.

"Listen, Mom, you don't want to do what you're thinking about," Michael explained. "You don't want to turn Dad in."

Barbara disagreed.

"Mom, you don't want to see Dad go to prison, do you?" Michael continued. "Do you really want to see him in prison?"

Barbara was undeterred. "She was really pissed," Michael told me. "She said she was sick and tired of him screwing her around. She had had enough."

"Mom, listen," Michael told Barbara. "This is more than you can handle. You are going to destroy this family if you do this. The entire family will be ruined."

"That seemed to calm her down," Michael said later. "I didn't tell her that I was involved and I don't think she thought, at that point, that I was."

Rachel had gone to work, and when she got home that night, she demanded to know what Barbara had decided. Michael laughed off the incident.

"She's got a drinking problem," he said. "She does this every once in a while. It's no big thing."

"I can't believe you," Rachel responded. "She almost went to the FBI today. She could have turned him in and you too!"

Michael wasn't in the mood to fight. He wanted to make love, but Rachel declined. She walked out onto the back porch of their apartment because Barbara was asleep on the couch in the living room. Michael followed her outside.

"What's wrong?" he asked.

"I don't want her here tonight," Rachel said.

"She's leaving on Sunday," Michael said.

"Tell me that you'll quit," Rachel said. "Promise me."

"I have," Michael said, lying. "And I'm going to talk to my father tomorrow about Mom."

The night before she left, Barbara made an Italian dinner for Michael, Rachel, Margaret, and some of Margaret's friends. The meal required more than $50 worth of special ingredients that Rachel paid for with her tip money. The next morning, Michael drove Barbara to the airport. On the way home, he detoured to John's house.

"I went over to my dad's and I told him what had happened," Michael recalled.

"Mike, we got a real problem here," John said.

"Hey, *we* don't have a problem," Michael replied. "You have a problem."

Recalling the conversation later, Michael said, "I told my dad that I worked for him. My part of the deal was to get the shit and he was supposed to take care of Mom."

Michael's assertiveness apparently surprised John.

"Mark is a problem too," Michael told John, "and Mom is a problem. What are you going to do about them?"

"Look," said John, "you're the one who has to tell Mom that you are involved, 'cause she ain't gonna believe me."

"No," said Michael. "You tell her, because if I tell her, she might kill herself. You do the damn thing. It will kill her, Dad. It will kill her if I tell her."

"I tried to tell Mike that Barbara wasn't going to kill herself," John told me later. "I said, 'Listen, Mike, your mother isn't going to kill herself. She is too fucking weak to do that. Now you've got to quit thinking about it and just tell her.' "

John reminded Michael that they could both be in trouble if Barbara talked to the FBI. "If she rats on me, they are going to be suspicious of you." John promised to find out when Barbara planned to return to Norfolk and to arrange a meeting between her and Michael so he could tell her that he had joined the spy ring. "It's got to come from your lips," John said.

Three weeks later, Michael was promoted from the recreational department aboard the U.S.S. *Nimitz* to the legal office on the carrier. He worked harder than ever to impress his superiors, particularly those in the operations administration department.

"I didn't hate my dad at this point," Michael told me later, "but I was just tired of his pressure and bullshit. He just kept pushing me to get that transfer."

After Michael had worked for one month in the legal office, a job in the operations administration office became vacant and he was selected to fill it. He stole his first classified document from that office within the first week and delivered it to John. Soon he was stealing documents regularly by hiding them in the backpack he carried to work each day. He hated his uniform, so he kept a change of clothes in the backpack, and put them on after work. He hid the stolen documents in the bottom of the backpack under his uniform.

One afternoon, Rachel emptied Michael's bag while collecting laundry. Inside were several documents with the word *SECRET* stamped on them.

That night, Rachel confronted Michael.

"You said you'd quit."

"I can't, we need the money," Michael replied. "Sending you to school isn't cheap."

"Neither is surfing," Rachel replied.

"I remember telling Rachel to get off my back," Michael recalled later. "I said to her, 'Rachel, don't worry. I've got everything under control so just stop sweating it.' "

# 58

Janet Fournier was working the complaint desk at the San Francisco FBI office on May 9, 1984, when the letter from "RUS" arrived. As an investigative assistant, Fournier was responsible for screening telephone calls and reviewing letters not addressed to specific agents. It was not glamorous work. Most of the time, she got stuck on the phone talking to disturbed callers who insisted on reporting their own murders. Fournier knew that most anonymous tips were worthless, but occasionally one paid off. RUS sounded legitimate so Fournier hand carried the letter to the office's foreign counterintelligence squad and showed it to Special Agent John Peterson. He was also impressed. RUS used words like *keylists, tech manuals,* and *intelligence messages,* terms that weren't generally known outside the government. The spelling and punctuation of the letter were terrible, however, and that raised immediate questions. Was the writer trying to appear less intelligent than he was, or was he poorly educated?

Peterson put the letter in a plastic envelope to preserve possible fingerprints and sent it to the FBI's laboratory in Washington. He also sent a copy of it for review to Dr. Murray Miron, a Syracuse University psychologist who was a consultant to the FBI in espionage cases.

As directed by RUS, Peterson placed an advertisement in the *Los Angeles Times* on May 21:

> RUS considering your offer. Call weekdays 9:00 A.M. to 11 A.M. Telephone number (415) 626–2793, or write. Signed M.E., San Francisco.

The telephone number was a special line the FBI had installed on Peterson's desk that enabled agents to trace an outside call instantaneously. But Jerry didn't call. With his electronics background, he knew calls could be traced and a caller's voice tape-recorded. Instead, he wrote another letter:

> Dear Sir,
> I saw your note today and was encouraged, however, I'm not going to call for obvious reasons. I'll admit that my most earnest desire is to talk to someone (like yourself) about my situation, but I feel that I'm unable to trust any kind of personal contact—phone included. Nor have I begun to look for an attorney. Where does that leave us or more specifically me?
> I'll be very open. It took me several months to finally write the first letter. Yes, I'm remorseful and I feel that to come forward and help break the espionage ring would compensate for my wrongdoing, consequently clearing my conscience. But there are other emotions: the difficulty of ratting on a "friend", and the potential of getting caught up in a legal mess (public disclosure of my involvement and a possible double-cross on immunity, assuming it was granted in the first place).
> I would guess that you are conferring with higher authority and possibly other agencies. I'm wondering if my situation is really considered serious enough to warrant investigation and to give me due consideration (immunity & etc.)!
> I'm going to begin looking for an attorney, which will be tricky from my view, to discuss my situation. And I will keep an eye on the *LA Times*, Monday editions, for any additional word/instructions from you.
> It would certainly be nice for people in my predicament to have a

means of confidential consultation with someone in a position of authority without the possibility of arrest.

My contact will be expecting more material from me in a few months, if I don't I'm not sure what his response will be. I'm going to come clean with him at that time (assuming no deal is made with you) and tell him I'm finished with the "business". And then get on with my life.

More info on him: he has been in "the business" for more than 20 years and plans to continue indefinitely. He thinks he has a good organization and has no real fear of being caught, less some coincidential [sic] misfortune; in that regard he feels safe also. I agree with his assessment.

Why haven't I discussed my desire to come clean (with you) with my contact and/or possibly convince him to do the same? It would be sure folly—dangerous to my health.

One line in Jerry's letter stuck out when Peterson and his superiors at the FBI office read it: RUS's contact had been "in 'the business' for more than 20 years."

The FBI responded with an ad in the June 4 edition of the *Times*:

RUS: Understand your concerns, but we can help. Must have dialogue with you or proxy, if you are serious. ME. SF.

Each day Peterson waited by the special telephone and searched the mail, but nothing happened. As usual, Jerry was vacillating. He didn't know whether or not to turn in John. He wasn't worried about John or anyone else in the spy ring. He was worried about himself. How could he nail John without incriminating himself?

Becoming impatient, the FBI placed another ad in the June 11 edition.

RUS: Considering your dilemma. Need to speak to you to see what I can do. This can be done anonymously. Just you and me at 10 A.M. June 21 at intersection of the street of my office and Hyde Street in my city. I'll carry a newspaper in my left hand. We will only discuss your situation to provide you with guidance as to where you stand. No action will be taken against you whatsoever at this meeting. Respond if you cannot make it or if you want to change locations. I want to help you in your very trying situation, but I need facts to be able to assist you.

The offer was tempting. The FBI promised it wouldn't arrest the mysterious RUS. But Jerry had read the note closely and noticed the FBI's caveat: "No action will be taken against you whatsoever *at this meeting*." Whom did the FBI think it was dealing with? Jerry correctly guessed what the FBI had planned. At ten A.M. Peterson waited at the designated corner as he had promised, but he wasn't alone. Several FBI agents were hiding nearby. The FBI intended to follow him if he appeared, and after the meeting, nab him.

Once again, Jerry replied by letter:

Sir: I won't be meeting you the 21st. A letter will follow in a week or two.

The FBI waited, but nothing appeared. Meanwhile, Peterson received an evaluation by Miron of the first RUS letter.

This communication exhibits a number of characteristics which suggest that it should be considered to be highly credible. It is quite likely that anyone engaged in espionage would be expected ... to be psychopathic in character. Idealists who might try to aid or abet our enemies would be expected to eschew any money for themselves so as to better prove their 'nobler' intentions. The author of this letter exhibits the language of the psychopath. His passing reference to conscience is both glib and superficial. Even the protestation of remorse is mitigated by the notion that the author wishes to be free of what we can presume to be some pressures consequent of an earlier attempt to demur from further participation. The author's psychopathic bent is further supported by his ending request that he be compensated for 'interruption' of his 'livelihood.' All of this is entirely believable.

Based upon the content and style of the author's language, it is my judgment that he is a technically trained Caucasian male approximately between the ages of 30 to 45. There are indications that the author is familiar with cryptography, codes and radio/computers apparatus. Although he is, in my judgment, clearly psychopathic, he can be expected to be sufficiently shrewd and wily to have avoided detection for other schemes in which he may be involved: i.e., he would not be expected to have a criminal record and have received relatively high fitness reports on the job.

On August 13, Peterson tried to flush RUS from hiding once again:

RUS: Haven't heard from you, still want to meet. Propose meeting in Ensenada, Mexico, a neutral site. If you need travel funds, will furnish same at your choice of location in Silicon Valley or anywhere else. Please respond to the above.

Jerry responded with another letter:

Dear Sir:
I saw your note in todays [sic] LA Times. Since my last note to you I've done a lot of serious thinking and have pretty much come to the conclusion that it would be best to give up on the idea of aiding in the termination of the espionage ring previously discussed.

To think I could help you and not make my own involvement known to the public, I believe is naive. Nor have I contacted an attorney. I have great difficulty in coming forth, particularly, since the chances of my past involvement ever being known is extremenely [sic] remote, as long as I remain silent.

Yes, I can still say I would prefer to get it off my chest, to come clean.

The above notwithstanding, I'll think about a meeting in Ensenada. Funds are not the problem.

My contact is pressing for more material, but so far no real problems have occurred. I haven't explicity [sic] told him, I'm no longer in the business.

By now the agents in the FBI office in San Francisco were convinced that RUS was legitimate. They believed he was a spy for the KGB and that, unless he was exaggerating, somewhere in the country, someone had been operating a spy ring for two decades. It was chilling and frustrating. RUS had surfaced and then disappeared. What the San Francisco FBI office didn't know was that their counterparts in Norfolk had found another source by late 1984, and she wasn't interested in rewards, immunity, or playing games by corresponding in newspaper advertisements.

Her name was Barbara Walker.

# 59

In the fall of 1984, Marie Hammond's relatives asked her and Laura to leave the farm outside Buffalo owned by Marie's grandmother. One of the incidents that had sparked discontent involved Laura. Marie's grandmother sometimes suffered from memory loss and disorientation, so one afternoon, when Marie went on an errand, she asked Laura to watch the old woman. "Laura spiked shut my grandmother's bedroom door so she couldn't get out of her room," Marie said later. "I just about died. Laura said she had some things to do and didn't have time to watch my grandmother so she simply spiked my grandmother's bedroom door shut."

Marie rejoined her husband, who was still in the Army. Laura headed north to Buffalo and enrolled in a beauty school. It wasn't long before she was broke and deeply depressed about Christopher.

"A guy literally took me in off the street," Laura told me. "He had fallen in love with me and I let him know that I didn't love him, but he wanted to do these things for me—help pay my rent and help with transportation—and he feigned being a Christian, so anyway, I moved in with him."

That November, Laura decided to end her seventeen-month, self-imposed excommunication from her family by calling Barbara, who now lived near Cynthia in West Dennis, a town near Hyannis, Massachusetts.

Laura and Barbara have given me different accounts of what was said during this conversation. Parts of their stories are also inconsistent with what they have testified to under oath.

When I spoke to Laura about the telephone call, she told me the same story that she had told other reporters after her father's arrest. She always began by saying that she had called her mother on November 23, Barbara's birthday.

"I said to her, 'Happy Birthday,' and then I apologized for not calling her sooner. I said, 'Maybe now you know how I feel about Chris. Maybe now you understand what it is like not to know where your child is.'

"It was very important to me that my mother knew how sorry I was for what I had done. We didn't say much else because we were in too much pain. She was in too much pain and so was I. We didn't even talk about Christopher. I was too upset and we certainly didn't talk about Mark.

"The next night, and I'll never forget this, it was November 24, 1984, and I was blindly watching television when my mother telephoned and she said, 'Laura, I turned your father in.' This is the very next night. She had gotten off the phone with me on her birthday and called the FBI. There wasn't any discussion about turning Dad in. She did this entirely on her own without telling me what she was going to do. She said, 'Laura, I did this for you. I did this so you could get your son back.' She said, 'Will you cooperate with the FBI? Will you tell them everything?'

"Her objective was that the FBI would believe that Mark had blackmailed me for x number of years, and the courts could not possibly grant Mark custody under those conditions. Somehow Mark would be brought out in the light and my dad would be brought out in the light, and somehow I would get Chris. That was her main objective and you could go to the bank on it.

"I never dreamed that my dad would get arrested. I never knew beforehand that my mother was going to do it. I didn't think he was spying anymore and I knew that I didn't have enough to hang him and I knew that my mother didn't either.

"When she told me this, there was an excitement in me, and I knew there was going to be a move, and I knew that God was going to do it. I just knew it, but I knew it wasn't going to be the FBI that got my son back. It was God working through my mother, guiding her hand. Don't you see the irony of it all?

"My mother turned in my father to save her grandson and get my son back to me."

Barbara Walker's version to me contradicted her daughter's story on several counts. Barbara said she and Laura actually spoke twice on the night that Laura first called and, contrary to what Laura had said, they spoke extensively about Christopher and Mark. Both women, Barbara told me, were worried about what might happen if Mark took action. During their conversation, Barbara began to realize that Laura really missed her son.

"I called Laura back that evening after she called me and we talked," Barbara told me, "because it had always bothered me that she had left Chris when we were in Skowhegan and gone to California. I asked her, 'How can you walk away from a child?' I knew she was in pain and we talked, and this is when I began to sense that maybe all this wasn't an ego thing with Laura. Instead of her saying, 'This is *my* child!' maybe she was saying, 'This is my *child*!' and there is a difference between wanting something because you own it and caring about someone because you love them. I began to believe that Laura really was hurting and she really did want Chris back.

"After the second telephone call, I went into the living room to be alone, and I sat there in the dark and I thought about the spying, and for the very first time I saw the whole picture. I suddenly could see everything clearly.

"You see, we weren't talking about Laura and Christopher. We weren't just talking about John's spying. We were talking about all of it. In the past, I had, in my desperation, only focused on one thing at a time. How could John serve with these men in the Navy and do what he is doing? Or how could he socialize with them and act like he's their best friend? Or how could he do this to his family? Or how could he do this to God? For the first time that night, all these things came together! I could see it all for the very first time because before that I didn't. I really didn't. All of those years, I was only seeing certain things and would only think about certain things, the pieces. But I saw it all that night in that room. I saw John and what he had done to his country, his friends, his children, his God, and to me, and all the pain and suffering that he had caused. Oh God! The men who have died because of what he had done. And me too, by going along with him."

Barbara Walker began crying at this point while talking to me. She had drunk several large tumblers of scotch during the afternoon and she was emotionally upset. It took her several minutes to regain her composure. "I was just as guilty, just as wrong, and I hated it. I hated it, and I couldn't stand it anymore, and I had to call the FBI. I didn't care what happened to me. I didn't care what happened to anyone. I just wanted it to stop.

"I had to call Information because I couldn't see the phone book because I'd been drinking. I called the number and I was glad. You don't know how many times I had wanted this over with. I wanted it to go away. I didn't want the pain. I do love my country, and I just got tired of carrying this load on my back.

"That's why I called the FBI that night. It *wasn't* Christopher or Laura. It was John. I just couldn't live the lies any longer: his lies and mine. It was time for it to end."

Laura's version of her conversation with Barbara is contradicted, in part, by two documents. A letter written by John to Michael, and later found by the FBI, indicates that Laura resurfaced *before* Barbara's birthday on November 23. The letter, dated November 18, said:

Dear Mike: Just a short note to give you some good news: Laura is alive and well. She telephoned Cynthia—Mom and informed everyone that she had never left New York. She has been going to school and basically living there. Apparently, her friend that called and said she had boarded a bus was lying: Laura was living with her all the time and just wanted to "drop out of sight," I guess. I knew you would be interested in hearing this right away. Sorry I don't have more details. Needless to say, I am glad Laura is okay, but I have mixed emotions in general. Obviously, it was a shitty thing to do, and I am sure she has enjoyed making us all feel like bastards.

A telephone log maintained by the FBI also showed that Barbara first called the bureau on November 17, six days before her birthday.

These documents suggest that Laura placed her call before November 23, most likely on November 17.

Laura's memory of her conversation with Barbara also is contradicted, not only by Barbara, but by Laura's own testimony at Jerry Whitworth's trial. Laura told me that she and her mother spoke only briefly, and never discussed John or mentioned the alleged threats made by Mark Snyder. But when asked during Whitworth's trial about her telephone conversation with Barbara, Laura acknowledged that she and her mother were worried that Mark might attempt to incriminate them if either of them crossed him. One of the reasons that Laura was worried was because she had applied for a job at the CIA and was concerned that the FBI might think she was trying to help her father.

Barbara Walker insisted in all of her interviews with me that her motivation for calling the FBI had nothing to do with her trip to Norfolk or her demand for $10,000. The FBI accounts indicate otherwise. When she first met with agents, Barbara specifically mentioned that John owed her $10,000 in unpaid alimony, and she told the FBI she had just come from seeing John in Norfolk, where he had a young girlfriend and such luxuries as a houseboat and an airplane. It was these comments, in fact, that initially made FBI agents suspect that Barbara might have made up the spy charges against her husband out of anger, seeking revenge.

Even members of the Walker family aren't certain what happened on the night that Laura telephoned Barbara. "I was told by Michael, after we both were arrested, that Barbara had turned John in because she was angry at him," Arthur Walker told me several months after the spy ring was broken. "She'd just taken all she was going to take. Then she called Laura for support, and together they came up with all this stuff about Christopher so they wouldn't look so bad for squealing on everyone."

Because of the various discrepancies, it is impossible to reconstruct accurately the conversation, feelings, and possible motivations of Laura and Barbara during their emotional telephone call that night in November.

But the result is clear. For whatever reason, Laura's telephone call that night prompted Barbara to call the FBI, and marked the beginning of John's downfall.

# 60

The operations administration office was on level 3 of the enormous U.S.S. *Nimitz* and was considered one of the most important chambers in the carrier. Anything that had to do with the ship's operation, destination, or mission passed through this office and generally found its way to Michael's desk, because he was the yeoman responsible for routing messages, filing memos, and typing orders.

Besides working in what the Navy called OPS-ADMIN, Michael also was assigned to the office next door, known as STRIKE-OPS, which is where the carrier's top echelon of officers meet to plan and coordinate actual combat operations.

The Navy recognized the importance of Michael's job even though he was technically a low-ranking yeoman. Only persons with a *secret* clearance or above were supposed to work in the center. After his arrest, the Navy would announce that Michael had such a clearance, but, in truth, he had never undergone a background check.

"When I reported to work," Michael told me, "I was told that I had to get a clearance to work in the office. I said, 'Okay, no problem,' but I never put in for one and no one ever followed up on it. They just believed me when I told them that I had one."

Michael's promotion to the OPS-ADMIN office and subsequent failure to obtain the proper clearance was a major breach of Navy security that was not publicly reported but was later substantiated by FBI and Naval Investigative Service agents.

"Somebody really screwed up even letting him in there," an investigator confirmed later.

The room where Michael worked was spartan. Along one wall to the left of the door were three large file cabinets containing classified messages and orders. A copy machine and supply cabinet sat next to the file cabinets. In the center of the room stood a large steel table holding four large clipboards, each of which contained various messages about the ship's maneuvers and operations.

Michael's desk faced the wall directly across from the door. It was one of a row of five desks, each belonging to someone of progressively higher rank.

The wall to Michael's right had a high-speed computer printer in front of it and an MPDS, or Message Processing Distribution System, machine. It reminded Michael of a teletype machine as it printed various messages sent to the office.

On the same wall as the door was a computer terminal and the duty officer's desk. It was Michael's job to tear messages off the MPDS machine, deliver them to the five senior officers in the office, and do whatever secretarial chores were required. He also had the mundane task of picking up the seven burn bags in the office and carrying them to a fan room. These bags looked much like standard grocery store bags, except that they were unmarked. Every secret and confidential document received by the OPS-ADMIN office was supposed to be placed in a burn bag once it was no longer needed.

The burn bags were stored in the fan room off the STRIKE-OPS office. This office was an even more sensitive assignment for Michael. It was guarded by a cipher lock, and no one was supposed to be inside without a specific reason—no one but Michael, who could come and go as he pleased since he needed access to the fan room where the burn bags were stored.

The STRIKE-OPS office was the closest thing to a "war room" on the carrier. Around a huge table the admiral and his officers made their major decisions. One wall had an enormous chart that showed the location of every missile and bomb aboard the carrier. Another wall contained a special audiovisual screen capable of showing within seconds a detailed map of any country in the world. The room also contained a telephone with a direct line to the Pentagon and, if necessary, the President of the United States. There were also several safes where various secret documents and reports were kept.

It was in the fan room, actually a closet off the STRIKE-OPS office with a ventilation fan in it, that each day's burn bags were stored. This was where Michael did most of his work as a spy. The carrier only burned the bags when necessary, and only after 11:30 P.M., when it was not launching aircraft. This schedule gave Michael time to sort through each burn bag and remove whatever secret documents interested him. It also enabled him to circumvent Navy security. As far as the Navy knew, all the items in the burn bags were destroyed. Michael never had to worry about signing for documents or even copying them.

"OPS-ADMIN and STRIKE-OPS were gold mines for spying," Michael recalled. "Classified shit was lying everywhere, and most of it eventually hit the burn bags. If you couldn't find something out by going through the messages and classified reports in these two rooms, then it just didn't exist or wasn't happening."

Michael began stealing classified material within days after reporting to work in OPS-ADMIN. The burn bags proved to be easy to ransack. Once a bag was full, it was stapled shut by Michael and taken to the fan room for storage. What no one knew was that Michael simply tore open the bags once he was alone in the fan room and took out whatever he wanted. "I kept a stapler in the fan room in plain sight and no one ever said a word," Michael recalled.

Michael was caught once going through a burn bag in the fan room.

"What the hell are you doing?" an officer who had been looking for Michael demanded when he discovered the yeoman looking through classified material that he obviously had removed from a burn bag.

"I got to get a message that the captain wanted," Michael answered quickly. "Someone threw it away by mistake."

"Okay. When you get done, I need you to run an errand," the officer replied.

"I was always cool about things," Michael told me. "The entire office ran on trust. You did your job and no one even thought about the guy next to them being a spy."

The longer Michael worked in the two offices, the more daring he became. He found a classified report in the OPS-ADMIN office that he wanted to copy for his dad. It was more than four inches thick and the copying machine could only duplicate twenty-five pages at a time, so Michael took it apart and carefully stacked it in sections.

When he was about halfway through his copying project, the duty officer came over to the machine with an order that he needed to copy.

"Jeez, Walker, what's all this shit?" he asked.

"Gotta make a copy for the captain," Michael said. Then he offered to interrupt his task so the duty officer didn't have to wait.

"Thanks," the officer said, handing Michael the order.

"This guy walked back to his desk," Michael recalled, "so I made two copies and kept one for myself, and then I finished copying this secret report. As long as you were cool about it and acted like you knew what you were doing, you were okay. The key was not panicking."

Michael took the report home to his father by hiding it in his backpack. "He couldn't believe that I had copied this huge report right under everyone's nose."

"You've got balls," John told Michael.

"I decided," Michael recalled, "that I was going to drain that ship of every secret it had."

In the fall of 1984, the U.S.S. *Nimitz* left Norfolk for a short cruise in the Caribbean. On October 12, John sent a tape-recorded letter to Michael. The two spies had agreed to refer to classified material by the code name *pictures*.

Dear Mike, How you doing? I miss you. Where are you? I just tried to call Rachel, wasn't home. Called her mother and said she's on some field trip up in Pennsylvania. . . . Don't know what you're doing. I guess you're having fun. Hope you're getting me some good pictures. . . . I'll be interested in looking at your photographs . . . that's what I like to see. I'd say like hang onto them. Let me see them when you come back in . . . and remember to get what you can, okay? . . .

Michael began enjoying himself. The U.S.S. *Nimitz* was participating in a secret and sensitive war game, Michael had discovered, which involved a simulated invasion of Cuba. The operation began at two A.M. and was supposed to be a surprise for the crew, but the officers in the OPS-ADMIN office didn't want to run any risks so they had tipped off Michael and warned him to be ready.

As a result, Michael reported to the OPS-ADMIN office before two o'clock, and was the first person there when the exercise began. Within minutes, a radio operator arrived at the office with a top secret message. Unlike secret and confidential messages, top secret messages are so sensitive that anyone who reads one is required to sign a log that is kept with the top secret message until it is destroyed.

"You got a clearance for this?" the radioman, who has since left the Navy, asked Michael.

Michael took a chance. "Yeah, sure."

"Okay," the radioman said, handing it to him.

"I couldn't believe this dumb ass gave me a top secret message and then didn't have me sign for it," Michael recalled. "Another yeoman was in the room and I told him to go next door. 'Hey, you go in STRIKE-OPS—that way it will look like we are manning both offices. That'll impress the captain,'" Michael said to him.

As soon as the other yeoman left, Michael locked the OPS-ADMIN door and raced to the copy machine.

Just as Michael pushed the copying button, someone pounded on the door.

"I hid my copy and opened the door," Michael recalled, "and it was the captain and he was pissed. 'I'm sorry, sir, I must have locked the door by mistake,' I said. I thought I was busted. 'Don't ever lock this door again,' he yelled. I gave him the top secret message and he was so busy, he didn't even ask if I'd signed for it."

During the entire mock invasion of Cuba, Michael sat at the computer terminal in the STRIKE-OPS office and printed out messages for the admiral and other brass.

"We were launching aircraft," Michael told me enthusiastically, "and directing cruisers and submarines and doing all kinds of exciting shit just as if we were at war and actually attacking Cuba, and what was really neat was that I was hitting the 2 key on my keyboard whenever I printed messages. I was printing one message, like I was supposed to, and then another one for myself. I did that all night long and no one noticed."

When the carrier returned to port, Michael delivered his package of messages to John.

"Ever wonder how we'd invade Cuba?" Michael asked John, tossing the stolen documents on his desk. John was impressed.

"Michael was really turning out to be a better spy than I ever expected," John proudly told me later. "He was really innovative about getting me stuff."

Michael's biggest achievement was yet to come. Once while working a relaxed night shift, he went into the STRIKE-OPS office and began snooping through various desks there. On top of one was a Rolodex telephone file.

Michael gave it a spin and noticed a woman's name on one of the small white cards. The card read "Jodie," followed by several digits, but there were too many to be a telephone number. Michael wrote the name and numbers on a pad and continued looking through the directory. He found "Sarah" next and copied down her name and number. When he finished going through the Rolodex, Michael counted the names and then looked around the room. "There were exactly the same number of safes in the room as names on my pad," Michael recalled. "Bingo, I knew exactly what had happened. Someone had been afraid they might forget a combination to the safes, so they had written them down and tried to disguise them as telephone numbers."

Michael began methodically trying each combination until he linked a girl's name with each safe.

After John was arrested, the FBI searched his house and confiscated a film typewriter ribbon that agents were able to use to reconstruct his correspondence. John had used his typewriter to type a list of the documents Michael had stolen from the *Nimitz*. The list included classified material about the Nuclear Tomahawk Land Attack Cruise Missile, spy satellites, newly developed underwater mines, and thirty-three messages concerning intelligence operations.

The FBI would wonder later how Michael had removed documents from the *Nimitz* safes and copied them. But no explanation was needed for another item that they found on John's typewriter ribbon. It was a brief note that he had written to Michael:

Dear Mike ... Everyone liked your pictures and it appears that you are becoming an excellent photographer. Keep up the good work. ...

# PART SIX

# *EXPOSED*

**The surest way to be deceived
is to think one's self more clever
than others.**

**LA ROCHEFOUCAULD**
*Maximes No. 127*

# *61*

---

The telephone operator gave Barbara the number for the FBI office in Boston when she telephoned for information on November 17, but the agent in Boston told her to call the FBI office in Hyannis, one of the bureau's smallest outposts. Barbara called Hyannis and spoke with Special Agent Walter Price, a fifteen-year FBI veteran who had been assigned there all but two of those years. Within the FBI, the Hyannis office was considered an anachronism, opened when John F. Kennedy was president and scarcely one of the bureau's choicer assignments.

Based on her speech, Price suspected that Barbara had been drinking, and when he asked, she acknowledged that she had poured herself a few drinks to calm her nerves. Price promised to drop by Barbara's West Dennis apartment and conduct a follow-up interview in person, but he didn't set a specific date.

As soon as Barbara replaced the telephone receiver, she called John in Norfolk. "I wanted to tell him about Laura and also warn him," she explained later. But their conversation quickly turned sour.

"She demanded the ten thousand and began threatening me again," John told me. "It was the same old story." John noted Barbara's call in the November 18 letter to Michael that the FBI found later.

> Your mother called . . . with her usual threats, and didn't really say much. Everything normal here except for Mom's endless threats. As usual, try to communicate with her and try to get her to STOP.

When Barbara finished talking to John, she telephoned Arthur.

"I'm going to turn your brother in," Barbara said.

Arthur figured she was drunk. "She had called prior times," Arthur said later, "and always said that she was going to do it. I was going to be a little flippant and say, 'Ha, ha, what are you going to turn him in for? He isn't doing anything.'" Instead, Arthur handed her over to Rita.

The next day, Arthur called John.

"Barbara called again," he reported. "She says she's gonna turn you in."

"Yeah, she's drunk again," John replied. "That crazy bitch."

"John, you had better take good care of her, okay?" Arthur said, but he knew John wouldn't give Barbara any money. "I sometimes wondered how he kept operating with that hanging over his head," Arthur recalled. "Evidently, his own ego convinced him that she wasn't going to do it."

During the next few days, agent Price stopped by Barbara's apartment twice but she wasn't home. They finally met November 29, and a few minutes after Price began questioning Barbara, she politely excused herself and returned with a large tumbler of scotch. Price dutifully took notes as she described traveling to Washington with John and delivering classified documents to KGB agents during dead drops. During the two-hour session, Barbara told how John had tried to recruit Laura and her suspicion that Mark Snyder was threatening Laura to prevent her from gaining custody of Christopher.

"It was obvious to me," Barbara said later, "that this agent didn't believe a word I was telling him."

Barbara decided to confront Price. "What if I had someone who could testify about all this?" she asked. "What if Laura told you about her father trying to recruit her as a spy?"

"That would help," Price said.

Back at his office, Price noted in his initial report to Boston that Barbara was an admitted alcoholic and angry ex-wife. He also noted that she had talked about John's spying in the past tense, which, he felt, indicated that John hadn't been spying since 1976 when he and Barbara were divorced and John retired from the Navy. How, Price wondered, would the FBI prosecute someone for a crime allegedly committed nearly a decade earlier? There was another problem with the case. What kind of a witness would Barbara make? Would a jury believe a jilted divorcee who had a drinking problem and was angry because her ex-husband owed her $10,000 and was living with a woman half her age? Price reacted by typing the numbers 65–0 on his report. The 65 indicated the subject of the report was espionage and the zero signified that no case number had been assigned because the agent considered the information not worthy of further investigation.

When Price's report arrived in Boston, a clerk there filed it in the "Zero file," a place for complaints that, more often than not, are more fiction than fact.

Barbara Walker telephoned Laura a few hours after the interview with Price and asked her for support.

"Would you be willing to testify against your father?" Barbara asked. "I'll try to make it easier for you. Your sisters and brother are not going to be happy with what you do, so I'll arrange it so it looks like I forced you into it by giving the FBI your name. I won't tell them that you agreed."

Laura volunteered to talk to Price.

Barbara immediately called Price and gave him Laura's number in Buffalo. "At last, I figured something would happen," Barbara recalled. "I kept waiting and waiting for someone to telephone me, but nothing happened. I couldn't believe it! After all these years of worrying and trying to turn him in, and then I finally call and no one believes me."

Laura was also surprised. She kept waiting for Price to telephone her, but he didn't. Finally she telephoned Barbara.

"Why hasn't anyone called?" Laura asked. "What's happening?"

"I don't know," Barbara said. "Maybe you should call Walter Price and ask him." Barbara gave Laura the agent's number and she promised to call him.

"Now, something is going to happen," Barbara said. "You promise to call him, Laura."

Laura telephoned Price, but she became squeamish when he began asking her specific questions. She began to panic.

"What my mother says is true!" Laura told him. Later she admitted that she was getting worried about "squealing" on her father. "I beat around the bush," Laura told me, "because I just didn't want to come out and say everything that I knew."

Finally, Laura told Price that she didn't want to talk anymore. "Look, I know my mother called you and I just want to tell you that I'm here to confirm what she said."

Price agreed to add Laura's statement to his original report, but she was so vacillating that their conversation helped persuade him an investigation wasn't warranted.

Laura began to worry. "I couldn't believe that I had called the FBI on my dad and I decided, in my own mind, that I wasn't going to cooperate with the FBI," she said.

"Instead, I called up my mom and I said, 'Mother . . . I want to call Dad and let him know that we've called the FBI.' I was going to blackmail my dad! I said, 'Mom, I want to call Dad and tell him that we called the FBI and we are going to cooperate unless he goes down and gets Chris for me. He's got an airplane and he's a private investigator. Boy, he would hop on that plane and go get Chris in nothing flat if we threatened him like that.'

"And my mother says to me, 'No, we are not going to do it,' but I said, 'Yeah, I'm going to do it. I don't want Dad to go to jail, but I want him to go and do it. I want my son, and Dad should do it.' And my mother said, 'Laura, don't be an asshole,' and I said, 'Mom, that's what I want to do,' and she said, 'He'll never buy it.' See, I didn't realize that he probably wouldn't have done it because my mother had already tried that umpteen times—threatening to turn him in. But that's what I wanted to do. I wanted to blackmail my own dad, but she talked me out of it."

Barbara continued to wait for the FBI to investigate. She was confident that Laura's call to Price would convince the agent that John was a spy. Day after day, she waited for a telephone call. At night she drank herself to sleep. Christmas approached and passed. New Year's Eve came, and there was still no word from Price or the FBI.

Finally, Barbara gave up.

"I decided that no one really cared. John had gotten away with it, and there wasn't anyone who was going to stop him."

# 62

Three months after Barbara alerted the FBI, John went to Vienna for his eleventh face-to-face overseas meeting with a KGB agent. He brought more than one dozen rolls of film with pictures of documents Michael had stolen from the U.S.S. *Nimitz*.

The weather on January 19, 1985, was, as always, bitter cold, and as John walked the usual route, he began to wonder once again why the Russians insisted on meeting in the streets rather than a safe house. With a chuckle, John did notice a change in scenery. Two blocks away from the Bazala store was now a McDonald's restaurant. John had been spying long enough for American fast food to invade his turf.

For the first time, John's KGB handler was apologetic. The photographs that John had delivered earlier from Jerry had turned out perfectly. The KGB now had all of the secret message traffic that Jerry had stolen during his duty aboard the U.S.S. *Enterprise*.

"Please tell Jerry that we will pay him," the Russian said. "He will get all of his money at the next exchange in your country."

Sensing a hint of apology, John protested at meeting in the middle of winter on the sidewalks of Vienna.

"Why the fuck don't you guys take me somewhere where we can talk comfortably in private?" he asked. "Don't you have a safe house here?"

"The Russian told me," John recalled later, "that it was safer to walk the streets." The CIA and other intelligence organizations are constantly trying to find Soviet safe houses. Taking John to one would be too risky.

John was insistent. He was tired of the cold.

"He told me that he'd arrange for me to go to a safe house the next time I came to Europe," John recalled. The plan called for John to be taken across the Czechoslovakian border when he returned in the fall.

The agent asked about Michael. "He's about to leave on an extended

Mediterranean cruise," said John. "He'll get as many messages as he can."

The KGB agent told John that Michael should try to get as much information about the Israelis as possible. John brought up Rachel. "She's graduating from college and I'm trying to get her to join the Navy, become an officer." With Rachel's interest in oceanography, John told the Russian, "she'd be able to find out about SOSUS [the network of ocean hydrophones]."

Women, the KGB agent replied, rarely are suspected of being spies. Recruiting Rachel would be good. What about Arthur?

John lied. Arthur was working hard to get a new job with better access, he said. Hopefully, Arthur would find a job where he could tell when the DEFCON changed.

"The Soviets were paranoid about us attacking them," John told me later, "so anything I could offer them that had to do with the DEFCON was always good."

The rest of their conversation had to do with Jerry and his intentional bungling of the photographs from the U.S.S. *Enterprise*.

John had come prepared. "I wasn't about to be caught in a fight between Jerry and the Soviets," he recalled, "and I wasn't going to stick my neck out for him or defend him."

John simply handed the KGB agents copies of the letters that Jerry had written to him, including his resignation letter, and John's responses.

Typical was a letter that Jerry had written John on August 14. He didn't yet know what kind of work he would be doing, and he acknowledged that his leaving the Navy had been done against John's advice. But he asked John to understand and respect his decision. ". . . there's been something missing," he wrote. "In all honesty, I was happier in the '60s and early '70s than I've been since."

The KGB agent was clearly worried. Why had Jerry quit? Would offering him more money bring him back into the ring? Could he get access once again to keylists?

John played it safe.

"I don't know," he said. "Jerry's sitting out in California masturbating with his computer while Brenda finishes her degree, and the truth is, I don't know what the fuck he is doing or thinking."

Was there any chance that Jerry might contact the FBI?

John paused deliberately. He wanted his KGB handler to know that he took the question seriously. No, John finally answered, he didn't believe Jerry would do that. He was too deeply involved.

Jerry's value had diminished now that Michael had joined the spy ring, the KGB agent said, but if there were a chance that Jerry might reenlist and once again have access to keylists, it should be pursued. John should be careful, his handler warned, because often when a spy stops getting money, he begins to worry about being caught and looks for a way to exonerate himself.

"Jerry must be paid the money he is owed," the agent said. "Tell him we are sorry it took so long."

It was arranged that John would make a dead drop delivery and collect more than $200,000 that the KGB owed him, Michael, and Jerry, on May 19.

Back at his hotel that night, John wasn't so sure that Jerry was owed an apology. After all the stunts he had pulled, John wasn't even certain Jerry was due his full amount, John said later. "He sure as hell didn't mind putting my life in danger."

His session that day with the KGB also had convinced John that, if necessary, the Russians would eliminate Jerry. All John had to do was persuade them that Jerry had become a threat to the spy ring.

John reached a decision: Jerry was going to have to pay for the trouble he had caused, and since John was the only person who knew for certain how much money the KGB had left in a dead drop, taking a percentage of Jerry's earnings would be easy.

All John had to do was tell Jerry that the Russians had cut his monthly salary because he had retired. "I didn't really need Whitworth anymore at that point," John said. "He was nothing but trouble."

# 63

Michael was bringing John so many secret documents from the U.S.S. *Nimitz* in the spring of 1985 that he didn't have time to photograph them all. Instead, John began putting them in a closet in an upstairs bedroom. It wasn't long before they began spilling out into the room.

One afternoon Michael dropped off a thick report with the word *SECRET* stamped in red letters on the cover. Two days later, when Michael stopped by his father's house, the report was sitting out in the open near a telephone book in John's den.

Michael was angry about his father's sloppiness.

"Dad, what the hell is this?" Michael complained. "I can't believe you are leaving this shit lying around in the open!"

"Don't sweat it," John replied. "No one's going to see it."

"I was really upset," Michael told me later. "I mean, he had been careless for years. That's how my mother found out. But he just ignored me because he was busy and convinced no one would ever catch him. I felt that way too, I guess, but I didn't leave stuff laying out at home."

Michael and John had been getting along poorly for months. Michael's dislike of P.K. was just one reason. John was pestering Michael to tell his mother that he was a spy and Michael didn't want to. John also had been urging him to help recruit Rachel, and originally Michael thought the idea was great.

"We could do it as husband and wife," Michael told Rachel one night. "Mr. and Mrs. James Bond."

But Rachel had been cool to the suggestion.

"You think it would be funny if I joined the Navy and became an officer," she told Michael, "because then you could tell your pals, 'Hey guys, I have to salute my wife before we go to bed.' But think about what you're suggesting, Michael. What if the Navy sent us to different parts of the world?"

Besides, she added, didn't Michael understand that John was simply using them? "He's asking us to do his dirty work. It's our butts on the line."

Michael disagreed. "He's just cutting us in on the action."

On March 7, the day before the U.S.S. *Nimitz* left for the Mediterranean cruise, John telephoned Rachel several times at the apartment and asked if Michael was there.

"I've got to see him," John said. "I want him to stop by and talk to me."

Michael knew what his dad wanted.

Barbara had been making threatening calls to John and Arthur. John wanted Michael to telephone his mother and get her off everyone's back. John also wanted to tell Michael how to hide documents aboard the carrier during a long cruise.

"I knew he didn't want to come over," John recalled later. "He wanted to stay home with Rachel and I can understand that. But I had been bugging him for weeks to come over and he hadn't, even though I told him it was vital that we talked. It turned out to be a major screw-up because Michael ended up leaving Norfolk without my having a chance to tell him how to hide documents."

Michael had ignored John's telephone calls on purpose.

"I didn't want to listen to my dad bitch about me telling Mom I was a spy," Michael told me. But John's calls also irritated him for another reason.

By then Rachel thought Michael had given up spying, because he had stopped bringing classified documents home. But John's frantic calls had convinced Rachel that Michael had simply been doing a better job of hiding things from her.

What Michael and Rachel both hoped would be a romantic evening together before the *Nimitz* deployed on March 8 was quickly blighted by an argument.

"You promised me you'd stop," Rachel said. "Michael, you're going to get caught. This isn't worth it."

"Look Rachel, we need the money!" Michael said.

"We don't need it that bad."

That night, Rachel refused to sleep with Michael. Instead, she slept on the couch. The issue was no longer Michael's spying. It was John's influence over his son.

# 64

FBI agents in field offices report to their regional headquarters every 120 days, and when Walter Price flew to Boston in the spring of 1985, he told his supervisor about Barbara Walker's charges. The supervisor sent an overnight letter to the FBI headquarters in Washington and mailed another copy to the FBI office in Norfolk.

No one at the J. Edgar Hoover Building on Pennsylvania Avenue paid any attention to the correspondence about Barbara Walker. Once again, the FBI dismissed her charges without bothering to investigate.

But in Norfolk, her accusations interested two agents: Joseph R. Wolfinger and Robert W. Hunter. They were an unlikely pair.

Wolfinger looked like an uncomplicated good old southern boy. At age thirty-nine, he had a slight paunch, ruddy complexion, witty demeanor, and a Virginia drawl that came from being born and raised in Norfolk.

In contrast, Hunter stood ramrod straight and at age forty-nine worked out daily at a local exercise club. His graying hair was always neatly combed, his clothes well tailored, his manner slightly reserved.

Their backgrounds also differed. Even though he rarely mentioned it for fear of sounding pretentious, Wolfinger had grown up the son of a wealthy and prominent Norfolk businessman. He decided early on to become a criminal defense attorney, but after graduating from the University of South Carolina Law School, he joined the FBI. He thought a three-year stint as an agent would give him an edge later in private practice when defending the accused. "I always had the impression that there were a lot of innocent people out there being charged with crimes," Wolfinger recalled, "but what I discovered as an agent was that there were a lot of sick people out there doing a lot of depraved things and very few of the ones who had been arrested were innocent."

Wolfinger had done well as an agent and was highly regarded for his skill at handling complicated cases. He had a knack for skillfully weaving evidence together in such a fashion that even a dense juror who didn't quite understand the nuances of a trial would still get the point: the FBI had found the guilty man.

Hunter had spent his youth in a small southwestern Pennsylvania town where his father had toiled at a steel mill. After he graduated from high school, his family moved to Florida, where he enrolled in college. But he didn't take the work seriously. He flunked out. Later, he returned to a junior college and ultimately graduated with honors from a state university. Hunter spent two years as a junior high school teacher and worked as an insurance investigator before joining the FBI. He arrived in Norfolk in late 1967, the same year as John Walker.

An uncompromising but compassionate man, Hunter genuinely liked people, and he had the unusual ability to empathize with them. This frequently gave him an edge when conducting investigations—people would tell Hunter things that they never intended to. But this trait also proved risky. Sometimes it was difficult for Hunter to keep from becoming totally immersed in his work, and it had cost him personally; he and his wife had separated.

Wolfinger was the first to see the Boston report on Barbara Walker, and was openly skeptical because she was an admitted alcoholic and angry ex-wife looking to nail her husband. But Barbara's descriptions of clandestine dead drops were uncannily accurate, and Wolfinger suspected that she had not gained such knowledge from pulp spy novels. As supervisor of the foreign counterintelligence squad in Norfolk, Wolfinger wanted to know more, so he showed the report to Hunter.

"This is definitely worth a few phone calls," Hunter said.

"It's all yours," Wolfinger replied.

Hunter contacted Walter Price in Hyannis and asked if Barbara Walker would voluntarily take a polygraph test. Hunter also requested that agents in Buffalo interview Laura—immediately.

On March 7, the day before the U.S.S. *Nimitz* left Norfolk for its extended Mediterranean cruise, FBI agents Paul Culligan and Charles B. Wagner knocked on the door to Laura's apartment. Culligan had talked to Laura earlier on the phone and decided he and Wagner had to approach her as friends, rather than federal agents. As part of that philosophy, Culligan and Wagner both changed from their suits into casual clothes for the interview with her.

"We wanted our interview to be as nonthreatening as possible and do everything we could to gain her trust and confidence," Culligan told me later. "Laura made it clear that she had some natural resistance to talking about her dad. The common bond between us was her son, Christopher, and we recognized early on that he was really the key to getting Laura's cooperation. If she wanted her son, she had to get John off her back."

During their interview, the telephone in Laura's apartment rang. It was Michael, who had called to tell Laura good-bye since he was scheduled to leave the next morning. Laura cut the conversation short without telling Michael that the FBI was there.

"We knew that she had been speaking to Michael," Culligan recalled, "but she didn't seem at all concerned. I doubt if she would have acted that way if she had known Michael was involved."

Culligan, a thirty-eight-year-old, nine-year FBI veteran, coaxed enough information from Laura to write an incriminating statement about John. He asked her if she would be willing to sign the statement and also, if necessary, testify against her father. Laura agreed.

Culligan called Hunter after the interview and told him that Laura seemed credible and was willing to testify. Culligan also had an idea: Why not ask Laura to telephone her father and tape record the call?

"It would be one way we could answer the one question that was on everyone's mind," Culligan recalled, "which was, 'Is John still doing this or is he inactive?' "

Culligan, Hunter, and Wolfinger discussed it and decided to ask Washington for permission. Culligan returned to Laura's apartment a few days later and explained why such a call was necessary.

"She said she'd do it," Culligan said.

One week after Laura first talked to the FBI, she wrote Michael a letter apologizing for her abruptness when he telephoned.

"But I never told Michael about the FBI," Laura told me later, "because I was afraid he would tell my dad." At the time, Laura said she didn't believe Michael was involved. "Of course, I assumed that my father had tried to recruit him," she explained, "but I figured he had said no because that's what I had done."

Even after Michael joined the Navy, Laura said, "I never dreamed he might have said yes."

Before Hunter left for Buffalo to interview Laura personally and oversee her telephone call to John, he received more good news. Barry Colvert, one of the FBI's polygraph examiners, had tested Barbara Walker in Hyannis and she had "passed." She was not lying about her ex-husband's being a Russian spy.

Hunter arrived in Buffalo on March 25 and was taken by Culligan to meet Laura that afternoon.

Hunter was impressed by her willingness to help. "Laura was quite honest and frank about her family's secret," he told me later. "She didn't have to cooperate with us. She could have told us, 'This is all I know and that's all I'm doing,' but she wanted to help. She *wanted* to call her dad."

The agents attached a listening device to Laura's telephone and showed her how to turn on the recorder.

"We had already decided," Culligan recalled, "that we would leave when she made the call. We were going to have a tape of the conversation so there was no point in us being there and upsetting her or making her nervous."

But before they left, the agents suggested two possible stories that Laura could use to entice John into once again trying to recruit her as a spy.

"You could tell him that there is an opening at Eastman Kodak," Culligan said, "which is a world leader in photography and optics. Or that you want to join the Army Reserves."

Hunter and Culligan told Laura that they would return for the tape recording at eleven P.M. that night.

"There was no doubt in my mind," said Culligan, "that she would make the call. She wanted Christopher back."

That afternoon and evening, Hunter tried repeatedly to put himself in Laura's shoes. "My heart went out to her," he recalled. "I tried to imagine how hard this must be for her. Here was a girl who hadn't spoken to her father in more than one year, yet she was willing to telephone him and let us tape record the conversation."

Hunter also tried to picture John Walker. What kind of a father was he, and what had he done to his own daughter that would make her turn so strongly against him?

# 65

"My name is Laura Mae Walker Snyder. Today's date is March 25, 1985. . . . I'm going to be calling John Walker . . . in Norfolk, Virginia."

JOHN: Hello?
LAURA: Um, hi.
JOHN: Hi.
LAURA: Do you know who this is?
JOHN: No.
LAURA: This is Laura.
JOHN: Laura?
LAURA: Yes, a voice—
JOHN: Laura *Walker*?
LAURA: Yes, that Laura.
JOHN: Well, I'll be damned. I didn't figure I'd ever hear from you. . . .

As the tape recording of Laura's telephone call to John indicates, she fulfilled her promise to the agents. Once John got over his surprise, his conversation ranged over familiar territory, berating Barbara with his usual profanity and assailing Laura for the way she had run her life. She turned the subject to spying, as she had promised Hunter and Culligan, and talked about her veteran's status and about the Kodak plant. When the subject shifted to Mark, John was furious again about Laura's "telling that guy something as private as what we discussed."

"Well, I got desperate," Laura said. "But I think now . . . he's so stoned and so gone that he doesn't even know his name anymore."

"Well, the problem is that makes him dangerous," John answered.

Despite Laura's bait, John didn't say anything incriminating. Still, the call convinced the FBI that John was someone to be taken seriously.

Though signed statements by Barbara and Laura, even though they had been verified by polygraph were not sufficient for the FBI to seek criminal charges against John, the FBI and the Justice Department agreed that the tape recording and the statements were enough to request permission to tap John's telephone. On April 5, a court approved the placing of wiretaps on telephones in John's house, office, and houseboat. It would take the FBI six days to install the wiretaps and begin its twenty-four-hour monitoring. In the meantime, the FBI faced a problem that threatened to unravel its investigation. Barbara Walker announced that she was coming to Norfolk to visit Margaret.

Hunter and Wolfinger were uneasy. At the time, all they knew about Barbara was that she was an alcoholic who had tried in the past, according to her statements, to turn John in. If she backed down now and alerted John, he could destroy whatever evidence might exist at his home and cover his tracks. Barbara arrived at Margaret's apartment during the first week of April, and Hunter and FBI agent Beverly Andress telephoned her immediately to arrange a clandestine meeting. Hunter had asked Andress to join him because he knew some women felt more comfortable talking to another woman rather than a man. It was crucial that he and Andress not upset Barbara.

They met Barbara at a parking lot near Margaret's apartment, motioned her into the back seat of Hunter's sedan, and sped away to a section of Norfolk where they felt confident she wouldn't be recognized.

Hunter was startled when he met Barbara. He hadn't expected her to be well tailored, attractive, and articulate. After listening to John's tape-recorded telephone conversation with Laura, Hunter expected Barbara to be as uncouth as her ex-husband. "It was hard for me to believe that he talked to his own daughter the way he did, using the language he did," Hunter told me later. "I heard an anger, an arrogance, particularly in the way he referred to women as bitches and cunts. I thought John was one of the most profane guys I'd ever heard."

But Barbara had a certain polish.

Hunter and Andress both had studied the six-page investigative report that Walter Price had written after a follow-up interview he had with Barbara on March 19. At that point, Barbara had told the FBI that John had two spying partners: Arthur Walker and a close friend of John's named "Jerry Wentworth." Laura had said Jerry's last name was "Wittemore." Neither Hunter nor Andress pressured Barbara for more details; instead they worked at gaining her trust by sympathizing with her. Although Barbara was noticeably tense, she clearly wanted to follow up on her accusations. She wanted John stopped, she said. But just as the two agents began to relax, Barbara announced that she had telephoned Arthur on the same night that she had called the FBI and had warned him. She also had called John that night and threatened to turn him in to the FBI.

Near panic, Hunter quizzed Barbara about how John and Arthur had responded. Did they believe that she had called the FBI? Did she think either of them was aware of the FBI investigation? Barbara didn't know.

"That interview was the beginning of a very stressful week," Hunter recalled. "We had a real control problem with Barbara."

Back at the Norfolk FBI office, Hunter and Wolfinger decided to literally hold Barbara's hand every day to make certain she didn't flip-flop. Margaret Walker also scared them. Barbara had told the FBI that Margaret knew about the investigation. Barbara had also said that Margaret had a good relationship with her father and was caught between "a rock and hard place—her father and me." Which, the agents wondered, would Margaret choose?

The morning after their first meeting, Barbara telephoned Hunter to tell him some details she had remembered about the mysterious Wentworth. Hunter kept the conversation upbeat and thanked her repeatedly for calling.

But the next day, neither Hunter nor Andress could reach Barbara on the telephone. Both were concerned, but they decided there was little that they could do. They couldn't drive to Margaret's apartment. What if John showed up unexpectedly?

Another day passed and Barbara remained out of communication. Now the agents were alarmed. Where had Barbara gone? What had happened? Had she changed her mind? Had she met with John?

On April 8, Barbara resurfaced. "I've seen John," she announced over the telephone. Trying to remain calm, Hunter arranged an immediate meeting. Whenever Hunter and Andress conducted an interview, they filed a written report on government form FD-302, referred to as 302 statements by investigators. The 302 statement that Hunter and Andress wrote after meeting with Barbara Walker was quickly classified as secret and sent overnight to the foreign counterintelligence office in Washington for review. In part, it said:

Barbara Walker saw her former husband, John Anthony Walker, Jr., on April 7, 1985, when he visited their daughter, Margaret . . . at her home. John told Barbara he wanted to talk to her for a couple of hours before she went home . . . Mrs. Walker advised that during her last visit in August . . . she talked to Michael Walker about his father's illegal activities. Mrs. Walker advised that Michael talked her out of reporting John Walker to the FBI because it would hurt Michael's Navy career. She does not believe that John Walker has recruited Michael to commit espionage, but advised that Michael has worked for his father doing surveillance connected with his private detective business.

Mrs. Walker advised John Walker has talked to their daughter, Margaret, concerning comments Barbara made about reporting his activities to the FBI. She advised that John Walker has commented to Margaret that he was surprised he had not been arrested yet, and that he had "done something good and the kids would hate their mother for turning him in."

Based on that 302 statement, the FBI began a discreet investigation of Michael Walker.

Both Hunter and Andress urged Barbara to stay away from John and stressed repeatedly how important she was to their investigation and how much they appreciated her patriotism. The Justice Department also made it clear that in return for Barbara's cooperation, she would be granted total immunity from any prosecution.

Hunter felt more squeamish than ever about his case. The wiretaps still hadn't been installed and he knew John was pressuring Barbara to meet with him. The fact that John had discussed Barbara's threats with Margaret meant he was aware that the FBI could be watching him. Obviously, he would be on guard. Something else Barbara had said also worried Hunter—that her son Michael was in the Navy and had urged her last fall not to turn John in. Yet she claimed Michael wasn't involved in the spy ring. Her thinking seemed naïve, but Hunter didn't press the point. He didn't want to do anything that might spook Barbara. Turning in an ex-husband would be difficult enough. If Barbara realized she was also turning in her son, she might withdraw.

On April 9, Beverly Andress and Barbara held another secret session. Andress's 302 statement recounted the meeting:

Mrs. Walker advised she never understood why John Walker would "commit treason." She believed that while he was successful in his naval career, he could not accept the business failures. Barbara Walker stated that she lived with the knowledge of her husband's treason and that concern for her family kept her from contacting the FBI. . . . Laura's estranged husband, who has some knowledge of John Walker's espionage activities, has stated to Laura that if she attempts to gain custody of their son, Christopher, he will turn John Walker in. Mrs. Walker stated she could not justify John Walker's activities and finally could not accept how his actions were affecting their daughter as well as their grandson.

Back at the FBI office in Norfolk, Hunter and Wolfinger went over the facts as they knew them. By now, they were confident John and Arthur were Soviet spies, that John had tried to recruit Laura, that Michael knew about his dad's espionage, and that Laura's husband was allegedly blackmailing her to maintain custody of their son.

On April 10, Hunter and Andress telephoned Barbara and held another parking lot rendezvous. Barbara told them she had agreed to meet with John that evening. Once again, they urged Barbara to put off the meeting. Even if she didn't intend to tip John off, she might accidentally warn him by appearing nervous.

"Okay," Barbara said. "I'll try to cancel."

Hunter and Andress could do little but return to their office and pace. John was scheduled to pick up Barbara at seven P.M., and Hunter and Andress waited anxiously. Hunter's telephone rang shortly after five P.M.

Mrs. Walker advised that she called John Anthony Walker, Jr., and told him she would not be able to meet him at 7 P.M. this evening as planned. Barbara Walker advised that John Walker was angry because she would not meet him and stated during their conversation, "We'll hook up before you leave here. It is vital that we talk. There are things that cannot be discussed on the phone."

The next day, April 11, Barbara telephoned Hunter again.

"I've got to meet John," she said. "Otherwise, he'll be suspicious. He's picking me up tonight at seven."

Hunter and Andress scurried to the now-familiar parking lot and picked up Barbara for another meeting.

"You must tell John that you haven't turned him in," Hunter told Barbara. "Tell him you lost your nerve. Tell him you just couldn't do it."

Barbara agreed and then she stunned the agents.

"I want to wear a wire," she said. "I want you to fix it so you can listen to what we say."

"Barbara, what if he pats you down?" Hunter replied. As part of their investigation, he and Andress had both read local newspaper clippings about John in which he claimed to be an expert at detecting electronic bugs. "What if he has some device in his car that can detect microphones? It's simply too dangerous."

"I might be able to get him to talk about his spying though," Barbara said.

"No way," said Hunter. "It just wouldn't be safe."

John arrived at seven P.M. that night, as promised, and picked up Barbara at Margaret's apartment. He drove her to a McDonald's restaurant.

Back at FBI headquarters, Hunter and Andress huddled nervously in Wolfinger's office and debated whether Barbara Walker could remain calm enough to fool John. In a moment of gallows humor, a fellow agent suggested they begin taking bets. Would Barbara tell John? Or would she keep quiet? The entourage, which had instinctively gathered around Wolfinger, Hunter, and Andress, began taking an impromptu poll. When it came time for Hunter to announce his bet, his peers became quiet.

"What's she gonna do, Bob?" someone asked.

"Damn if I know," he finally said. "I'll be goddamned if I know!"

# 66

Barbara Walker was scared. "It was very hard playing the part that I was to play," she recalled. "I tried to be blasé and avoided looking in his eyes."

John was also nervous. "Barbara was clearly pissed about the ten grand and that scared me. It was the most money she had ever asked for; most of the time it was for a couple hundred or so, but this was the biggest amount and it was the first time I'd really turned her down. I had to make it clear that Michael was involved but I just didn't want to come out and say, 'You stupid cunt, your son is part of the spy ring,' because I figured she wouldn't believe me."

Inside McDonald's, John pleaded poverty.

"Jesus Barbara, if I had the money, I'd pay you," he said, "but goddamnit, I don't have it right now. I really don't."

Barbara didn't believe him.

"Look Barbara," John said, "there is something you should understand. If I ever get arrested, a lot of people are going to get hurt. A lot of people—not just me."

"I'm aware of that," Barbara replied.

"Are you sure?" John said, "Because I don't think you understand what I am saying to you."

"Are you telling me that Michael is involved?" Barbara asked, point blank.

"Yes, and no. I'm not saying that," said John. "You'll have to ask Michael that. Why don't you ask him?"

Once again, John had dodged the question. He told me later that he was afraid Barbara wouldn't believe him if he gave her a direct answer.

That night at McDonald's, John asked Barbara outright: "Barbara, have you gone to the FBI?"

"No, I haven't turned you in," she replied.

"Good, 'cause you wouldn't want to see your fifty-year-old husband in prison," John replied. "I don't think our kids would like it either."

On the drive back to Margaret's apartment, John pulled over to the side of the street.

"I asked Barbara why she was doing this to me," John recalled. "I said, 'Barbara, we've been divorced for ten fucking years! Why do you keep aggravating me? This is like a sickness. People get divorced all the time in this country. They don't have to destroy each other. Why can't you leave me alone?' And Barbara's voice changed, and I know Barbara and I know she was being totally honest, maybe for the first time in years, and she said to me, 'I just want to get back at you!' That says it all! Her decision to turn me in to the FBI had nothing to do with my spying or fucking America and homemade apple pie. It didn't have anything to do with Laura or her kid either. I had betrayed our marriage vows. I didn't love Barbara anymore and she couldn't stand that. It was destroying her and she was going to take me down with her."

When Barbara stepped from the car that night, she turned and told John, "Talk to you later." But Barbara knew, she told me later, that she wouldn't. She had done it. She had met with John and not tipped him off, but rather than feeling good about it, she felt sick. She couldn't get to sleep that night on the couch in Margaret's apartment.

Barbara Walker gave me this explanation: "You see, I never wanted to hurt John. It is hard to explain but it is like primates, you know, monkeys picking each other off the branches of a tree. This is how the game is played. 'Do you like me?' 'No, I don't like you!' 'Then I knock you off the tree.'

"It took us a long while when we first started dating before John and I could say, 'I love you!' The first time I said anything emotional to him, I said, 'I hate you!' because he had violated the protection that I had built around myself. Saying 'I hate you' is very much like saying 'I love you.'

"During our talk that night in McDonald's, John reached out several times and touched me. I didn't reach out to him, but he touched me. You see, I knew that deep down he really cared. It was just that he was showing it with anger and hostility. It was like we were the monkeys on that tree limb and I was asking him if he cared. When he said 'No,' I pushed him off. But it didn't mean that I hated John or wanted to hurt him. It meant that I was his best friend.

"You see," Barbara concluded, "I was sick that night because I still love John."

As far as John was concerned, his meeting that night with Barbara was a success. He returned home and tape-recorded a letter to Michael in which he mentioned his encounter with Barbara and his recent telephone chats with Laura.

Barbara's visit in Norfolk came to an end the next day, April 12, and Hunter volunteered to drive her to the airport and put her aboard an airplane. By now all of the telephone taps had been put in place, and Wolfinger had drawn up a schedule for each agent to work the round-the-clock wiretap.

"This is the most bizarre case," Hunter told Wolfinger after returning from the airport, "and it's getting worse." Usually an agent conducts an investigation by interviewing witnesses, collecting evidence, and then arresting a suspect. But the FBI was afraid to interview anyone but Laura and Barbara for fear that John might hear about the investigation, and, so far, there was absolutely no hard evidence that John had committed a crime. "I don't know if we can get this guy or not," Hunter continued. "He's been doing this for twenty years, Barbara's warned his brother, we don't know what the hell Margaret might do, and John's supposedly an expert on wiretaps and bugs. You've got to wonder if he is going to screw up."

"I don't know, Bob," Wolfinger said. "Sometimes you get a case where everything seems to fall together no matter what you do. It's almost as if it's inevitable. Fate. It's like a person's time has come. It's time for them to be arrested."

"Maybe John Walker's time has come," Wolfinger said.

# 67

By late April, FBI agents had monitored John's telephone lines nearly twenty days and had not heard any damaging evidence. They had, however, listened to one conversation that Hunter believed contained a clue.

At 7:12 P.M. on April 18, Rachel telephoned John at his home to ask about his encounter with Barbara.

The reason I was calling is to see what's going on, you know. . . . I talked to Maggie a couple of times and I understand that Barbara was upsetting Maggie a little bit with her problem. You know what I mean.

Rachel's comment, "You know what I mean," seemed significant to Hunter, who decided that she also knew about John's spying. He added Rachel's name to his list of suspects. Another remark in that call also interested Hunter. When Rachel invited John to attend her college graduation ceremony on May 18, he replied:

Oh Lordy . . . I can't believe it. I know that I'm gonna be busy that weekend. Can you goddamn believe it!

John seemed genuinely upset. What was he doing that weekend that he couldn't reschedule? Hunter circled the date on his calendar.

Wolfinger and Hunter both knew John was being discreet on the telephone and everyone in the Norfolk FBI office, except Hunter, was becoming impatient with the wiretap. In order to monitor John's calls, nearly every agent in the office had to work extra hours, and none of them was paid overtime. Some of Hunter's colleagues wondered if the wiretap was worth the trouble. Even novice agents knew that convicting someone of espionage was extremely difficult. Unlike crimes that involve a culprit and a victim, espionage involves two co-conspirators, and only a dolt would think a foreign intelligence operative, like a KGB agent, could ever be forced into a courtroom or, for that matter, even questioned. As a result, Hunter was going to have to catch John either actually stealing classified documents or delivering them. And if the telephone tap was an accurate indicator, that was going to be difficult because John Walker was being very careful.

While other agents grew weary of listening to John's often mundane and always profane conversations, Hunter found them fascinating. Day after day, he read the transcripts of John's calls and listened to selected tapes. He heard John lie to his clients, chide employees, brag about his sexual prowess. Hunter studied not only what John said, but also his choice of words and even the rhythm of his sentences. Hunter tried to think like John Walker, to place himself in John's mind, and the endless hours of telephone conversations supplied hundreds of clues. Like piecing together the shards of a broken vase, Hunter began shaping an "image" of John Walker, and what Hunter developed disturbed him.

"John's conversations with members of his own family were just unbelievable," Hunter recalled. It wasn't only the profanity. There was something more that went beyond the gutter. John Walker had a sinister, sneering side to him. "I was beginning to see that this was a man who was not only devious and untruthful, but also evil," Hunter said. "I really came to believe that. He was a truly evil person."

Each conversation Hunter reviewed seemed to buttress his analysis that John seemed to bring out the worst when he spoke to his family— even his own mother, Peggy. During one tape-recorded conversation between the two of them, Hunter heard Peggy and John speak viciously about other family members. Even more biting was John's conversation with his daughter Margaret, who gave vent to her feelings about her mother and sister.

The longer Hunter listened to taped conversations, the more upset he became. It was as if the entire Walker family had been stricken with a sickness, the children mimicking the twisted love–hate relationship of their parents.

*   *   *

In early May, the Washington headquarters of the FBI sent several of its foreign counterintelligence experts to Norfolk to have a strategy session with Hunter and Wolfinger. "This was becoming a tremendously complicated case," recalled Jack Wagner, the supervisor of the Norfolk FBI office. At this point, the FBI suspected that four people besides John could be directly involved in the spy ring, including the enigmatic "Jerry Wentworth" in California. There were other problems too. "John owned an airplane that was faster than the airplane that we owned," recalled Wagner. "He owned a boat. We had to figure out what we were going to do if he used either of them. What if John flew to New York and boarded an airplane to Europe where we don't have jurisdiction? Do we have an agent follow him? If so, he'd better have a valid passport."

The Washington and Norfolk agents spent one afternoon discussing various procedures and scenarios, and found themselves agreeing about everything but one issue. The Washington agents wanted to plant an electronic tracking device on John's new minivan in case he got away from agents during surveillance. Hunter strongly opposed the idea.

"He might find it," Hunter said. "This guy is an experienced detective."

"Right! A real James Bond," one of the Washington agents replied mockingly. Hunter had become the butt of some jokes in Washington because he had written in a 302 statement that he considered John to be an "armed and dangerous" suspect. Some agents in Washington thought Hunter was overestimating Walker's skills and making him more of a villain than he actually was.

After a brief argument, the Washington agents gave up and accepted Hunter's advice. It was his case.

Before that meeting ended, Hunter asked theoretically what he and other agents should do if they followed John to an actual dead drop delivery. Should they arrest him? Should they confront John's Soviet handler?

His questions were answered by a loud laugh from one of the Washington-based agents. No one in the history of the FBI, the agent explained, had ever followed an American spy to a dead drop and arrested him making a delivery.

"I don't care," Hunter responded. "Guys, we got to plan for this, just in case."

"Bullshit, Bob!" the Washington agent said. "It will never happen. C'mon, these things just don't work that way."

# 68

Like Hunter, FBI agent John Peterson was not a man to give up, especially when following the scent of a self-admitted Russian spy who claimed to be part of a twenty-year-old espionage operation. For eight months, Peterson doggedly tried to find the mysterious RUS who had written to the San Francisco FBI office. Several times, Peterson thought he was on RUS's trail, but he had been wrong. Each time, he hit another dead end. Finally, Peterson decided to try once more to lure RUS from hiding by placing yet another advertisement in the personal section of the *Los Angeles Times*. It ran on three consecutive Mondays, beginning in April 1985.

RUS didn't respond. Unknown to Peterson, Jerry Whitworth had changed his mind about confessing. He was busy trying to find a career and, as usual, was floundering. When he had retired from the Navy, Jerry planned to become a stockbroker. When he failed the test, he decided to become a computer salesman. That didn't work either. On March 25, Jerry wrote his old patron, John Walker, describing his problems. He was again considering being a stockbroker, he said, but admitted he brooded about his decision to retire from the Navy. Still, he professed optimism once he and Brenda were settled in their new careers.

John nearly laughed out loud when he read Jerry's letter. He saw what was coming. Jerry was so damn predictable. "Jerry couldn't cut it outside the Navy," John told me. "I sensed that when I met him. I knew he was failing and was setting the groundwork to come back to me and the spying." Still bitter about Jerry's shenanigans with the fogged film, John decided against answering Jerry's letters. He wanted to let Jerry sweat awhile.

In late April, at about the same time Jerry was trying to mend his friendship with John, the FBI's analytical unit in the foreign counter-intelligence office in Washington made a startling discovery. While reviewing ongoing investigations, agents noticed a similarity between RUS and John Walker. Both men had been linked to a spying operation that had operated for twenty years. Was it possible that RUS and John Walker were linked somehow?

Agents reexamined Barbara and Laura Walker's statements, particularly their comments about "Jerry Wentworth."

Mrs. Walker advised Jerry Wentworth is a white male in his forties and is an enlisted man and may be a chief petty officer. She has neither seen nor heard from him since 1976. She believes his wife's name is Brenda and she described Brenda as being young, in her twenties, and possibly attending a college in Berkeley, California. She noted the Wentworths got married in approximately 1977, and that Jerry Wentworth had been married previously and had gotten into some trouble with the U.S. Navy because he continued to accept allotment payments for his ex-wife after they were divorced, and he had to pay that money back to the U.S. Navy. . . . Mrs. Walker noted she is confident that Jerry's last name is Wentworth [not Wittemore, as Laura Walker said.]"

Washington had already asked the San Francisco FBI office to locate "Jerry Wentworth" as part of the bureau's probe of John Walker, but no one in California had linked Wentworth with the RUS letters.

An urgent message, classified by the FBI as top secret, was sent to the San Francisco FBI office: "Wentworth may be RUS!"

Suddenly, finding Jerry Wentworth became an even higher priority, but despite the San Francisco office's efforts, no person by that name could be found. Frustrated, the agents asked if Barbara and Laura Walker could be interviewed again about John's obscure friend.

When FBI agents in Buffalo asked Laura for her help, she quickly volunteered: "I think I have his telephone number." She found it in a pile of papers, and gave it to the surprised and excited agent, who immediately notified San Francisco.

An FBI agent there dialed the telephone number in San Leandro and asked for Jerry Wentworth. No, there was no person living at that address named Wentworth. With the number in hand, agents began searching old directories. In a 1982 telephone book, next to the number Laura had given them, the FBI found the name Jerry A. Whitworth.

Both Laura and Barbara quickly agreed. Yes, the name could be Whitworth instead of Wentworth. In a matter of hours, the FBI had obtained copies of Jerry's motor vehicle records, listing his current address and his Navy record. In Washington, the analytical unit quickly established that Jerry had once worked for John at the Naval Training Center in San Diego. RUS had been identified. He was Jerry Whitworth. The net around John Walker was beginning to close.

On May 16—three days before John's prearranged exchange with the KGB—the wiretaps on John's telephone paid off. And it was fate, just as Wolfinger had predicted, that caused John to slip up and tip off the FBI.

It began with a telephone call from his mother, Peggy, who told him his favorite aunt had died in Buffalo. The funeral had been scheduled for that Saturday, May 18, and Peggy wanted John to attend. Despite Peggy's pleas, John couldn't. He had something important that he had to do.

John telephoned P.K. Carroll's number as soon as he hung up on Peggy.

JOHN: My Aunt Amelia just died . . .

P.K.: Oh, my God.

JOHN: What a mess. A funeral I should really go to and I can't get away.

P.K.: I think you'd better get away for this one, John.

JOHN: I can't. Um, shit. I'm gonna call Art right now. . . . See, I lived with her. Jesus Christ, when the family broke up, you know . . . um, I gotta try to collect my thoughts, get my schedule together. Tomorrow's Friday, isn't it. . . . Jesus, I suppose I could fly in. Huh?

P.K.: Yeah.

JOHN: God, if the weather catches me, Jesus Christ. You know, there's some things I just can't change the schedule of. . . .

P.K.: Oh, I know that.

JOHN: They're just unchangeable.

P.K.: I know that, but if it's possible for you to go, I know you want to.

JOHN: Um . . . damn it.

P.K.: I can't believe it, John. Amelia is the one who, who made me feel like a part of your family up there.

JOHN: Yeah. She was something. Well, let me get off the phone, 'cause I'm gonna now have problems getting, getting my act together. Okay?

P.K.: Okay.

John called Arthur next and told him of the funeral.

The next day, a Friday, May 17, John unwittingly gave the FBI another crucial clue. At 4:13 P.M., John called his employees at Confidential Reports into his office and took his telephone receiver off the hook to keep from being interrupted by calls. "It was like giving us a microphone to listen in," Hunter recalled.

Listen, I'll be in late Monday. I'll be driving in Monday morning from down around Charlotte, so I'll be getting in around noon. . . . See you all Monday, have a good one.

Hunter and Wolfinger reviewed the tapes. What could John be doing in Charlotte that was so important that he had to miss Rachel's graduation and his Aunt Amelia's funeral? Both of them suspected it was a spy-related meeting. It had to be.

"It looks like John is finally making his move," Hunter said. "God, if we don't catch this guy, we better hang it up."

Wolfinger smiled. "We will."

# 69

Spying aboard the U.S.S. *Nimitz* was child's play. Alone in the fan room, Michael could pick through the burn bags from OPS-ADMIN and STRIKE-OPS unmolested. But this easy access created a new problem: storage. Just like John back home, Michael was having trouble finding room for all the documents he intended to steal. At first, he simply started hiding messages in his desk, but that was both risky and stupid. There wasn't enough room and if anyone saw them, they might wonder why he was keeping them. The solution came one afternoon when he was loading a new box of computer paper into a printer in the OPS-ADMIN office.

"I looked at the empty box and bingo," Michael recalled. "I realized it was the perfect size for documents."

Michael took the empty cardboard box to his desk and began filling it with copies of messages and other classified documents. He put several sheets of stationery and some small boxes of envelopes on top of the classified documents to help hide them.

One morning, Michael arrived at work a few minutes late and found an officer looking through the box.

"What's all this stuff, Walker?" he asked.

"That's stuff I'm working on," Michael recalled. He paused and then he said, somewhat crossly, "Hey, you didn't get it out of order did you?"

Michael had learned as a private detective that one of the best ways to keep from answering a question was by asking one in return, especially one that implied that someone had screwed up.

"No, I didn't mix anything up," the officer replied, and then, defending himself, added, "I was looking for some big envelopes."

"No sweat," Michael said, "here, let me get them for you."

Recalling that encounter, Michael told me, "That proved to me that I was in control, man. I could handle anything."

Still the exchange alarmed him. He decided to move the box somewhere safer. This time, he placed several pages of blank computer paper on top of the stolen documents, which now filled the entire box, making it look as if the box was filled with unused paper. He placed the lid on the box, sealed it the same way other boxes of computer paper were sealed, and carried it down the hallway to his berthing area.

Michael slept in a bottom bunk in a room that he shared with two other sailors. He had found a good hiding place one day, at the foot of his bed between the wall and a large air duct that rose from the floor to the ceiling. There was just enough room behind the air duct for the computer box, and when he had pushed it behind the duct, it was impossible to see from anywhere in the room except on his bunk.

Just like John, Michael believed that money could solve all problems. Ergo, not having money obviously caused problems, particularly in his marriage. Michael was convinced that his marital spats with Rachel were related to their tight finances. If he could earn more money, then Rachel wouldn't have to work as a waitress and she wouldn't be so tired and they wouldn't get into fights about never having time to spend together. The real reason why he and Rachel didn't have sex on the night before he left Norfolk was not because of his spying, Michael convinced himself, but because of money. His spying was just a red herring. Once Michael got paid by his dad, he and Rachel would have plenty of money and their personal problems would vanish.

Michael also decided while he was at sea that espionage was not really that dangerous. "My father had been doing this for twenty years and hadn't got caught, and I was more cautious than he had been," Michael recalled. "I didn't see why I couldn't do it for a while, just until we got on our feet. Then I would quit."

The U.S.S. *Nimitz* was scheduled to stop in Naples during June, roughly midway in its eight-month cruise, and Michael and Rachel planned to rendezvous there. John also planned to meet Michael in Naples to pick up documents and pay him. This time, Michael expected more than a $1,000 token payment.

On April 1, he wrote Rachel an affectionate letter.

Two days later, he wrote her again and began what soon became a foolish habit; he made a disguised reference to his spying. "I need to be careful," he told her.

Michael received a chatty tape-recorded letter from Rachel soon thereafter. The thirty-minute tape contained news about her upcoming college graduation, work plans, mutual friends, and Michael's family. It also revealed how much Rachel had changed during the three years she had known Michael. Gone was the bashful and naïve coed who dressed modestly and hid behind a pair of thick glasses. Rachel may have feared Michael's spying and asked him to stop, but she still loved him and she wanted to please him. Her appearance and personality had changed so dramatically that people who had known her in high school frequently didn't recognize her when they happened to meet. Rachel enjoyed her punk rock image. She wore three dangling earrings in one lobe and two in the other, and her hair was multicolored and spiked. Going bra-less, which had once embarrassed her, now was as natural as the skin-tight miniskirts and the black fishnet stockings that she favored. Sometimes her language was coarse and abrasive.

By mid-April, more than a month since he had left Norfolk, Michael started to worry because he hadn't received a single letter from his father. Michael wrote Rachel and told her he had had no word, had "a lot of supplies" for John, and was counting on a steady flow of cash as a result.

A few days after Michael sent his letter, John's April 11 tape recording arrived. Michael listened carefully to his father's description of his meeting with Barbara, but couldn't decide from it whether the meeting had gone well or poorly. John also had updated Michael on other members of the family in his tape recording, including Cynthia; he complained, as always, about money troubles, and made an oblique reference to Michael's spying. He was looking forward, he said, to good pictures of "those ports" Michael had been visiting.

By the end of April, Michael was becoming concerned about how much he would be paid for his spying. He wrote his father a letter asking for advice, and waited patiently for a reply, but John didn't respond. By early May, Michael still didn't have a clue about what was happening back home. Rachel, busy with college final exams, also hadn't written. Michael reacted with a short angry note to Rachel. "Sometimes I feel I am missing everything. . . . I get the feeling that something bad is going to happen."

# *70*

Based on its wiretaps, the FBI knew that John rarely rose early on Saturday mornings, so Hunter and Wolfinger decided to begin the stakeout at John's house on May 18 at seven A.M. Because as a private detective John had himself conducted surveillance, Hunter ordered the six-car FBI stakeout team to place themselves at major intersections through which John would have to pass if he left home. An FBI airplane circled above at 3,500 feet. The agents were excited. Finally, they were going to be doing something besides listening to John talk on the telephone.

They didn't have to wait long. Early that morning, John got in his minivan, and started to drive. The FBI team carefully followed, anticipating that John was en route to a clandestine meeting. When he parked near his houseboat and spent the next hour painting, the agents' excitement waned.

By mid-afternoon some of the team began to grumble. The thrill of tracking a possible KGB spy to a dead drop was being surpassed by the need to mow lawns and spend time with families. By four-thirty P.M., there was enough dissatisfaction to warrant an impromptu meeting in a nearby parking lot. "There was some griping so we decided to call it a day, but we agreed we had to continue the stakeout on Sunday," Hunter recalled.

Hunter felt fairly certain that John wasn't going anywhere that night because agents monitoring his telephone calls had heard John tell callers that he and P.K. intended to go out on his boat that evening and watch a Memorial Day fireworks show. Even so, Hunter was nervous. If John left town that evening, it would be difficult to organize a tracking team in time to follow him. By this time P.K. Carroll had left John's detective agency and had become a plainclothes vice officer on the Norfolk force. Her hours were irregular and usually began late at night, when prostitutes and other purveyors of illegal activities were the busiest. This had taken a toll on her relationship with John, particularly after he announced that he didn't "wait up until three A.M. for anybody."

So Saturdays were special because it was the one day of the week when John felt fairly confident that he and P.K. could get together. He tried repeatedly to telephone her during the day, but didn't reach her until 7:40 P.M. He was peeved when she refused to come over and spend the night with him because she was tired.

A few minutes after John finished calling P.K., he telephoned another woman. After complaining about P.K., he asked her out for that night. The girlfriend had plans, but said she was free the next night.

JOHN: Ah shit, as it is, I'll be out of town. I gotta work on a goddamn case tomorrow and, uh.

GIRLFRIEND: Where you gonna go?

JOHN: Down to North Carolina . . .

GIRLFRIEND: What part?

JOHN: Down to, let me think, what's the name of it again. It's a little town just beyond Elizabeth City . . . I've forgot the name of it. It's a little, ah, just on the outskirts.

The agents monitoring John's call telephoned Hunter and reported that John had just said he was going to a small town near Elizabeth City—not Charlotte as he had claimed earlier. Hunter considered the discrepancy a good sign. Obviously, John was up to something.

The FBI stakeout team arrived at their positions at seven A.M. Sunday.

Two cups of coffee later, Hunter needed to find a bathroom. He drove to McDonald's and, out of habit, surveyed the patrons as he left the men's room. "Goddamn if John Walker wasn't sitting there eating breakfast and reading a newspaper," Hunter recalled. "He had ridden his bike to the restaurant and no one had seen him!"

Back at his car, Hunter barked into his two-way radio: "Goddamn it, why didn't we know that he had left the house?"

John bicycled home. At ten A.M., John W. Hodges, the pilot of the FBI plane, radioed Hunter and explained that the plane was getting low on fuel.

"Okay, bring her down, but try to be back in the air by eleven-thirty," Hunter said.

Shortly before noon, Hunter received another call. What time, one of his agents asked, were they going to call off the stakeout?

Hunter knew weekend work was hard on morale. After yesterday's tedious watch, his agents were getting impatient.

"Okay," Hunter announced. "We'll keep this up until one o'clock, and then if he hasn't gone anywhere, we'll go home."

Unknown to Hunter, at the very time he was making that decision, John was sitting in his den typing a note to his KGB handler. He referred to Michael, Arthur, Jerry, and Gary Walker by the code letters the KGB had assigned them: S, K, D, and F, respectively.

Dear Friend.

This delivery consists of materials from S and is similar to the previously supplied materials. The quantity is limited, unfortunately, due to his operating schedule and increased security prior to deployment. His ship departs in early March and they operate extensively just prior to deployment. The situation around him looks very good and he is amassing a vast amount of material right now. His last correspondence indicated that he now has material that will fill two large grocery bags. Storage is becoming a problem. As is obvious, I did not make a trip to Europe to pick up material for this delivery.

His schedule does fit fairly well with our meeting and I plan to meet him during a port call which will give me two days to make it to our meeting. I will arrange to pick up the best of his material and deliver it in bulk; photographing it while on the road does not seem practical. Also, the entire amount he has would be impossible to safely transport and I plan to deliver that at the schedule you will provide. I hope his ship doesn't experience a schedule change which will put me in the same situation we once faced in Hong Kong. I did not make the primary date and we met on the alternate. So I have to make a decision and here it is: If his schedule changes and I cannot make the primary date, I will collect the material and make the secondary date.

D continues to be a puzzle. He is not happy, but is still not ready to continue our "cooperation." Rather than try to analyze him for you, I have simply enclosed portions of two letters I've received. My guess?

He is going to flop in the stockbroker field and can probably make a modest living in computer sales. He has become accustomed to the big-spending life-style and I don't believe he will adjust to living off his wife's income. He will attempt to renew cooperation within two years.

F has been transferred and is in a temporary situation giving him no access at all. He is having difficulty in making a career decision in the Navy. He is not happy and is experiencing family pressures with our father who is 73 and in poor health. He married—his father—a younger woman who has a significant drinking problem. F feels obligated to support them. He may come around and good access is possible.

K and I have discussed your proposal and I will pass on some extensive details when we meet. Briefly, he is involved in carrier and amphibious ship-maintenance planning. He would instantly recognize unrealistic repair schedules or see that ships were "off their normal schedules." This may provide a basis for the information we seek. Otherwise, he has no useful material.

So I will see you as scheduled and hope I will make the primary date with no problem. I'm sure you have access to S's port schedule and can anticipate my moves in advance. I am not providing his schedule in this note for obvious reasons.

Good luck.

Since S is providing a large quantity of material, the quantity of film to shoot is also becoming large. I have been trying to figure out an alternative method that will decrease the size of the packages to deliver. I have a super 8mm movie camera which is capable of single-frame shots. There is 50 feet of film in each cassette which, unless my math is off, would consist of over 9,000 frames.

I have enclosed a short sample of a document shot with the camera using different focusing methods. The first two were shot from 1.5 feet and measured: then two from two feet, then two while focusing normally. They don't look very good to me, but I thought you may have an idea on how we could make this method work.

John was not to meet his KGB contact until after dark that night, but since he had nothing planned for the afternoon, he decided to leave early. He walked out of his house at 12:10 P.M.—fifty minutes before Hunter had promised to call off the stakeout.

Hodges, who had returned to the air with a full tank of fuel, contacted Hunter by radio when he saw John get into his van. "He's on the move!"

Recalling the wild goose chase of the day before, Hunter tried to keep from getting excited. But within a few minutes, Hodges was on the radio again.

"He's driving evasively."

John was doubling back, riding in circles, and performing other maneuvers to detect if he was being followed. The six FBI cars, under the direction of Hodges, carefully kept out of sight, and Hodges pulled his airplane up to four thousand feet into a position he hoped John wouldn't notice.

John drove west onto Interstate 64 toward Richmond. FBI agent Beverly Andress, who was part of the stakeout team, called Hunter on the radio.

"Are we having fun yet?" she asked. Obviously, John was driving in the wrong direction if he was going to North Carolina.

"Not yet," Hunter replied. "I'll let you know when."

When John reached the outskirts of Richmond and turned north on a bypass that feeds traffic to Washington, D.C., Hunter grabbed his radio microphone.

"Bev," he said excitedly, "now we are having fun!"

Meanwhile, Wolfinger pulled away from the chase and drove to a telephone to call FBI headquarters in Washington. "Operation Windflyer," the code name the FBI had chosen for this case, he reported, "is under way."

Hunter wanted to get to Washington before John Walker, so the agent pushed down on the gas pedal of his Jeep Cherokee and soon found himself behind John's Astro minivan. Fighting the urge to turn and stare at John, Hunter sped past. He wanted to reach a special communications center that the FBI had set up in Washington to monitor the operation.

John didn't notice anyone during the drive. Just before Washington, he pulled into a highway rest stop to use the bathroom. Hodges quickly warned the remaining four FBI chase cars to pull off the highway. When John returned to the interstate, one of the chase cars sped into the rest area. Two agents dashed into the bathroom and amid startled travelers, searched for any packages that John might have hidden. There were none.

As John got closer to Washington, the FBI put into operation some of the plans that Hunter, Wolfinger, and the experts from FBI headquarters had agreed upon only a few weeks earlier.

Perhaps the most extraordinary action involved the flooding of the area around John with tracking vehicles. Trying to follow John in heavy traffic with one or two cars was just too risky, the FBI had decided. There was always the chance that he might notice a car on his tail. Using one or two cars was also dangerous because they might get trapped behind cars at a traffic light or lose John if he made a series of sudden turns.

So the FBI called upon forty-one persons in twenty vehicles to trail John when he arrived at the Beltway that circles Washington. It was one of the most massive surveillance operations ever undertaken by the agency.

It also didn't work.

The hitch occurred after John crossed the Potomac River and began driving through a rural section of Maryland on a narrow road. The sudden appearance of twenty cars in such a sparsely populated area might spook John. So the FBI pulled back its network of cars and decided to rely on the plane. By this time, a fresh pilot and crew had taken over. The new aircraft kept on John's trail, but it soon became difficult to find John's minivan as it rode along the curves and dips under a protective cover of foliage. After several minutes, the pilot and crew lost sight of John's van in the canopy of trees. The plane quickly dropped lower to give its passengers a better look, but that didn't help. John was gone.

Every second counted now. It was crucial to get the ground search started, but because the Soviets frequently monitor FBI broadcasts through the antennae on their embassy, the pilot decided not to risk using his radio to contact the communications post where Hunter and Wolfinger were waiting. Instead, he raced to a nearby airport, where he landed and telephoned the command center. It was 4:55 P.M., and by the time the FBI unleashed its ground crew, John had disappeared.

"We didn't have the faintest idea where he was," recalled Hunter. Anger and frustration began to build. People began looking for someone to blame. No one said anything aloud, but everyone was reminded of Hunter's decision not to place an electronic tracking device on John's car. The Norfolk office had successfully followed John to Washington, and agents in that jurisdiction had lost track of him. But it didn't matter. Hunter was the case manager, and now that John had vanished, Hunter was the agent who would have to bear responsibility.

For three hours the FBI inspected the rural Maryland countryside where John had last been seen. No one could find him. Back at the command center, frustration led to second-guessing. Hunter held to one thin hope. Barbara Walker had said John always drove through a dead drop area on a practice run when she accompanied him on dead drops. If true, there was a chance that John might return.

While Hunter fidgeted, John was dining peacefully at the Ramada Inn in Rockville, confident that this drop would go as smoothly as the rest.

At 7:45 P.M., the FBI airplane spotted John's minivan returning to the rural Maryland road where he had earlier disappeared. A cheer went up at the FBI command center and Hunter was immediately transformed from dupe to sage. This time the FBI flooded the area with tracking cars.

John later recalled being suspicious of the increased traffic. "I stopped at one small intersection and there was a car on each of the other three roads." But he ignored the warnings and placed his 7-Up signal can for his KGB contact at the prearranged spot.

The FBI rushed in as soon as John left. Thinking that he might have dropped off a container of film for the Russians, a special search team of FBI agents quickly explored the area and found the 7-Up can. The FBI said later that members of its highly trained foreign counterintelligence squad knew that the 7-Up can was a signal by John to his KGB handler. They knew that disturbing the can could jeopardize the dead drop exchange and they gave instructions for the can to be returned unmolested to its original location after agents were confident that it didn't contain any film.

But the FBI screwed up. Because of what later was described as "an innocent miscommunication," the can was confiscated by the FBI and removed as evidence.

This proved to be a major blunder, because it ruined the FBI's chance of catching both a KGB agent and John, and of proving without any doubt whom John was meeting. Luck, however, was on the FBI's side. At 8:20 P.M., an FBI unit spotted a 1983 blue Malibu sedan driving in the area where John had left his signal can. The car had a diplomatic license plate—DSX 144—and was being driven by a man with a woman and child as passengers. No one had to tell the FBI which foreign country the letters DSX represented. It was the Soviet Union. Back at the command post, Hunter watched as the number 144 was run through a computer. Within seconds, the computer identified the car as one assigned to Aleksei Gavrilovich Tkachenko, third secretary of the Soviet embassy since January 7, 1983.

"We got really excited when we saw the Russian in the area because it confirmed everyone's suspicion," Hunter explained. "There was no reason for a Russian to be out at the very edge of the twenty-five-mile restricted area in the middle of the night."

At that moment, Hunter and the other agents figured they had a good chance of catching both John and Tkachenko. But to their horror, Tkachenko began driving away from the dead drop area. It was then that the FBI realized that one of its agents had picked up John's signal can. Three days later, Tkachenko, his wife, Olga, and two daughters, Mariya and Oksana, were escorted to National Airport by Aleksandr Vasilyevich Shcherbakov, Viktor Vladimirovich Volkov, and Yevgenity Gennadyevich Vtyhrin, three beefy embassy security guards. The family boarded a flight that took them first to New York City and then to Montreal, Canada, where they were able to fly aboard a Soviet Aeroflot airplane to Moscow. The Tkachenkos left Washington so suddenly that when FBI agents searched the family's apartment, they found half-cooked hamburger in a pan on the stove. They also found a bumper sticker in the master bedroom that Tkachenko had retrieved from the 1984 presidential campaign and attached to a bathroom mirror in a bit of black humor. It said: "President Reagan: Bringing America Back."

Because Tkachenko had dropped off his signal can before John, there was no way for John to realize that Tkachenko had aborted the drop. So John drove to his drop site and tucked his delivery behind a telephone pole. His grocery bag contained the 129 classified documents that Michael had stolen before the U.S.S. Nimitz left Norfolk, John's incriminating letter to the KGB, and copies of recent letters that Jerry Whitworth had written John.

FBI agent Bruce K. Brahe II found the grocery bag a few minutes after

John hid it near the telephone pole. "I touched it with my foot," he recalled. "It had a crumply dry sound." Opening the bag, Brahe noticed the trash inside had been cleaned. "The caps were on the bottles; the bottles were rinsed out . . . I immediately knew this was the package; I couldn't believe that it wasn't."

When he reached into the bag, Brahe found John's package of documents wrapped in a white trash bag, sealed with tape.

"I got it," he yelled.

"Are you sure?" asked a fellow agent.

Spicing his reply with expletives, Brahe made clear that he was certain.

John, meanwhile, could find neither his package from the KGB nor, when he returned to the telephone pole, his documents. He returned to his room in the Ramada Inn.

FBI agents tailed John to the hotel and shortly after three A.M., the Justice Department gave Hunter permission to arrest John on charges of espionage.

The only problem was getting John out of his room. Breaking through the door was simply too dangerous. "We really need this sucker alive," Hunter said. "John Walker has too much to tell."

Hunter remembered listening to a taped phone conversation between John and his mother in which John bragged about his new minivan. Hunter and the other agents at the hotel decided to stage an accident. Agent William Wang would pose as a desk clerk, telephone John, and claim that John's new van had been hit by a drunk driver. When John came out into the hotel hallway, he would be arrested.

It was an old trick, but the agents felt confident that it would work. Hunter and James Kolouch put on bullet-proof vests and carefully got into position near the elevator bank closest to John's room. If possible, John was to be taken alive. Both agents drew their guns and waited.

At precisely three-thirty A.M., Wang telephoned John's room.

A few minutes later, Hunter and Kolouch heard John's door open.

# 71

The U.S.S. *Nimitz* was in the Israeli port of Haifa when it received a secret encrypted message about eight hours after John's arrest. The FBI was afraid that Michael Walker might have friends or accomplices working in the carrier's radio room so the message referred to him by a prearranged code name: Brown. John Walker was referred to, rather appropriately, as Red, and only the top-echelon officers, whom the FBI had alerted a few weeks before, knew the two men's real identities. The Naval Investigative Service had assigned the code name Cabin Boy to its probe of Michael.

SECRET
NOFORM SPECAT

REF: CABIN BOY
WINDFLYER / ESPIONAGE
REQUESTED BY FBI/ NORFOLK VA.

Brown's father, herein called Red, was arrested by the FBI early am 20 May for 3C activity after FBI surveillance disclosed him loading a dead drop in Poolesville, Md area . . . FBI subsequently recovered 129 secret-confidential documents. Information from FBI reflects material seized came from Brown and that Brown allegedly has similar material, enough to fill two grocery bags, stashed somewhere on his ship which he was to deliver to Red at a port call. The recovered papers consist of 80 secret and 49 confidential documents. FBI was advised that preliminary review reveals that most, if not all, came from Brown's ship and are dated February 1985 before the ship's deployment. One of the documents is entitled 'Nimitz Mediterranean Pre-Deployment News' classified 'Secret.' It has the handwritten notation on the lower right corner 'OPS Admin Secret Board.' . . . Evidence indicates that Brown has provided additional documents in the past to his father. It is not known at this time how long Brown has been involved in this activity with his father. Interrogate Brown using the following warning: "Violations of the espionage statutes: Improper handling of classified material: and theft of U.S. government classified material and property." Attempt to obtain permissive search of Brown's personal effects, his locker, his work space, desk and other logical spaces for classified material, cameras, film, notes, letters, letter writing materials ... and any other materials indicative of espionage activity.... Recommend pre-trial confinement for Brown, arrange to have all his spaces secured until a command authorized search can be obtained. Ensure Brown has no access to his spaces and that his every movement is monitored to prevent destruction of evidence.... It is possible that Brown has additional accomplices aboard the Nimitz and this should be explored....

Michael was not aboard the carrier when the message arrived. He was in a bar getting drunk with some friends. He returned to the dock riding his skateboard.

"I was sick," Michael Walker recalled. "Riding the waves on the boat that took us out to the carrier was too much for me to take. I thought I was going to throw up. It was about twelve-thirty A.M. when I got to my room and climbed in my rack. I turned on the light and when I lay down I could see that box glowing behind the air duct. It was like the damn thing was saying, 'Move me! Move me!' I had this strange feeling that something was telling me to move that damn box, but I said to myself, 'The hell with it,' and rolled over and went to sleep.

"The next morning, at around six A.M., this guy wakes me up and says my commander wants to talk to me. I went to the berthing area and called the yeoman on duty in OPS-ADMIN on the telephone and told him that it was my day off and I was hung over and could I come up at eight A.M., and he checks with the commander and says okay.

"I climbed back in my bunk and that box is really glowing now and it's like screaming at me, 'Move me, you dumb shit!' but I went back to sleep. I could have carried it to the burn room and destroyed it, but I just felt too bad.

"I got up two hours later and shaved and got my hair combed and locked my locker and went up to OPS-ADMIN and people are going through my desk and basket and no one wants to talk to me, and I suddenly knew what was happening. I felt like I had E-S-P-I-O-N-A-G-E written across my face. I was about to barf when someone said, 'Michael, the captain wants to see you.' All of a sudden, three big guys from the Master at Arms office came in. 'Walker, come with us,' this guy says. I thought, 'This is it!' I felt like dog shit!"

Michael was taken to the brig and ordered to sit. He was not allowed to speak to anyone or leave the chair except to go with two escorts to the bathroom. "I figured I had screwed up somehow. I didn't think my dad was busted, I thought they had caught me. Someone had seen something."

Michael asked for a pen and paper and began a letter to Rachel.

Hello Bunny, I love you. Today is our third day in Haifa. I would have had the day off today, however, I am still on board trying to take care of a *BIG* problem, which is why I am writing this letter.

Currently, I am sitting in the Master at Arms office waiting to speak with the executive officer among other NIS [Naval Investigative Service] agents, etc. At this time I have no idea what has come up, although I would imagine it is pretty serious.

I will finish this letter once I have had my little discussion with the XO. If I end this letter on an unhappy note, please contact my father as soon as possible. Needless to say I am not in any trouble with drugs, fighting or any other sailor type bullshit. *YOU AND I* could only begin to wonder what kind of trouble I am in.

I will close this letter for now and get back with you later. The time now is 0930.

Michael was taken to the ship's legal department, where he was briefly questioned by Gary Hitt, an investigator for the Naval Investigative Service.

"He asked me if I knew why I was there," Michael recalled, "and I played dumb and said that I didn't have a clue. 'Your father has been arrested for espionage and we have reason to believe you are involved,' he tells me. 'No, I'm not involved,' I said, but I knew that I had the word *GUILTY* tattooed on my forehead. He says to me, 'Okay, you want to say anything?' and I said, 'No,' and then he asked if he could search my bunk and I said, 'Sure,' 'cause I didn't think they would find the box. I had hid it too well. They made me strip and that's when they found my letter to Rachel and my reference to getting in touch with my dad. What a stupid mistake. Hitt reads it and shakes his head 'cause he knew exactly what the letter meant. Then they had me show 'em where my bunk was. They took me back to the Master at Arms office while they searched it."

Hitt carefully logged what he found during the search of Michael's bunk, locker, desk at OPS-ADMIN, and the fan room where Michael had hidden several documents he was saving.

Hitt found 195 classified documents hidden in the fan room, 665 documents in the computer box behind the air duct at the foot of his bunk, and 316 documents in his work area. In all, Michael had stolen 1,176 documents during the cruise.

"Around eleven that night," Michael recalled, "they took me back up to see Hitt. I was smoking like crazy. I had given up cigarettes a long time before, but I had to have one that day and I'm sitting there, nervous as hell, and Hitt says, 'Tell me about the box,' and I said, 'What box?' but by this time my eyes are dilating and my ears are turning red and I'm realizing that I'm not such a hot poker player after all. And he got angry and said, 'Don't play games with me,' so I said, 'Oh, that box, well I was going to put it in the burn room but the burn room was closed so I stuck it behind there and forgot about it.' He says to me, 'Walker, that's bullshit.' "

Michael was taken to a cell in the brig. A guard was stationed outside the bars to watch him.

"I began crying and couldn't stop," Michael said. "I couldn't sleep. I was really scared. All that night, I cried and cried. The next morning, I threw up. I was totally humiliated. I asked to see Hitt and boom, like that, they put a yellow band on my arm that meant I was in the brig and marched me up to see him.

"I said to him, 'Hey, are they going to kill me?' And he says, 'I don't think so.' I was worried about being executed, man! I mean, I was in the Navy and my dad wasn't. They could court-martial me on the spot and blast my ass right there. So I confessed. I was so nervous I couldn't even type my confession and I can usually type eighty words a minute."

In order to prove Michael had engaged in espionage, the government had to show that he had stolen classified material, that such material was going to or was intended for a foreign government, and that releasing the material was harmful to the United States.

Michael admitted all three during his confession.

"My father never said who he sold classified documents to, but when he suggested I furnish him with classified documents from my work I believed he must be selling them to the Russians or some other Communist country. When my father asked me to give him classified documents from my work place, I remembered that when I was still in high school, he commented to me one day that someday he would tell me how he makes his money. I now concluded that selling classified documents to the Russians must be what he meant. My father's request of me to furnish him classified documents wasn't a total surprise to me, but I really can't explain why not. I knew he had done other illegal things like smoking pot freely in front of us at home. . . . I knew when I was taking the classified documents that the unauthorized disclosure of them to a foreign government could harm the United States."

After Michael signed his confession, he was taken back to the brig, where he had a change of heart. "I decided that I wanted them to kill me," he told me solemnly. "I wanted them to do it right there on the ship. Go up on the deck and shoot me! Get it over with! It would have been easier than having everyone know what I'd done. I began to cry like a baby again. I couldn't stop."

Something else happened when Michael got back to the brig. "My dad had paid me one thousand dollars," Michael recalled. "That's all. He had told me that we would make thousands, up to fifty thousand per year working together, but all I ever received was a lousy thousand dollars. My entire life had been screwed and ruined for a lousy fucking one thousand dollars!"

The next morning, ten Marines wearing helmets and carrying M-16's formed a human wall around Michael and marched him from the brig to the carrier deck. News of his arrest had spread through the ship, and as Michael was led away, he felt as if all six thousand men aboard were watching him. "I knew I had betrayed those guys," he said. "I knew each and every one of them hated my guts."

During the flight to Andrews Air Force Base outside Washington, Michael was allowed to read a copy of a newspaper and for the first time he learned details about his father's arrest. It was not until just before he arrived at the air base, however, that he heard a radio broadcast that explained that Barbara and Laura were the tipsters. Michael felt betrayed.

"I wanted to kill them both," he told me. "I really wanted to kill them with my own hands. I was so pissed off. How could they do this to me without any warning. That's when I decided again that I just wanted to die. Shit! My own mother and sister had been plotting this and the entire time, neither one of them told me a thing. Why hadn't they told me they were going to turn him in? They had to have known I was involved. They just didn't want to admit it.

"I thought about it a lot, you know, what kind of a family I had, and I just couldn't believe that they had done this to me. They had completely ruined my life and not even given me a warning. I think I would have jumped ship and come home and machine gunned every last one of them if they hadn't caught me! Then I would have gotten on my surfboard and just paddled out into the ocean and let the sharks eat me. How could they do it to me?

"If they would have told me, Rachel and I could have disappeared somewhere, gone to the West and lived with Indians or something. But they didn't give me any warning because I think they both were afraid that I'd tell them I was involved. They didn't want to know that. They wanted to turn my dad in and they didn't really give a damn about me, but they didn't want to admit that. They wanted to act shocked and horrified later. I was screwed."

Agent Hunter was at the foot of the airplane's stairway when Michael's sneaker touched the runway. "Mr. Walker, I'm with the FBI, you are under arrest," he said, before whisking Michael into a waiting car. Surrounded by police cars, the motorcade headed for Baltimore.

Rachel had driven to the air base with a friend as a sign of support for Michael and had tried to get his attention, screaming as loudly as she could. But he hadn't heard her, and there were so many reporters and television crews there, she couldn't get close enough to wave.

The day after Michael was arrested, Rachel had written a letter to him, but she didn't know where to send it, so she simply asked the FBI to deliver it. They kept it as evidence. Its tone was panicky, and it was full of poorly disguised attempts to cover her own knowledge. In that letter, Rachel told Michael about her questioning by the FBI and the NIS.

They had asked her whether he had ever brought anything home from work. They had questioned her about the family—Laura, Cynthia, Margaret, Barbara—and asked whether John had ever given Michael large sums of money. "I said no, because that's the truth," she wrote. She ended with assurances of her love and support.

After she missed making contact with Michael at the air base, Rachel telephoned the Baltimore FBI office. An agent told her that she could visit Michael there, so she left immediately for Baltimore, where she got lost and had to be led by an agent to the FBI field office. When she was taken into a room to see Michael late that afternoon, she burst into tears. The FBI tape-recorded the couple's conversation and didn't allow them to be alone, so neither said anything incriminating. Michael had already confessed, of course, but he didn't mention that to Rachel. "I didn't want the FBI to know that Rachel knew about the spying and I didn't know how she would react."

Rachel stroked Michael's arm and tried to find out if he had said anything to them about her. He tried to hint that he hadn't, but she didn't seem to understand.

"I really didn't want her there trying to make me feel good," Michael said. "I didn't want to see Rachel or anybody. I wanted to be in my own little world and to be left alone. She kept saying, 'Now Mike, take it easy and everything will be okay,' and I didn't want to hear that bullshit. I immediately brought up getting a divorce and that upset her, but I knew it was something we had to do. I just wanted to get on with it all and get it over with."

Rachel promised Michael that she would be strong and stick with him, and then he was taken into another room for interrogation. Rachel found herself being questioned, too. Exhausted and emotionally distraught, Rachel was only able to make a few statements before she began sobbing. She said that she knew nothing about the spying, but when an agent showed Rachel the letter that Michael had been writing to her on the *Nimitz*, she became frightened.

The sentence, "YOU AND I can only begin to wonder what kind of trouble I'm in," jumped out at her. She asked if she could call her father in Norfolk, and when he got on the telephone, Rachel pleaded, "Daddy, I want to come home."

Rachel's father calmed her and suggested that she check into a motel in Baltimore and not risk driving five hours back to Norfolk, since it was late. Embarrassed, Rachel told her father that she didn't have enough money for a motel. She was broke.

Without being asked, an FBI agent stepped forward and gave Rachel $50 for a room. It was money from his own pocket.

Rachel was not the only person who had asked for permission to see Michael. Barbara Walker also wanted to visit her son, but Michael refused repeatedly to see her.

Instead, Michael sent her a brief note: "Mother," he wrote, "you are the biggest BITCH I've ever met!"

# 72

$F$our FBI agents arrived at Arthur's house at 6:50 A.M. on May 20, about four hours after John's arrest, and asked Rita for permission to come inside.

Arthur walked into the entryway in his pajamas to see what was going on.

"Your brother John was arrested this morning and charged with espionage," an agent explained.

"What?" Arthur demanded, faking shock over the news that John was a spy.

Agents Beverly Andress and Carroll Deane questioned Arthur in the den while two other agents quizzed Rita in the kitchen.

"I felt safe," Arthur told me later, "because only John and I knew about what I had done, so I figured they were talking to me just because he was my brother."

Arthur was worried about publicity more than being implicated. "My thought was, 'Oh shit! The newspapers are gonna have in there: JOHN WALKER, SPY CAPTURED, etc. . . . which is exactly what happened later on, and then all the neighbors will know he's my brother.' "

Unlike John, Arthur had always been concerned about his standing in the neighborhood.

"I had always told my kids, 'If you get into any kind of trouble, don't say nothing until you talk to an attorney,' but I didn't want to give the FBI any inkling that I was not fully cooperating," Arthur explained later. "I was afraid they might be suspicious if I did."

So Arthur acted as if he wanted to cooperate.

"I don't want to be the one who nails my brother," he told the agents, "but if I can help, I certainly will. I certainly have nothing to hide."

"Of course," Arthur told me later, "I was lying."

Arthur didn't know that Barbara had already implicated him in the spy ring and that the FBI was fairly confident by that point in its investigation that Arthur was the cryptic $K$ in John's dead drop letter. Arthur was about to dig himself a very big hole.

"In a sense, I really wasn't lying when I told the FBI that I wanted to cooperate," Arthur claimed later. "I *really* did want to cooperate, as strange as that may sound. You see, I had taken an oath and part of my oath was not to betray my country. I didn't have the moral courage to turn John in or at least punch him out or do whatever would be necessary and . . . I felt guilty about that, I really did, so I thought, 'John is nailed now, so why not help them. Why not do the right thing.' I thought it might help ease my own conscience about what I had done."

At nine A.M., Beverly Andress asked Arthur to accompany her and Agent Deane voluntarily to the Norfolk FBI office for more questioning. He agreed and during the next six hours, Arthur attempted to satisfy the FBI and also keep from incriminating himself. It proved to be a tightrope that he couldn't walk.

Arthur began by admitting that John had once asked him about various documents at VSE Corporation, but he "categorically denied" any knowledge of John's espionage and claimed to have never "passed on anything."

"It's something I wouldn't even consider," he said. "Even for my brother."

But the longer the questioning went on, the more overwrought Arthur became.

"I began to do a damage assessment," he explained to me later. "As I'm talking to the feds, I'm thinking . . . how could I tell them stuff about John without telling them about myself? Because, you see, all I know about John is what I did. I started telling them and soon I was sliding right down into it. I was giving myself away." Shortly after three P.M., the agents took Arthur home and asked if they could search his house. "Sure," he said, knowing there was nothing incriminating hidden there. Afterward, he returned voluntarily to the FBI office and agreed to take a polygraph examination.

By this time, Arthur was afraid to stop cooperating, even though he knew that he was getting himself into trouble. "I didn't want the FBI to be suspicious of me because I still didn't think they knew about what I had done," Arthur said. "How could they? Only John and I knew. So I agreed to a polygraph to keep up that appearance. Oh God, was that a mistake. But my feeling at that point, when I agreed to take the polygraph, was that I had told them enough truth that . . . that I could pass it."

But when he was attached to the polygraph, before the test began, Arthur said that he wanted to amend his story. In "hindsight" he recalled that he had become "suspicious" of John six months earlier during a "bullshit" session when John asked him about information concerning the overhaul of Navy ships and explained that "some people might be interested in something like that."

"That made alarm bells go off in my head," Arthur told the agents, "and on a scale of one to ten, I was approximately nine point five suspicious that John was doing something wrong because the only people I know of that would be willing to pay for that kind of information are those people in eastern bloc countries."

Arthur went a step further. He acknowledged that he had given John a document, but claimed it was unclassified, very old, and totally useless. In his own mind, Arthur told me later, he was convinced that he had told enough of the truth to protect himself. Surely, he thought, the polygraph machine wouldn't be sophisticated enough to detect the subtle differences between his admissions and the truth.

Arthur was wrong. The polygraph indicated that he had been "deceptive."

Arthur was genuinely astonished when told this. "It can't be!" he said. Hoping to clear himself, Arthur elaborated on his first story. This time, he admitted that he had once allowed John to see a single page of a ship's casualty report, which is classified as confidential, and he said that he first became suspicious of John two years ago, rather than six months earlier. The FBI suggested that Arthur hire a lawyer.

Back home that night, Arthur admitted to Rita for the first time that he was involved.

"I've told the FBI that I gave John something," he said.

"What?" Rita replied. "Arthur, how could you?"

"Now don't worry," he replied. "It wasn't anything serious."

Rita panicked. Was he going to be arrested?

No, Arthur replied. The document that he gave John was insignificant. "I think it will be okay."

The next morning, Arthur drove to the FBI office and said that he wanted to "start over from the beginning."

"By this time," Arthur recalled, "the FBI had told me enough for me to know that John was nailed and Mike had been arrested, so I figured it was time to stop evading and to tell them everything I knew about John. I still believed that I hadn't done anything serious enough to be prosecuted."

Arthur also thought that if he squealed on John, the FBI would be convinced that he had cooperated and readily accept his own story. Arthur told a bit more of the truth. He admitted showing John several pages of two confidential documents and told the FBI that John had paid him $2,000.

Then Arthur volunteered to take another polygraph test and, once again, it indicated that he was lying.

During the next few hours, Arthur revealed more and more. By evening, he was chain-smoking so heavily that the tiny interrogation room in the Norfolk office became dense with smoke and the FBI agents had to excuse themselves to go outside and breathe fresher air.

Hunter had returned to Norfolk by this time and checked periodically on the questioning of Arthur during the day. Shortly after eight P.M.,

Hunter lost his temper. "I felt Arthur was an intelligent man and I thought he was simply trying to find out what we knew about him. The smoke was pouring out of the room and all we were hearing was bits and pieces of crap."

Hunter stormed into the interrogation room and jabbed his finger on Arthur's chest.

"Get your ass out of here and don't come back until you want to tell us the truth!" Hunter yelled. "You're lying. You're not telling us the truth. You're jerking our chain, so just get the hell out of here!"

Hunter lifted Arthur from his chair and pushed him out of the door.

At eight-thirty A.M. the next morning, Arthur reported to the FBI office on his own without an appointment.

"I want to clear my name," he told the agents.

"That polygraph was driving me crazy," Arthur explained later. "I had to pass that damn polygraph."

During the next five hours, Arthur told how he was recruited by John, how much he was paid, and what documents he had passed. Agent Andress listened carefully and then asked Arthur a question that shocked him.

"Have you ever slept with Barbara?"

"No," Arthur immediately responded. Later, Arthur explained, "I was embarrassed to admit to a woman that I had slept with my brother's wife, but a few minutes later one of the male agents asked me and I said, 'Hey, I'm not an angel. Yeah, I did it, but only once.'"

The fact that the FBI knew about Barbara was the most terrifying discovery of all for Arthur.

"The impact hit me. This is the FBI. They really do know all and see all," he said. "They had checked me out. I figured that they even knew if I had peed in the alley as a kid. It finally hit me that I had said too much. I had done myself in. . . ."

That night, Arthur and Rita sat down and made eight pages of notes about everything Arthur knew or had given to John. The next morning, May 24, Arthur once again came to the FBI office voluntarily to make a statement. The interview lasted more than five hours, and this time Agent Andress asked him about his girlfriend, Sheila, and other sexual relationships that Arthur allegedly had with other women.

"Who told you about that?" he asked, bewildered.

"Arthur," an agent replied, "we know more about you than you know about yourself."

Arthur gave the FBI a long and thorough statement that afternoon and after Hunter read it, he was convinced that during Arthur's thirty-five hours of interviews, he had "confessed bit by bit." The Justice Department disagreed. Arthur's admissions were not corroborated and some of his statements were contradictory. More importantly, Arthur insisted throughout the interviews that he didn't believe the documents that he had passed really had harmed the government.

The next morning was a Saturday and when Arthur awoke and went into the kitchen, he found Rita crying at the breakfast table. The FBI had been questioning her and she felt the interrogations were demeaning.

"I haven't done anything," she said, "but I still feel guilty."

"Rita, you didn't do anything," Arthur said. "I'm the one they're after."

"But you're my husband," she replied.

After a few minutes, Arthur said, "Rita, there's something I got to tell you and you're not going to like hearing it."

Arthur figured that sooner or later the FBI would tell Rita about his sexual act with Barbara. It was better, he decided, that it came from him. In the next few minutes, Arthur admitted infidelity with both Barbara and Sheila.

"I'm sorry I did it," he said when he had finished. "But I did." Then Arthur began to cry.

Rita was in shock. "I had been upset that morning," Rita recalled later, "because, and I got to be honest, because my personal conviction was that anyone who was a spy should be hanged and killed. I felt that strong about it. But when the person is your husband, the man you have been married to for twenty-nine years and you cared about and who was the father of your children, it is a different situation, and I was in a funky mood and he helped me snap out of it. I had assumed that he had told me everything at that point and then he says, 'Rita, there's more,' and I looked at him and he told me about the women. I was blown away emotionally. That was it. How could he have done that? How could he have done that to me and the children? It was too much."

Rita began to cry, too. Within five days her entire life had been turned upside down.

A grand jury was meeting in Baltimore on May 28, a Tuesday, to review evidence against John and Michael. Rita had been called as a witness, but Arthur hadn't. Arthur told the FBI that he would drive Rita to Baltimore if that was okay because she was afraid of driving on major highways. He let her out a block away from the courthouse and drove back to the motel. The phone was ringing when he got there.

"Art, come get me," Rita said. She was crying. "They don't want me."

"I had broken down," Rita recalled. "They asked me some simple questions about how long I had been married and then said, 'Well, we don't need you this morning.' "

Arthur raced back to the courthouse and went inside without drawing any attention from the media. As he waited outside the U.S. Attorney's office while someone fetched Rita, he was approached by Hunter and Assistant U.S. Attorney Michael Schatzow. They took him into a conference room and asked if he wanted to volunteer to appear before the grand jury.

"Okay," he said.

Later that afternoon, Arthur answered a series of carefully worded questions posed by Schatzow before the grand jury.

SCHATZOW: Since 1980, have you had occasion to provide your brother, John Walker, with documents, which contained classified information?

ARTHUR: Yes, sir.

SCHATZOW: Approximately how many occasions have you done it?

ARTHUR: I believe I have previously stated two occasions of classified information, perhaps three. I don't remember off hand what we have been going over . . .

SCHATZOW: At the time you gave those documents to your brother, you knew that he was going to give them to somebody else for money, is that right?

ARTHUR: Yes, sir. I knew they were, there was certainly the possibility that they were going to be passed on, yes, sir.

SCHATZOW: And you knew also that the somebody was a foreign government, isn't that correct?

ARTHUR: Yes, sir.

SCHATZOW: And you assumed that to be the Soviets?

ARTHUR: My assumption, I don't remember him ever mentioning them specifically, but my assumption was he certainly was going to somebody who wanted to buy information about the U.S.

SCHATZOW: You knew the reason that these people were buying information about the United States was to either hurt the United States or to help that foreign country, isn't that right?

ARTHUR: It's obvious, yes, sir.

Schatzow later acknowledged that his questions were designed to give the FBI a foolproof case against Arthur. Until Arthur appeared before the grand jury, the government did not have much of a case against him. Arthur's admissions could not be used against him in court because the FBI could not confirm them. The FBI, in fact, couldn't even prove that a crime had been committed. No documents were missing from VSE's files, and no one had seen Arthur do anything wrong. The only proof that he had done something came from his own mouth, and any attorney fresh out of law school would be able to knock down a confession that couldn't be corroborated. Testimony before a grand jury, however, doesn't need corroboration to be admissible in court. It was one of those legal nuances that Arthur Walker didn't recognize. When Arthur volunteered to testify before the grand jury, however, Prosecutor Schatzow knew exactly what he was doing. He questioned Arthur skillfully and made certain Arthur admitted to each of the key elements necessary for the government to charge him with espionage. Before he understood what had happened, Arthur had admitted that he (1) had stolen classified documents; (2) had delivered them to a foreign country or its representative; and (3) had done so while knowing full well that they "would be used to the injury of the United States."

Arthur's statement before the grand jury was as valuable as Michael's confession.

During the drive home from Baltimore on Wednesday, May 29, Rita turned to Arthur. "I think we've been duped," she said. "I think the only reason they subpoenaed me was to get you to Baltimore so they could get you in before that grand jury. I think you're really the person they wanted up there."

The telephone was ringing when they got home. It was the FBI. They needed to stop by. Arthur opened the door a short time later. "Mr. Walker, you are under arrest."

Rita watched the agents put Arthur into the back of a car after handcuffing him. After they left, she went into the garage and found a sledgehammer. Then she walked into their backyard and found the grill that Arthur had admitted buying with money that John had paid him for spying.

She lifted the sledgehammer and began hitting the grill with it, over and over again, until her thin arms were too tired to lift it anymore.

She stood there, physically exhausted and emotionally drained, and she wept.

# 73

Five hours after John was arrested, FBI agents John Peterson and Michael McElwee knocked on the door of Jerry Whitworth's trailer in Davis, California, and told him that John had been accused of being a spy.

Peterson didn't mince words. He told Jerry that the FBI believed he was John's accomplice.

"That's really heavy stuff," Jerry replied. "Ah, I need a drink of water."

The three men were sitting in the dining room of the trailer when Jerry stood, excused himself, and walked into the kitchen toward a bottled water dispenser. But when he reached it, he kept on going into his den. Alarmed, McElwee jumped up and followed him, entering the den just in time to see him remove a floppy disk from his IBM computer and hide it under the machine's keyboard.

McElwee escorted Jerry back into the dining room and suggested that he refrain from leaving their presence again. Jerry agreed, and said that he wanted to explain his relationship with John.

Peterson stopped him. This was too important a case to screw up on some legal technicality. Before Jerry said anything about himself and Walker, Peterson wanted to make certain that he had been read his rights. During the next two hours, Jerry gave the two FBI agents a disjointed review of his Navy career. While he was truthful about checkable facts, such as his duty stations and access to classified material, Jerry lied about his friendship with John, saying he did not really like him and did not trust him.

When Jerry finished, McElwee showed him a copy of the first RUS letter and asked if he recognized it.

"He stared at the letter for ... what seemed like a long time," McElwee recalled later, "about ninety seconds or so, and then he looked up ... and said he didn't want to answer that question." Clearly unnerved, Jerry told the agents that he wanted to speak with an attorney.

"I felt like I was under a great deal of pressure," Jerry complained later. "I felt like I was being bombarded psychologically."

Peterson and McElwee were in a quandary when Jerry cut off the interview. They knew that if they left the trailer, Jerry would destroy whatever evidence might be there, but if they kept questioning him, they could jeopardize their case. In a rather unusual move, Peterson asked for permission to use Jerry's telephone to call his boss for instructions, and while he was talking to him, McElwee asked Jerry if he would consent to a search of his trailer.

"What if I say no?" Jerry asked.

Then, McElwee explained, the agents would get a search warrant.

It seemed futile, so Jerry agreed. As soon as Jerry signed the proper waiver of rights form, McElwee rushed to the den and confiscated the floppy disk that Jerry had tried to hide earlier. It contained a letter that Jerry had been writing to John when the FBI agents appeared at his door. In it, Jerry was asking John for permission to rejoin the spy ring.

The FBI put Jerry under round-the-clock surveillance, but despite its best investigative efforts, there still was only circumstantial evidence that Jerry had once spied. The FBI had the floppy disk, John's incriminating note, and the letters that Jerry had written to him, but the Justice Department needed to be able to prove that Jerry had given John a classified document if it was to authorize Jerry's arrest.

One week passed and then another. Back in Norfolk, Wolfinger and Hunter began to worry. The arrest of John, Michael, and Arthur had been international news. Congress had reacted by passing legislation in the House of Representatives to make espionage during peacetime a crime punishable by death; and the Pentagon threatened to recall John and Arthur to active duty in the Navy because the military still had the necessary authority to execute spies. But the biggest hoopla centered on the search for other members of John Walker's spy ring. After Arthur was arrested, the Justice Department disclosed that one of the items found during the FBI search of John's house was the small card that John had filled out while walking in Vienna with his KGB handler. It contained the letter designations for each member of the spy ring, and it didn't take the media long to realize that someone with the code name *D* was still on the loose. Several times a day, Wolfinger received telephone calls from reporters with questions about *D*, and some of the callers were getting close to discovering Jerry Whitworth's identity.

"I could just see a television crew showing up outside Jerry's trailer to do an interview," Wolfinger recalled. "I was afraid such a fiasco would blow our case against him."

The Washington headquarters of the FBI contributed to the media hunt by disclosing that *D* was a "California man." It was not the only mistake that the Washington FBI made while trying to win accolades for its handling of the probe. FBI Assistant Director Bill Baker claimed that agents had "patiently watched [John Walker] for six months" and had intentionally waited to catch him in the act of passing documents. To say the least, those most familiar with the case registered surprise at Baker's misstatements. Eventually, his comments to the press became so irksome to John Walker's attorneys that they asked a federal judge to cite Baker for contempt of court.

Wolfinger, meanwhile, was trying to put together a case against Jerry Whitworth based on documents seized at John's house. It wasn't easy and on June 1, when a reporter called and told Wolfinger that he knew that *D*'s first name was Jerry and that he lived in the San Francisco area, Wolfinger recognized that time was quickly running out.

"We had to do something and fast."

Wolfinger decided to play a long shot. One of the 150 boxes of documents seized from John's house and business had contained an envelope with John's handwriting on it. Wolfinger wanted to know what the scribbles meant because they looked as if John had been referring to secret documents and some sort of advanced radio message system. So he telephoned Washington and arranged for several experts in cryptology from the National Security Agency to fly to Norfolk and examine the envelope that same day.

What Wolfinger didn't learn until later was that John had used the envelope as a note pad when he debriefed Jerry about the documents that he had stolen from the U.S.S. *Enterprise*. One of the NSA officials immediately recognized John's hieroglyphics and told Wolfinger that the writing on the envelope contained information that was so sensitive that the envelope itself should be classified as a secret document to prevent the information from being disclosed.

Wolfinger next rushed the envelope to John C. Saunders, a fingerprint expert at FBI headquarters, who spent most of Sunday examining it. At two A.M., Saunders awakened Wolfinger at his home.

The envelope contained two sets of fingerprints, Saunders reported. One set belonged to John Walker and the other matched Jerry Whitworth's prints!

In effect, John Walker had given the FBI exactly what it had been looking for to arrest Jerry—proof that Jerry Whitworth had passed classified information to John Walker. Some defense attorneys might consider it shaky evidence at best, but Wolfinger thought it would be enough to convince the Justice Department to authorize Jerry's arrest, and that would keep the media from interfering with the case. The Justice Department agreed. The next morning, it issued a warrant. The last major player in the spy ring had been unmasked.

# 74

Laura Walker was fixing dinner with Marie Hammond when she heard NBC anchorman Tom Brokaw announce John Walker had been arrested. "Oh my God!" she shrieked.

Laura had moved in with the Hammonds in early May. "She was depressed again and having money problems," Marie recalled, "so my husband and I went down to Buffalo and got her." At the time, Bill and Marie were living in Canton, a small New York town near the Canadian border. After Laura arrived, Marie took her to the Christian Fellowship Center, where they sang, prayed, danced, and spoke in tongues. That seemed to cheer up Laura.

"She told me that she had called the FBI and turned in her father," Marie Hammond told me later. "Laura told me about the lie detector tests the FBI had given her."

After the FBI captured John, Laura was called before the grand jury and dozens of reporters began arriving in Canton.

"Laura," Marie exclaimed, "you've got to get a lawyer!"

"But I'm broke," Laura said. "How am I going to get a lawyer?"

"Let's call Pat," Marie said. "He'll know what to do."

Once again, the two women turned to television evangelist and *700 Club* founder M.G. (Pat) Robertson for help. Marie dialed the long-distance prayer line for the Virginia Beach-based headquarters. It took her eight calls before she finally reached someone who promised to tell

Robertson that Laura Walker wanted to talk to him. A producer for the television evangelist called back a short time later and asked if Laura would be willing to fly to CBN (the Christian Broadcasting Network) and grant *The 700 Club* an exclusive interview.

Yes, Laura replied, if Pat Robertson promised to help her. Within a few hours, Laura, Marie, and Marie's two sons, Jonathan, twelve, and Billy, eight, were on their way to CBN.

"Laura was upset because one of the stewardesses had recognized her," Marie recalled. "She had a brother on the U.S.S. *Nimitz* with Michael and she told Laura, 'I hope they tear your brother to pieces and feed him to the sharks.' "

Laura and the Hammonds received an impressive guided tour of CBN's two hundred-acre tract. "It was so exciting to see it in person," Marie recalled. "I told Laura, 'See, the Lord is working. He's keeping His promise to you. You are going to get Christopher back.' "

The televised interview was done in private, not before a studio audience, as usual. The tapes of the interview were then rushed to Los Angeles, where Pat Robertson was staying. Marie made certain that the show's producers understood that it was a *700 Club* counselor who had started the chain of events that led to John's arrest by speaking in tongues to her over the telephone.

After Laura's interview, Marie demanded to know what CBN was going to do to help Laura. "She needs legal advice," Marie explained. The two women were taken to see Guy C. Evans, Jr., one of three corporate lawyers at CBN.

Evans had been on the telephone all morning trying to check Laura's story. "The truth was that Pat [Robertson] didn't think Laura was the real Laura Walker. He thought she was a ringer because her story was just too slick," Guy Evans recalled, "so he instructed us to hold up the tapes until he could see them personally and then he still wasn't convinced."

Evans believed Laura and her story about Mark Snyder. He had already verified that her Social Security number had been issued to Laura Walker. But he still needed more proof. During the next two and a half hours, he quizzed Laura about her religious values and life. During their conversation, Laura told Evans that she had seen Mark Snyder when he appeared before the grand jury in Baltimore but she still didn't know where he lived.

Evans suggested that Laura call the U.S. Attorney's office and ask for Mark's address. "I dialed the number for the office in Baltimore and asked for the attorney, and then handed the telephone to Laura," Evans told me. "I listened to her end of the conversation and was further convinced that Laura was genuine."

Laura spoke with Michael Schatzow. "I told him that Mark had given me his telephone number and his address when I saw him at the grand jury. It's true that he had given me his phone number, but not his address. I said to Schatzow, 'I've misplaced Mark's address.' I lied. It was a lie, but I did it anyway. I had to have that address and Schatzow gave it to me. I was so excited."

"Listen," Evans said, "the law says that where no one has filed any petition for divorce, then the court has rendered no decree about custody, then either parent can claim custody. In other words, Laura, you can do exactly what Mark did. You can go steal your child back."

Evans called his secretary.

"I need a car for these two ladies, something nice, and also some cash, say five hundred dollars each." After he finished talking on the telephone, he turned to Laura and Marie.

"Now," Evans said, "go get your child."

It was dark by the time that Laura and Marie arrived in the Washington suburb where Mark lived. The next morning, they drove into his apartment complex.

Marie sent her son, Jonathan, to telephone Mark's apartment. "I wanted to wake up everyone in the house and get them moving," she recalled. "I told Jonathan not to ask for Chris but to stay on the phone long enough that whoever answered wouldn't be able to go back to sleep."

A short time later, a small boy came out on an apartment balcony. It had been three years since Laura had seen Christopher and she wasn't certain it was her son until she saw Mark come out and get him. At about the same time, she saw two boys playing on the lawn in front of the apartments.

"I tried to manipulate the situation," Laura Walker said. "I told Jonathan to go tell one of those boys to knock on Chris's door and tell him to come out and play. But the boys wouldn't do it, and then a voice spoke within me. It wasn't from the heavens, like you see on television, but it was clear as a bell. It said, 'Christopher is going to come out and play,' and I said, 'Marie, I know what is going to happen. Chris is going to see those boys and come out to play,' and sure enough, Chris comes out with a toy in his hand."

Laura and Marie moved quickly. Jonathan took Christopher's hand and led him to the car. Laura opened the door.

"Hi, Chris," she said. "I am your mother."

"He looked at me bewildered and he didn't know what to do," Laura Walker recalled later, "so I picked him up, he put his arms around me, he looked at me and started to cry, and I got in the car and said to Marie, 'Go!' . . . I won't deny it, it was traumatic. He kept saying that he wanted his daddy, but I felt it was the right thing to do and I knew that in the long run it would be for the best even though he cried for the next twenty miles."

Mark Snyder was looking out the window of his third floor apartment when he saw Christopher being taken. "I ran down the stairs and ran outside, but he was gone, and I asked the kids standing there what had happened, who had taken Christopher, and they said that some woman had said she was Christopher's mommy," he recalled. "I hoped it was her and not some nut, but I was still furious. I called the police. It wasn't fair. I had taken care of him all those years and she didn't give a damn and then she had him."

In Virginia Beach, CBN flew Laura and Marie and their children to Los Angeles to meet Pat Robertson. "When he met Laura and saw that she had gotten Christopher back, he was convinced we had the real thing," Guy Evans, Jr., recalled.

The next day, Robertson introduced Laura and Christopher to his viewers on The 700 Club and recalled how a 700 Club counselor had given Laura a message from God. The network televised the first half of its interview with Laura. It was the first televised interview with a member of the Walker family, and it received worldwide attention.

Laura described her father as "arrogant, self-centered, and egotistical," but she ended the interview on an upbeat note by saying that she hoped John would turn to Jesus for forgiveness.

CBN flew Laura and Marie back to Virginia Beach, where the religious organization set Laura up in an apartment and gave her a job.

"It was all God's doing," Laura said afterward. "He had kept His promise and returned my son to me. I never dreamed He would do it in such a dramatic way, by having my mother turn in my dad and then leading me to take Christopher, but He did it."

John Walker, Jr., watched Laura's interviews on CBN from jail.

"Laura needed a crutch," he told me later, "and that phony Pat Robertson gave her one. She couldn't just say, 'My dad was a fucking spy so I turned him in.' She had to claim it was for Christopher and that God had made her do it. She was so silly I couldn't believe it. She was a Nazi cunt."

# 75

Arthur Walker's court-appointed attorneys, Samuel H. Meekins, Jr., and J. Brian Donnelly, knew they didn't have much of a defense. Their only hope for keeping Arthur out of prison depended on whether or not they could convince a federal judge to throw out Arthur's incriminating statements to the FBI and his grand jury confession.

On July 12, Meekins tried to convince Judge J. Calvitt Clarke, Jr., during a court session closed to the public, that Arthur's statements were taken illegally. A confession, in order to be admissible, must be "free and voluntary," according to the U.S. Supreme Court, "and must not be extracted by any sort of threat or violence."

Meekins claimed the government misled Arthur by suggesting that he wouldn't be prosecuted if he helped the FBI buttress its case against John and if he, Arthur, could prove he didn't give away anything valuable. Meekins also suggested that Assistant U.S. Attorney Michael Schatzow had tricked Arthur by telling him that his testimony before the grand jury would be sealed and couldn't be used to prosecute him.

It was an easy defense for Meekins to argue because he believed it. Meekins had spent dozens of hours with Arthur at the Virginia Beach Correctional Center and had developed a genuine liking for him. He also had decided that Arthur was somewhat naive and easily manipulated.

Meekins did his best to undermine Agent Beverly Andress's credibility. She was young and inexperienced—this was her first major investigation— Meekins pointed out. He also argued convincingly that the FBI had *intentionally* chosen not to tape record any of its interviews with Arthur so that only its version of those sessions could be presented in court.

Despite Meekins's efforts, Judge Clarke ruled against Arthur's motion. There was no evidence of government wrongdoing, he said.

Four days before Arthur was scheduled for trial, Meekins and Donnelly met to finalize their defense. There was none. Both men were former prosecutors and both agreed that a jury would convict Arthur based on his own statements. Regardless of what they did, Arthur was going to be found guilty of the first count filed against him—conspiracy to commit espionage—and it carried a potential life prison sentence.

Meekins and Donnelly met with Arthur and suggested that he try to cut a deal with the government. Why not offer to plead guilty, sparing the government the cost of a trial, and agree to testify against John, in return for a lesser sentence?

Arthur agreed.

The Justice Department would later act as if it never seriously considered any plea bargain offer with Arthur. In truth, it offered in early July to drop all of the charges against him except the conspiracy charge in return for his cooperation. But that had been in July. Not August. During the next four days, the government and Arthur's attorneys talked round the clock trying to reach an agreement. They couldn't. And then, on August 5, one hour before Arthur's trial was scheduled to begin, Meekins and Donnelly made a last-ditch offer. Arthur would plead guilty to conspiracy and nolo contendere to the other six counts. In effect, Judge Clarke could sentence Arthur as if he had pleaded guilty to all seven counts. There would be no point to proceeding with the trial. The government had won.

Much to Arthur's shock, the Justice Department said no. The Reagan administration wanted full exposure. "We were not going to give up the public's right to see into an espionage case," Stephen S. Trott, an assistant attorney general at the Justice Department, explained. "You don't put a knife in your country's back and come in and ask for some kind of deal."

The government used Arthur's trial to outline its case, not only against Arthur, but John. At times, Arthur seemed like a mere accessory as prosecutors talked about John's role as ringleader.

During the third day, Arthur leaned over to Meekins, visibly upset.

"It's that damn picture," Arthur whispered, pointing to his left. Earlier in the trial, federal prosecutors had introduced a large portrait of John Walker as evidence and during the lunch recess, someone had leaned the picture against the jury box so that it was now facing the defense table. Regardless of how Arthur sat, he had to look directly into his brother's eyes.

Arthur's attorneys didn't call a single witness in his defense. It took Judge Clarke only fifteen minutes to find Arthur guilty of all seven counts filed against him. Outside the courthouse, prosecutors admitted that the government never would have had a case against Arthur if he hadn't voluntarily talked to FBI agents for thirty-five hours. Arthur Walker had literally talked himself into prison.

That night, Arthur was clearly shaken when he, Meekins, and I met together in the county jail. The folksy humor and blind optimism Arthur had shown on earlier nights was missing. At one point, he leaned close to the wire screen that separates prisoners and visitors. "I'm no spy! I never intended to hurt my country. No way! No way!" he told us.

Arthur continued to complain. "There is no fairness anymore," he said. "I mean, if you made a mistake and you were sorry and you tried to make up for it, everything would be okay in the end, right? Whatever happened to fair play? It just isn't out there anymore, is it?"

"You're wrong, Art," replied Meekins, trying to calm his client. "There is fair play for robbers and rapists and even murderers. The court can cut them some slack, but not you. This case got too big, Art, too many headlines, too much television. It got bigger than you, Arthur, bigger than you."

And then, Arthur asked a question that bewildered both Meekins and me: "What's the worst I can expect, Sam, from the judge? What do you think, maybe a two-year suspended sentence? I won't have to go to prison, will I? I mean, come on, I didn't pass anything that was really valuable to John. The judge has got to realize that."

As incredible as it later seemed, Arthur's questions appeared to be genuine. He seemed to honestly believe that Judge Clarke would sentence him to a short jail term and then suspend that.

Meekins avoided answering. The next step was a presentence investigation, he explained. Arthur had to prepare for that. He had to think about what he was going to tell the court-appointed investigator who would come to analyze him.

After Arthur was taken away, Meekins and I left the jail and stepped into the cool night. Meekins paused beside his car in the parking lot as if to review one last moment of the day's traumatic events. He needed to explain some things, he said. Like Arthur, he needed to talk. He felt badly, he explained, because he had misjudged the government. Meekins had thought the Justice Department would go easy on Arthur if he cooperated. Instead, the government claimed Arthur was a veteran spy and alleged that he might have actually been the brains behind the spy ring. Meekins couldn't believe it.

Where was the physical evidence—the money that Arthur would have made spying for John? he asked.

Meekins had spent hours talking to Rita in the modest kitchen of the Walkers' home. He had seen their financial records and so had I. There was no hidden cash. Where was the proof? The only confirmation that Arthur Walker was a spy came from Arthur's own mouth. If Arthur had been smart enough to hide the fact that he was a skilled KGB spy, then why had he so stupidly confessed?

After several minutes of such conjecture, Meekins became quiet. He was tired. He would save his questions for later when he didn't feel so emotional. He would dissect his decisions like a scientist slicing open a frog, but not now. Not tonight. He was still emotionally raw. He wanted to go home to his wife and children. He wanted to have a few scotches to unwind.

But before he left there was still something that he had to say. Meekins felt queasy about what he had just witnessed in the jail. "I really don't believe, in my heart, that Arthur Walker truly understands what's going to happen next," Meekins explained. "I don't think Arthur understands that he's about to be sent to prison for the rest of his life."

"Do you think Arthur Walker was a spy?" I asked.

Meekins didn't answer quickly. A big man, with bright red hair, an instantaneous grin, and self-effacing laugh, Meekins had served in the Air Force in Vietnam during the bloody Tet Offensive and had lost several friends there. He had been decorated for gallantry. He had no sympathy for spies, but on that night, Meekins had sympathy for Arthur Walker.

"My feeling was this: if you define a spy as someone who intentionally set out to injure his country or to help a foreign power, then Arthur Walker isn't a spy. I just don't believe Arthur gave John those documents because he intended to hurt the United States," Meekins said. "Arthur did it because he wanted to please his brother. He did it for John."

# 76

John wasn't about to be represented by a public defender. He knew what they were—liberal, long-haired lawyers anxious to protect the poor. "Screw 'em!" John wanted the best, some nationally known defense lawyer who, he believed, would take his case for free just to get his name in the newspaper.

But when John met Fred Warren Bennett on May 23 in the Baltimore City Jail, he changed his mind about public defenders. Bennett, a short feisty man with a carefully trimmed beard and moustache, gave John what he later described as an awe-inspiring pitch.

"What kind of attorney do you want representing you?" Bennett asked. "There are three things to consider. First, is he a criminal lawyer or some guy who does civil and tax work too? Is he any good? Does he get people off? Is he respected and feared by prosecutors?

"Second, is he familiar with the Baltimore courts? Does he know the prosecutor and the judges? Does he know how the game is played here?

"And last, can he put in the time and financial resources necessary for a big case like this?"

The Federal Public Defender's office in Baltimore could do everything John needed and do it better than anyone else, Bennett claimed. It had two full-time criminal investigators at its disposal, huge financial resources, sufficient time, and, best of all, it had Fred Warren Bennett.

At age forty-three, Bennett had spent nearly half his life practicing criminal law—always on the side of the defendant. "I'm too liberal to prosecute," he explained to me later. "I wouldn't be comfortable getting up and asking for *one* day of jail time for anybody."

After graduating from American University in 1966, Bennett spent twelve years in private practice, often taking criminal cases that no one else would touch. Even his wife frequently tired of Fred Bennett's penchant for defending the dregs of society, particularly after one sensational rape–murder case when a neighbor said that she hoped Fred Bennett "fried" along with his client in the electric chair.

But Bennett never questioned his own motives, and he met anyone who criticized him with the coolness of an attorney with justice on his side.

Most of the time Bennett was able to convince his critics that everyone deserved a fair trial and the best attorney possible. The fact that he taught Sunday school at a Lutheran church and slept well at night attested to his own satisfaction with his reasoning.

In 1978, Bennett moved into public defender work in a crime-infested suburban county of Washington, D.C. His office oversaw five thousand cases per year, and he handled the most sensational of them. Often he became so emotionally involved in the cases that it threatened his health. Once he sobbed openly in court after a client was convicted during an emotional trial. Later, he took over the Federal Public Defenders Office.

John was impressed by Bennett's enthusiasm and obvious salesmanship, but that wasn't the deciding factor.

"Fred believed me when I told him something," John explained later. "I liked that."

Bennett quickly realized the case against John was persuasive. Wolfinger and Hunter had done a masterful job. So Bennett approached John about negotiating a guilty plea. He explained his plan in nautical terms.

"We are on a sinking ship," he told John. "So are Arthur, Michael, and Jerry Whitworth. Whoever gets off the ship first and gets to the U.S. Attorney is going to get the best deal. Whoever is left on the ship after a deal is cut gets screwed and sinks."

The trick, Bennett explained, is knowing when to jump ship.

"If we appear too eager," he said, "then we aren't going to get as good a deal as if we hang in there for a while and file motions, threaten to litigate, and make them come to us. But we've got to be careful not to overdo it or we'll be the ones who go down."

The only person that John really had to worry about, Bennett added, was Jerry Whitworth.

Arthur didn't have much to offer in exchange for a deal and Michael already had confessed. But Jerry had provided John documents for ten years and the government was anxious to know how much harm those classified secrets had done.

Bennett put in a telephone call to Whitworth's two attorneys and talked openly to them about plea negotiations. Both sides agreed to keep each other informed about such dealings.

With John's approval, Bennett launched a two-prong defense. Publicly, Bennett attacked the government's case full force. Unlike Arthur's attorneys, Bennett's posture was to make life as difficult as possible for federal prosecutors.

But behind the scenes, Bennett worked hard at trying to cut a deal for John.

"I knew I was down the toilet," John recalled. "The press and politicians were responsible for that. It was going to be impossible for me to get a fair trial with all the leaks by the Navy and fucking politicians calling me the worst spy in history. So Fred suggested we adopt what he called a 'slow guilty plea.' We were going to drive them insane by appealing everything for the next ten years. Obviously, I'd refuse to testify or talk about what I had given to the Soviets or about the tradecraft that we used unless a deal was cut."

John knew he was headed to prison for life, but he also knew that the parole board and prison system operate under mandatory guidelines that could make it possible for him to be paroled, no matter how unpopular he was, if he played his cards right. He also wanted to do something to help Michael.

"I didn't want Michael behind bars all of his life," he said. "Michael had to be the first one out and later I could join him."

So John agreed with Bennett about negotiating and on July 2, they held their first secret meeting with the government. "We had agreed to a very limited debriefing of John to show his bona fide credibility," Bennett recalled. The government was anxious to find out the identities of John's fellow spies because some questions had been raised about the appearance of the letter A in John's notes.

During the four-hour debriefing session, John insisted that only Arthur, Jerry, and Michael had provided classified information to him. Gary Walker, he said, hadn't passed anything, and the letter A meant nothing. It was just another code name for Whitworth.

When asked to describe the kinds of documents that he had stolen, John announced glibly, "If I had access to it, color it gone."

But John became nervous when he was asked how he started as a spy.

"John started telling us this wild and totally ridiculous story," Hunter recalled later, "about how he went down to apply for a job at a Yellow Cab Company in Norfolk and met these two mysterious characters, and it was so awful, I felt funny writing this stuff down. It was just total nonsense."

John was given a polygraph test after the briefing.

The machine indicated that John had been deceptive in two areas. He had lied about the number of persons helping him spy and about how he got started.

The lie detector results alarmed Bennett. The government was not going to be interested in plea bargaining if John intended to lie. He quickly huddled with his client in the corner.

"What the hell happened?"

"I once strapped a money belt on my mother when we were in Europe," John said, explaining why the machine had indicated John was deceptive when asked about his spying partners.

"How about the other?"

"I lied about that, Fred, 'cause I got started by walking into the Soviet embassy," John explained. "How can I tell them that without blowing our defense?"

"At that point," Fred Bennett recalled later, "John hadn't even told me about the Soviet embassy. That was one piece of information he hadn't been candid with me on. He had told me the story about the cab company."

Bennett returned to the bargaining table.

"Okay," Bennett said, "my client assures me that there are no other people involved. John had trouble with the polygraph machine because of some guilt feelings about his mother and a money belt and that's all there is to that. There is no A.

"Secondly, my client can't go into how he got started as a spy because it would reveal the cornerstone of our defense."

Bennett thought he had been convincing, but as he surveyed the faces in the room, he had a sinking feeling. "The debriefing had turned into a fiasco," he recalled. "Here we were trying to show how credible John was and he blew the polygraph."

The government held another debriefing session with John shortly before Arthur's trial in August. This time, federal prosecutors wanted to talk about Jerry Whitworth. John had plenty to say.

"I never would have squealed on Jerry," John told me later. "I would have simply adopted a policy of hanging tough and telling the government, 'Fuck you!' But when Fred showed me the RUS letters, I was really pissed. Jerry had tried to sell me out, so as far as I was concerned, all promises were off."

John was convincing, Hunter recalled, when he described Jerry's participation as a spy. He made it clear that if the government gave him a chance, he could provide more than enough rope to hang Jerry. Still, the government held back.

John had followed Arthur's trial in the newspapers and on television and had been furious with the outcome. He later bitterly accused the government of using Arthur to get to him. "I knew exactly what they were doing," John said. "That trial was a demonstration put on for my benefit. It was like they took Art in a room and tied him to a chair and beat him with rubber hoses and then said to me, 'See, you motherfucker, see what we did to your brother. Now just watch what we're going to do to your son.' I hated those bastards for what they did to Art."

The trial scared John. If the government could convince a federal judge that Arthur, who had never met with any Russians, was guilty, then how hard would it be to convict John?

Bennett made one more effort to cut a deal. He spoke with several persons in the U.S. Attorney's office in Baltimore. He was told that John's case was simply too political for a plea bargain. No one at the Justice Department was willing to negotiate a deal because of the heat they'd get from the press, Pentagon, and Congress.

On September 4, Bennett received an angry telephone call from James Larson, one of Whitworth's two attorneys. Larson had just learned from the U.S. Attorney's office in San Francisco that John Walker had been cooperating with the government by squealing on Jerry Whitworth. Larson was furious because he thought Bennett and he had agreed to advise each other before either entered into plea negotiations. Why had the government told Whitworth's attorneys about the debriefings? Obviously, the Justice Department was playing an old game. It was telling Jerry that John had talked in the hope that Jerry would offer to testify against John.

After he received Larson's call, Bennett decided there wasn't much chance of a plea bargain and he began preparing for John's trial in late October. But for the first time in his career, Bennett was stumped.

"Finally I decided that we would concede everything during my opening statement and then say, 'So what?' We were going to argue that the FBI couldn't prove John was meeting the Soviets. It wasn't much, but it was all we had."

What Bennett didn't know was that the Justice Department was also worried about John's trial. The problem was Jerry Whitworth. Jerry was claiming he was innocent and refusing to cooperate. He seemed to think he could beat the charges against him, and several Justice Department attorneys regretfully agreed. There was simply not enough evidence to convict Whitworth—unless John Walker testified against him. John was the only person who could prove that Jerry had spied.

The only person who wasn't distressed before his approaching trial was John. "I was really getting excited about it," he told me later. "I wanted to see fucking Barbara's lying face and Laura's fucking lying face. I know I am bad, and I know what I did, but these bitches didn't have to lie about me and Art to the FBI, the way they had, you know, adding a bunch of stuff to their stories that didn't happen."

John was beginning to enjoy the notoriety. A national magazine sent him a letter naming him one of the ten top newsmakers of 1985. Every major television network and news program had requested an interview.

Five days before John's trial, the government contacted Bennett. If John would testify against Jerry, a deal would be cut to help Michael.

John quickly agreed.

"I told Fred that he had timed it perfectly," John recalled. "We weren't going to be the ones that sank with the ship."

# 77

One month after Jerry Whitworth was arrested, he wrote a letter affirming his innocence to Geneva Green, his longtime friend and loyal supporter in Muldrow. Geneva was only one of Jerry's friends who figured the government had made a mistake. Nearly everyone who knew Jerry took his side. His mother, Agnes Morton, led the way. "Jerry loves the United States," she explained. "Why, he was born right here in Oklahoma . . . he was no New York person, no Los Angeles person. He was raised in the country. He's well thought of by everyone, no meanness, no trouble. These charges are enough to drive anyone to an insane asylum."

Jerry perpetuated the myth by writing dozens of letters to people he had known and asking them for help. But whatever their previous differences, it was Agnes who provided Jerry with his strongest support.

"My mother and I became very close," Jerry confided to a friend later. "I was able to make peace with her." In Jerry's mind, the support that Agnes gave him after his arrest finally convinced him—his mother *really* did love him as a son.

They didn't have much time to enjoy their new relationship. Six weeks after Jerry was arrested, Agnes was killed in a car accident outside Muldrow. She was returning home from Sallisaw, where she had met with a lawyer on Jerry's behalf.

After Agnes died, Geneva Green became Jerry's most vocal defender back in Muldrow. She wrote to him religiously and filled three huge scrapbooks with newspaper clippings about him. She was confident that once he was free, the two of them could sit down together on the couch in her living room and look through the clippings and laugh about how silly the entire incident had been. Geneva even offered to mortgage her modest home in order to help Jerry financially.

Jerry's defiant attitude changed once James Larson told him that John had agreed to testify. Like attorneys Meekins, Donnelly, and Bennett had done before him, Larson now told his client that winning acquittal would be nearly impossible. In February 1986, Larson and Jerry's other attorney, Tony Tamburello, contacted the U.S. Attorney's office with a plea bargain. Jerry would submit to complete debriefing, freely undergo polygraph exams, and would plead guilty to "a combination of counts," including a charge that carried up to a life sentence. In return, Jerry wanted to be promised that he would not be recalled into the Navy and court-martialed, and that Brenda would not be charged.

It seemed to Larson and Tamburello to be a reasonable request, but U.S. Attorney Joseph P. Russoniello quickly ruled out any deal. In a short response, he wrote:

> It is the position of the Department of Justice that . . . a full exposition of the entire conspiracy in a public trial is of paramount importance. . . . In our view there is a compelling need for an accurate public account of the scope of this conspiracy and Mr. Whitworth's role in it. Mr. Whitworth's strident and repeated assertions of having been framed by an overzealous FBI and a lying John Walker must be corrected. We firmly believe that public revelation of the overwhelming evidence against Mr. Whitworth will provide the true picture.

Once again, personal ambition and politics were playing a central role. The Justice Department's dealings with John and Michael Walker had outraged some Pentagon officials, particularly Navy Secretary John F. Lehman, Jr. In a highly unusual move in Washington, Lehman had publicly condemned the plea bargain. "We in the Navy are disappointed at the plea bargain," Lehman told the press. "It continues a tradition in the Justice Department of treating espionage as just another white-collar crime and we think that it should be in a very different category." John Walker's actions, he said, "were traitorous acts and ought to be treated differently than insider trading."

Defense Secretary Caspar W. Weinberger rebuked Lehman two days later. "Secretary Lehman now understands that he did not have all the facts concerning the matter before he made several injudicious and incorrect statements with respect to the agreement," Weinberger said.

Now that it had shaken John's hand, the Justice Department had no choice politically but to crucify Jerry Whitworth. It had to prove that the price it had paid by cutting a deal with John had been worth it.

Jerry's trial began on March 25, 1986, and it quickly turned into one of the most elaborate spy trials ever presented by the government. The Justice Department called dozens of witnesses, introduced hundreds of exhibits, and provided the public with an unprecedented look into the secret world of ciphers, cryptographic machines, and military communications. For the first time in history, the government brought an actual cipher machine into a courtroom to show jurors.

But the most explosive evidence came from John Walker himself, who revealed for the first time, in public, the inner workings of his spy ring during five days of testimony. While John's testimony grabbed the headlines, but it was his behind-the-scenes cooperation that, he felt, helped federal prosecutors the most.

"I really began to feel like part of the government's team," John recalled. "Before I left, I posed for pictures with the prosecution. . . ."

One night, John was moved into the same Oakland jail as Arthur, who also was a witness. It was the first time the two brothers had met since being arrested and, feeling rather festive, they called me at my home. "We're just sitting here in the recreation room watching television and having some coffee," Arthur reported cheerfully. "We're the only two in this cell block and they're treating us like celebrities."

"Hey, I'm famous!" John said proudly after Arthur handed him the telephone. Someone in the jail, he said, had asked him to autograph his picture in an encyclopedia's year-end review.

The defense called Geneva Green as a witness. "I truly believed Jerry was innocent," Geneva told me later, "and I was proud to get up there and tell everyone that he was my friend. I didn't understand, though, why Jerry didn't take the stand and defend himself."

On July 10, James Larson made what to Geneva Green was a shocking disclosure in his closing statement to the jury. "The writer of the RUS letters was Jerry Whitworth," Larson acknowledged.

Geneva felt sick! Jerry really was a spy! "I was angry at first," she recalled. "I'd been duped. We all had. We all had believed Jerry was really innocent, but now we knew. I felt betrayed, personally betrayed. Jerry had lied to us all."

After the trial, Jerry said during a presentencing evaluation that he was "extremely sorry" for passing classified information, but claimed that he did not pass John all of the documents that John had said.

> I wanted out basically all the time. I just couldn't keep doing it, but I did. I never really did what he wanted me to do, but only gave him what I thought would satisfy him. I would never go outside my duty area, which is what he wanted.

The person who conducted the evaluation of Jerry described him this way:

> Upon interview, Whitworth, for the most part, exhibits a flat effect. He is given to occasional inappropriate laughter, despite what appears to be a rather constricted emotional tone. His expressions of remorse are absent in emotional tone, and he becomes tearful only when discussing the subject of his wife and his marriage. It is quite clear that Jerry Whitworth exhibits very little insight into his behavior and psychological state and is prone to explanation and description, rather than understanding. . . . It will take time and professional assistance for him to accept, on the deepest levels, the gravity of his crime and the effects on the country and those around him.

On an emotional level, a review of Jerry Whitworth's life suggests an intense need for acceptance and an almost pathological need to please John Walker. . . . Equally clearly, John Walker preyed on Jerry Whitworth's vulnerabilities. Although there are many in our society who are equally vulnerable as Jerry Whitworth, few have been as manipulated. . . .

# 78

Special Agent Robert Hunter should have felt exultant on November 7, 1986, as he sat in a Baltimore courtroom listening to Judge Alexander Harvey II formally sentence John to life in prison. Hunter had played a major role in the successful investigation, arrest, prosecution, and debriefing of John. No other government official had spent as much time with John as Hunter.

By this time, Jerry Whitworth had been found guilty and sentenced to 365 years in prison with no possibility of parole until he reached the age of 107. Jerry also had been fined $410,000. The sentence came after the government made public a statement by a former high-ranking KGB official, Vitaly Yurchenko, who had defected and told the FBI that the Walker spy ring was "the most important operation in the KGB's history" and had allowed the deciphering of "one million" classified Navy messages. Jerry was described by the judge who sentenced him as "one of the most spectacular spies of the century" and a man who represented the "evil of banality."

"Jerry Whitworth is zero at the bone," said Judge John P. Vukasin, Jr. "He believes in nothing. His life is devoted to determining the wind direction and how he can make a profit from the coming storm."

Arthur Walker had been sentenced to life in prison and a $250,000 fine by Judge Clarke, who said Arthur's "greatest culpability is his silence."

Arthur should have "counseled John, at the very least . . . if he didn't want to tell on him."

Now John faced Judge Alexander Harvey II.

Based on the government's plea bargain, John's sentence already had been decided. He would be sentenced to two life terms, plus 100 years, all to be served concurrently, making him eligible for parole in ten years. Michael would receive two twenty-five-year terms and three ten-year terms, all concurrent, making him eligible for parole after serving eight years.

"One is seized," Judge Harvey told John, "with an overwhelming feeling of revulsion that a human being could ever be as unprincipled as you."

John said nothing, but he later recalled his thoughts.

"I figured Harvey would grandstand for the press," John told me later. "Fuck 'em!"

Hunter was troubled after Michael and John left the courtroom. The FBI had given Arthur another polygraph and it had indicated that he was being deceptive when he was asked if he had been a spy while in the Navy. John had failed another polygraph too when asked about how he had gotten started as a spy. Meanwhile, the FBI had reviewed John's story about going to the Soviet embassy in Washington and determined that there was no heavy iron fence around the embassy in late 1967 as John had claimed. John's version of his encounter with an embassy employee also was amazingly similar to an account in *The Falcon and the Snowman,* which John liked so much. On the other hand, Hunter had asked John to draw the floorplan of the embassy for him, and what John drew matched perfectly with the FBI's records. "There is no question in my mind that John Walker had been in the Soviet embassy," Hunter recalled. But when?

What troubled Hunter most was that no one might ever be able to discover the truth because of a mix-up months earlier before Arthur's trial. Shortly after John and Arthur were arrested, Fred Bennett had telephoned Samuel Meekins, Jr., and requested copies of all of Arthur's statements to the FBI. Meekins obliged and Bennett showed the statements to John. When it came time for Hunter to question John about Arthur, John told the exact same stories as Arthur had.

"He knew exactly what Arthur had told us," Hunter said, "and John did not deviate on it at all. It was impossible for us to catch them in lies after that."

His FBI colleagues told Hunter that none of this mattered. The good guys had won. Hunter had done his job. All the spies had been captured and imprisoned. Hunter received a letter of commendation from FBI Director William H. Webster. It felt good, said Hunter, but it also was incomplete. Hunter had always been able to empathize with people and he had developed a genuine warmth for Barbara and Laura, and even Michael and Arthur. But not John. There was an invisible barrier around John that Hunter couldn't pass through. During one of their final interviews, Hunter had tried to talk on a personal level with John.

"We had spent a lot of time together," Hunter recalled. "A lot of time, and I had been wondering. I mean, this was just incredible, here was a guy who had been in espionage all these years and gotten his best friend, and brother, and then his son involved. He had tried to get Laura involved too and I had yet to see any remorse, so I decided to ask him."

Hunter approached John gingerly.

"John, we have been together a long time now and talked about a lot of things together, but I've never seen any indication of remorse. Do you feel remorse, any sorrow about what you've done?"

John's face became red.

"Remorse?" he replied. "What are you talking about? Even if I had any, I wouldn't display it to you. What do you want me to tell you, that I have remorse so you can go home and say, 'I got John Walker to admit he was remorseful'?"

"I knew just about everything you could find out about John Walker," Hunter recalled later. And yet Hunter felt at that moment that he really knew "nothing at all" about him.

After they were sentenced, John and Michael were allowed a few minutes together.

"I'm going to kill myself," John told his son. "When I get to a penitentiary, I'm going to do it."

Anyone else might have been suspicious, but Michael believed him.

"Don't do it, Dad, please," Michael said.

"I've done everything I wanted in life," John said. "Now it's time for me to just get the fuck out of here."

"Dad, I know you're gonna think this is stupid," Michael said, "but I've been reading the Bible and it helps. It really helps, man. Perhaps—"

John cut him short.

"I've tried that, Mike, it don't work for me, but, hey, it's a good idea with you. It will help with your parole."

Then John told Michael about a dream.

"I had a dream about us, Mike," John said. "You and I were together in this room and I kept telling you to lay down on this bed of nails. You didn't want to, but I said, 'Goddamnit, Michael, lay down!' and you finally did exactly what I told you."

"It's okay, Dad," Michael said. "We're still buddies, still partners, right?"

John nodded.

"It felt really good," John told me later. "Because Michael was willing to take care of me."

After he had been in prison a few months, Michael decided to meet with his mother for the first time since his arrest.

"I hated my mother at that point and, the truth was, I also hated my dad," he told me later. "I began to realize I had always hated them. I hated half of my mother—the alcoholic half, the cruel half. And I hated half of my father—the selfish half, the manipulative half.

"But they were my parents. My mother. My father. And I had no choice. I had to love them too—didn't I?"

# PART SEVEN

---

# *JOHN*

*Even so we should abandon
all sentimentality in our views of the
traitor, and recognize him as a
thief and a liar.*

REBECCA WEST
*The New Meaning of Treason*

# 79

The noisy electric motor slowly opened the prison cellblock gate. I stepped past the reinforced steel bars into a small waiting area as a ceiling-mounted camera watched. After the gate slammed shut, I heard a loud *thunk,* which meant the steel door to the right had been unlocked by an unseen guard. A voice through the speaker in the ceiling directed me to an interview room barely big enough for the two chairs and the metal table inside. The air had a smell of stale tobacco, and the fluorescent lighting was so harsh I had to squint. Burnt orange paint had been applied so thickly to the walls that the concrete blocks were smooth. There were no windows.

A half hour later, a guard brought in John Walker, Jr. We shook hands and the guard left. We spoke casually, and then he began to talk about the FBI's handling of his case. "After I was arrested," he explained, "I told the FBI it wasn't the Soviet Union I was dealing with, and they went ahead and prosecuted my brother Art. They convicted Art of dealing with the Soviet Union based on no information at all. He was railroaded. Fred and I were negotiating a twenty-five-year sentence for Michael. And Art, who is obviously a lesser player, is crucified and gets multiple life sentences and fines.

"I knew they did that to get to me and I knew Michael was next, so I confessed really. I said, 'What do you want me to say? I'll say it.'

"After Art's trial, I said to them, 'Okay, *you* tell *me* how I did it,' and they said, 'Your brother Art said you told him that you went to the Soviet embassy.' Hey, what a great idea! Fucking wonderful! So I said, 'Yeah, that's exactly what happened. That's how it was!' and they said, 'Good, now you're telling the truth,' and they wrote that down.

"Don't you see? The FBI wouldn't accept the fact that I might have been dealing with anyone else. The FBI is preconditioned to think it is the Soviet Union, and they wouldn't have believed me if I had said it was anyone else but the Soviet Union. Period! That's the way bureaucrats think. The Soviets are the enemy. It's got to be the Soviets.

"Okay, this time, I got to admit, they were right because it *was* the Soviets. I did go to the Soviet embassy. I'm not going to lie to you. I want to tell the truth. But just think for a moment about the case against me."

By this time, I'd been thinking about it for almost two years. I'd been thinking, too, that John Walker's dissembling, paranoid, convoluted reasoning and illogic were getting on my nerves. The FBI was stupid. John Walker was clever. The FBI was out to get him through Arthur. Arthur was convicted on no information at all. The FBI was paranoid about the Soviet Union. That's why they didn't believe him. And so forth, round and round until I drew a mental picture of John Walker like a dog chasing his own tail, wondering why no one else was impressed with his courage and ingenuity.

"Barbara called in November," John continued. "I went to Vienna in January and made a delivery. The FBI didn't know it, right? Or *did* they? How could they *not* know? How could they not follow me after she warned them? I didn't do anything fancy. Granted, I used a false name on the domestic flight and changed my real name a bit on the international flight. But it wouldn't have been that hard to follow me.

"Okay, how do you know that they didn't follow me? What if they actually did follow me to Vienna, saw who I was dealing with and decided not to arrest me there because of who I met? Maybe I wasn't really dealing with the Soviets after all and the FBI knew that but didn't want the public to know. Consequently, back in the United States, where they could have caught both of us, they somehow managed to fuck up."

I wanted to point out to John that the FBI has no arrest powers overseas, and that, if anyone had been following him, it was more likely the CIA at that time and not the FBI. But he was intent on pursuing his own logic and I had learned from earlier discussions that John didn't react well when challenged. So I let him continue. By this time, he was becoming animated and was mocking the FBI by pretending he was an agent explaining to a reporter in a shrill voice what had happened.

" 'Oh, golly, Mr. Reporter, we fucked up! We picked up the signal can at the dead drop! Isn't that a shame? And, gosh darn, we fucked up and only caught John, and the other guy, the Russian, got away because one of our agents ran away with the bag before the Russian could get it! Gosh, we are sorry about that!' "

Returning to his normal speaking voice, John continued, "Maybe I was set up. Think about it. Isn't it possible that the FBI went over there and watched me deliver documents to someone who I thought was a Russian, but who really was someone else? Maybe the FBI wanted me to make that delivery in January because they knew what Michael had stolen and wanted it delivered into someone else's hands. Maybe all of this is a giant charade to get the Soviets to take me in a prison exchange. Who knows, I might really be working for the CIA. What better cover than to accuse someone of being a Russian spy, trade him to the Soviets and then actually use him as a spy? Think about that."

I thought about it. I thought about how John had sold secrets to the Soviets for almost eighteen years, the incalculable damage he'd done to his country, and I started to feel angry. Angry at the distortions, angry at his inane and puerile suggestions that there was a "much larger game afoot." Angry that he had harmed those who had loved him, emotionally crippling his wife, manipulating his best friend and brother, corrupting his children until Michael became a warped image of himself.

"Even the fucking President of the United States of America," John continued, "thinks I'm a spy, but this all might be part of a great scam. Maybe I don't even know what is happening here. You see, nearly anything is possible."

And so it was.

I asked, "What about Michael, Arthur, and Jerry?"

He replied quickly, "What about them?"

"Do you feel responsible?"

"The worst thing I feel sorry about," John said, "so much so it is hard to talk about, is Michael. He is my son, and I did what no parent should do. I put him in danger. He couldn't say no to me, and I knew it. There is no justification for my action, except, as I have said, I really believed I did it for him, for his own good."

For a brief moment, as John said, "There is no justification," I thought I was about to see, perhaps for the first time, a human being. But then John added the rest. As always, there was an excuse, an out. His life was little more than layer upon layer of rationalization. His father was a drunk—that's why John became a teenage thief. Barbara nagged constantly—that's why he became a spy. Blah, blah, blah. The man was hopeless and, against all my instincts as a reporter, I wanted to tell him what a miserable human being he was. But something in his words kept me from responding. There is a certain fascination in listening to a deranged man who can excuse his own evil with the mere wave of his hand, as if shooing away a pesky fly.

"I regret what has happened to Michael," John continued, "but he was an adult, and I gave him plenty of chances to say no. You see, it is so easy to blame me, but what did I really do? In every case I was dealing with weak people and I was trying to help them out."

I looked at John and our eyes met. He paused and then looked away. He knew I didn't believe him. But he continued anyway.

"Art, when it comes to Art, yeah, I got some regrets, he's my brother. But I had loaned a ton of money to Walker Enterprises and Art didn't put the effort into the business that it required. You need to be a workaholic to make a business go. Sure, he damn near killed himself worrying, but he didn't put the time in the business. He worried, and he waited, like most fat-ass Americans, for good luck to come along. Well, I don't believe in luck. You make your own good luck and Art couldn't cut it. Worse yet, he didn't have the balls to say to his kids, 'Go get a job and earn your own money for college.' And he didn't have the balls to tell Rita to get off her butt and stop watching soap operas and get a job or help retarded kids or do something. He was stupid. His family used him. What did he ever get from them? What is he getting now? Rita is so angry now she won't send him any money, not even for cigarettes. My brother has to smoke cigarette butts that he finds on the fucking jail floor. 'Hey nigger, will you kick that butt over here for me to smoke?'

"I was Art's only real friend. Don't you see? Don't you get it? I had to salvage that dummy. I got him out of debt and he never paid me back. Never. There is no way Art should have been taking home a paycheck each week, but he did and it came from my spy money. And then Rita wouldn't even be in the same room as me.

"I feel bad about Whitworth. He was my best friend. I'm sure he views me as Lucifer for obvious reasons. But Whitworth enjoyed the spying and he was good at it. He worked at getting good access and was a damn good spy.

"On the other side of the coin, even though Whitworth was good, he was a flake. Don't you see it? He was weak too! He had to have a crutch. He wanted to believe he was doing something noble for the Israelis. What bullshit, but it was something he could grab onto to keep him from having to deal with reality. He and Art were living a fool's paradise. They didn't want to admit what they were doing and what kind of persons they really are. They still don't want to admit it even now. But come on. They were big boys. They weren't kids. They were veteran warriors. Top notch sailors. They knew what they were getting into and they did it, just like I predicted they would.

"You see, everyone wants to blame me, but who did they run to when they needed money? The FBI thinks I got money hidden somewhere. How stupid. My fucking family took it all. Now you tell me. Who was really lying the most? Art, sitting in suburbia with a witch and a *Better Homes and Gardens* house and all the time he had a fucking mistress and was a spy; Jerry, a patron of Israel and intellectual follower of Ayn Rand and all the time a fucking spy for the KGB? Or me?

"You see, I never pretended really to be anything but what I was. I knew exactly what I was and why I was doing it.

"You know, I gave every one of them at least twenty chances to say no. But they didn't, did they? That's because deep down every one of them wanted the fucking money! Just like every fucking American wants the money or a promotion or some edge on everyone else. Everyone has a scam. Everyone has an angle. You see in the end, Barbara, my brother Arthur, Whitworth, and even Laura, every one of them really except Michael, in the end they all wanted the fucking money. So why can't they admit it? If you want the truth, the truth is this. I told each of them whatever they wanted to goddamn hear, whatever crutch they needed, as long as it got them to do what I wanted them to do. I didn't give a shit what I said or promised. And it worked, until the money stopped. And that's the point, really. You see, what I did and said didn't really matter. It was the money, the money, that mattered. As long as they got paid, then it worked. The spy ring worked. But when Whitworth screwed up the payments, then everything went to hell.

"Take Barbara, my lovely ex-wife. Oh, did you know she still loves me? I heard her say it on television after my arrest. 'Oh, I still love him.' That shows how sick that fucker really is. If you dislike me, then I can understand you standing up and beating the shit out of me. I can handle that kind of confrontation. But this? She sleeps with my brother and turns me in to the cops and then says she loves me! Jesus! Tell me you hate me, Barbara, because I sure hate you. You know why she did it? For the money, man. The money. She wanted to get even with me for sleeping around on her, for not loving her, and she knew if she turned me in, there were going to be books and interviews and television programs that would pay her to be on them.

"I hate all of them and I don't need them. Any of them. You see, the truth is that I don't need people and that's what really makes me different. It makes me fucking powerful, man! My stupid daughter Cynthia writes to me and says, 'Daddy, I still love you! I want you to know that I will always love you!' Who needs that bullshit! Tell me something useful, information I can use. Tell me what Barbara and Laura are going to do next to screw up my life."

John seemed momentarily pensive, then continued. "Maybe it's something I learned from my father. My wonderful alcoholic father. He didn't need anyone unless they could buy him some booze. Then, he sure as hell needed you. You were his best goddamn friend, his favorite son. Fuck yes, he loved you when you bought him his whiskey.

"After my arrest, my dad told reporters that I and Art weren't his sons. Thanks, Dad. After all I did for him. Thanks a lot, Dad. But you see, I know. I know that if I was out of this fucking jail and I drove up to his house and offered to buy him a bottle, then I'd be good old Jack, his favorite son."

John always seemed to talk about his father when we met so I mentioned it to him, and he became irritated.

"Ahh, we're going to play shrink now, huh?" he said, mimicking a thick German accent. "It is clear that the subject Walker suffered from a neurosis caused during his early childhood." Then, in his normal voice, "Bullshit! Sure he fucked me up. He fucked up all his kids. So what?"

I handed John an article from *The Washington Post* in which several psychologists had evaluated John Walker based on what they had read about him and what they already knew about spies. John had read the article when it was published in June 1985, and remembered it with obvious spite.

"These son of a bitches don't even know me," he said. "Fred brought a shrink in here to talk to me to see if we could plead insanity as a defense, and when the guy got ready to leave, he says to me: 'John, you are one of the sanest men I've ever met.' I'm not the one with the problem, man. It's not *me*. It's *society* that's all fucked up. How can you not see that?"

I didn't reply.

John continued. "I keep reading about how I am the worst spy since the Rosenbergs gave away the bomb. Okay, show me. Where is the damage? Where's the invasion by the communists? Where is the Red Dawn?

"Guess what? There wasn't any and there's not going to be one. Guess what? All you fucking stupid Americans who sit around all day watching the boob tube—it ain't gonna happen. There isn't going to be a war. That's all a game, man, to keep the defense contractors rich.

"This is all we did. We let the Russians read our mail just like we read their mail. That's it. That's all. The United States monitors every international telephone call and every open circuit in the world. All I did was sell those poor bastards the same access.

"If a war started today, then you could say, 'Okay, Walker, you did your shit! You profited from what you did! A war has just started because of the shit you did!' I'd say, 'Okay, I agree with you. I sold stuff that caused a war. I fucked up. Take me out back and shoot me because of it.' That would be fair. I'd go even farther. If a war between us and the Russians started in the next three and a half years, then you can take me out and shoot me between the eyes or let me hang myself.

"But what has happened to me is *unfair*. I've been destroyed by the government for no real reason and so has Art and Mike. Our lives have been ruined and these prison sentences are just like salt in the wounds. If they let us out now, what would we do? They've taken all our money. Do you think anyone would hire us? It's really unfair.

"You see, it's like getting drunk and going ninety miles down the road. If a pedestrian is there and you hit and kill him, fine, then the state executes the son of a bitch for murder. But there wasn't any pedestrian there for me to hit. So my drunk driving didn't matter. For godsakes we aren't at war with the Russians! Doesn't anybody understand that?

"I sincerely in my heart felt that selling classified documents wouldn't do any damage and, you know what, history has *proved* me right. Nothing has happened! So how much damage did John Walker do? None. Absolutely none."

John Walker spoke with such conviction that I was convinced that *he* actually believed exactly that.

I stood. We shook hands and I left him. Outside, past the cellblock gate, beyond the reinforced steel bars, the sun beat down on the black asphalt. It was sweltering. How different that afternoon was from the first time that I had met John Walker.

As a young reporter, I had once spent fourteen months writing stories about convicts and prisons in Oklahoma, and during that period I met and interviewed dozens of inmates. One night in January 1977 I talked to several men on death row at the Oklahoma State Penitentiary. It was a special night because the state of Utah was about to execute Gary Gilmore, the first convicted murderer to be put to death in more than a decade after a U.S. Supreme Court ruling rendered most death penalty laws unconstitutional. Each man on death row had a radio and all of them were listening to the same station as I went from cell to cell. The radio kept giving news updates about Gilmore and last minute appeals to spare him. These men were Oklahoma's worst criminals, and yet I discovered something in their personalities that I later came to believe was lacking in John's.

I had liked John when I first met him. He seemed ordinary, if not pedestrian. He was reserved. He spoke intelligently and articulated his points with wit.

But the longer I spent time with him—listening to him talk about his life during a series of all-day sessions, relaxing with him at lunch over sandwiches and soup served to us in various county jails, speaking to him long-distance as he crisscrossed the country going from one federal prison to the next—the more I came to realize that his banality was more frightening than the hostility and anger that I had witnessed on death row the night Gary Gilmore was executed.

There was a shallowness and emptiness to John, a lack of any sort of spiritual dimension in his life, a lack of any notion of loyalty to friends, family, and nation. Betrayal came easily to John because he was loyal only to himself.

In doing research for this story, I interviewed various intelligence analysts and I began hearing over and over the same phrase: "attitudinal loyalty." Supposedly our citizens have it and citizens of the Soviet Union don't, especially the non-Russians within the Soviet empire. Attitudinal loyalty is supposed to be important. It is supposed to make soldiers fight for their country without threats or without ostentatious displays of state-organized patriotism. It is supposed to keep the average citizen from deserting or betraying his country. It's in the blood, so to speak.

John Walker, Arthur Walker, and Jerry Whitworth undoubtedly had an attitudinal loyalty to their country. They were superpatriots. John kept a photograph of President Ronald Reagan on his desk at Confidential Reports. Laura Walker and Barbara Walker considered themselves good Americans, as did Rachel Walker and Michael Walker. But they did not go to the authorities when they first discovered John's secret. They remained loyal to a man who gave them nothing in return. Michael Walker did his father's bidding without a thought to the question of right or wrong: that question never once entered into his decision to become a spy.

How could this be?

Perhaps it is time for intelligence experts to rethink this central concept of attitudinal loyalty, this idea that Americans don't betray their country to foreign powers the way that Europeans are perceived to do quite regularly. We trust our citizens to an extent that is almost unknown in history and unheard of in most other countries. This is as it should be. However, we live in a society where money is no longer a mere commodity, but a sacrament. Money is power, possessions, persona, sex, and status.

John was able to separate his patriotism and his spying, and rationalize both, as he rationalized everything in his life.

But what was it about John Walker that gave him a hold over persons that superseded their love of country? I am not a psychiatrist. As a writer, I am, at best, a chronicler of today's events, tomorrow's history. But at the risk of attempting to analyze, I believe there were occasions during my interviews with John when I saw into the soul of the spy. This is what I saw:

John Walker, Jr., had an uncanny skill to see the frailties of those around him. He was able to identify the flaws in their personalities and, like a chameleon, he became whatever he needed to become, whatever they wanted him to be, in order to take advantage of them, manipulate them, and profit from their weaknesses. This was not done by chance. It was calculated, precise.

Jerry Whitworth, Arthur Walker, Barbara Walker, and Michael Walker were drawn to John and did what he asked even though he openly abused them. He became their master, in part because he convinced each of them that without him, they were somehow incomplete. He was superior, had accomplished more, was successful. They welcomed him and, like a leech, he drew their blood.

John fled from strong persons. Whenever he met someone with a complete personality—from the unbending priests and nuns at St. Patrick's High School in Scranton; to Bill Metcalf, the Norfolk Navy officer who complained about John's morals and gave him his first and only poor evaluation as a sailor; to Mike Bell, the tough Wackenhut detective who refused to bend his rules to fit John's schemes—John immediately retreated.

John preferred a world where there were no white knights, no black knights, no knights at all. There were only gray people drifting in an atmosphere of moral weightlessness. It was this type of world that reflected John's own image, like a mirror. "Everyone is corrupt ... everyone has a scam."

John Walker was able to use his skill at discerning other people's weaknesses to destroy them, including his own son. John Walker had no moral center, only an unquenchable thirst to control, to obtain admiration and power, no matter what the cost, as long as someone else paid.

Most of the criminals whom I have met as a journalist seem to have had some moral code of conduct, however twisted and slim, beyond which they could not trespass without traces of guilt and occasional remorse.

John didn't.

He was totally without principle. There was no right or wrong, no morality or immorality, in his eyes. There were only his own wants, his own needs, whatever those might be at the moment. In John's world, only fools believed that they were their brothers' keepers.

John Walker did not show any remorse when Robert Hunter asked him about his crimes because he truly didn't feel any. This is why John could say to me, with all seriousness, during one of our last sessions together, "I have lived every fantasy that I have ever had. I've done everything I wanted to do. And the real mistake I made in life was letting myself be surrounded by weak people.

"My mistake was in caring about my brother, Arthur, and daughter, and best friend, and in trying to help them. In the end, they used me. Each of them used me. They brought me down. If anything," John concluded, "I am the real victim in this entire unpleasant episode."

This was John's truth, John's reality. And to John Walker that is all that really mattered.

As I walked to my car in the parking lot that hot afternoon after talking to John, I remembered something Barbara Walker had said about how John had changed during the early years of their marriage. "I had married a young sailor that liked to be called Jack, but Jack was becoming John and there was a difference." Jack had been playful, caring, loving. But John was none of those things. John worried only about himself and his gratification. The name change, she felt, was significant, and so do I.

Sitting behind the wheel of my car in the prison parking lot, I looked through the windshield at what now was John's home and I wondered: Whatever happened to Jack? If you were able to strip away all of the lies and rationalizations that surround John Walker's life, like a craftsman removing layers of old paint, would you find Jack Walker?

And then I answered my own question. No. Jack Walker no longer exists, if he ever did. There is only John, flashy Johnny Walker, private eye, daredevil pilot, KGB spy. If you removed the first layer of veneer, you would discover beneath it another, and yet another under it. And so on. In the end, you would learn that whatever had been inside had decayed long ago. John Walker's life had become nothing but a series of lies, myths, and illusions wrapped around an empty core. And that was all that remained.

I started my car and drove away.

# AUTHOR'S NOTE

This book is the story of John Walker, Jr., and the members of his spy ring. It is the result of over one hundred interviews with many of the people involved in this extraordinary affair, including members of the Walker family. I conducted twenty-three separate interviews with John Walker, lasting an average of seven hours each. I also met with Arthur Walker, Michael Walker, Barbara Joy Crowley Walker, Laura Walker Snyder, Cynthia Walker, Margaret (Peggy) Scaramuzzo Walker, Rita Frisch Walker, James Walker, Tina Walker, and John Walker, Sr. It is accurate to say that I have spent several hundred hours talking to immediate members of the Walker family, and many more with the other eighty-seven people interviewed.

From the start, John Walker's attorneys made it clear to me that John would only tell his story if he was compensated financially. As this book documents, John Walker does not do *anything* unless he benefits from it personally. John sold his country's secrets for money; he enlisted members of his family in his spy ring for money; and he would only tell his story for money.

Journalists do not like arrangements like this and I am no exception. But the more I learned about the case, the more I was convinced that a thorough and accurate account of one of the most heinous traitors in this country's history could not be written without full access to John Walker. It is for that reason that I entered into a personal contract with John and the other members of his family that remunerated them in exchange for their exclusive cooperation.

It should be noted as a matter of information that John Walker is very unlikely to benefit financially from our agreement. The Internal Revenue Service has placed a lien on John's assets and any income he receives for failing to pay income taxes on his earnings as a spy. Thus, ironically, any money received from this book will go to the United States government.

My contract with John stipulated that I have "sole discretion over the contents [of the book], which will not be subject to control or approval by John Walker." This is not "John Walker's book." All our conversations were on-the-record and I made no deals as to how John would be portrayed or what would be included in the book. Neither John nor any other member of the Walker family was permitted to read any of the manuscript before it was published.

In addition to the personal interviews I conducted, the book also relies on numerous trial transcripts and FBI reports, as well as documents that have not been made public previously, including John Walker's personal journals, family letters, grand jury testimony, and telephone conversations recorded by the FBI through wiretaps.

As noted above, besides the members of the Walker family I have mentioned, I interviewed eighty-seven other people who were involved in some aspect of this story. Among them were:

Philip Mark Snyder
Curt Christopher Walker
Frank Scaramuzzo
Roger Olson
Pamela K. Carroll
Charles "Chas" Bennett
Joseph "Joey" Long
Annie Crowley Nelson
Donald Clevenger
Bill Wilkinson
James Wightman
Frances Wightman
Robert Hunter
Jack Wagner
Joseph Wolfinger
Howard Sparks
Geneva Green
Willard Owens
Beulah Watts
Harold Watts
Sue Watts
Robert McNatt
Michael Bell
Philip Prince
Marie Hammond
Walter Price
Paul Culligan
Roberta Puma

Other persons who were interviewed but did not wish to have their names listed include teachers and friends of Michael Walker, naval co-workers of John Walker, former employees at Confidential Reports, persons investigated by John Walker, two relatives of the Walker family, and intelligence officials.

I interviewed Jerry Whitworth at the federal penitentiary in Leavenworth, Kansas. However, because he was in the midst of appealing his conviction, Whitworth declined to answer any questions about his relationship with John Walker. Therefore, my account of Whitworth's involvement in the spy ring is based upon information from the fifty-five-volume transcript of Whitworth's trial; interviews with his attorney, James Larson; a previously unpublished presentence report written by Dayle C. Carlson, Jr., who questioned Whitworth about his spying and friendship with John; interviews with FBI agents; FBI investigative reports; and interviews with John Walker. While my conversations with Whitworth were limited, I still found them valuable in studying his personality and background.

Readers should note that "Smiley," Bill Metcalf, Shirley McClanahan, Mary Ann Mason, Sheila Woods, and Windsor Murdock are pseudonyms used to protect the privacy of real persons. All quotes attributed to them are actual statements. All other persons in this book are identified by their correct names.

Statements by Michael O'Connor, Aaron Darnell Brown, Karen Margaret Barnett, Michael McElwee, and John Peterson were taken from their sworn testimony at Whitworth's trial.

At various times, I have chosen to let one person recall a specific incident. In such cases, these events were confirmed by at least *two* other persons, and usually more, before being included. The exception is John Walker's account of his meetings with the KGB. I have done my best to compare John's statements to me with his comments to the FBI, which used a polygraph machine to determine whether or not he was lying. I also have used John's financial records and personal journals to verify his trips overseas to meet the KGB. John showed an amazing ability to recall statements made to him by his two KGB handlers. Perhaps this is because he was always excited and keenly aware of what was happening when he met with them. In the few cases where I have been unable to substantiate what John Walker told me, I have used the words "John claimed" to warn the reader that his statements cannot be corroborated.

During interviews, I found that people often recalled the same events quite differently. I have noted major disparities in the book, usually by giving more than one account, but in minor cases, I have chosen the version that seemed most likely to be true.

I would like to thank several people for their help. My agent Nicholas Ellison spent countless hours working on this project. Author Nelson DeMille also read my initial drafts and made invaluable suggestions.

Without the help of defense attorneys Samuel Meekins, Jr., and Fred Warren Bennett, this book could not have been written. I am indebted to them for their candor and determination to see that all of the facts about the Walker case, even embarrassing ones, were made public. Attorney Christopher Brown also provided me with considerable help in regard to Michael Walker.

Walter Harrington, Patricia Hersch, and Gay Daly gave me excellent editorial guidance and moral support.

I would also like to thank Benjamin Bradlee, executive editor of *The Washington Post,* for granting me a leave of absence to write this book. My editors there, Jay Lovinger and Stephen Petranek, also offered valuable advice. Tony Germanotta, a reporter at *The Virginian-Pilot and The Ledger-Star,* proved a helpful source.

Others whose help I would like to acknowledge are Brian E. Crooks, Candace J. Vanderclute, Frank Fox, Linda Webb, Edward S. Stancheski, James Kalbaugh, Jay Myerson, Oliver Goodenough, Stanley J. Reed, Graeme W. Bush, Robert H. Powell III, John Y. Richardson, Jr., Raymond Teichman, Kathy Morris, Karen L. McClearyCale, Peter D. Miller, Lynn Smith, Dr. C.T. Shades, William Schwartz, John Fyfe, Jr., John Lefevere, members of United Christian Parish, and Fred Klein, my editor at Bantam Books.

My account of the murder of Georgi Markov was based on *KGB, Inside the World's Largest Intelligence Network,* by Brian Freemantle. Information about SOSUS came, in part, from *Running Critical: The Silent War, Rickover and General Dynamics,* by Patrick Tyler. I also referred to *The Puzzle Palace:* A Report on America's Most Secret Agency, by James Bamford, when questions arose about cryptology. Although I interviewed Dr. Murray S. Miron, his analysis of the RUS letters for the FBI was first published in *Breaking the Ring,* a book by John Barron.

Last, I would like to thank Carolyn Hunter and my parents, Elmer and Jean Earley, for their loving advice and financial support. I am also indebted to Barbara Hunter Earley, my wife, who spent hours reading the manuscript and offering suggestions, and to my children, Steve, Kevin, and Kathy Earley, who always kept my spirits up.

# INDEX